For Jack, Elsie, Lily, Wesley, and all who went before them.

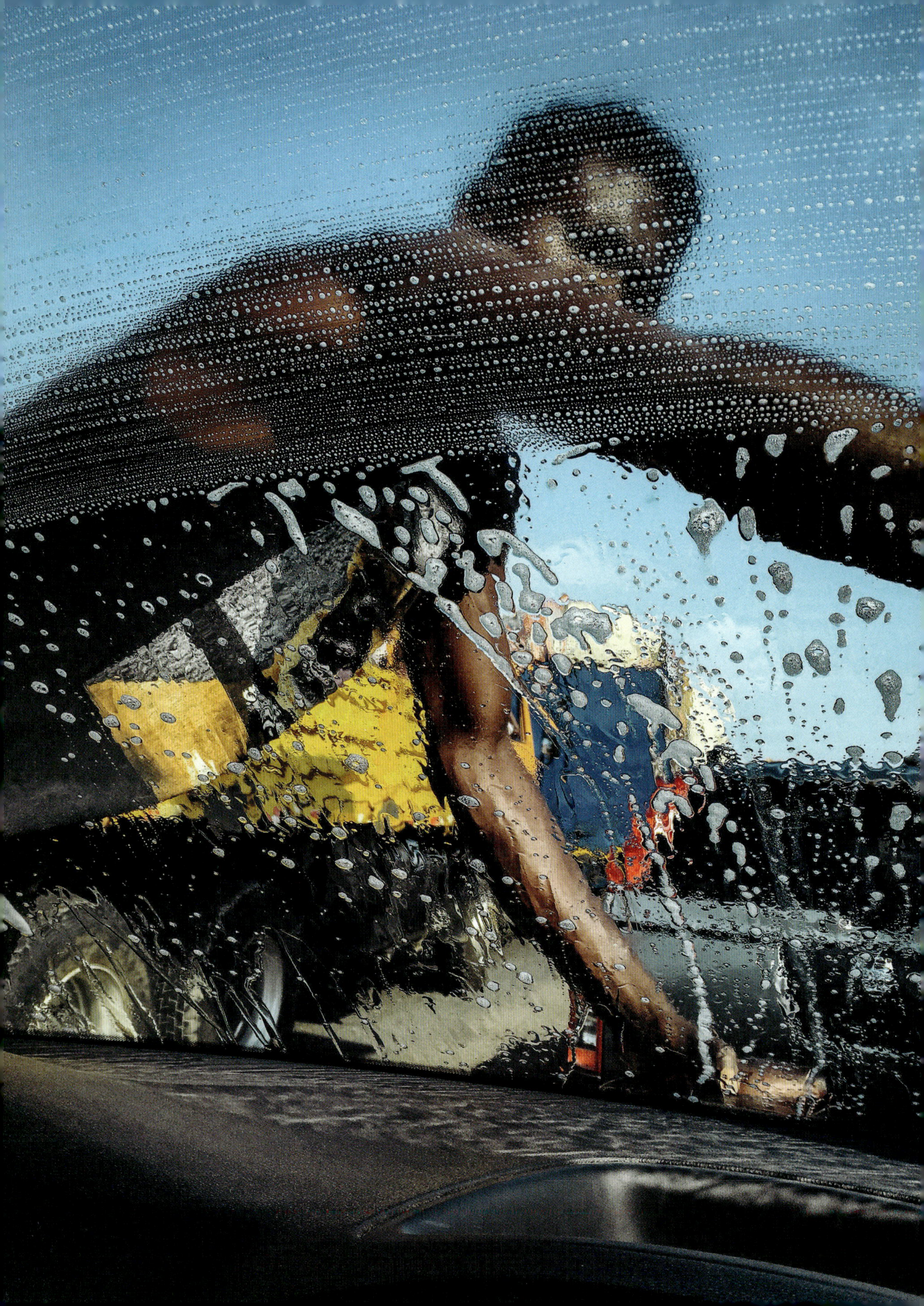

VIEW POINT

Human stories through the smartphone lens

Jo Bradford

ilex

CONTENTS

7 INTRODUCTION

12 Akhil Vilakkadan
Kozhikode (Calicut), Kerala, India

18 Alessandra Manzotti
Siena, Italy

25 Alexandra Cabral
Oporto, Portugal

28 Ana Carolina Fernandes
Rio de Janeiro, Brazil

33 Ann Hecht
Kleinemonde, South Africa

36 Barbara Januszewska-Piróg
Zielona Góra, Poland

42 Brendan Ó Sé
Cork, Ireland

47 Charlotte Mason-Mottram
Weybridge, UK

51 Dina Alfasi
Hadera, Israel

56 Elaine Taylor
Leeds, UK

60 Ernest Ankomah
Accra, Ghana

64 Ernest Rius Bonet
Badalona, Spain

69 Forough Alaei
Tehran, Iran

73 Franc Ortiz Rodrigo
Nules, Spain

76 Glenn Homann
Brisbane, Australia

83 Harshita Sabnis
Mumbai, India

86 Hasan Belal
Damascus, Syria

93 Hezron Chen
Singapore

94 Inga Dinga
Vilnius, Lithuania

100 Isaac West
New York and Wyoming, USA

105 Ismail Zaidy
Marrakech, Morocco

110 Joyz Kwok
Hong Kong

112 Julia Shatun
Belarus

118 Juliet Cope
Hove, UK

122 Jun Imaizumi
Tokyo, Japan

127 Karl Mansour
Beirut, Lebanon

130 Kelley Dallas
Denver, USA

137 Kgomotso Neto Tleane
Johannesburg, South Africa

141 Kim Abbas
Katy, Houston, USA

145 Laura Gorun
Brașov, Romania

146 Laurence Bouchard
Tokyo, Japan

152 Leonid Pryadko
Norilsk, Russia

158 LianYu Lu
Chaozhou, China

163 Ludovic Broquereau
Lyon, France

169 Maksim Goncharenok
Minsk, Belarus

172 Marcello Raggini
San Marino

177 Mariko Klug
Erding, Germany

182 Martina Loiola
Lecce, Italy

191 Mehrnoush Negahdari
Shiraz, Iran

197 Mobin Mayeli
Bandar Abbas (Gambron), Iran

200 Mohammad Nazari
Zanjan, Iran

204 Moises Levy
Mexico City, Mexico

211 Paulo Buncuga
Jelsa, Hvar, Croatia

214 Philip Parsons
Port Talbot, Wales, UK

218 Rachél Sela
Stockholm, Sweden

223 Raymond Baffour
Kumasi, Ghana

228 Renzo Grande
Lima, Peru

233 Robin Robertis
Carlsbad, USA

234 Sehin Tewabe
Addis Abeba, Ethiopia

238 Shihyu Tsao
New Taipei City, Taiwan

242 Taru Latva-Pukkila
Helsinki, Finland

247 Vincent Patrizi
Montreal, Canada

253 Wei Xiong
Wuhan, China

256 Acknowledgements
+ List of Contributors

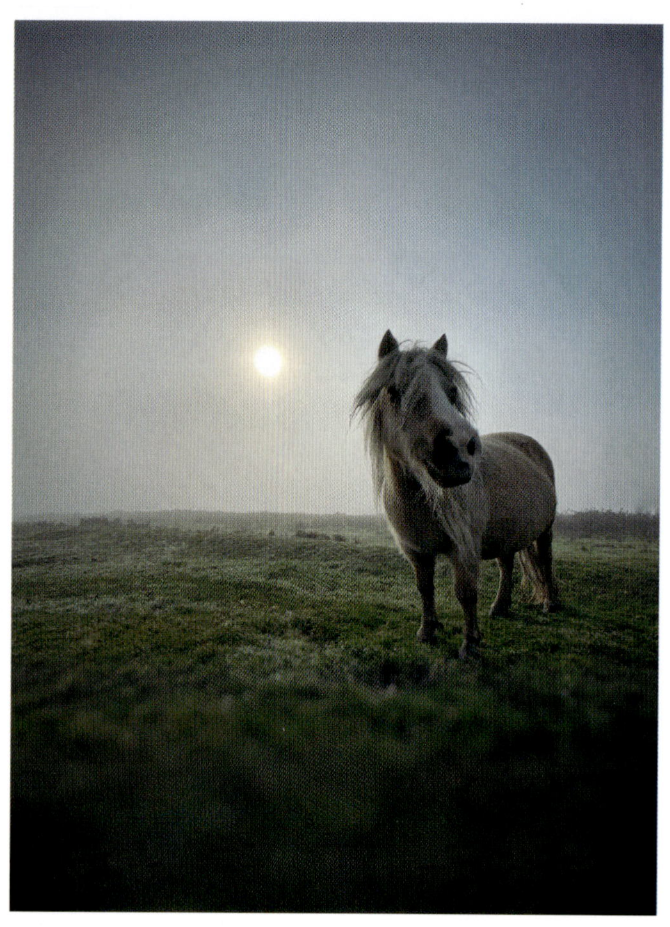

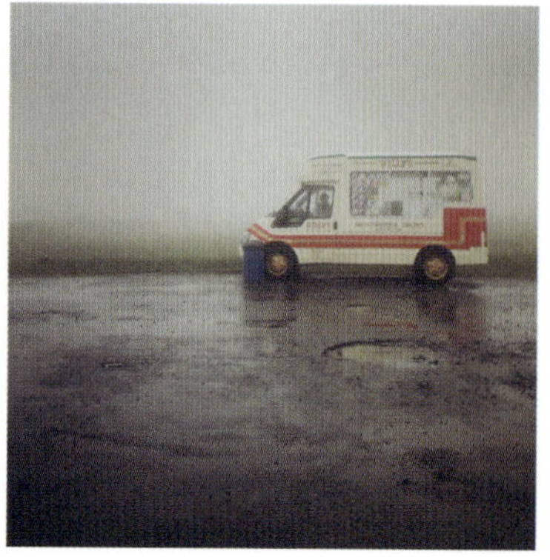

VIEWPOINT

Introduction
Jo Bradford

ViewPoint is more than a book about photography; it is a book about community and dialogue, presenting cultural offerings from a global perspective. We are accustomed to seeing the world through the lenses of professional travel photographers with expensive equipment, but this is not a true vision of the lives playing out on every continent. The advent of the smartphone camera has democratized photography, giving people all over the world the opportunity to photograph their lives with the camera they have to hand. Telling stories with photography has become possible for the many rather than just the few. This book was conceived from a desire to collect such stories.

The photographers presented here look at the world with fresh eyes, unfettered by the rules and preferences of the established gatekeepers of the medium. Their work does not seek to address what exists in the canon but, by its very nature, is more improvisatory and original. For many, photographing their daily life is habitual, necessary, the way that they understand their existence and make sense of the world. Their images serve as a record, memoir and historical artefact, too.

I tend to point my smartphone camera at the scenes I see unfolding in my own wild and windswept neighbourhood – I live off-grid in Dartmoor National Park, where I have colour darkrooms and large cameras and more lenses than I care to confess to buying – and have become increasingly aware of the way I use my phone to capture daily life, without artifice. This is why I wanted to make a book like this: to tell stories of life as it is, and to show how other people see the world through their phone cameras.

Curating this book has been a thrilling treasure hunt. Over 90 per cent of the 1.5 trillion digital photographs taken in 2022 were taken on a smartphone. There were a

lot of images to sift through – it felt like panning for gold.
Some of the initial selections were too small to print. For
other images, the original, larger version had been deleted;
the photographer had failed to see the value in keeping
anything other than a screen-resolution file size. And then
there was the not inconsiderable issue of language barriers
between myself and the contributors. But somehow we
found a way to communicate; the desire to tell stories
frequently overcame the need for words.

The photographs in the book include those by
professional photographers and by everyday people,
with a multitude of day jobs, united by their great eye
for a strong image and passion for the medium. Some of
the contributors shoot on traditional digital cameras for
work and reach for their smartphone camera to create a
daily diary; for others, a smartphone is the only camera
available. All of them produce compelling and intriguing
images.

The photographers all have their own story to tell. Some
drew me in with the significant political message in their
images (Forough Alaei, pp.68–71); others appealed with
the sheer joy of their viewpoint (Raymond Baffour,
pp.222–7). What they have in common is their ability to
give an honest account of life in a specific place on earth.

It has been an unfortunate reality that some of the
photographers in this book were unsure about being
named alongside their photographs of certain regions –
Tibet, for example – for political reasons. I got close to
securing images from people in Ukraine and Gaza and
the West Bank on several occasions. But the contributors
– preoccupied with difficulties happening in their lives
in these war-torn places – got cold feet or stopped
communicating completely. It felt churlish to press them
when they had greater issues to deal with.

Another difficult and worrying case is that of Wei Xiong
(pp.252–5). In 2020 I was grateful when he enthusiastically
agreed to send me his beautiful photographs of his home
in Wuhan, China, and a stunning image of a young monk
praying in Tibet at the Larung Gar monastic centre and
study institute. (This scene no longer exists, incidentally;

'The photographers
all have their own
stories to tell.'

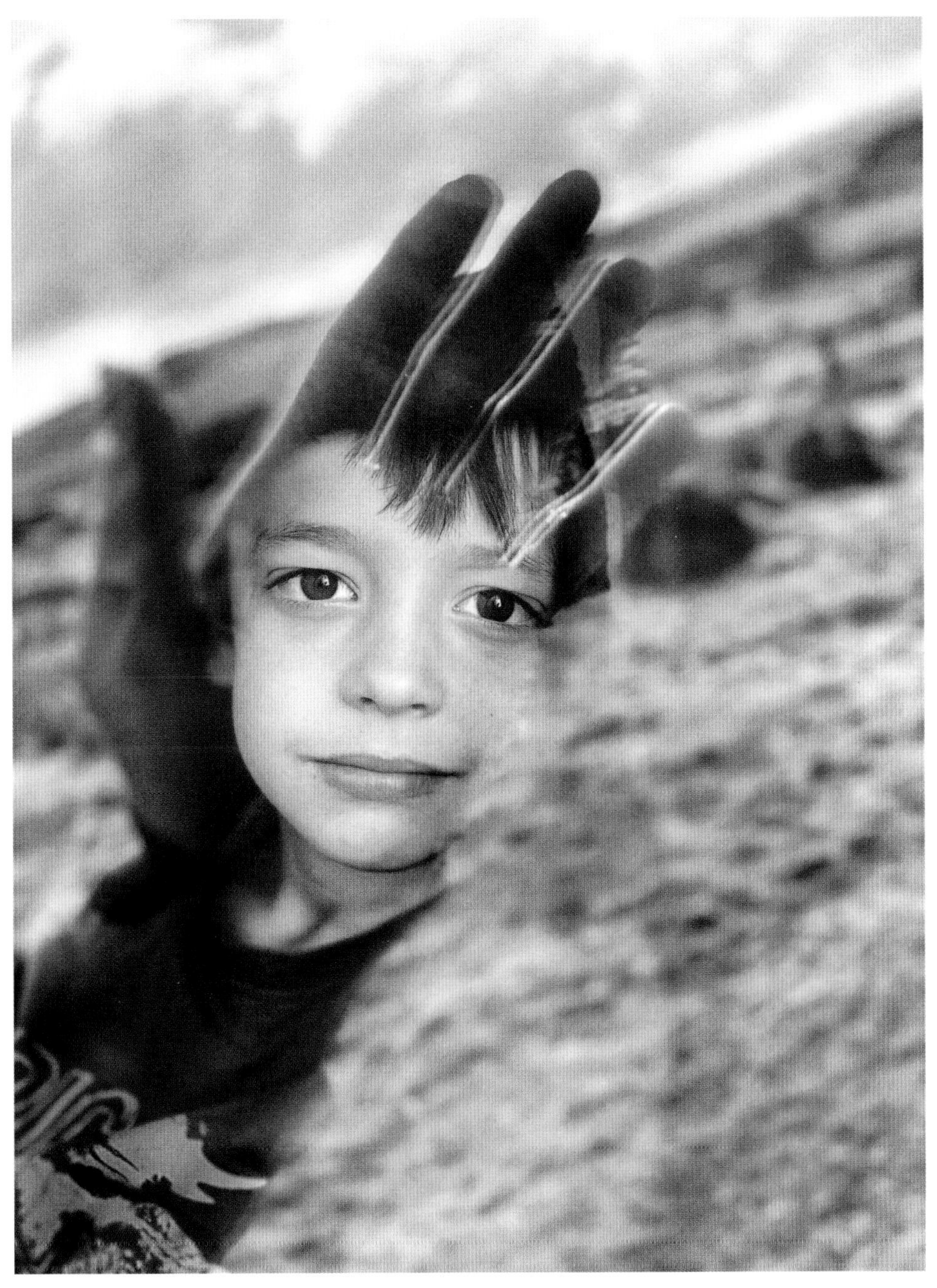

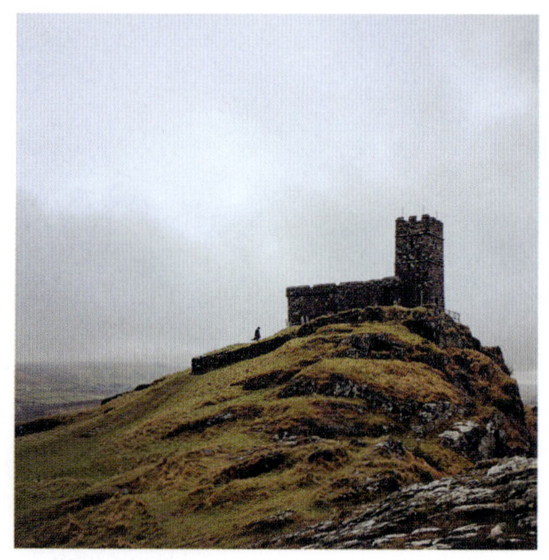

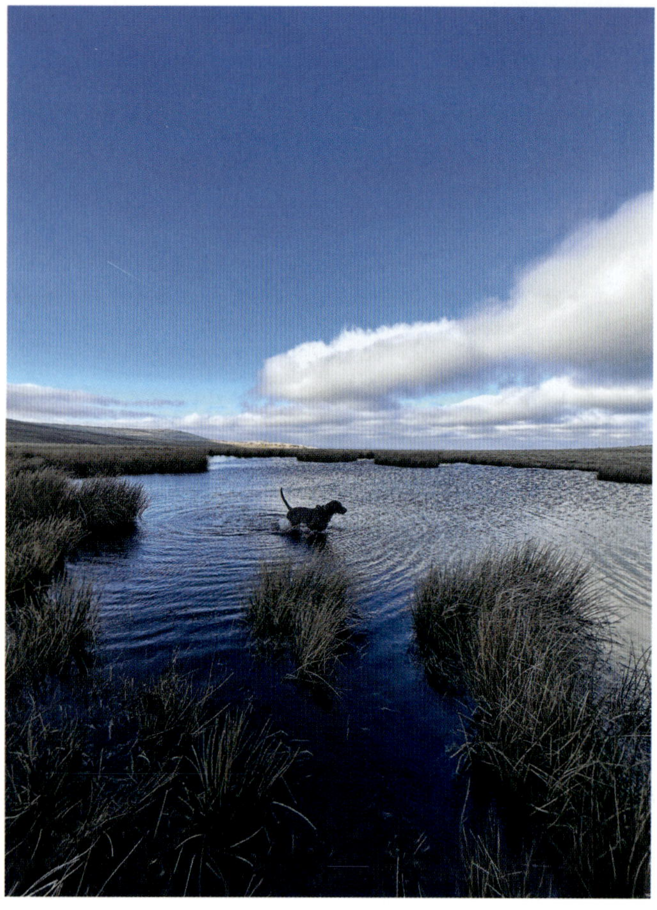

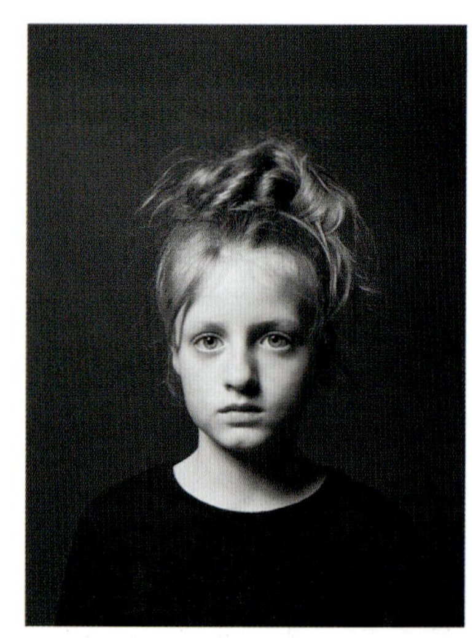

the area has been subject to a wave of demolitions.)
Unfortunately, shortly after he sent me the full-resolution
images, Wei Xiong disappeared, ceased all contact and
has not posted on any of his social media accounts since.
This is why his entry and the accompanying captions are
written in my voice rather than his. It felt important for
me to honour his wish to have his work included in the
book. I hope that one day I will be able to give him a copy
of the book and my thanks.

We all have different points of departure, but our shared
humanity shines through the stories told in the pages
of this book. Some of the images represent perspectives
historically consigned to the peripheral: the voices of
those hidden or marginalized due to their gender, location,
birth right, or sexuality. My wish was to make this book a
place for people to share their own narratives.

While some images present pastoral landscape scenes
of misty views (Mariko Klug, pp.176–81), showing
nature in all its glory, others challenge our view of the
infrastructure of urban life, reimagining it in saccharine
pastel colour palettes (Alexandra Cabral, pp.24–7)
or eerily clean scenes devoid of life (Glenn Homann,
pp.76–81). There are images that feel utterly banal yet
exude a beguiling confidence. Other contributors make
images as a starting point to explore the range of human
experiences: poetic examinations of family (Kelley
Dallas, pp.130–5); loneliness, love (Kgmotso Neto Tleane,
pp.136–9); sexuality (Ernest Rius Bonet, pp.64–7); gender,
race, exile (Julia Shatun, pp.112–17); physical difference
(Laura Gorun, pp.144–5) grief (Harshita Sabnis, pp.82–5)
and healing. They are poignant reminders of the quiet
but profound ways in which the way we occupy the
world is similar – a shared humanity that supersedes
our differences.

Akhil Vilakkadan
Kozhikode (Calicut), Kerala, India

Akhil Vilakkadan works as a quality assurance engineer for Gameberry Labs, a gaming company, in Bangalore. Alongside photography he has a passion for film-making and hiking.

He spends all his savings on travelling, mostly to hill stations where he can indulge his passion for watching sunrises and sunsets from the mountaintops, capturing all of the beautiful moments he experiences on these journeys with his phone camera. He has dreamed about buying a DSLR since childhood, but now, even though he can afford to buy one, he hasn't. Instead, he spends all his money on travelling, making the most of his adventures and using his mobile phone for photography.

Vilakkadan loves to capture the feeling and emotions of life. He has never had any intention of making money from photography, but was recently offered a chance to take photos at music festivals, which was something new for him.

Vilakkadan enjoys all types of photography, but his favourites are wildlife, landscape, underwater and street. He feels that, in essence, he is trying to convey a feeling and tell stories through his photos and is always striving to improve, to express himself photographically in the best way possible.

Currently, Vilakkadan uses an Apple iPhone 12 mini. In the past he has used an iPhone SE 2016, a Samsung Galaxy S10e and a Nokia Lumia 720. If he is shooting at festivals or for clients, he hires a DSLR. He does minimal processing to bring out the details in photos; increasing contrast, reducing highlights, slight colour corrections and reducing grain in low-light images. He prefers to use natural light.

RIGHT: Aside from photography I am also into film-making. The art in this picture is me trying to sketch out my abstract thoughts for the poster of my Malayalam short film, *Agaadham*. It was at the post-processing stage, and was later released on YouTube and MX Player. I was finishing the sketch from the balcony of my home in the evening, and the beautiful sun flare of the golden hour started to distract me. That's when I captured this beautiful moment using a Samsung Galaxy S10e. I used its wide-angle camera vertically to have maximum coverage to fit my own art and the art I was surrounded by into one frame, and clicked this picture single-handedly with my left hand. My right leg is covered with a bandage due to an injury caused during a football match.

'As far back as I can remember, I have always been curious and a close observer of the beautiful things that life has to offer.'

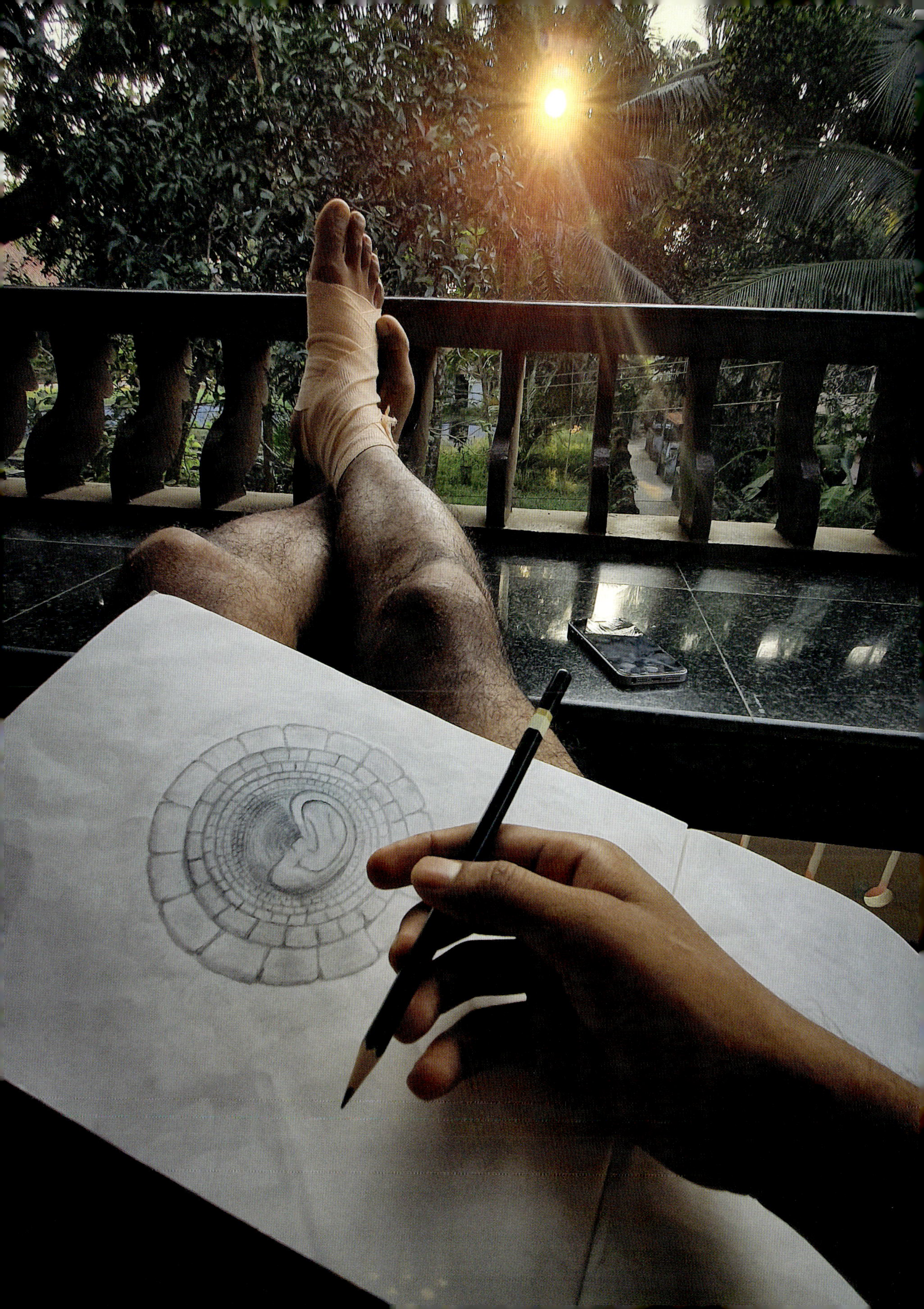

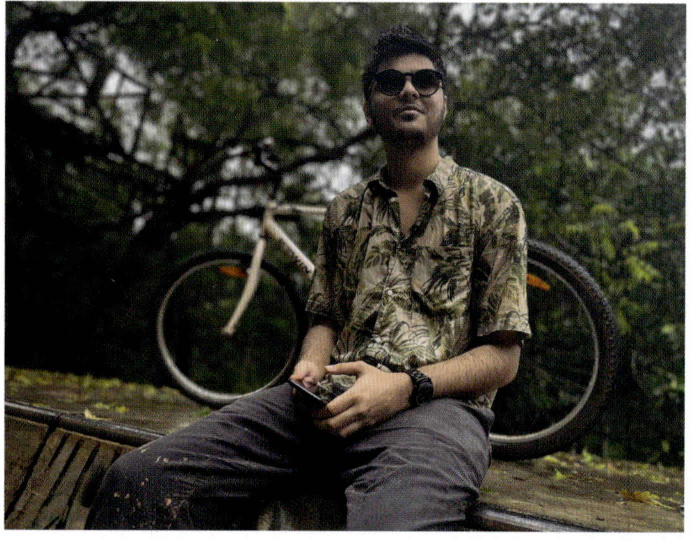

LEFT: I had been working from home for about a year due to the Covid-19 pandemic and decided that I wanted to do a 'workation' with my friends. We did it from Auroville, an experimental township in the Viluppuram district of Tamil Nadu. It's a beautiful city covered with manmade forest and amazing cycle trails and we rented cycles to get around. One morning, while we were exploring the trails, it started raining; we got drenched but decided to keep exploring anyway. We randomly took a trail and ended up in a skate park in the middle of the forest, where we decided to take a break. My friend was wearing a shirt which blended perfectly with his surroundings, and the moody lighting was perfect for a photograph. I parked his cycle behind him so the photo would show what he had been doing. This photo was captured using portrait mode on an iPhone 12 mini device. In post-processing the highlights were reduced slightly, and the contrast increased a bit to give it a cinematic look. Later we carried on exploring new places using the trails and returned home at lunchtime.

'I love to capture the feelings and emotions of life with my camera, and then I can share these tokens of my memories.'

RIGHT: My friend and I decided
to take a short trip, so early
in the morning we packed
our bags and started the
journey from Bangalore to
Kemmanugundi, which is
about 190 miles (300km) away,
on my friend's scooter. We
reached our destination around
4 p.m. and decided to try and
catch the sunset at the top of
a nearby peak called Z Point,
which was about an hour away.
I was feeling refreshed by the
greenery around me, taking
deep breaths to fill my lungs
with the cold air, when my
eyes caught this lung-shaped
muddy puddle. I started to
think about how forests are the
lungs of the Earth, and humans
are destroying it, and how I
could use the puddle's shape to
illustrate this with my camera
in a single frame. I was ahead
of my friend, so I took out my
iPhone SE, waited for him to
pass, and clicked as soon as his
reflection appeared in one of the
puddles. The green lungs of the
earth are being turned brown
by human negligence – that is
the message this photograph is
trying to convey.

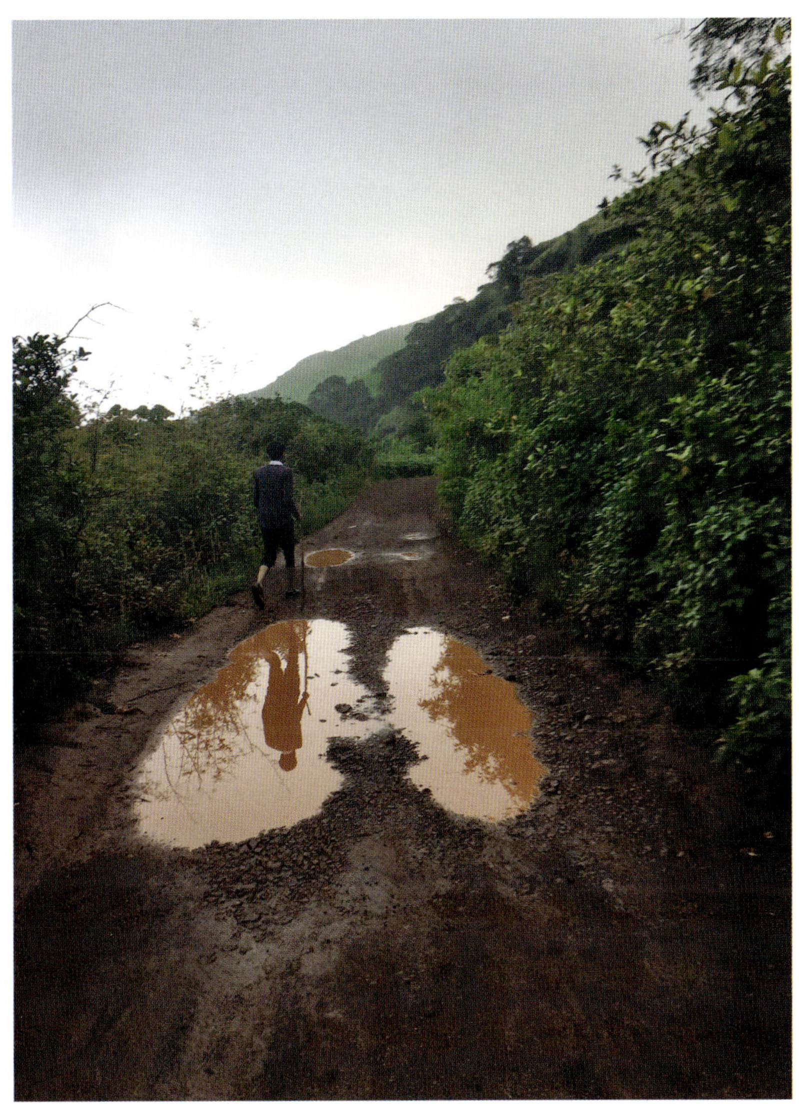

 I was on solo bike ride from Pondicherry (Puducherry) to Kodaikanal in Tamil Nadu. It is one of my favourite destinations and this was my sixth visit, but the first on my own. As I rode through the forest, the visibility was reducing due to mist and, when I finally reached the village of Poondi, I stopped at a small hotel for lunch. I was talking to the people who run the hotel when I saw this cute little puppy hopping around with a club foot. I asked them about him, and they told me he was Rambo, one of a litter born to a stray dog. They didn't have time to look after the litter, which would have been attacked by the other stray dogs, so they kept the puppies for a month, then took them to a town about 30 miles (50km) away and left them where people would find them. As Rambo wasn't strong enough to look after himself, they kept him with his mother. I took out my iPhone 12 mini and clicked this little man using portrait mode while he was resting after running around. The portrait mode helps to add depth and emotion to the subject.

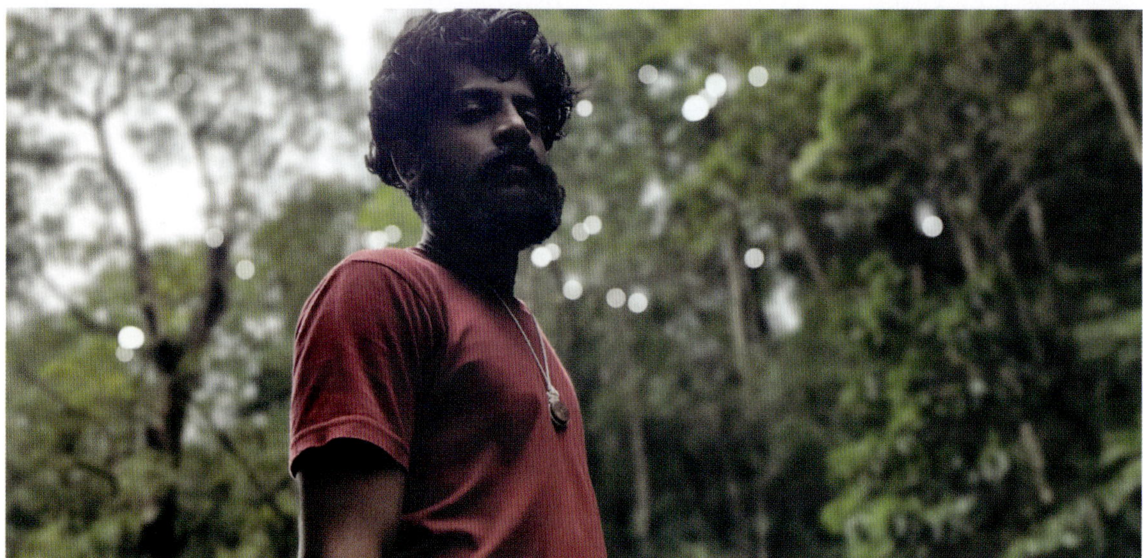

ABOVE: This is Swachu. We have known each other since the age of five and he is one of my best friends. He manages a property in a forest area in Kerala called 900 Kandi. Once in a while I go there to meet him and chill out. On this occasion my elder brother, Anoop, came with me. When we arrived we decided to go stream hiking and bathe in the small waterfalls. Anoop and I followed Swachu, who checked up on us every ten minutes as the terrain is rocky and slippery. The sky was a bit cloudy and the trees were cutting out the light, giving a moody effect, and I decided to take Swachu's picture while we waited for my brother. The red of his clothing stood out from the green of the trees. I chose portrait mode as there was only a bit of light falling on his face, and I used a lower angle to add a sense dominance. When he looked down at to me, I clicked my Samsung Galaxy S10e. Afterwards, we carried on hiking, took a good bath in the cold waters of the waterfall and returned before it was too dark.

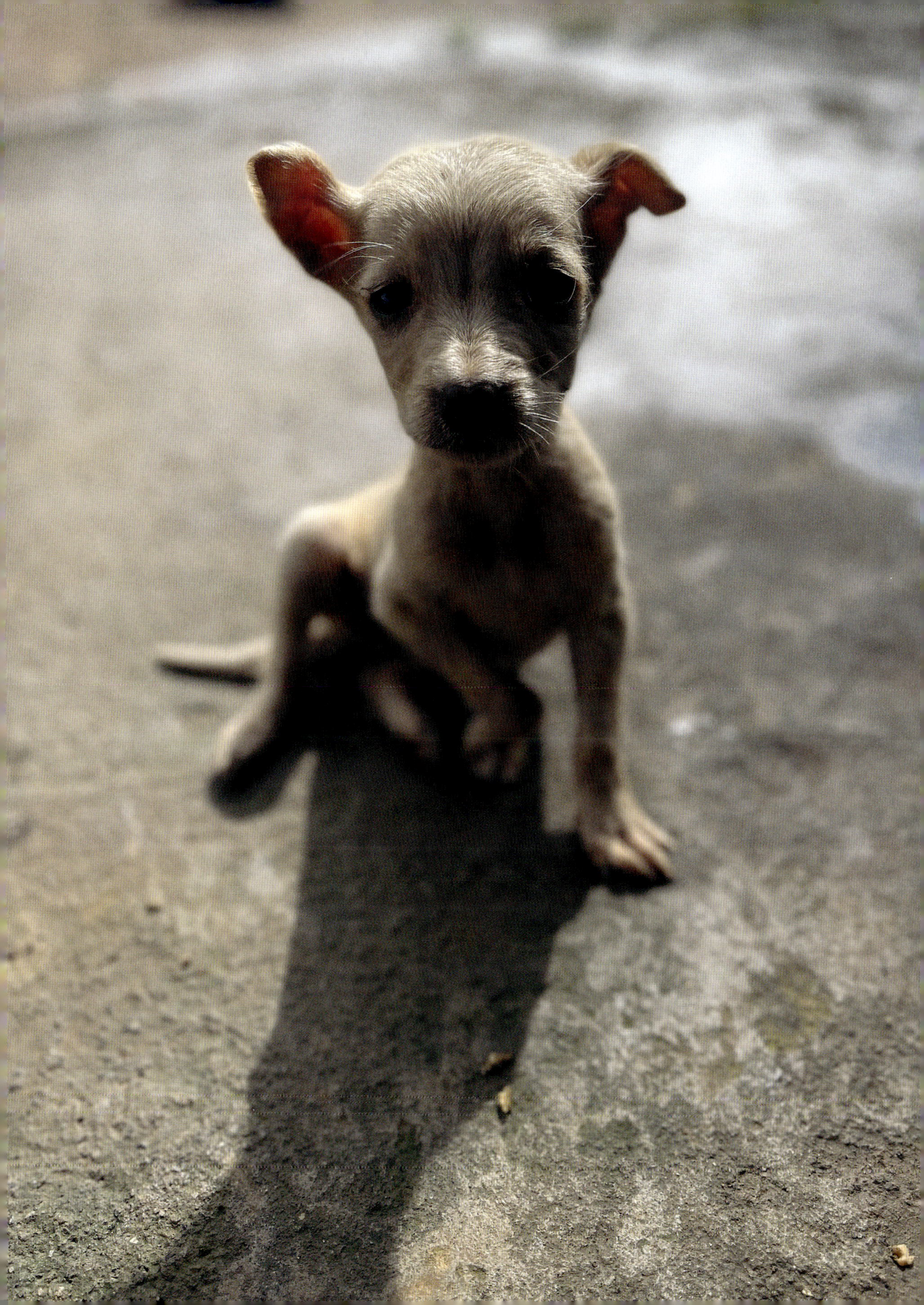

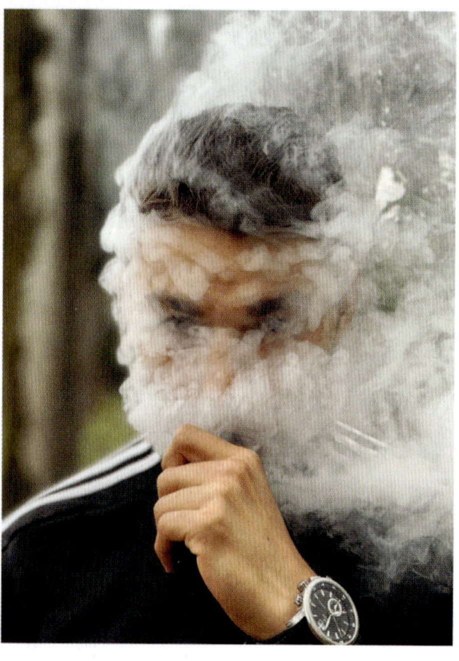

ABOVE: This is my neighbour's teenage son vaping. It was a cold day, and as I sat there trying to tell him how bad that was for him, he kept engulfing himself in thick smoke. So I snapped the picture. I loved how the smoke was circling around his face.

Alessandra Manzotti
Sienna, Italy

Freelance travel and portrait photographer Alessandra Manzotti was born and raised in Milan. After living in the United States of America for a while, she moved back to Italy to be close to her father.

She photographs anything that attracts her attention – horses, trees, people, street photography. Manzotti tries not to limit herself to a specific subject, especially when using her phone, but is inspired by memories of her childhood, the challenges of motherhood in her forties, and a never-ending curiosity and sense of restlessness.

Although photography is her profession, she first and foremost takes photographs for herself. Manzotti currently uses an Apple iPhone 12 Pro max, but in the past has used iPhones 4, 7 and 8, which were used to shoot some of the images shown here. She uses Mextures and Snapseed to edit the images.

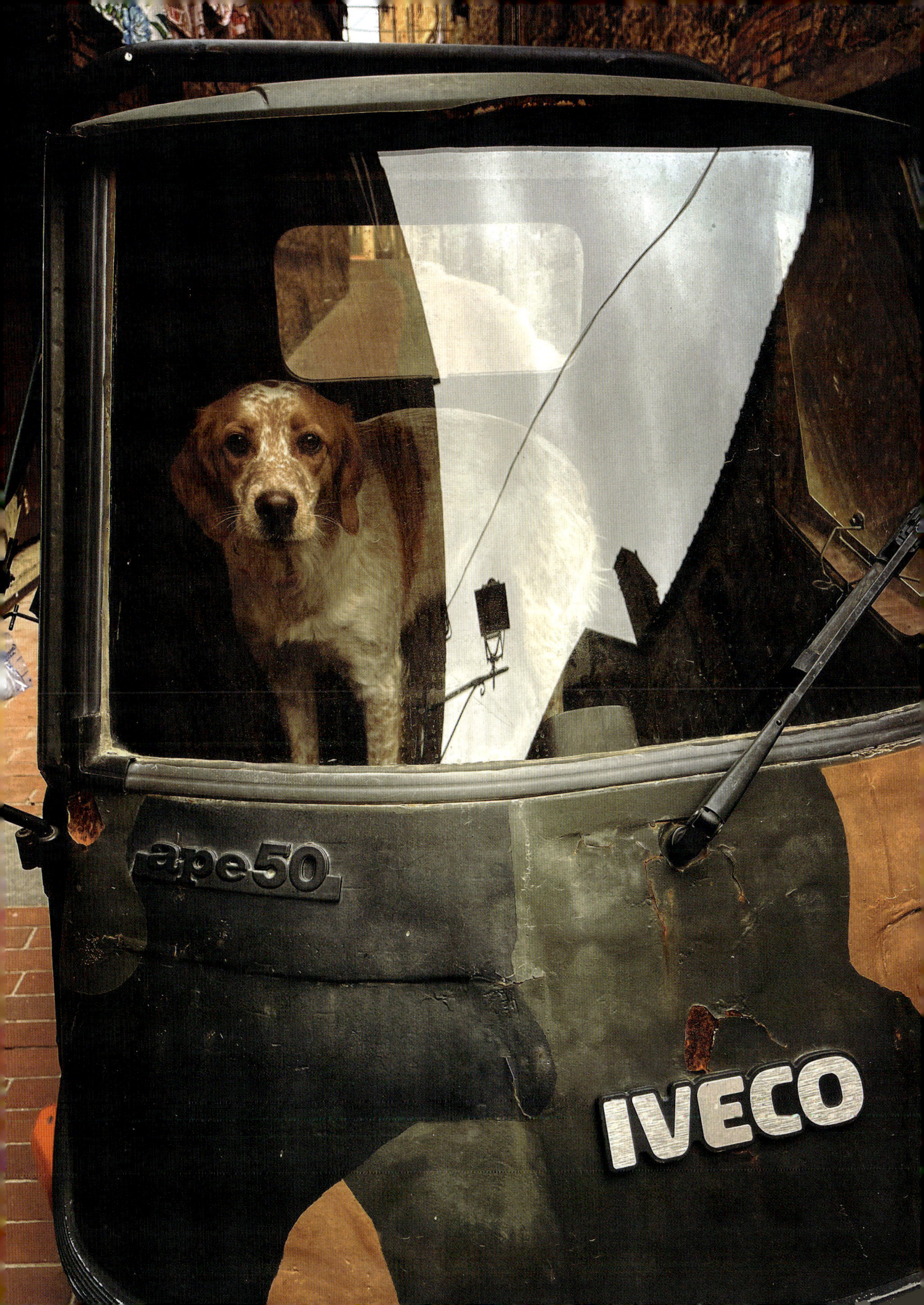

ape50
IVECO

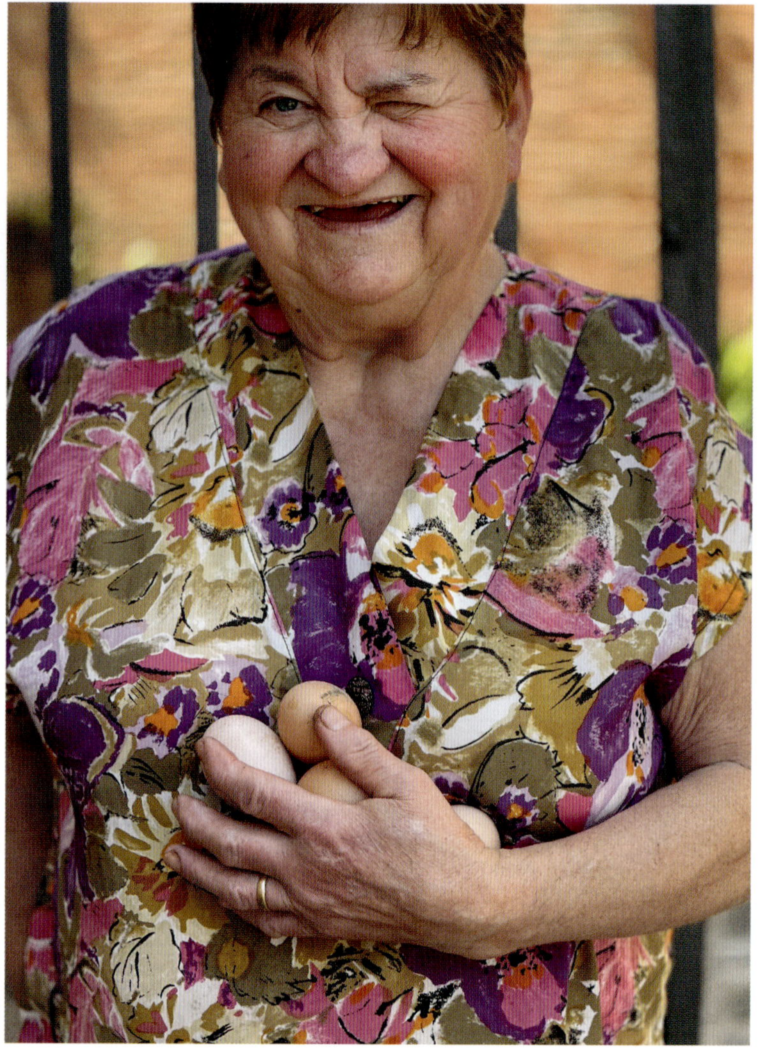

ABOVE: This is Franca, a farmer's wife. I have become friends with her through working at the farm, helping with the olive harvest. In exchange for my work she gives me eggs, vegetables and so on. In this image she had just gone to the chicken coop to get me some eggs. I had nowhere to put them, so I had to walk 3 miles home with the eggs in my hands! They are very, very generous people and I love that. Franca has a beautiful face; she is the salt of the earth.

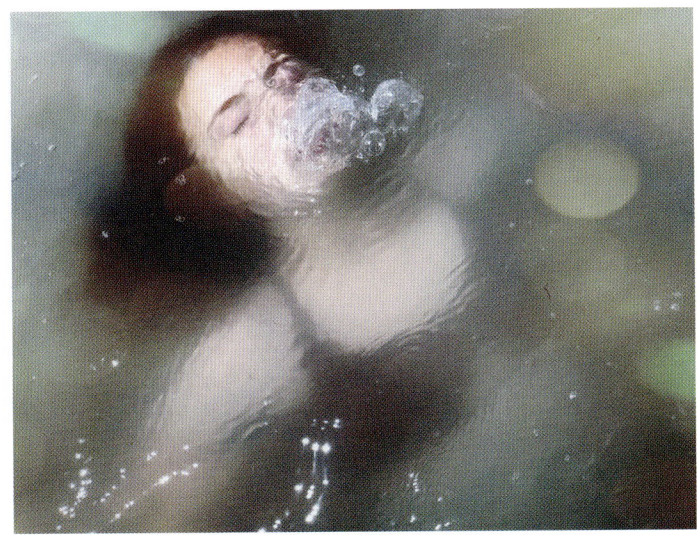

ABOVE: This is my daughter in
the sea at Maremma, Tuscany,
in the winter. She and her friend
just decided to brave it and
go swimming. I thought this
was a beautiful picture as my
daughter went over and under
and over and under the water,
blowing bubbles. I waded out
to her, and she didn't even see
me as I took the picture. I was
up to my waist in the water and
worried about getting my phone
wet, so it was a very quick photo
– I think it took me 3 seconds.
I loved the bubbles and her
expression. It looked very poetic.

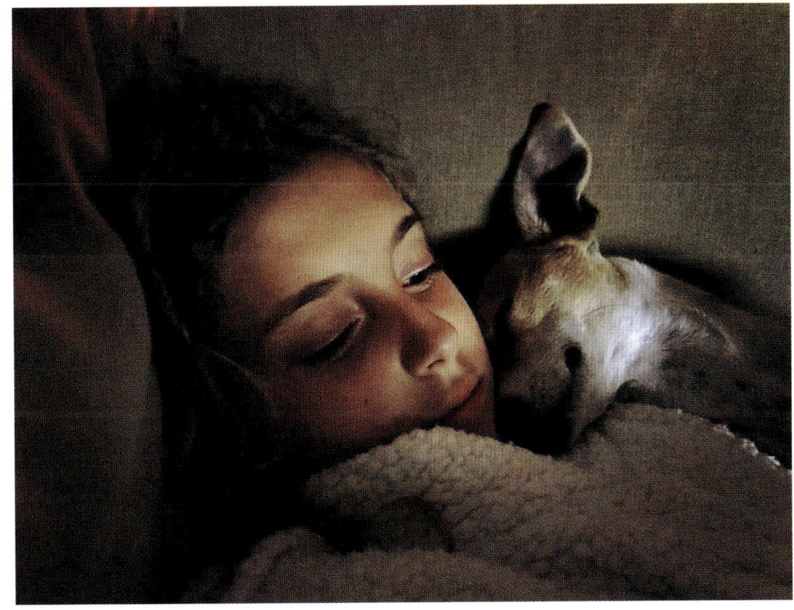

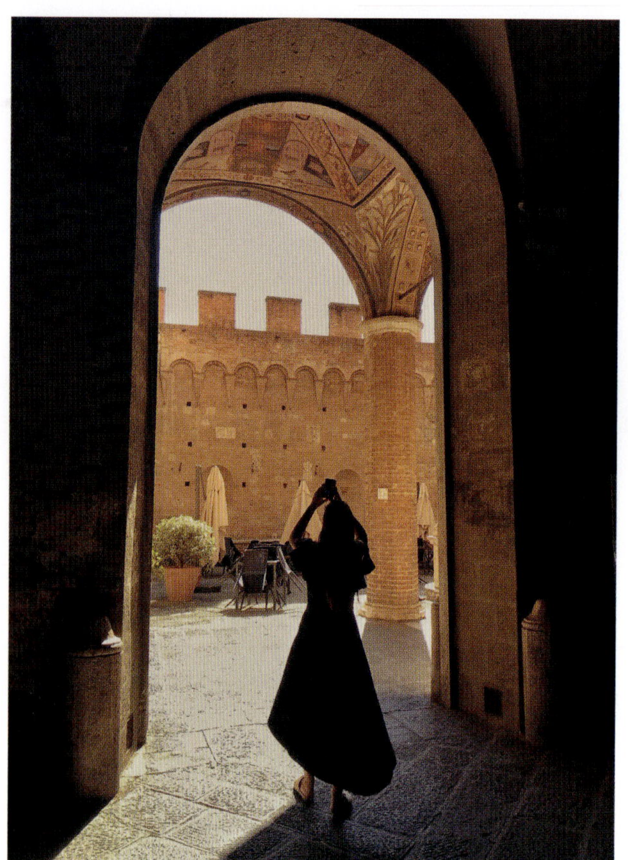

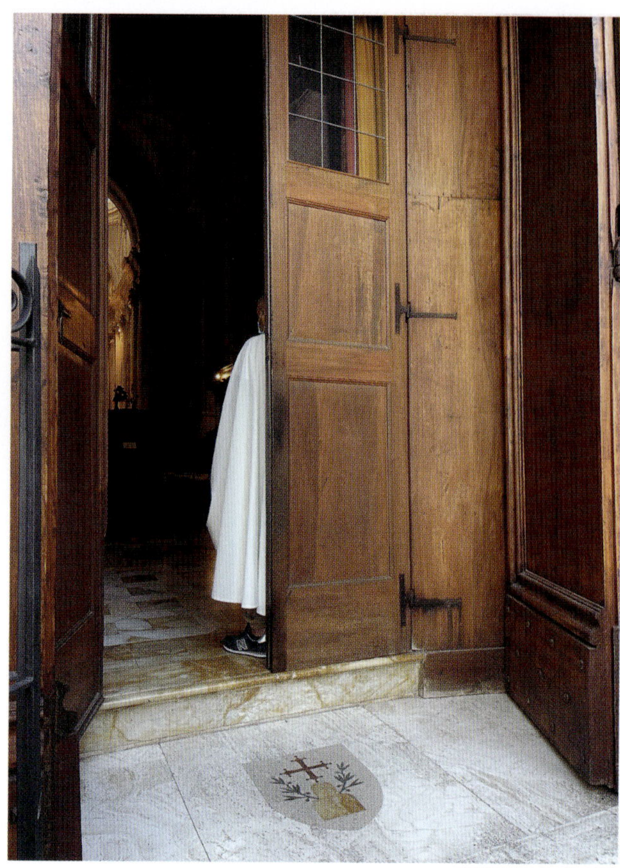

ABOVE: I was walking around Siena, and I was struck by the silhouette this lady created and the way the breeze made her dress flow.

ABOVE: The Abbazia di Monte Oliveto Maggiore, in the val d'Orcia in Tuscany, is a beautiful church, with calm, cool cloisters to escape the heat of the midday sun. The surrounding grounds are sublimely beautiful. I was touring with my husband, my daughter and my father and it happened to be the time for mass, so we walked around. I saw this monk standing outside and was struck by the fact that he was wearing trainers. It is not a big deal, but it was a very solemn moment with the elderly monks inside wearing their white tunics. My eyes went straight to this little detail.

'Sometimes you're very lucky and something happens that you weren't expecting. At other times you sit waiting for ages and nothing happens. It is about being present in the moment, going with the flow and letting things happen how they are supposed to happen.'

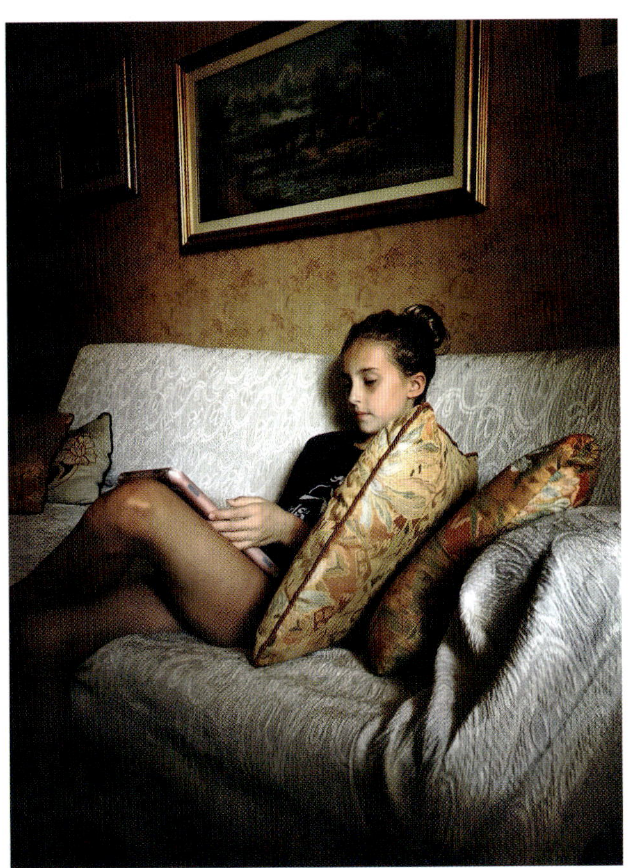 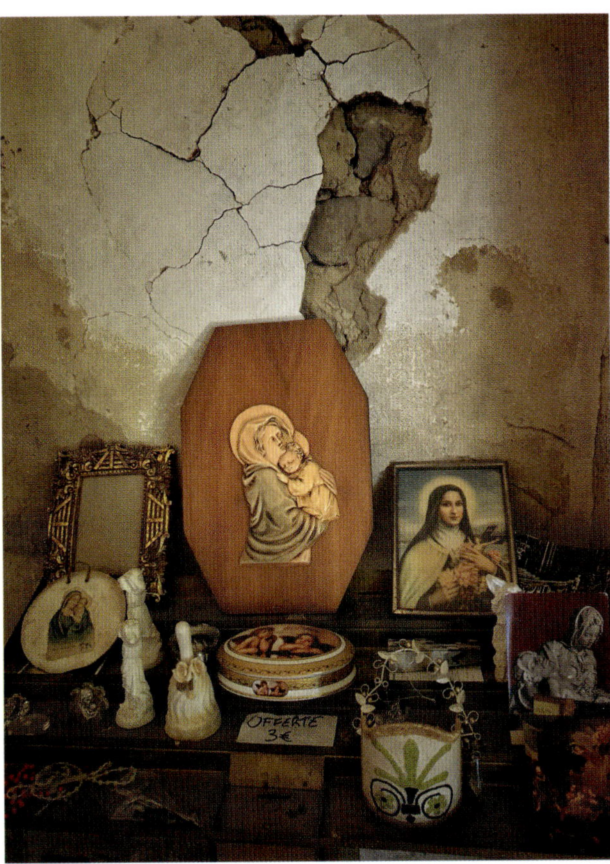

ABOVE LEFT + RIGHT: These two images were shot in different locations at different times. There is something that feels very old and also traditionally Italian about the tones and the light in both images. The one of my daughter was shot at my late grandmother's house. What caught my attention was that, at first impression, the scene is a very old one. Nobody lives in that house now, the couch is old, the painting is old and yet my young daughter is sitting watching something on a very modern Apple iPad. I love the contrast between the old and the new. The light from the window was beautiful – I love to shoot side lighting. It felt like a little Madonna scene. Likewise, the shrine image is full of older objects set against a modern euro sign, which puts it in the present. It was in Cortona, where there are a lot of shrines at which people make offerings. You see them everywhere. People could take the objects and the offerings, but they don't. Even without a human subject, the way the objects are neatly arranged means there is the sense of a human presence in this photo.

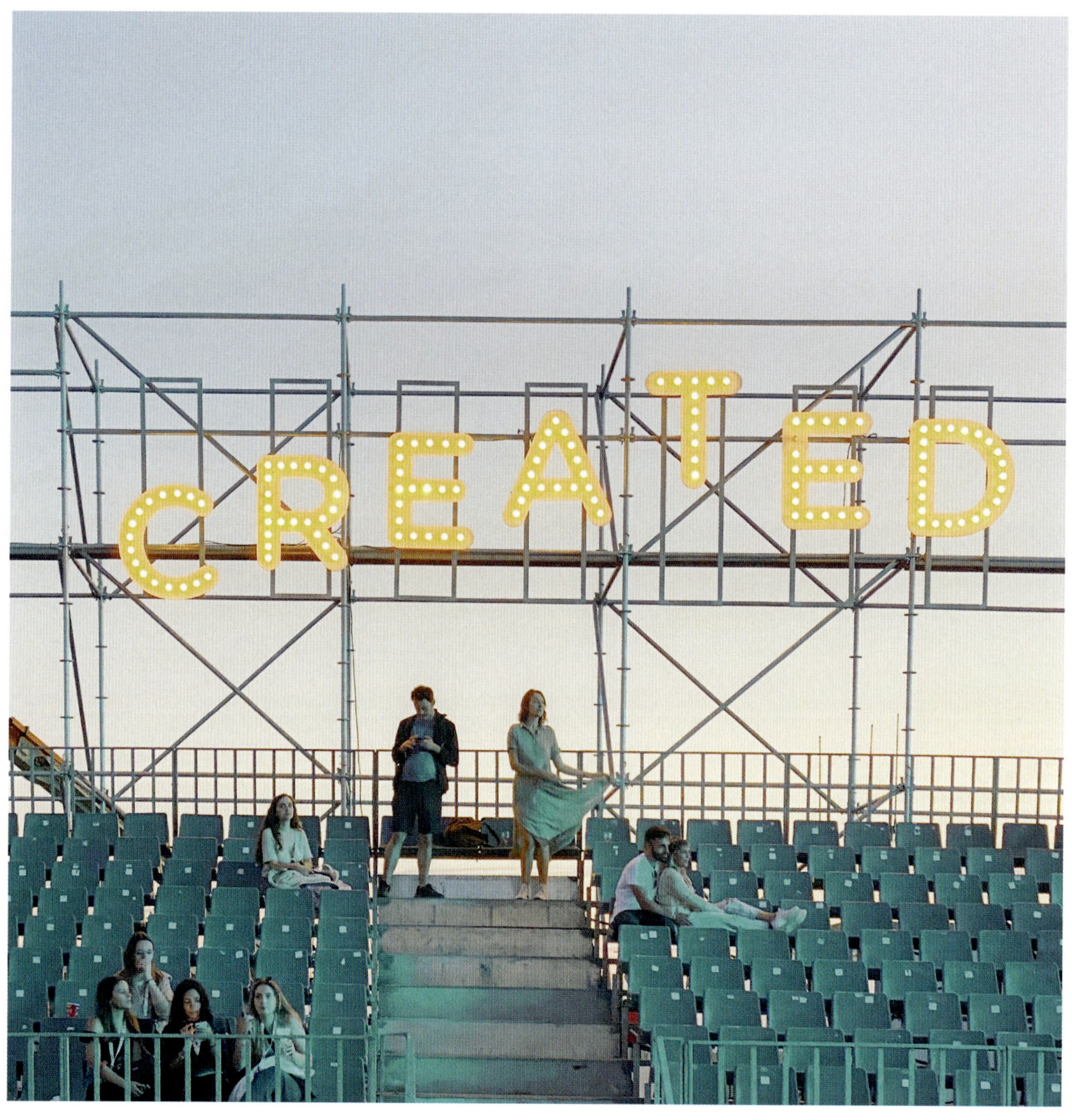

'Photography is an essential part of my daily work, and the immediacy of street photography is the best therapy.'

Alexandra Cabral
Oporto, Portugal

Graphic designer Alexandra Cabral lives with her cat, Xico, and works as the head of communication design at Gaiurb, the company responsible for urban planning, rehabilitation and social housing for the city of Vila Nova de Gaia. Her job involves creating corporate identities, editorial projects and exhibitions, as well as environmental and public space design.

Cabral received her doctorate in design from the faculty of fine arts at the University of Porto in 2018. She normally uses her Apple iPhone 11 Pro, and edits occasionally with VSCO and Lightroom.

She loves a minimal aesthetic and the random moments captured in photos. Much of her photography is captured during her walks. She loves to find the human scale of the city or the environment, and delights in capturing small details. Her characters are often framed in symmetrical compositions. This, combined with pastel colour palettes, evokes a sense of nostalgia and creates a dreamy atmosphere in her photography.

'Each photo appears as a visual diary, inspired by tiny instants, where the uniqueness of moments, shapes and colours stands out.'

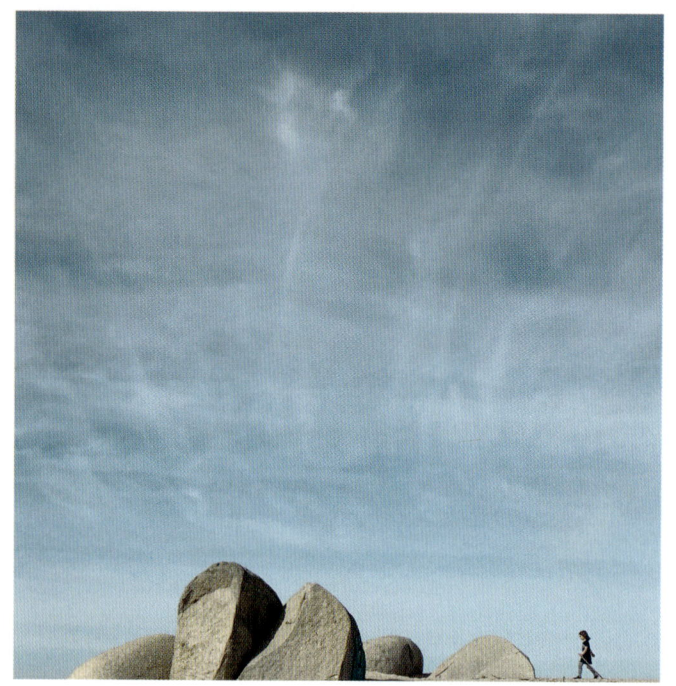

'With a more minimal
approach, I try to convey a
narrative in each image.'

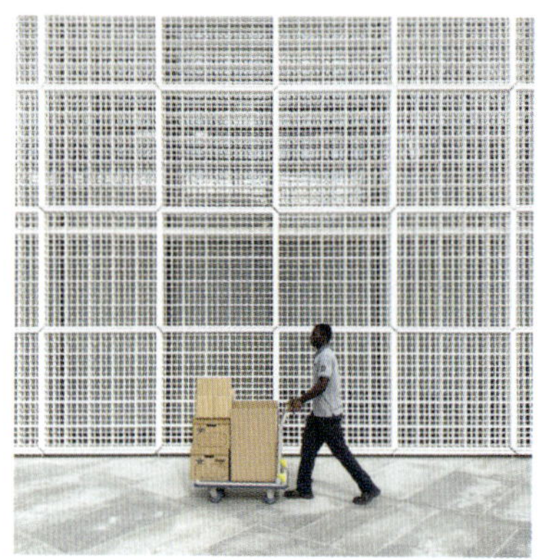

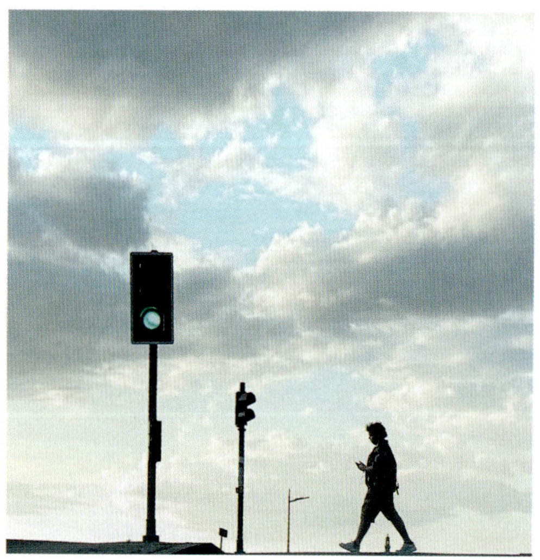

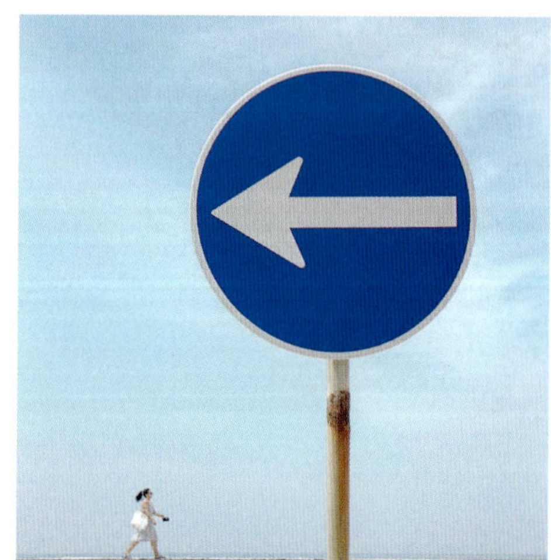

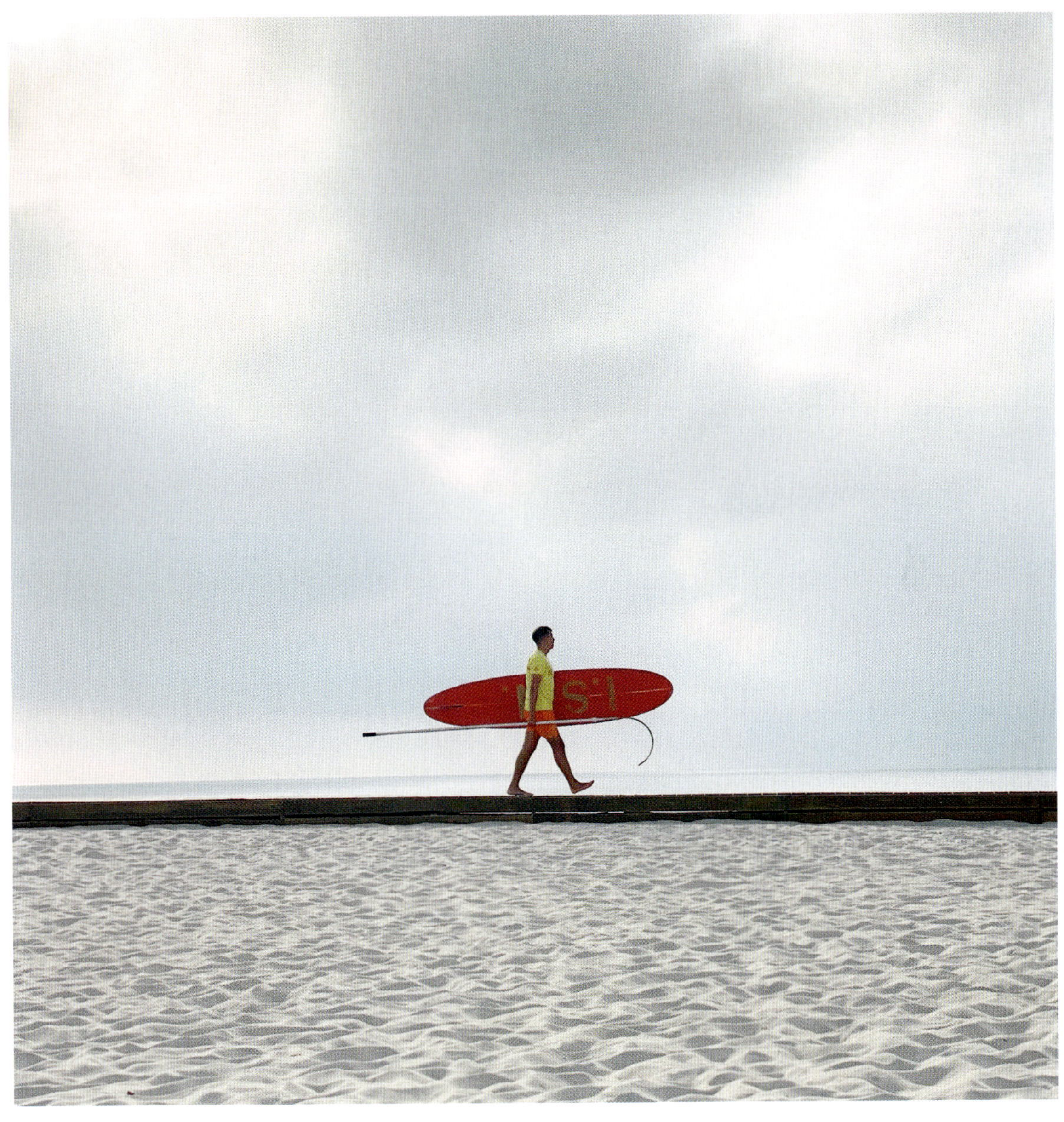

'The details of everyday life have
always caught my attention, and
can appear as the silhouette of a
passer-by, the simplicity of a shape
or the impact of a colour.'

Ana Carolina Fernandes
Rio de Janeiro, Brazil

At the age of 19, after studying photography at the School of Visual Arts at Parque Lage, Ana Carolina Fernandes started working as a photojournalist. For the majority of her professional life she has worked for some of the most important newspapers in Brazil, such as *O Globo*, *Jornal do Brasil*, *O Estado de S. Paulo* and *Folha de S.Paulo*. Fernandes has always used an Apple iPhone. A few years ago, the company offered her an organic partnership and now, every year, they send her the latest model even before it's in the shops. She uses Snapseed for all her editing.

Fernandes has spent the past decade developing authorial documentary work, telling the stories of the Brazilian people and their diverse cultures – always with a humanist eye – as well as focusing on environmental and ecological issues.

Her work has been published widely, and she has won several notable awards, including the Julia Margaret Cameron Award for Women. Fernandes believes that photography is extremely important for the balance of her whole being. It's not the mirror of reality for her, but the poetic extension of her eyes and soul. She needs photography to understand her place in the world, or sometimes her lack of place. It is as important to her as the air that she needs to live and breathe.

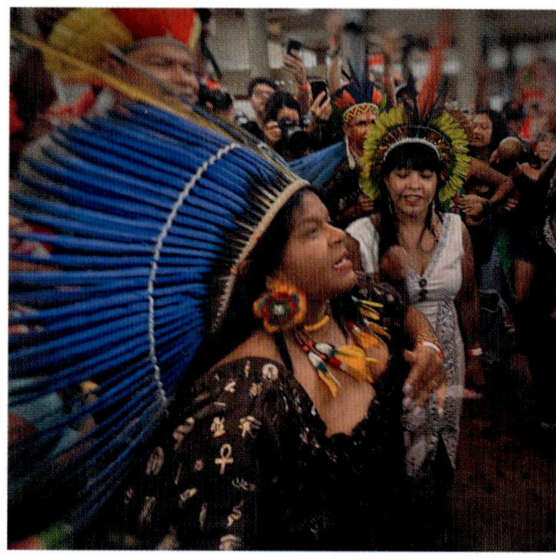

ABOVE: Sônia Guajajara, 49, is the first indigenous minister in Brazil. In January 2023, President Luiz Inácio Lula da Silva historically appointed her to lead the Ministry of Indigenous Peoples. In 2022, Guajajara was named one of the 100 most influential people in the world by *Time* magazine for being a pioneer in defending the land rights of the indigenous people and local communities, while also protecting the Brazilian Amazon rainforest. Here, she jubilantly visits a camp for landless rural workers who went to President Lula's inauguration ceremony.

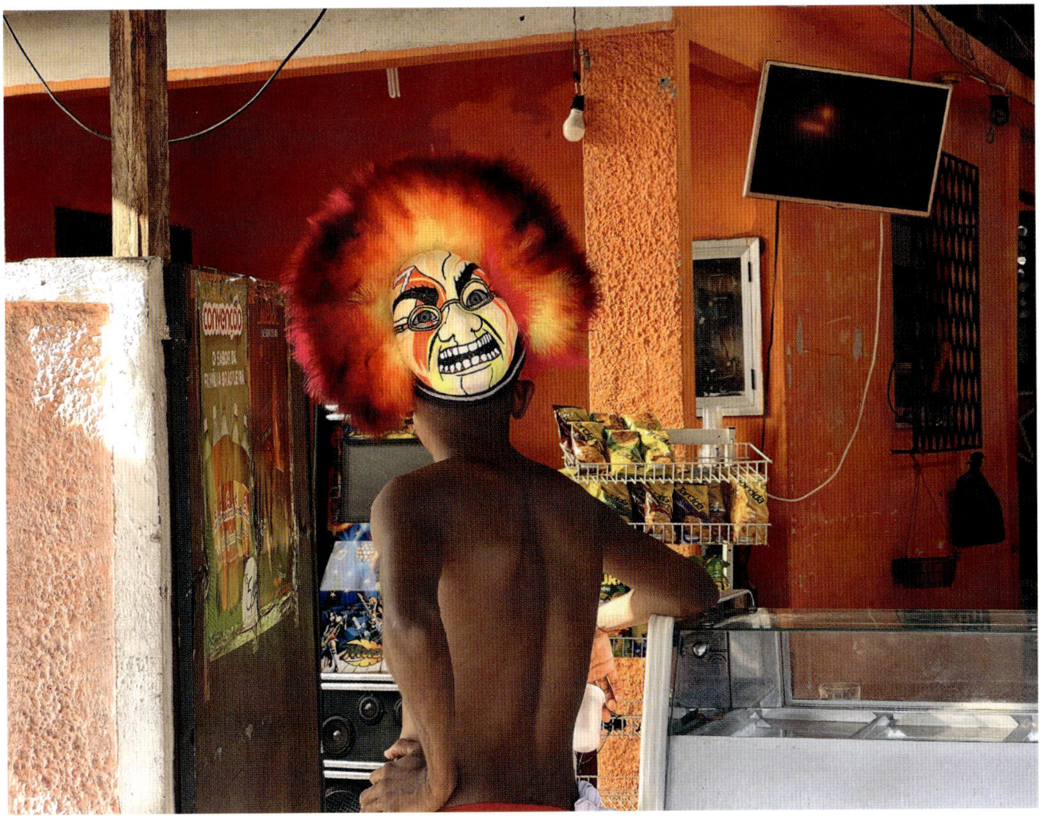

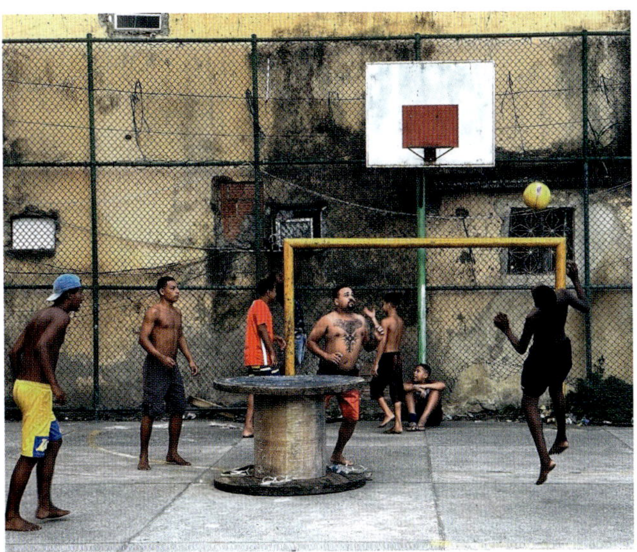

 A clown in Marechal Hermes, a suburb of the city of Rio, during the 2022 bate-bola carnival. Clown costumes are characteristic of this alternative carnival celebrated in the working-class suburbs (mainly the North and West Zones, and Baixada Fluminense) of Rio de Janeiro. The tradition, which dates from the early 20th century and exists in reaction to the more mainstream Rio carnival, may have been inspired by Portuguese colonizers. Others say that freed slaves, who were sometimes unfairly persecuted by the police, wore costumes to enable them to enjoy the carnival, protest oppression, ignore the rules and demonstrate.

LEFT: Residents of Favela de Ramos play teqball on a public court.

BELOW: Drag queen Hellena Borgys poses for a picture backstage at the 2018 Miss Gay Brasil contest, in Juiz de Fora, Minas Gerais state.

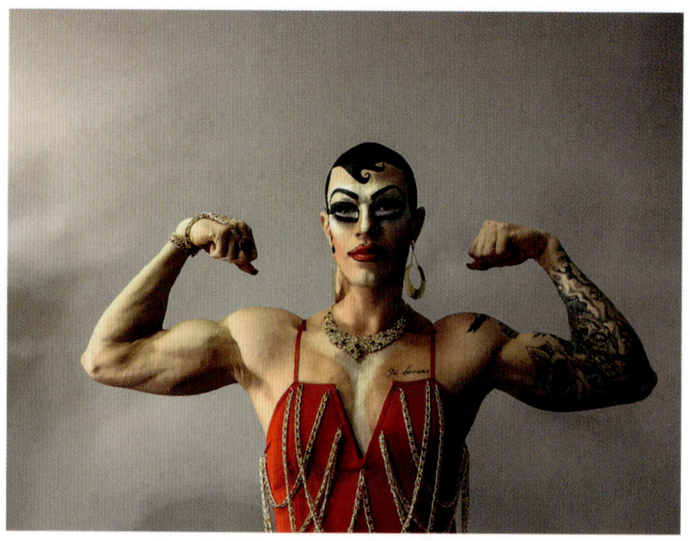

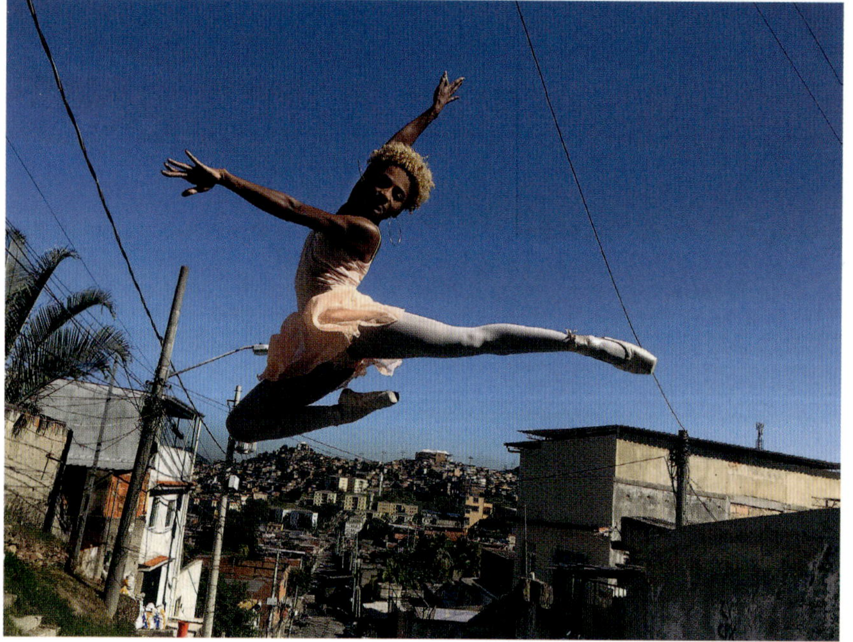

ABOVE: Tuany Nascimento became a very dear friend of mine after I started a photo documentary project about her and the wonderful school she runs that transforms the lives of hundreds of children in the favela who have no government support. Tuany is a Brazilian ballet dancer and dance teacher. She is the founder and director of Na Ponta dos Pés, a dance school that provides ballet training for underprivileged girls living in the favelas of Complexo do Alemão in Rio de Janeiro.

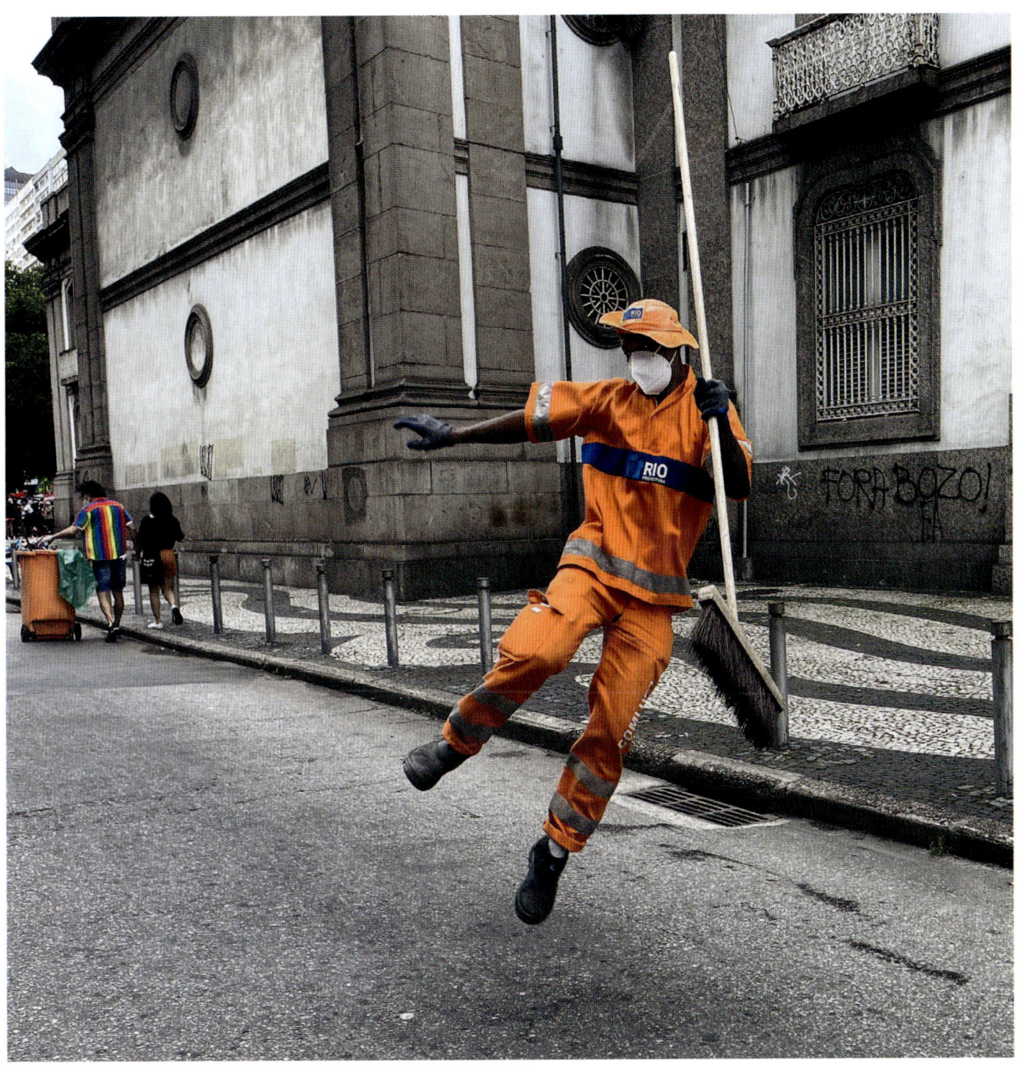

ABOVE: This cheerful street sweeper works for
Rio's Municipal Urban Cleaning Company.

Ann Hecht

Kleinemonde, South Africa

Every morning artist Ann Hecht walks along the beach near her home on the Eastern Cape and she never leaves her Apple iPhone 11 Pro Max behind. Hecht edits in Snapseed, and often plays with images in Instagram before posting too. Her artwork is mostly created in pencil or black ink, and her black-and-white photography echoes this aesthetic.

'I really enjoy photography because there are no strings attached. I am not trying to sell my photos as I am with my artworks, so I can just go with the process and the beauty of my surroundings.'

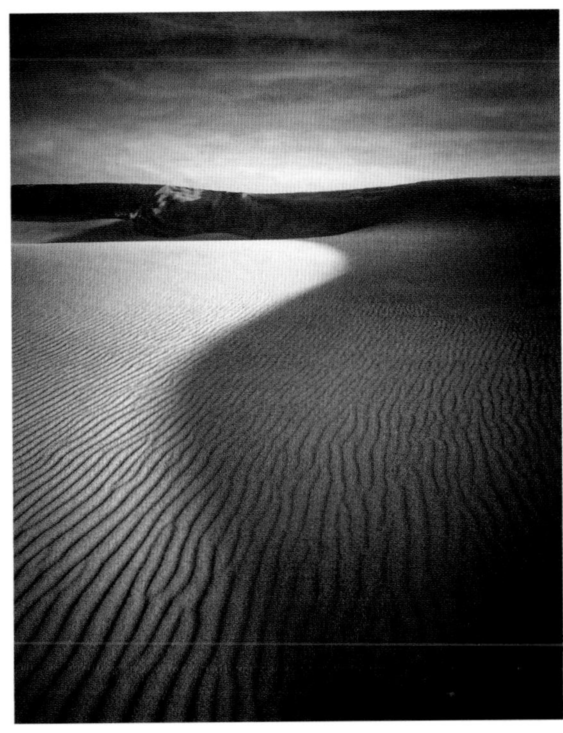

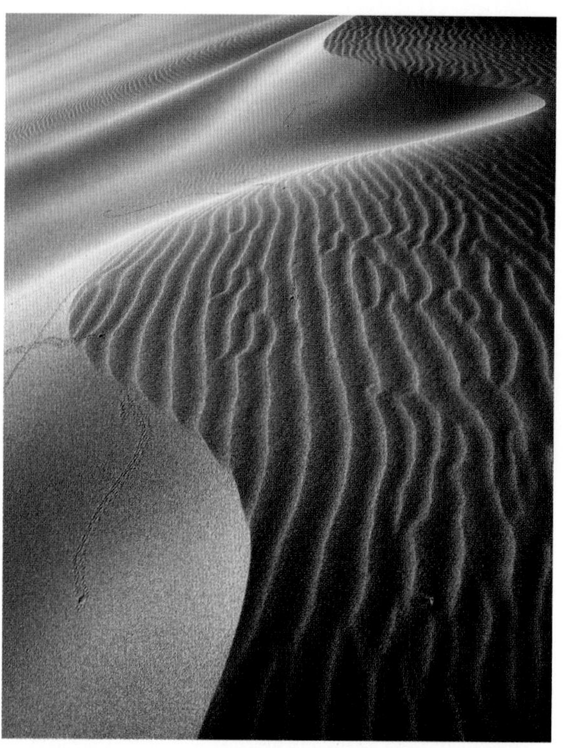

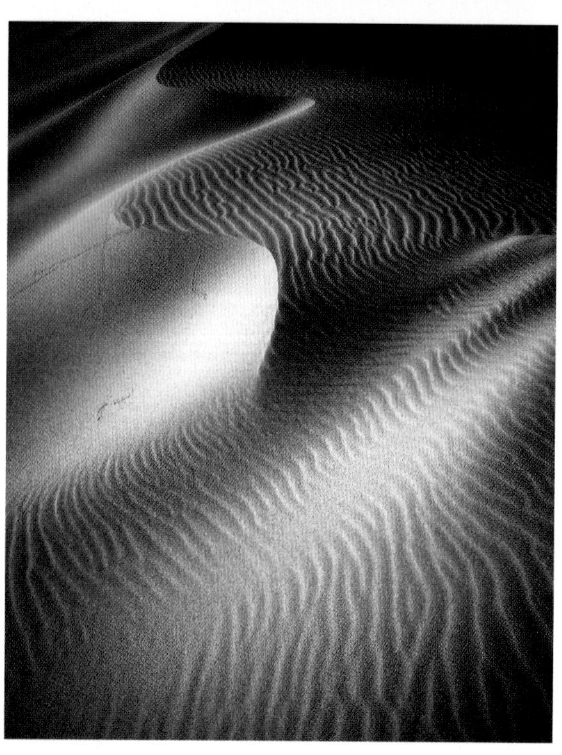

RIGHT: Sophie and I love our walks through the dunes. I like to try and photograph her at the top of a dune, but it is impossible to stage a shot as she doesn't stand still. I like the paw prints and the way they lead the eye to Sophie, the patterns in the dunes and the clouds above.

FAR RIGHT: This is the view from the top my favourite big dune. The wind has sculpted this perfect combination of curves, patterns and shadows and there is not a single footprint in view.

LEFT TOP + BOTTOM: I find it is a good idea to move around the dunes as I am taking pictures because everything changes from a different angle. I try to make the most of the soft light before the sun gets too high.

RIGHT: This photo is the view looking back up at my favourite dune. At first I was disappointed to see my footprints, but when I converted the image to black and white I decided that they provide a wonderful leading line. I also love the contrast between the light and shadow.

FAR RIGHT: This is the result of gales which blew for days. It was easterly one day and south westerly the next, then easterly again, and so on, which made sandfalls like this one. We had had no rain for months and the sand was bone dry. I liked the contrast between the south westerly stripes and the easterly sandfall.

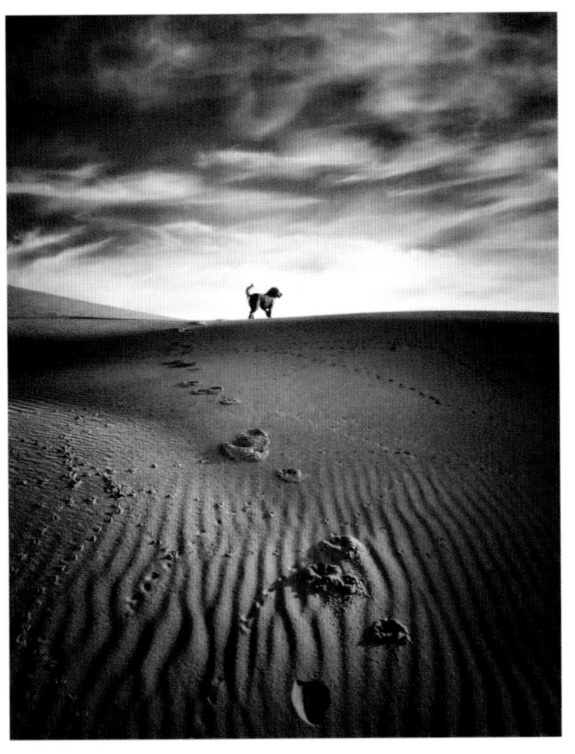
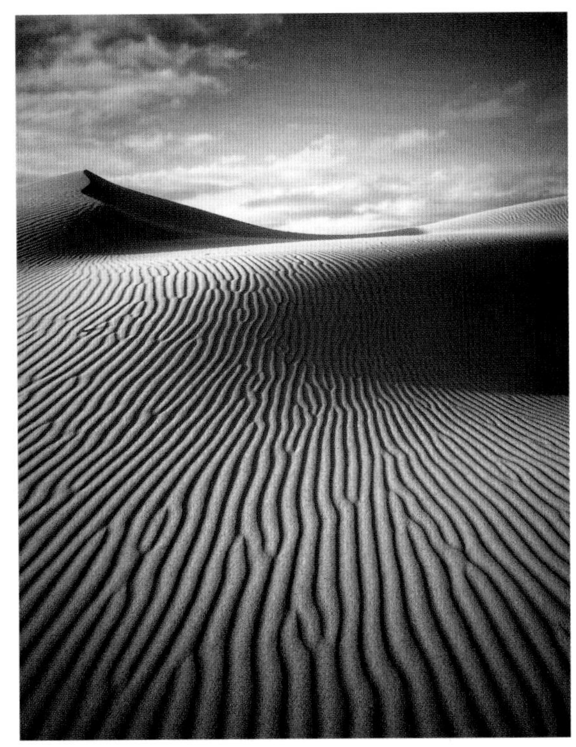
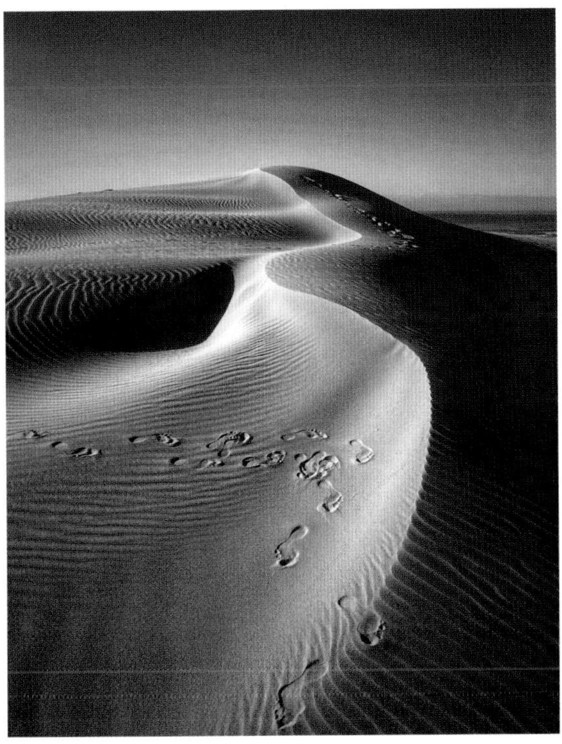
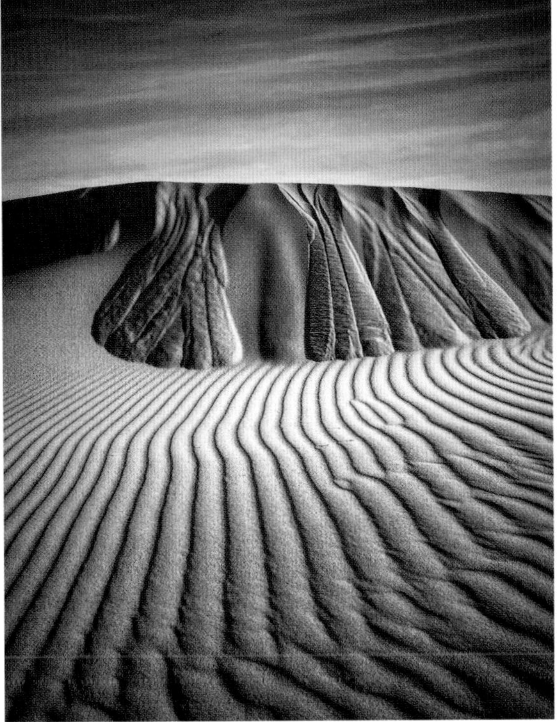

Barbara Januszewska-Piróg
Zielona Góra, Poland

A favourite part of Barbara Januszewska-Piróg's job as a real estate broker is photographing the properties she rents and sells. She also loves to travel and use photography to document what she sees. During the Covid-19 pandemic she became interested and 'totally absorbed' in taking photographs with her camera phone.

At work, Januszewska-Piróg uses a Sony A6000 camera, but when she is travelling she prefers to take photos with her smartphone; it is much lighter and always with her. She is faithful to Samsung phones; she started out with a Galaxy S8 and now has a Galaxy S21. She edits with Lightroom, and sometimes also uses Snapseed for retouching and SKRWT for fixing perspective and leaning verticals.

Januszewska-Piróg enjoys photographing cities because she loves their 'architecture, buildings, streets and people'. She is drawn to symmetry and appreciates the aesthetics of Wes Anderson's films, and the way he frames and composes images. She also likes minimalism and playing with photos in Photoshop to create more or less unreal compositions with buildings in the lead role.

RIGHT: I was looking forward to a trip to Görlitz in east Germany, where almost the whole of the movie *The Grand Budapest Hotel* – my favourite Wes Anderson film – was shot. I have a huge hunger for this city. I only spent two or three hours there and it was not enough. But I'm comforted by the fact that I visited it on Saturday afternoon, during my favourite golden hour. I took a picture of the beautiful Barockhaus building, which houses a museum and an amazing library that I only know from photos. I stood on the other side of the street, prepared the camera on the phone, set the parameters, and waited for someone to walk that way to take a perfectly symmetrical photo, with a passing person in the centre. I am sure that I will visit this city again because I still have a lot of sightseeing to do and photos to take there.

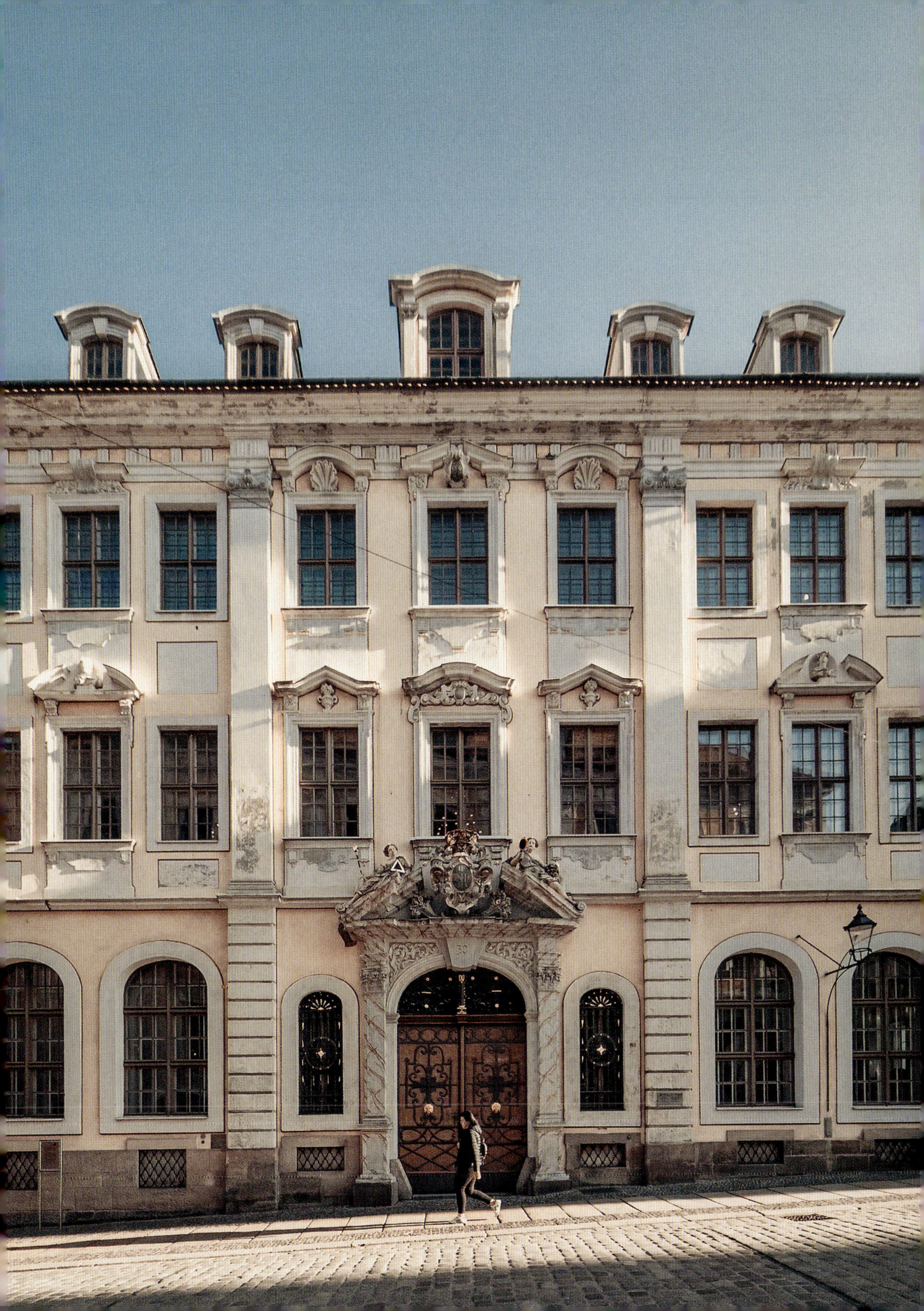

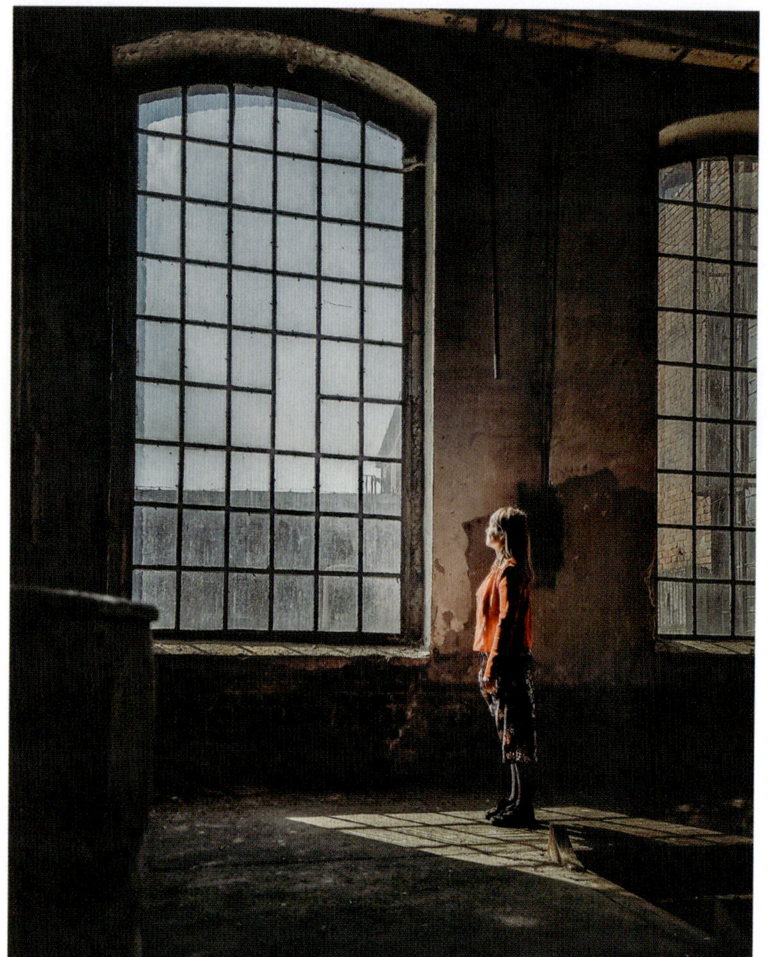

'I am a fan of Wes Anderson and his style, especially his perfect symmetry and perfectly matched colour palette.'

 The golden hour is every photographer's favourite time to take photos. I took this image at the beginning of July in Zielona Góra, my home city. I had planned to take something completely different, but I left for the city centre too late, the sun had almost set and nothing resulted from my planned photos. Dissatisfied with my tardiness, I wandered along Fabryczna, a street where old post-industrial buildings have been converted into apartments, and I took a photo of the most beautiful one, made of red brick. While taking the photo, a boy was passing by, so I had my 'human factor'. In the evening I sat down with the phone to edit this photo (usually I use Lightroom). This is how one of my favourite photos was created. It is also one of the photos I am most proud of.

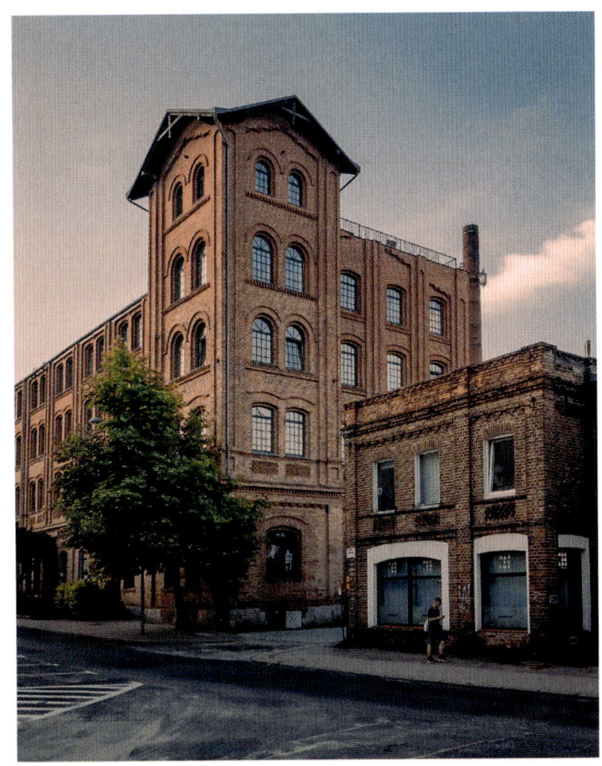

RIGHT: Shadows cast by trees on the wall of a beautiful tenement house. I had only noticed them a few days earlier, although I must have passed them thousands of times because it is on my route to and from work. The key to the micro-delight? Mindfulness and a clear head. You won't notice these little miracles when you are stressed and the phone is constantly ringing. But once you notice it is amazing what you feel: joy and happiness. Micro delight and macro emotions.

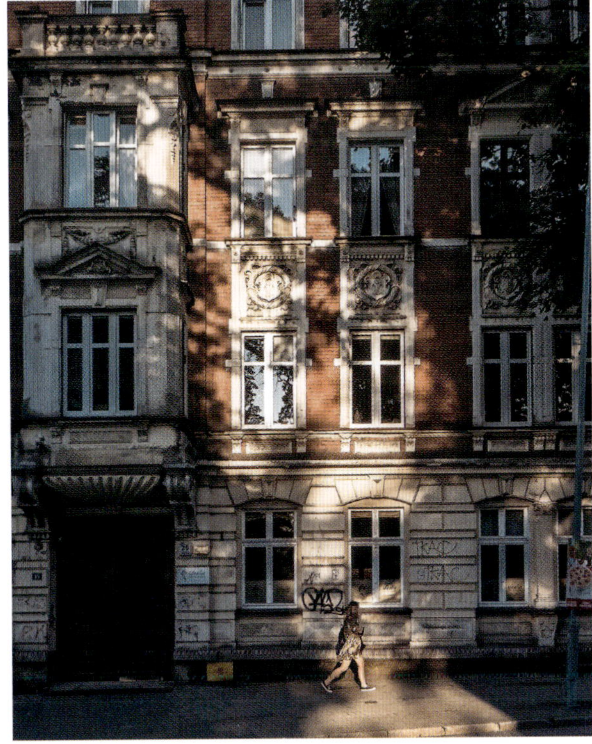

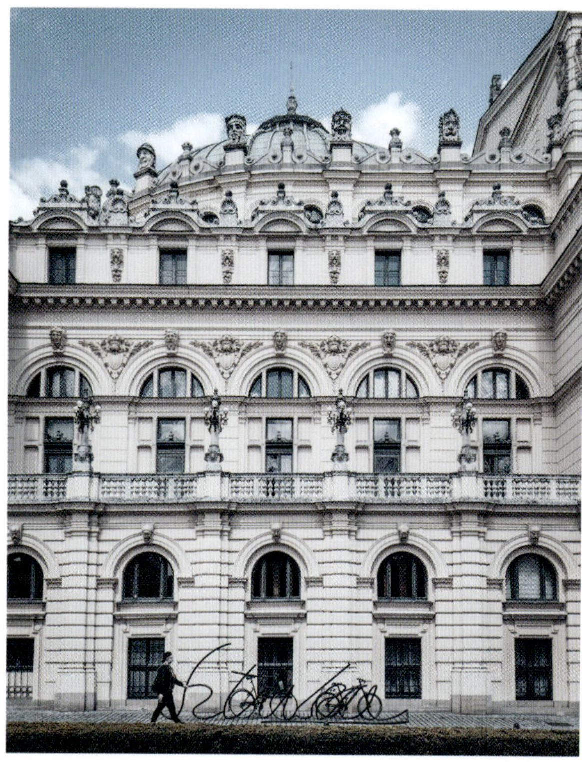

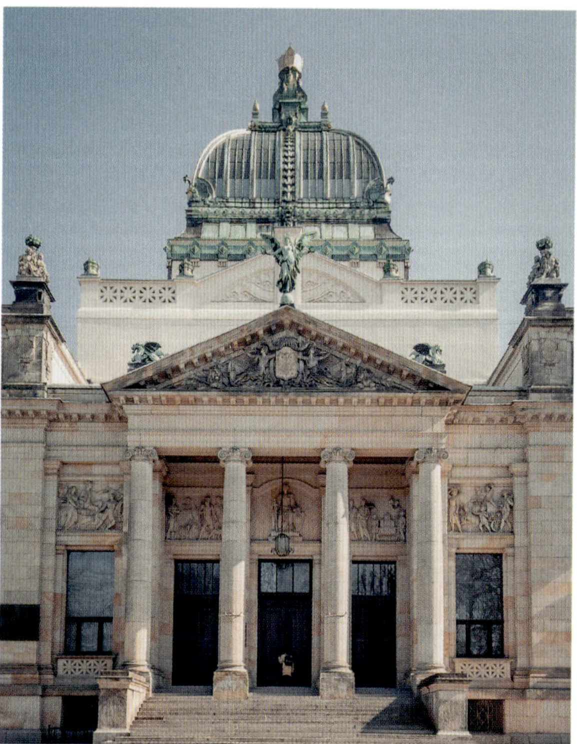

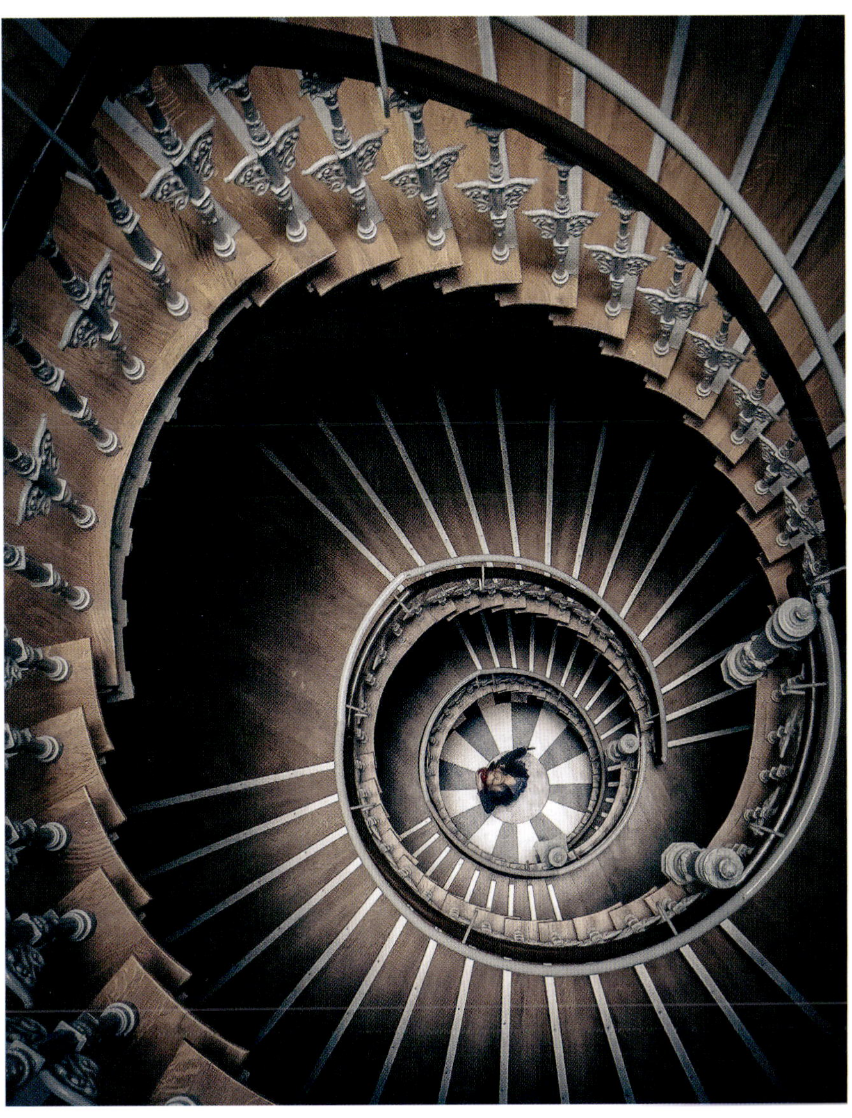

BARBARA JANUSZEWSKA-PIRÓG

Brendan Ó Sé
Cork, Ireland

Brendan Ó Sé is interested in street and abstract photography but, he says, only as a 'truly wonderful leisure activity'. He is the head of development in the Language Centre at University College Cork. Ó Sé is glad he is not a professional photographer as he suspects it would suck the joy out of it. His street photography gives him the chance to zone out and be in a 'visually charged' state of mind. Ó Sé shoots mainly on an Apple iPhone 11 Pro Max, and edits on his phone using Snapseed.

RIGHT: This was shot in Cork, very much in the moment, as the bus passed by. I liked the gesture and the sense of mischief, that idea of avoiding regret and taking risks. It has a lovely story attached to it in that after posting the photo on Instagram, the daughter of the main character contacted me to tell me the two men in the photo were her dad and uncle. They would have been in town enjoying a few drinks, and when she saw this photo it really brought home to her how life had changed during the Covid-19 pandemic, with simple things like two brothers meeting up for a social drink now not possible. I emailed her a copy of the photo, and she now has it framed in her home.

LEFT: This is another street photo, shot in the moment in Cork. I liked the reflections and the layers achieved in creating this composition.

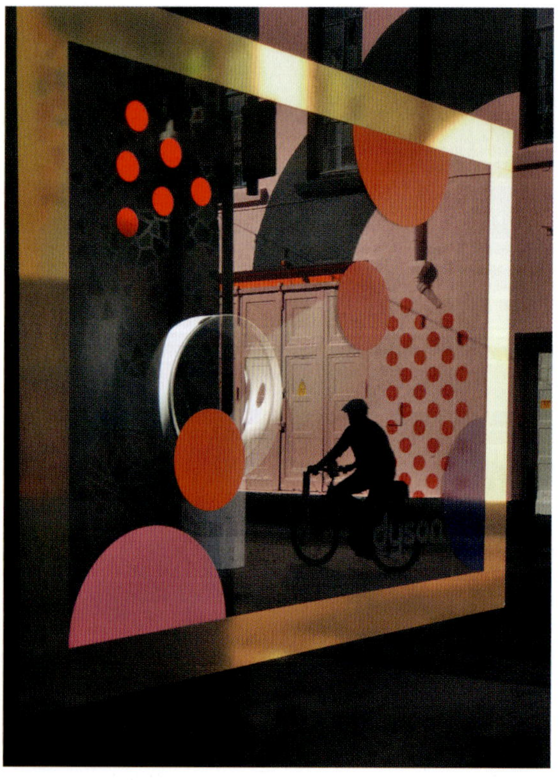

'I love exploring creativity and vision in my photography.'

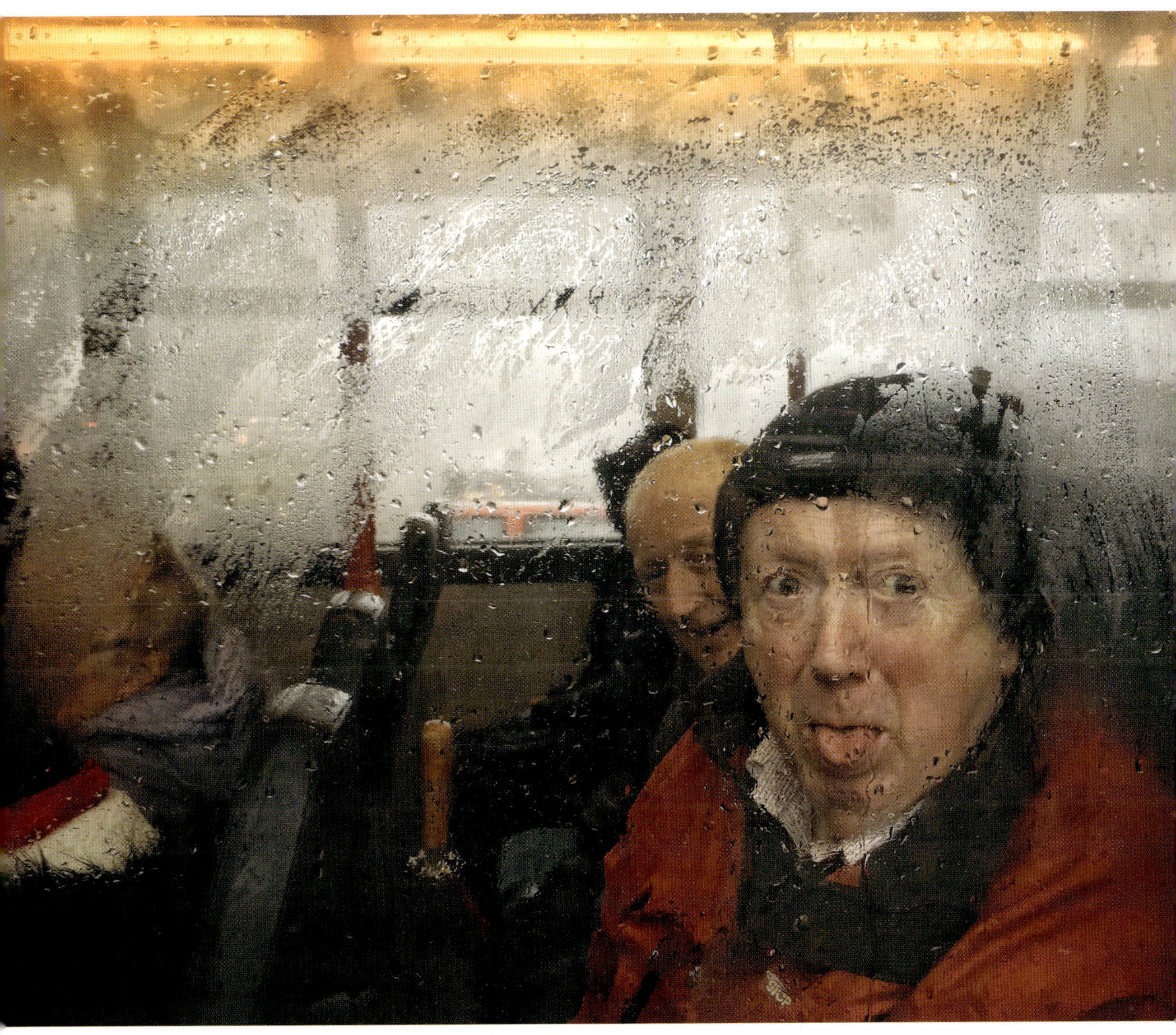

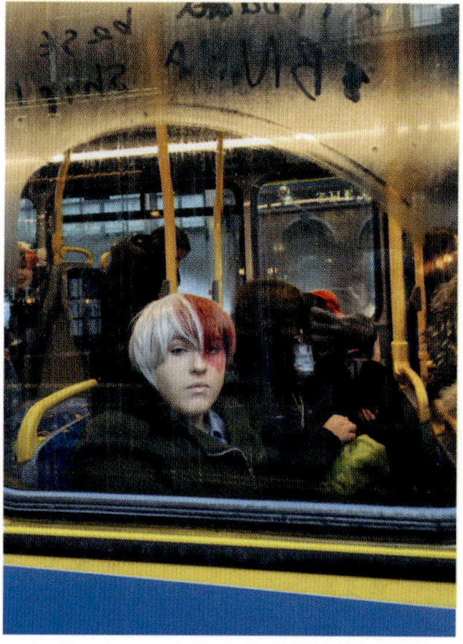

LEFT + BELOW: In the first image, I loved the frame created by this Dublin bus window and the lines and textures of the colours and condensation. The bus window provided a similar frame in the second photo. The layers and depth and distortion created by the condensation on the bus window and the fabulous look of surprise on the subject's face were brilliant.

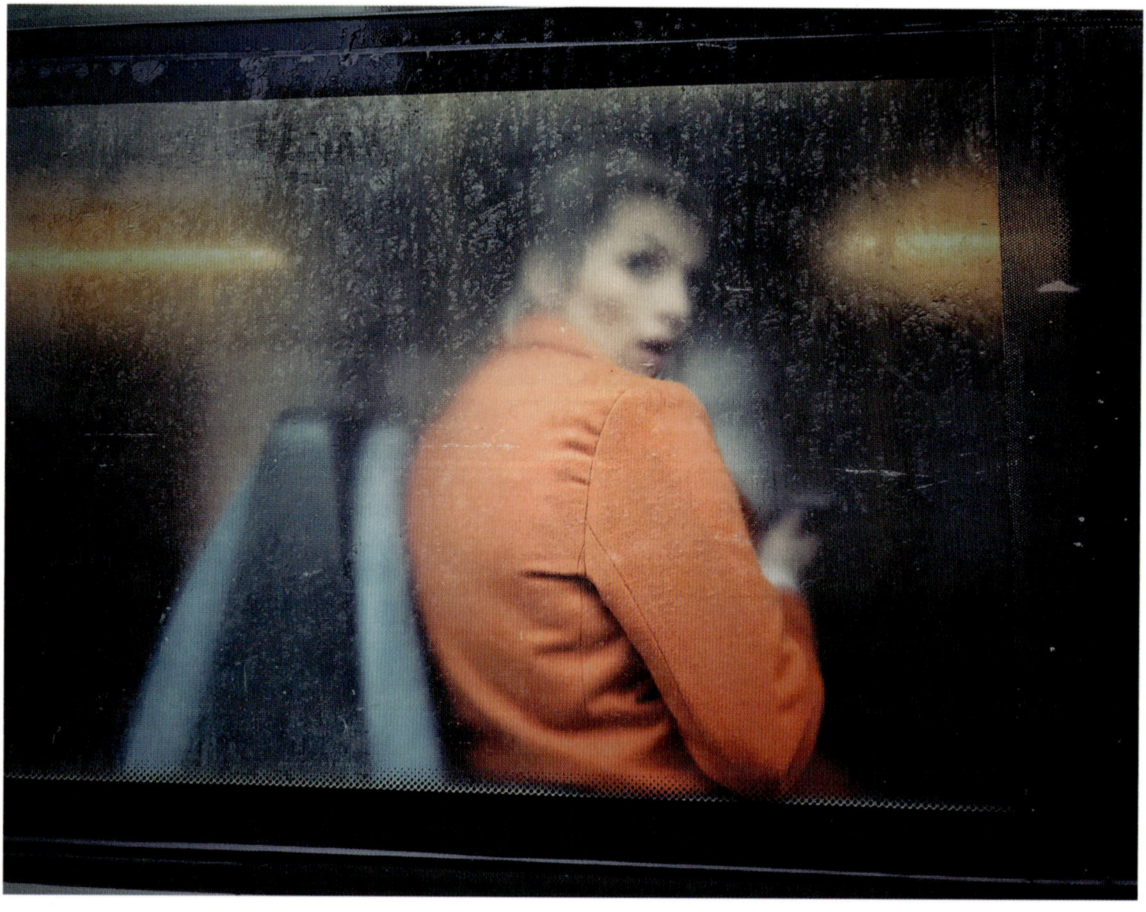

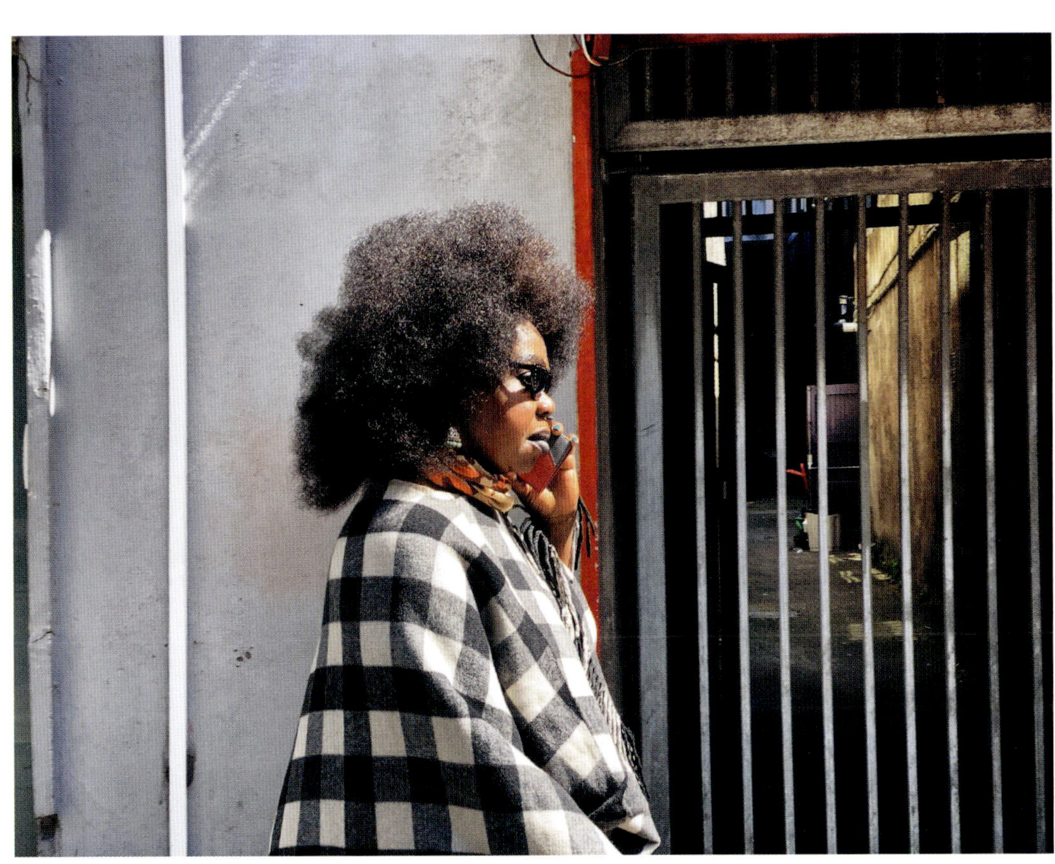

ABOVE: I saw this lady in Cork and was attracted to her style and how wonderful she looked, though I don't know her. For me the act of taking street photos of people is primarily about my sense of empathy towards them, as much as the idea of risk-taking and finding adventure.

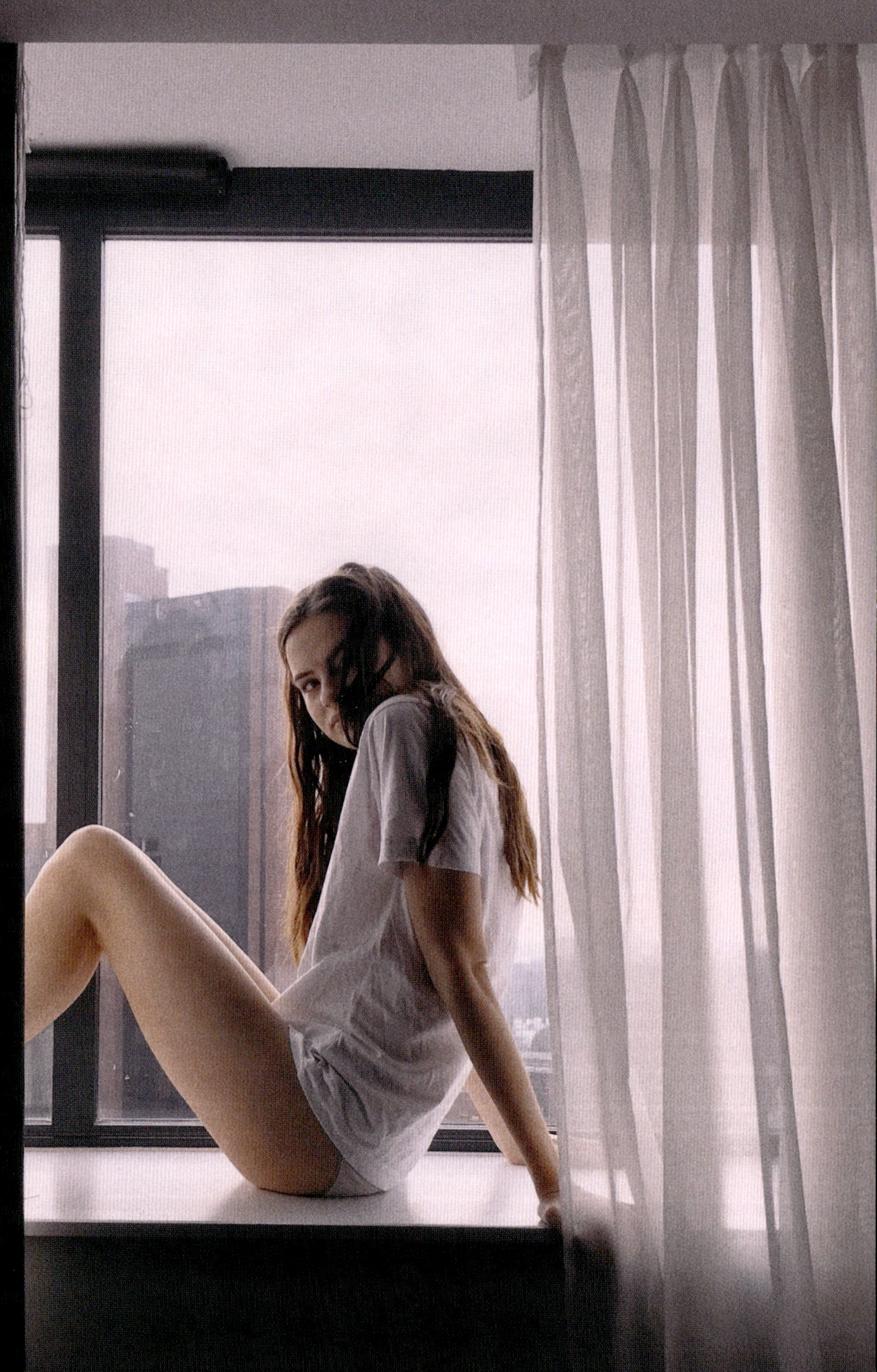

Charlotte Mason-Mottram
Weybridge, UK

 Georgie is my sister and best friend. This photo was taken inside a hotel room in Birmingham. She was working in Pryzm, a night club in Brighton, while studying, and won the opportunity to stay overnight with another person in a hotel in any city that had a Pryzm night club. She asked me to come with her and we chose Birmingham because it had the biggest Pryzm in the country. I had never been to Birmingham before, and we had a great view of the city from our room. The lighting was particularly captivating, as there was a stark contrast between the daylight and the darkness of the bedroom (we were yet to turn on the lights and were extremely hungover). I asked Georgie to sit on the windowsill because I saw an opportunity with the lightning.

Social media manager and copywriter Charlotte Mason-Mottram spends most of her time and money travelling, and she rarely visits the same place twice. With working from home no longer taboo, she makes the most of her employers' 'work from anywhere' scheme to achieve her perfect work/life balance. When the lease on her home in London came to an end in 2022 she moved in with her grandparents. It made much more sense given her lifestyle, and she says she has a wonderful relationship with them, even though they can't quite believe how often she is away. She says: 'they ask me if I'm likely to get fired from my job!' Mason-Mottram says that photography is her passion in her free time. For as long as she can remember, she has taken photos exclusively with her Apple iPhone. Her photography captures people in moments when they aren't expecting to be photographed, and she points her camera at both strangers and friends. Mason-Mottram photographs her travels and her friends on an iPhone 13 Pro, and often uses VSCO to finish them.

'I seem to like photographing people in hotel rooms. I think it's because the lighting can be controlled and manipulated to stage the perfect shot.'

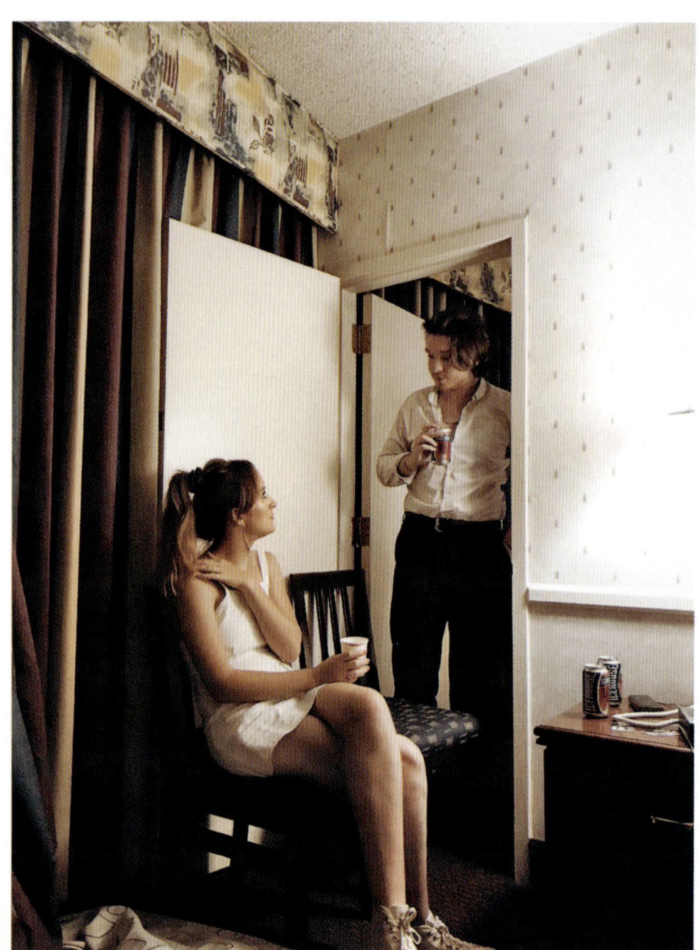

LEFT: I went to school with Katie and Joe. They are two of my best friends and have been together for 11 years. We were on a three-week road trip around America and I took this photo when we stopped in Las Vegas, Nevada. We chose this hotel because it was cheap, and we knew we were about to spend a lot of money! I shot it in the moment, as Joe appeared in the connecting doorway to another of our rooms. We were drinking cans of cheap beer ready to head downstairs to the casino inside the hotel. I knew they would like this type of candid photo. I love the colours and the way Katie is looking up at Joe from her chair. I used the filter M5 on VSCO. Katie and Joe currently have the image framed in their flat in east London, which makes me very happy.

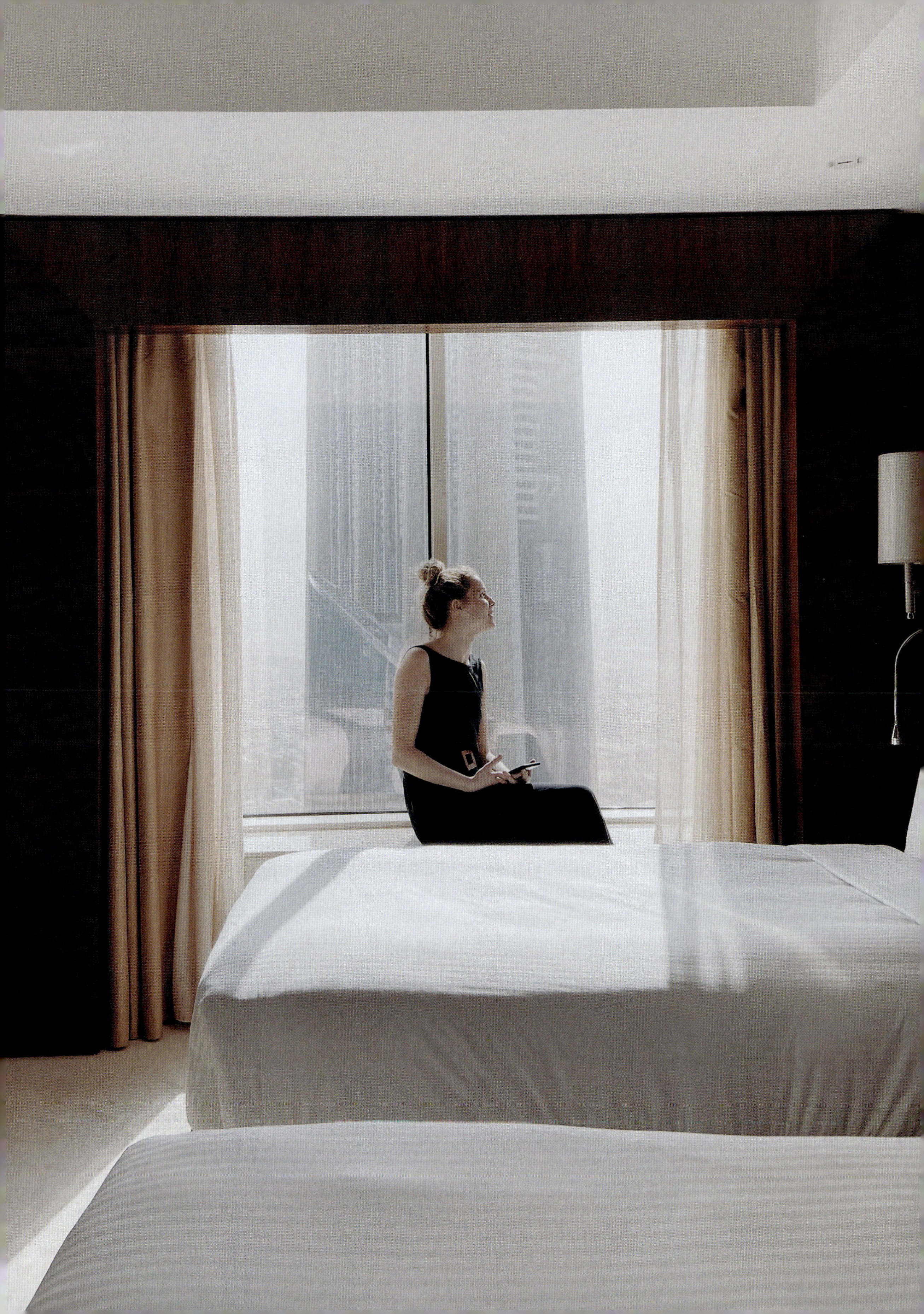

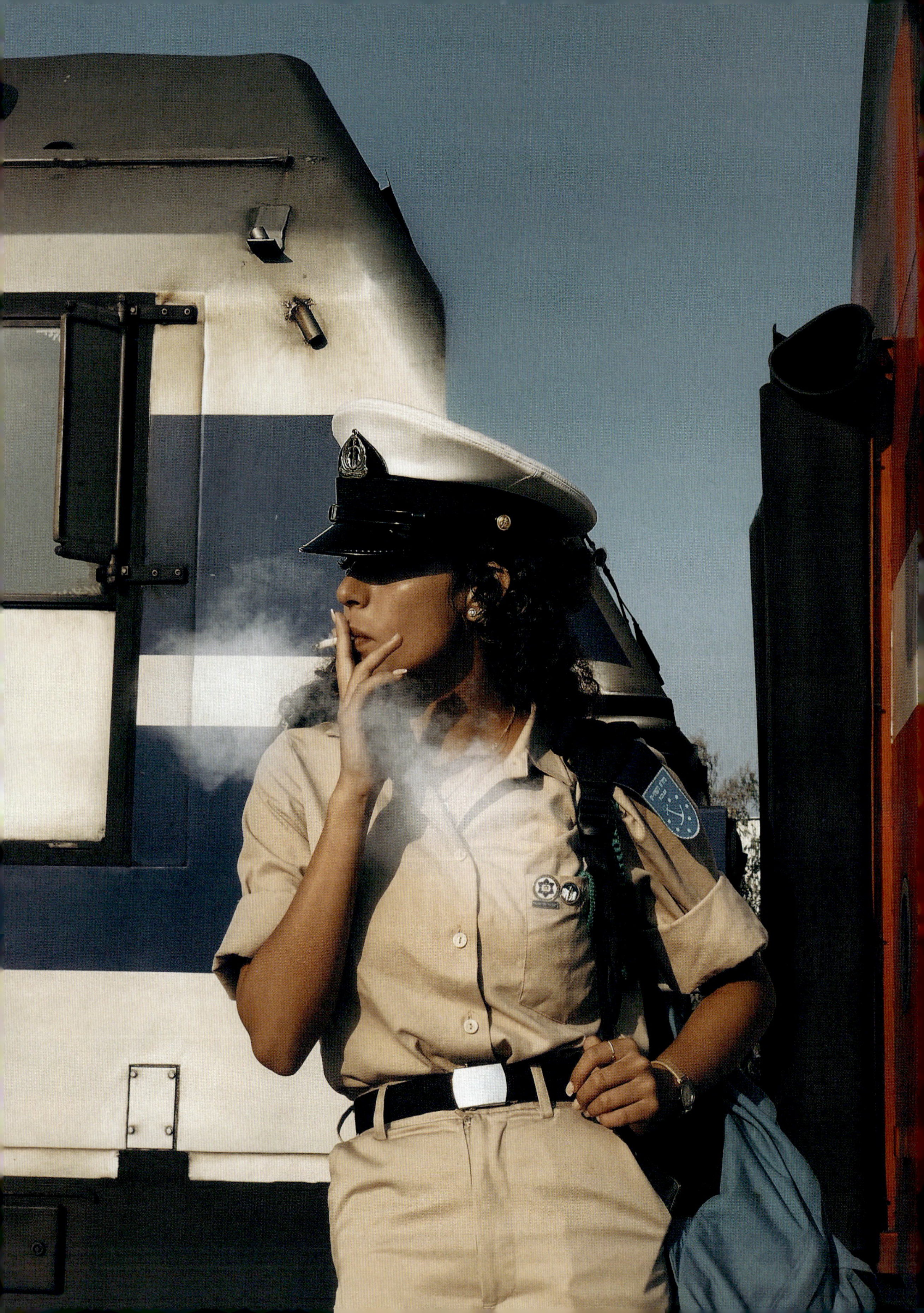

Dina Alfasi
Hadera, Israel

LEFT: A young sailor looking super cool at the train station.

'I take pictures almost on a daily basis, and I look forward to these opportunities for creative moments on my way to work and back.'

Dina Alfasi is an architectural engineer and works in a large hospital in northern Israel. The city where she lives was established in 1891 as a farming colony by members of the Zionist group Hovevei Zion, who had emigrated from Lithuania and Latvia. Today, the city's population includes a high proportion of immigrants who have been steadily arriving since the 1990s, mostly from Ethiopia and the former Soviet Union.

Hadera lies along two of the main Israeli railway lines, one of which is the Coastal Line, which Alfasi uses for her commute to work. As she frequently uses public transport, most of her photos are taken on trains and buses during her trips to and from work. She uses this time creatively, and as a chance to expand her photography. As a result, she takes pictures almost daily. She currently uses an Apple iPhone 14 Pro, Snapseed and VSCO. Her main interest is taking photos of people, and she describes her style as being mostly like street photography.

All the photos Alfasi shares are moments that made her think, get excited, intrigued, happy or sad. She hopes that she will be able to convey these feelings to people who view her pictures so that they can discover the story in that single image and feel excited too. Perhaps they will feel the same magic she felt in the moment as she captured the photograph.

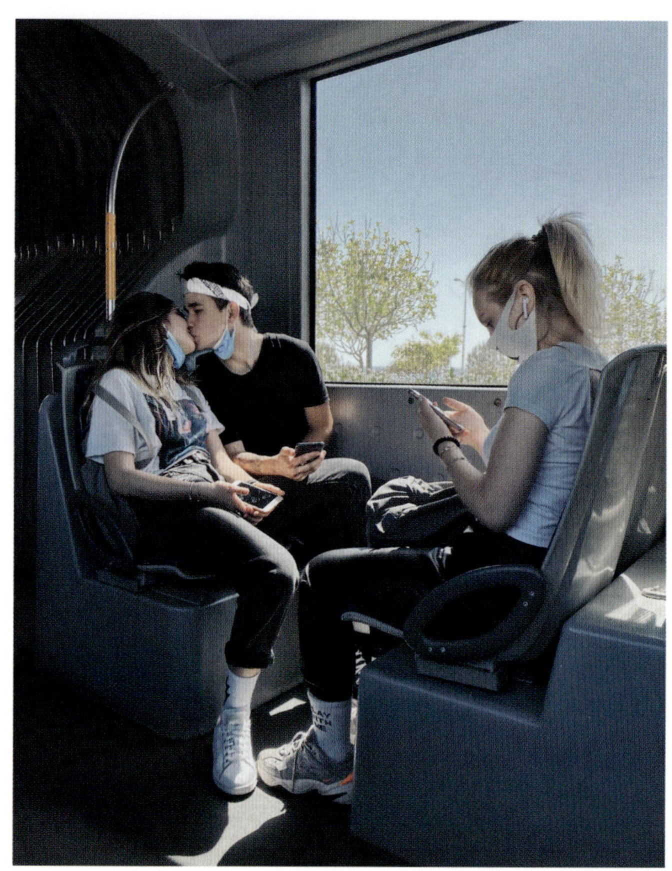

BELOW: A priest presides over a religious ceremony of the day of the Epiphany at the River Jordan.

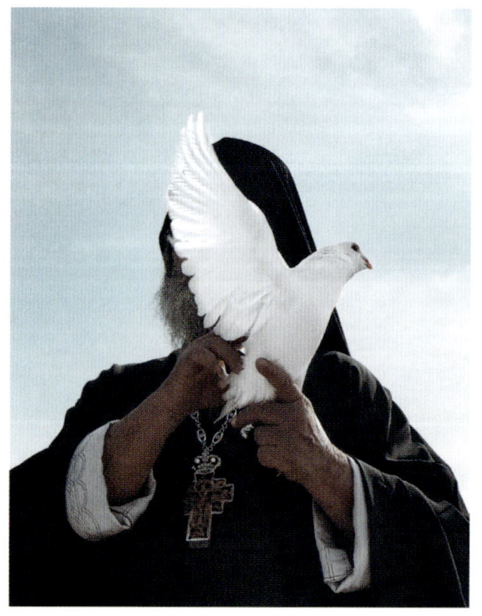

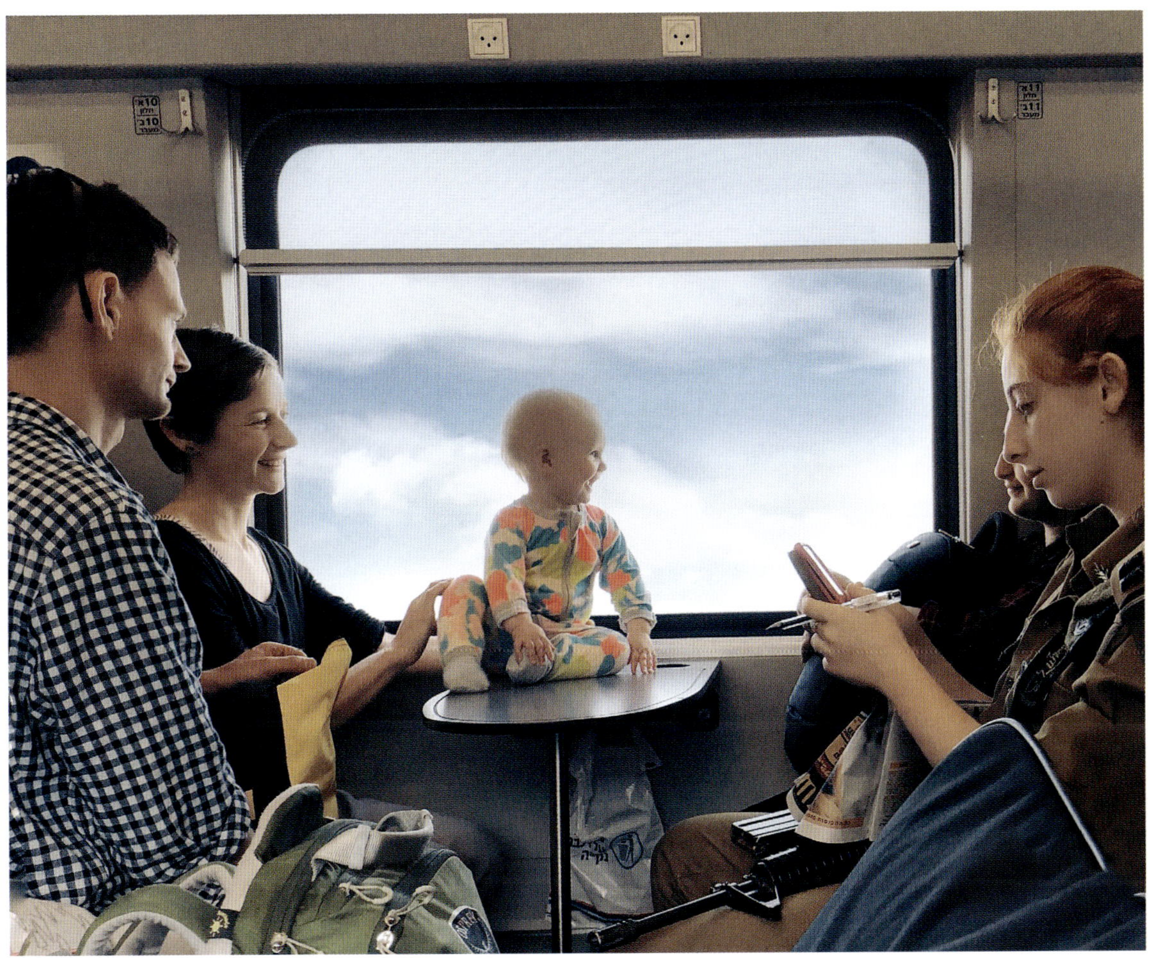

ABOVE: A cute baby girl charms all the passengers in a train carriage and makes everyone smile. The young woman with the gun is a conscripted soldier. In Israel there is mandatory conscription for all young people starting at the age of 18; both young men and women serve in the military and some of them regularly carry weapons.

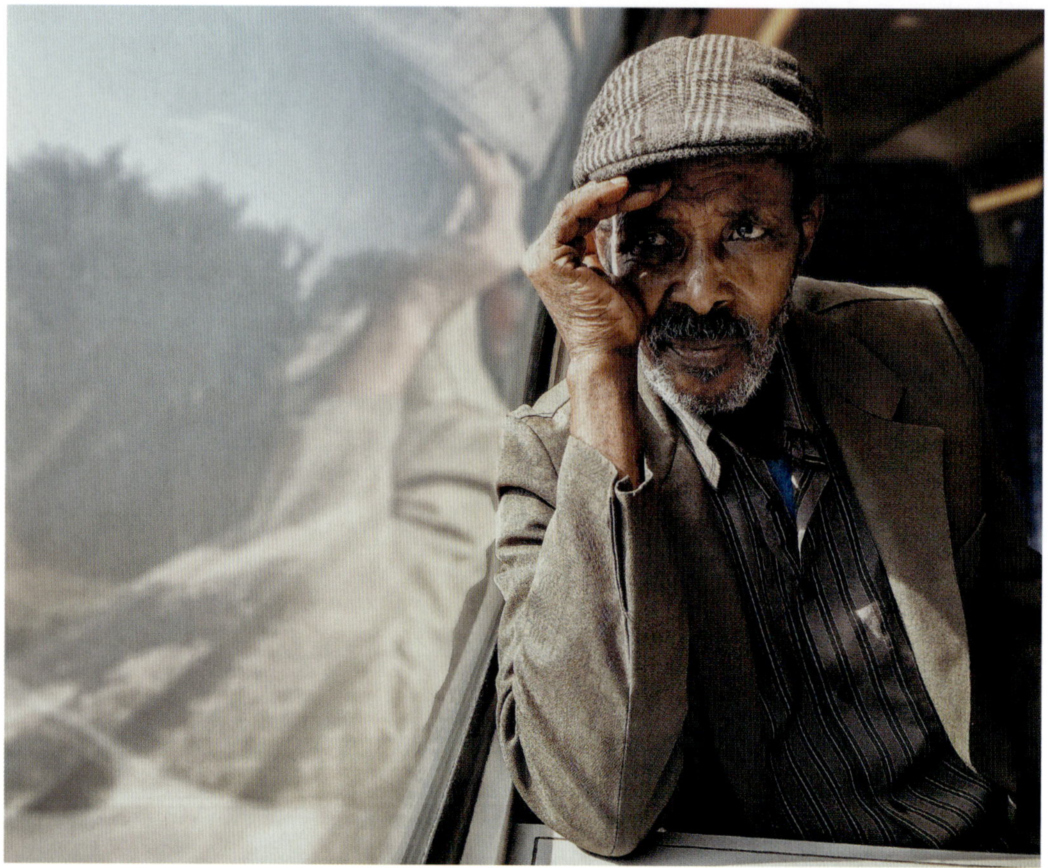

ABOVE: An elderly Ethiopian
man is lost in thought while he
watches the passing view from
a train window.

RIGHT: At sunset, a daydreaming
train traveller enjoys the warm
evening light.

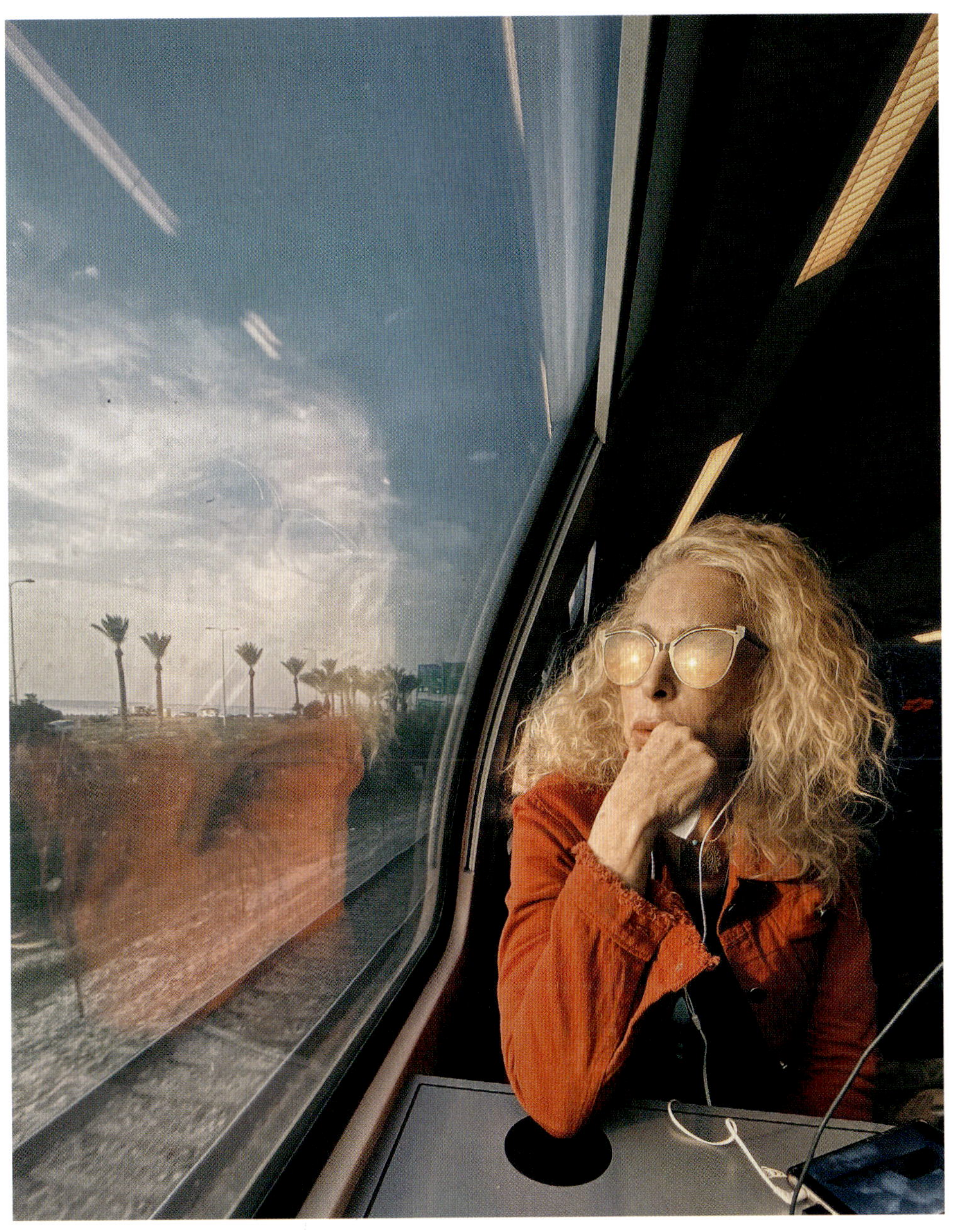

'iPhone photography has given me a way to bring creativity into my everyday life.'

Elaine Taylor
Leeds, UK

A mum of two teenage boys, Elaine Taylor has spent most of her career in university administration management. But over the past few years she spent time as a volunteer in education settings and with St John Ambulance, a first aid charity.

She is passionate about mobile phone photography. Taylor's Apple iPhone has been her only camera for over 12 years. Through her mobile photography, she has been on the jury of mobile photography awards, is a beta tester for a range of mobile apps and has delivered smartphone photography workshops. Her iPhone photos have been exhibited, published and received recognition in international photography competitions.

If needed, Taylor uses the iPhone's native editing tools or Snapseed for initial edits such as cropping and straightening. However, she tries to get those things right when she takes the photos. She also uses Hipstamatic a lot; in 2010 it was the first app she had ever used and is still her favourite. Every now and then she uses TouchRetouch to remove small unwanted items and blemishes.

RIGHT: I was away with my family and had been walking around looking for interesting photographic opportunities. I sat on a bench and noticed the railings in front of me and lots of different characters walking past. I love the contrast between the gentleman with the walking stick with his head down walking away from the shot and the couple standing still looking out at the sea.

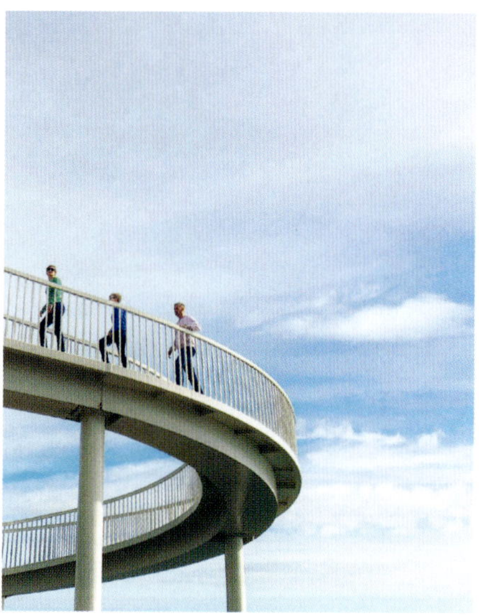

ABOVE: I didn't want my friends and family who were on the bridge to know I was going to take this photo, so I ran ahead of them. It turned out that they 100 per cent knew what I was doing as soon as I ran ahead with my camera and had slowed down on purpose. So this photo was staged without me knowing it. In reality there was a lot going on to the left and underneath the bridge, so I was very careful about cropping to keep it clean.

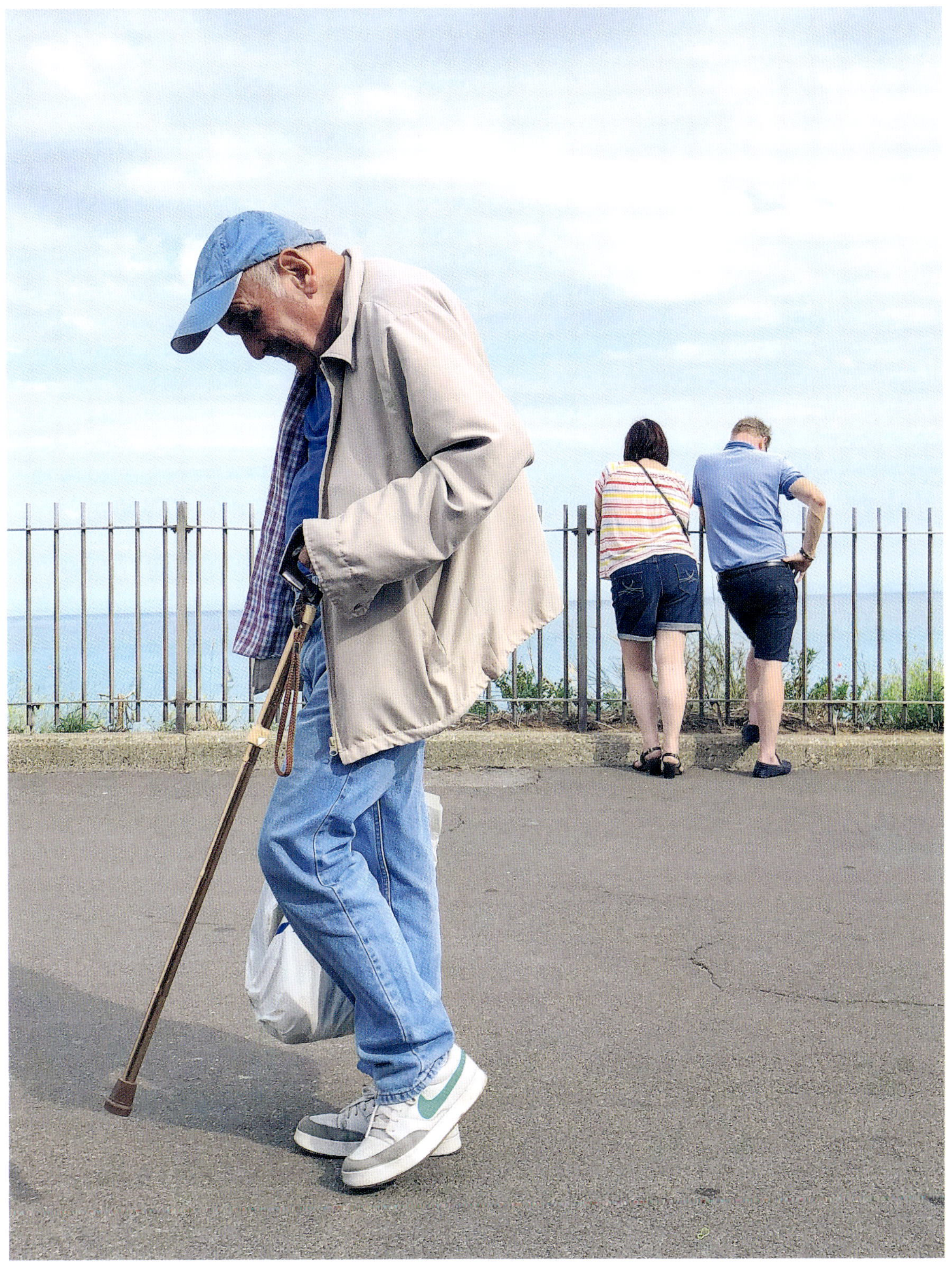

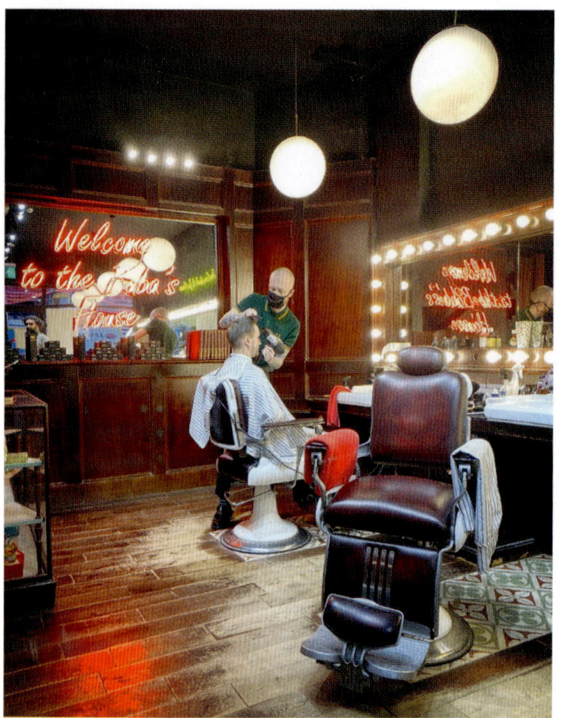

BELOW: I'm really attracted to colour. I am always looking for it and it is one of the first things I spot. At the time I took this photo I was often attracted to the colour blue, but I wasn't fully aware of this until I looked back at my photos later on. It was a lucky 'right place at the right time' shot. I was on a pedestrian crossing in the city centre and I noticed the two women chatting and the mannequins in the shop behind them. I noticed the contrast between them straight away and thought it would make a good photograph. I had to be a bit canny because I was on the crossing and on the move.

ABOVE: This is one of my favourite images. I shot it as part of the 24 Hour Project, when a couple of friends and I took a photo on the city streets of Leeds every hour for 24 hours, starting at midnight. This was a very early morning shot. I felt brave and went in and asked if I could take a picture. I was mindful of the composition; I was very aware of the lighting, the signs, people's faces.

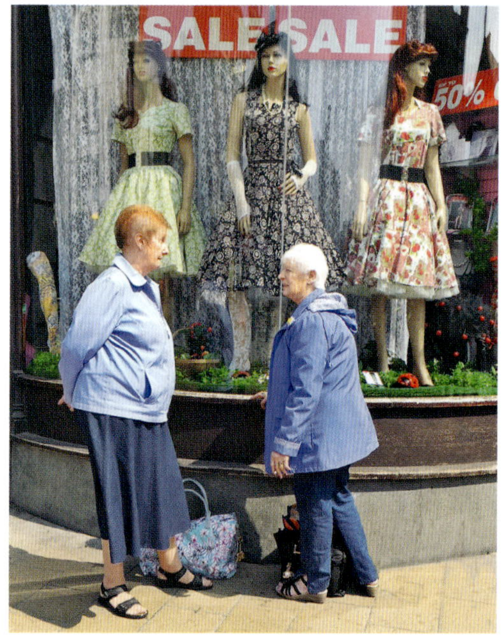

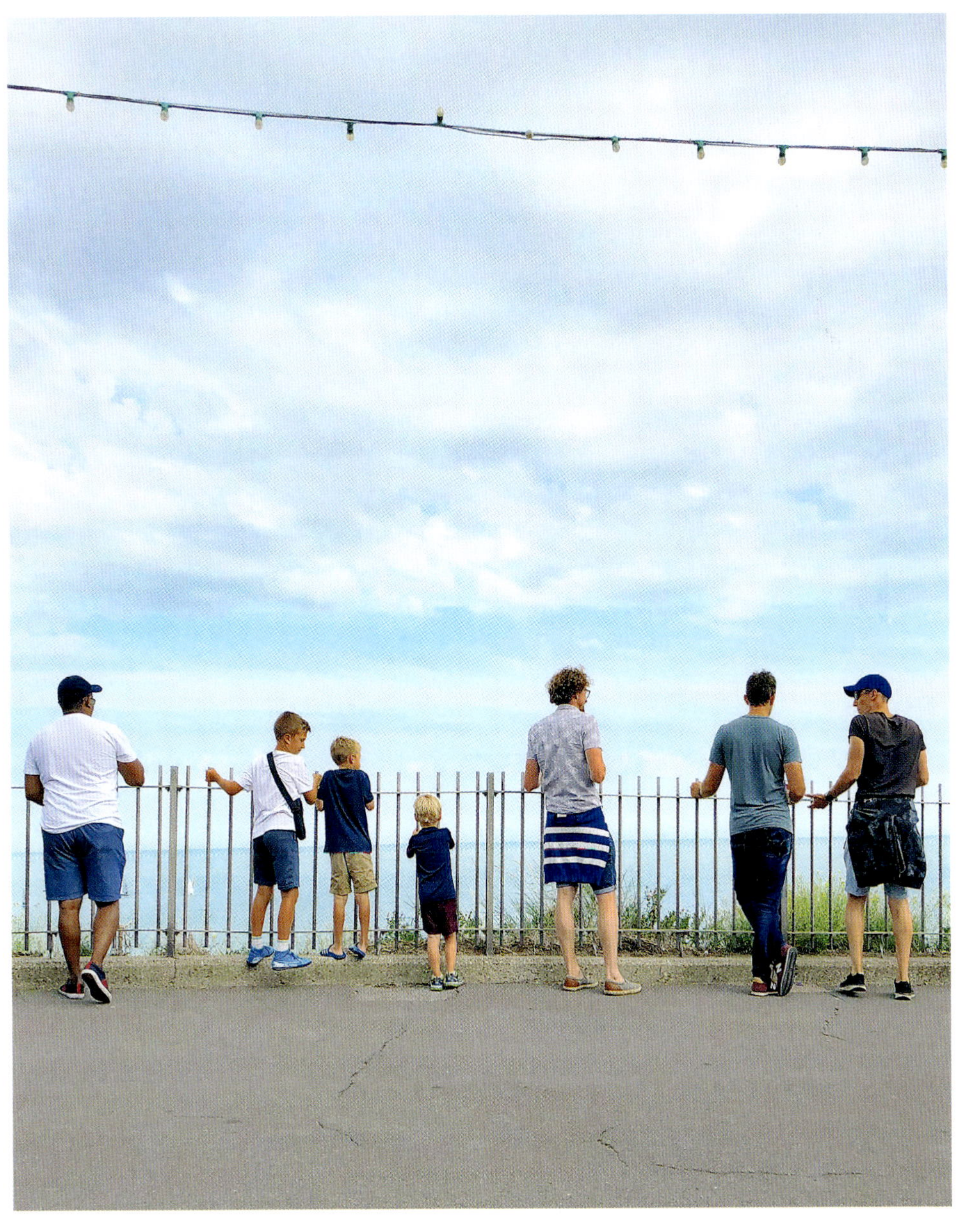

ELAINE TAYLOR

Ernest Ankomah
Accra, Ghana

Ernest Ankomah is a full-time freelance photojournalist. A large percentage of his work is commissioned by the World Health Organisation. He also works for other non-profit organisations, pitches work to international newspapers such as the *Guardian* or *Le Monde,* and works on assignment for Getty Images. Ankomah likes the fact that he has no idea of who around the world is looking at his work. He uses an Apple iPhone 12 Pro, and edits with Lightroom, VSCO and Snapseed.

As a child Ankomah read novels and drew pictures while his sisters told him he should read biology textbooks. There was a sense that creative activities would not lead to a secure profession. He did some photography at high school. He travelled around the country performing as a member of the school choir and used point-and-shoot digital cameras to take photos of his fellow choristers to sell back to them.

After graduating with a degree in biomedical engineering, he spent five years working as a surgical instruments engineer. This gave Ankomah the chance to travel around the country, exploring beautiful places and meeting people with interesting stories to tell. His interest in photography grew and he quit his job to focus on it.

Today his working life as a photographer is in stark contrast to his past life as an engineer. He enjoys this spontaneous way of working but has had to adapt since he got married. In Ghana, quitting a full-time job to be a photographer is unusual, and photography isn't considered a profession. For Ankomah, it was a big step; his mother worried he wouldn't be able to support himself, but she sees that photography makes him happy and knows that's what is important.

RIGHT: In Winneba, a coastal town an hour from Accra, this lady, with her yellow socks pulled up to her knees, is selling a local delicacy *kosua ne meko* (hard-boiled chicken's eggs with onions and hot pepper sauce sandwiched in the middle). I bought a few eggs (one is never enough) and chatted to her a bit about her work. She carries the pepper sauce in the blue tub on her head.

'Photography is everything to me.'

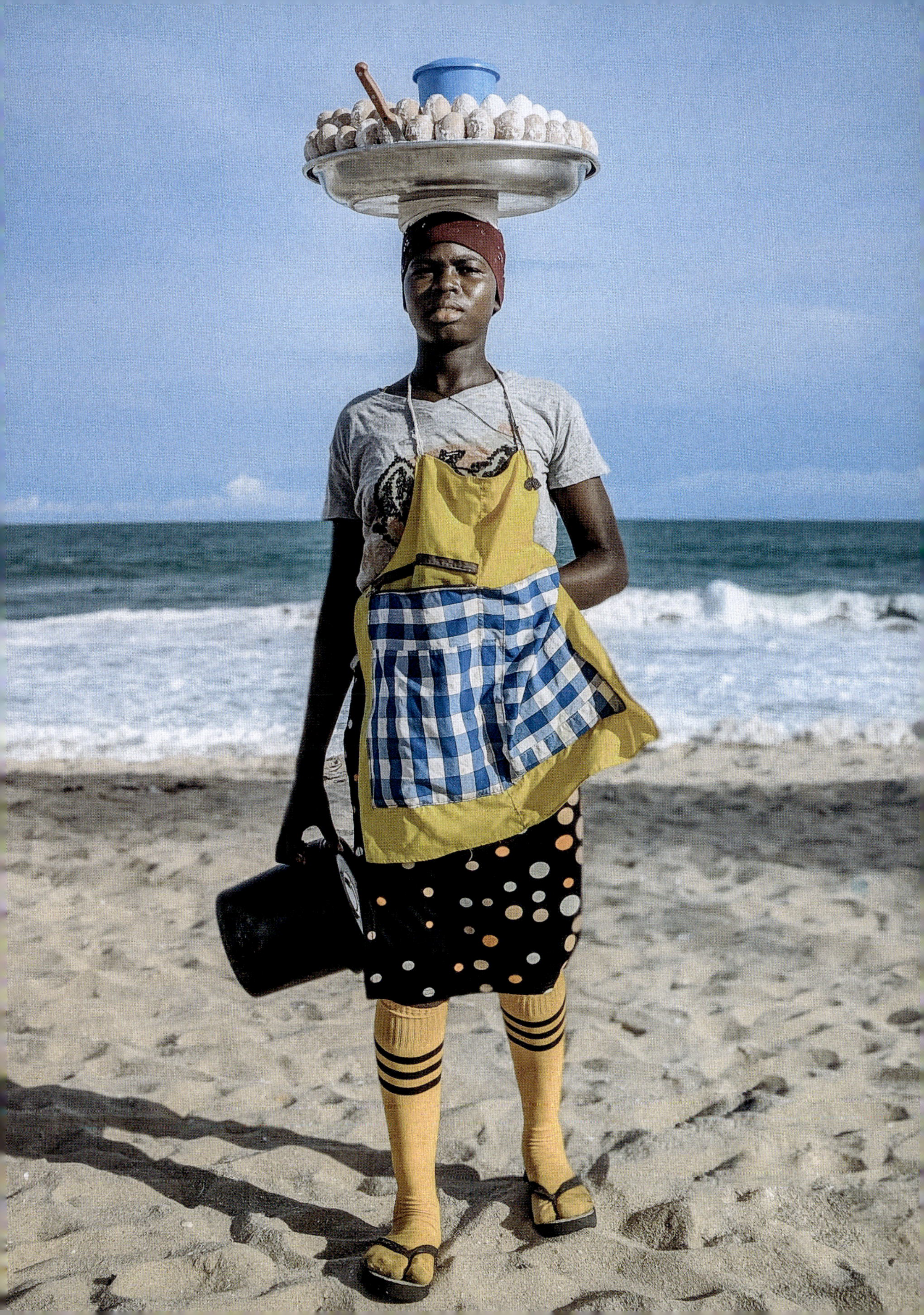

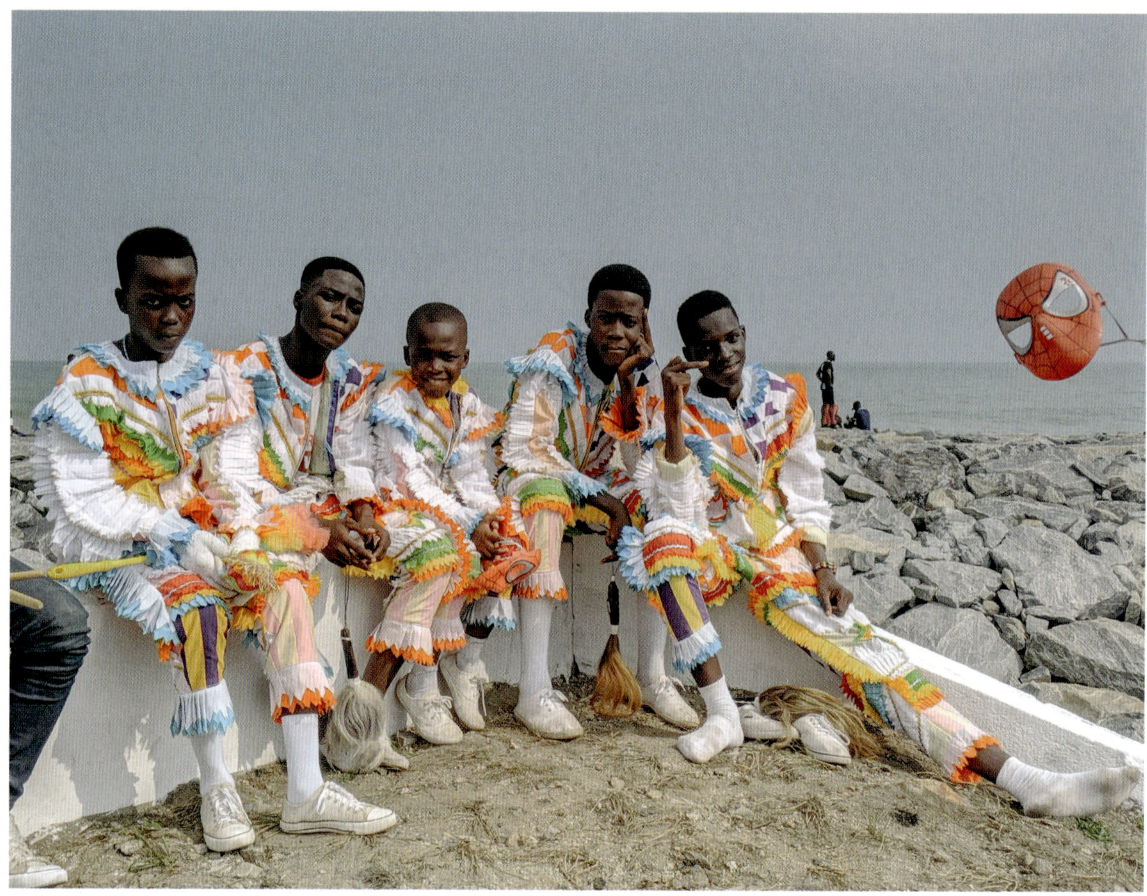

 Elmina, a coastal town with a large fishing community, hosts the annual Bakatue Festival, which celebrates the founding of the town. As Tuesday is considered to be the day of the sea god, it is held on the first Tuesday in July every year. These young men are taking a break from their 'masqueraders' acrobatic street performance. Groups of masqueraders move along the coast to perform at all the local festivals. They have cow's tails – *nan twi podua* – at their feet, which are used as part of their performance. The *podua* were originally used by priests and witch doctors and their exact origin is unknown. They use them purely for fun with no real connection to their history. The young man in the centre is holding a Spider-Man mask, as does an unseen performer standing to the side and holding his mask into the frame. The whole group would have worn Spider-Man masks for the performance; they freely mix cultural references like the *podua* and superhero masks.

BELOW: I was being driven by a company driver when we hit traffic. This boy took the opportunity to give the windscreen a wash before we had a chance to say no. I grabbed my phone and took a few shots, the traffic cleared, and we moved on. My only interaction with the boy was to tip him two cedi notes. I like that the boy's face is not showing so there is a bit of mystery to the whole image. You can see the figure and exactly what he is doing but not who he is, something of a visual metaphor for the class system and the visibility of people working on the streets.

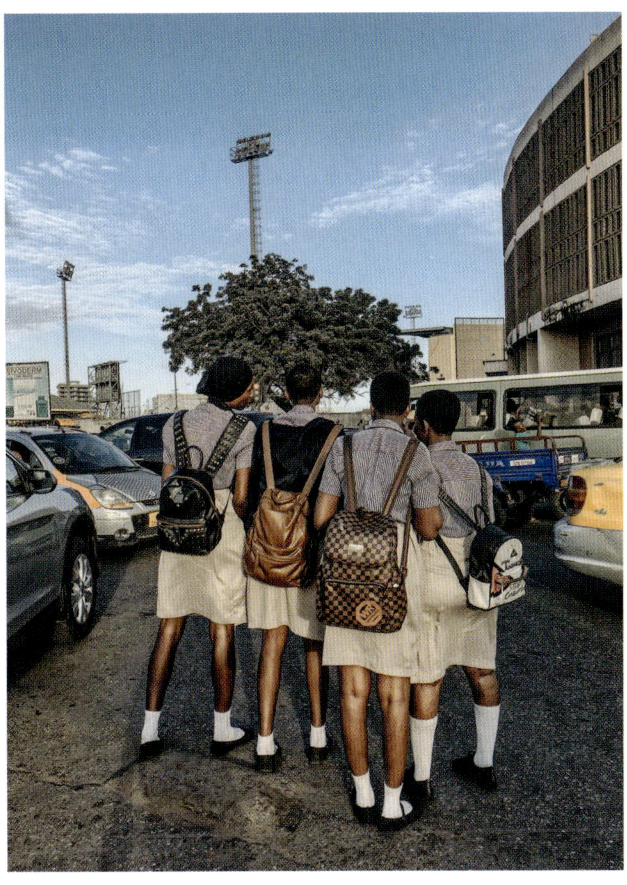

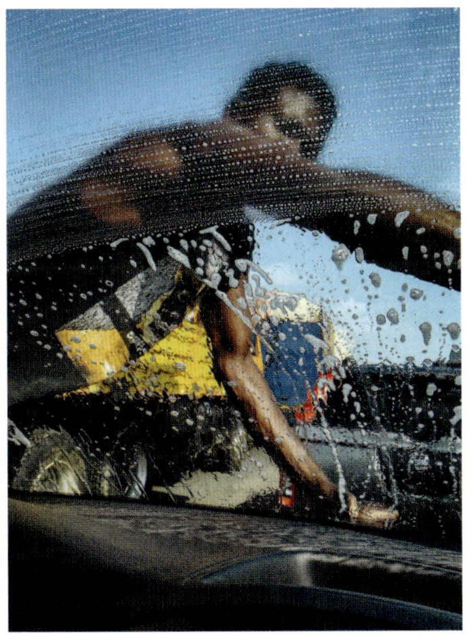

ABOVE: The girls in this photo were on their way home from school in Accra. The traffic is chaotic, and the cars don't give way to pedestrians. The girls have come together to signal the drivers to stop. I saw it as a statement of unity or togetherness. When there's only one of you it would be impossible to get the cars to stop for you, but this group had managed to get two cars to stop in the time it took me to take this photo. There is a uniformity in the group, as the girls all wear their bags in the same way and are wearing school uniform. This is heightened by the fact that in Ghanaian high schools it is obligatory for students to keep their hair short.

Ernest Rius Bonet
Badalona, Spain

Nurse Ernest Rius Bonet works at a Catalonian hospital and a blood donor centre in Barcelona. He was brought up in Valls, a small town that is rich in Catalan culture, but moved to Badalona (which is north-east of Barcelona) because there were more options for work and so he could take dance classes. When Rius Bonet was younger he wanted to be a vet, but he did not get the grades required to pursue his dream. He chose nursing without really knowing if he would like it, and now he loves it. Outside work his passions are creative, with a love of dancing – a passion sparked when he joined a nursing classmate at a contemporary dance class – and photography.

Rius Bonet uses an Apple iPhone and lightly edits some of his photos using the Lightroom app. His pictures often feature his partner, Aleix. He takes engaging photos of their lives and travels with the express desire of capturing memories of their love and time together that will last forever. His vibrant, colourful photographs feel full of the joy of a life led to the fullest. They exude his passion, the intense emotional connection he has with Aleix and how much being a positive person means to him.

Rius Bonet proudly came out at the age of 16. Until then he needed to hide his homosexuality. He says that in Spain, bigger cities such as Madrid and Barcelona are generally more accepting of the LGBTQI+ community than the smaller towns, but happily both Badalona and Valls are gay-friendly these days. Although he was supported by his friends when he finally felt ready to come out, his family took more time to accept his homosexuality. Fortunately, they soon saw how happy he is and now they support the LGBTQI+ community of which Ernest is so proud to be a part.

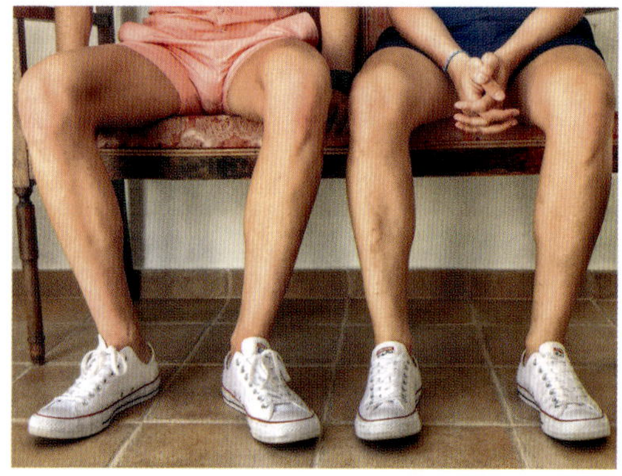

ABOVE: I took this self-portrait to mark the first time Aleix and I were invited to a wedding as a couple. I wanted to make the viewer wonder about the subjects' story. 'Are they looking at each other? Are they happy? Are they kissing?' We were definitely two of those in that particular moment.

'I am a positive person. I do not usually take "sad" pictures. I like to show myself as a happy person.'

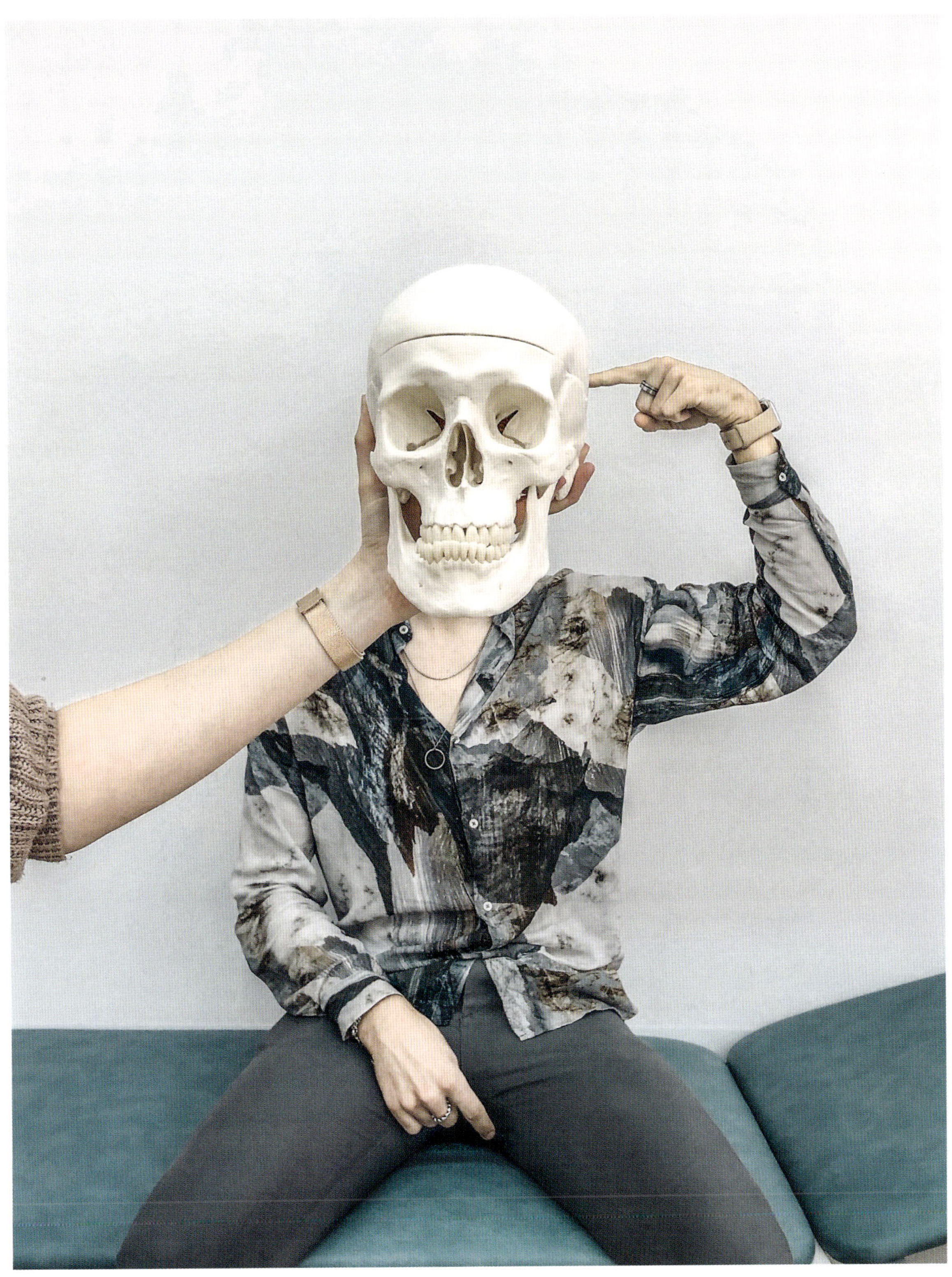

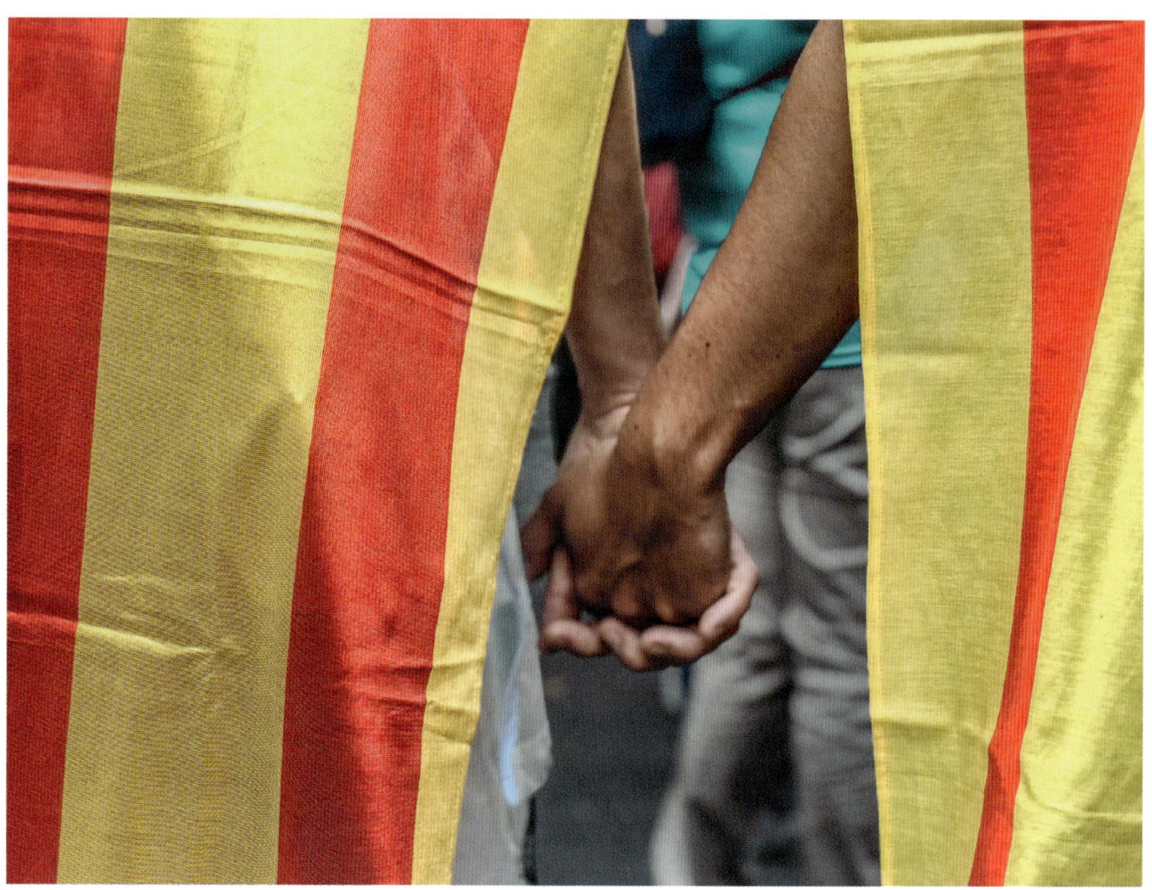

ABOVE: Two men holding hands and 'wearing' Catalonian flags on 11 September, Catalonia's national day, known in Catalan as the *Día Nacional de Cataluña*. The day commemorates the end of the War of Spanish Succession, the fall of Barcelona when the Catalonian army was defeated by the Franco-Spanish army and the subsequent loss of Catalan institutions and laws. Both Aleix and I want Catalonia to become an independent nation. I wanted the photo to show a couple who share beliefs and ideals.

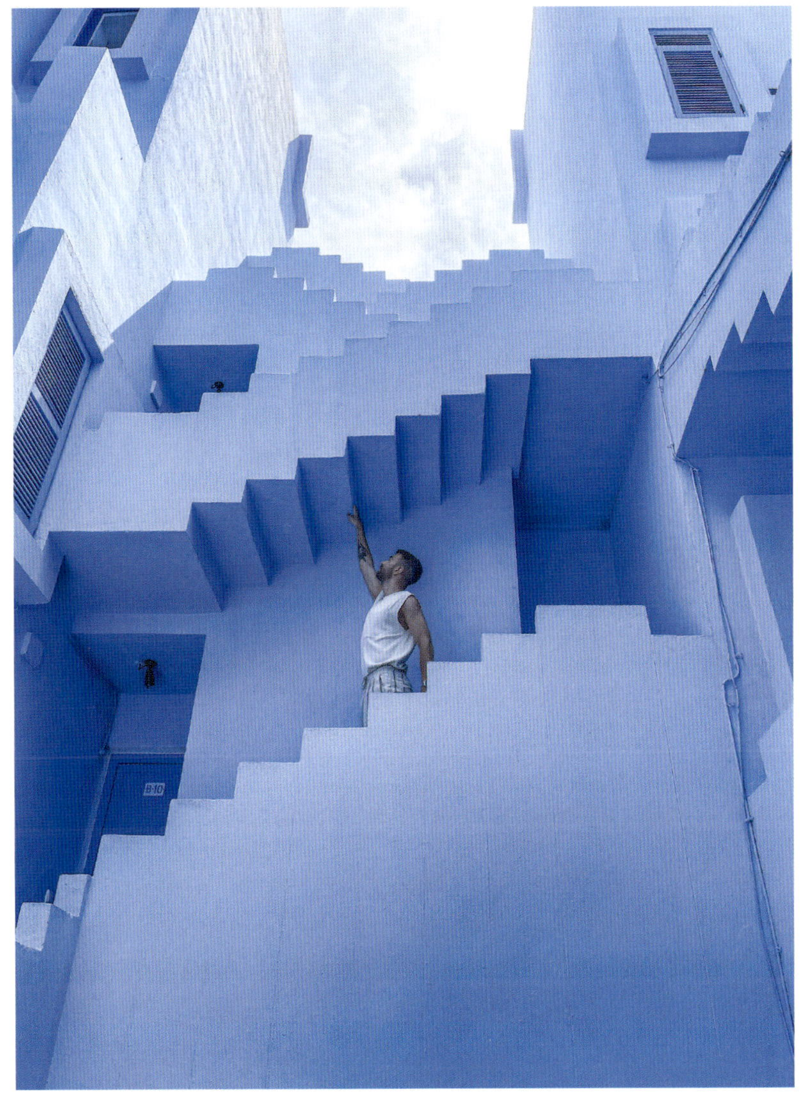

'When I was at school I was bullied by some classmates. It made
me realize at a young age that there was something different about
my sexuality. As I grew up, and as I moved to Barcelona, everything
changed. The city is more cosmopolitan.'

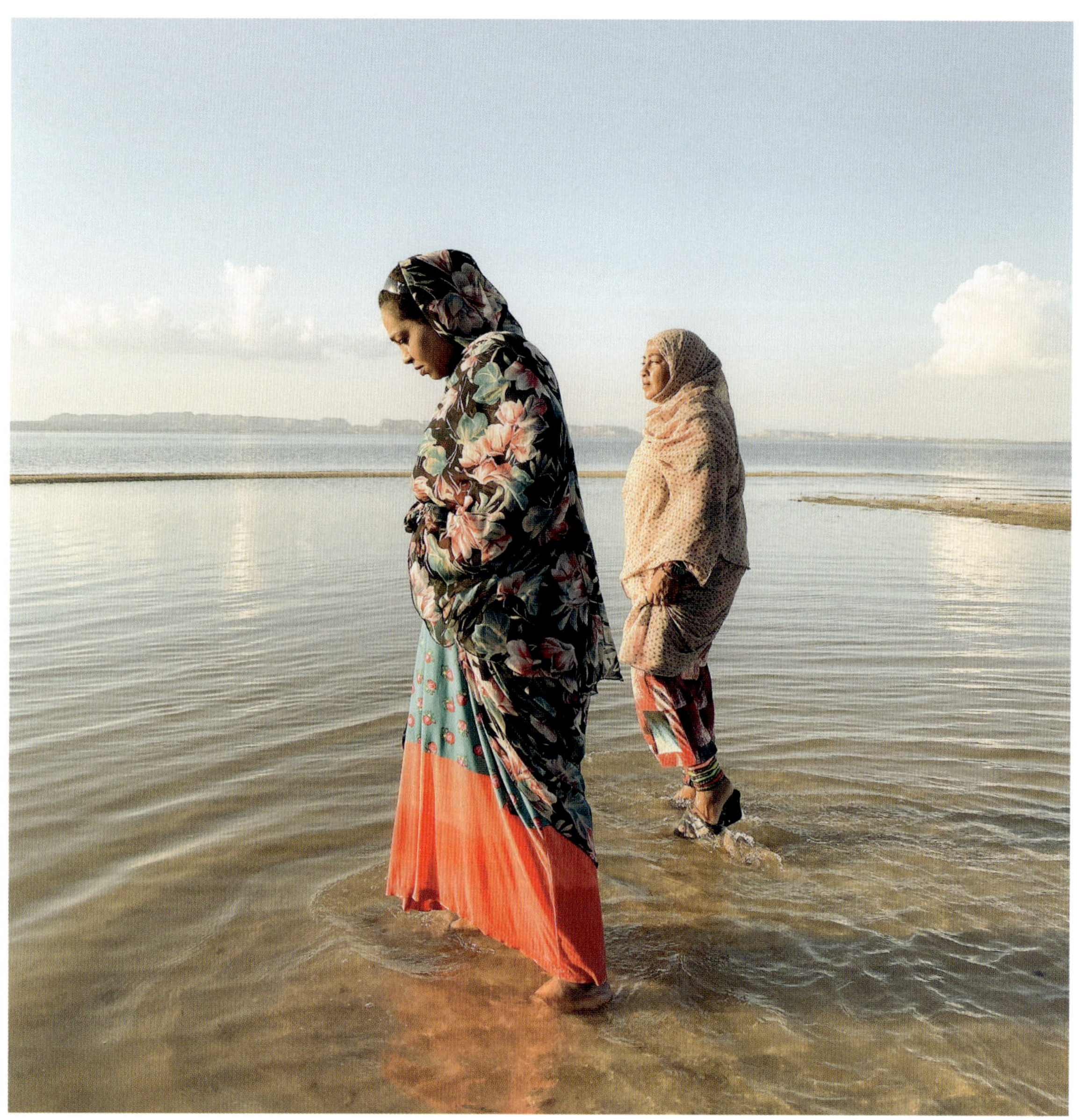

ABOVE: Kobra is a fisherwoman. She lacks any insurance or social support. Kobra broke her wrist in a terrible accident a few years ago when she was out fishing with her sister and was involved in a collision with a fast boat. Now that she has recovered, she's been able to go fishing again. Kobra said 'I grew up in the sea, so I couldn't leave it, I had to return to it.'

'I mostly take photos that tell stories of Iranian women and the economy. I'm a woman from an ordinary family and so I feel and understand these two issues strongly. I think these are the most important issues within Iranian society and I try to be a voice for them and hope that my stories reach far to share our truth.'

Forough Alaei
Tehran, Iran

Freelance photojournalist Forough Alaei was born in 1989 and works for a daily newspaper. Her photography explores women's rights and social and cultural stories. Growing up as a woman in a conservative country, she experienced and tolerated the stigma of being female and the daily oppression that is her birth right as an Iranian woman. She studied law at university and has always been interested in exploring how Iranian women survive the immense inequality, as well as the small things they do to alleviate the hardships of their lives.

Alaei's photography has achieved major success. In 2019 she won the highly prestigious World Press Photo award for sports stories with a photo project about female football supporters who dressed as men so that they could watch live football matches. She was arrested for disguising herself as a man to gain access to the stadium to make this fascinating body of work – a harsh reminder of the realities for an Iranian woman daring to explore such a culturally sensitive subject matter. Although Alaei feels she has not yet recovered mentally and emotionally from the ordeal, she is determined to continue her work because she feels that life must go on.

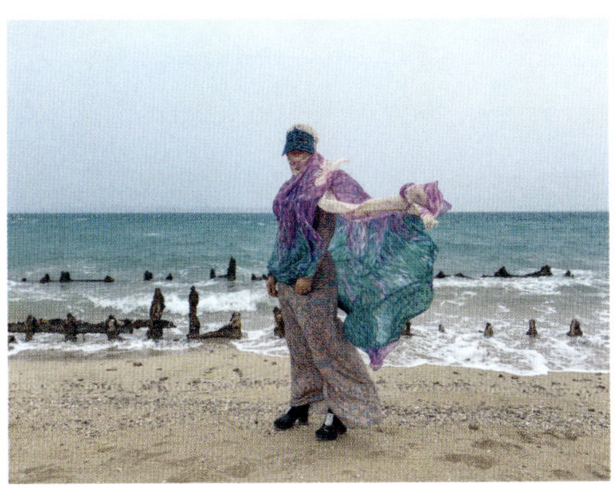

ABOVE: Soghra Arbabi and her sisters had the misfortune of being involved in a violent encounter with smugglers which saw their boat torn apart and them struggling for their lives for hours. They survived, but when they reached the shore they could not get any compensation for their loss. Nevertheless, these strong island women still contribute financially to the household by fishing in the manner they learned from their ancestors. Lately, Iran's fisheries organization has promised to give these women the permission to fish, which I hope will come to pass so they can have safer working conditions.

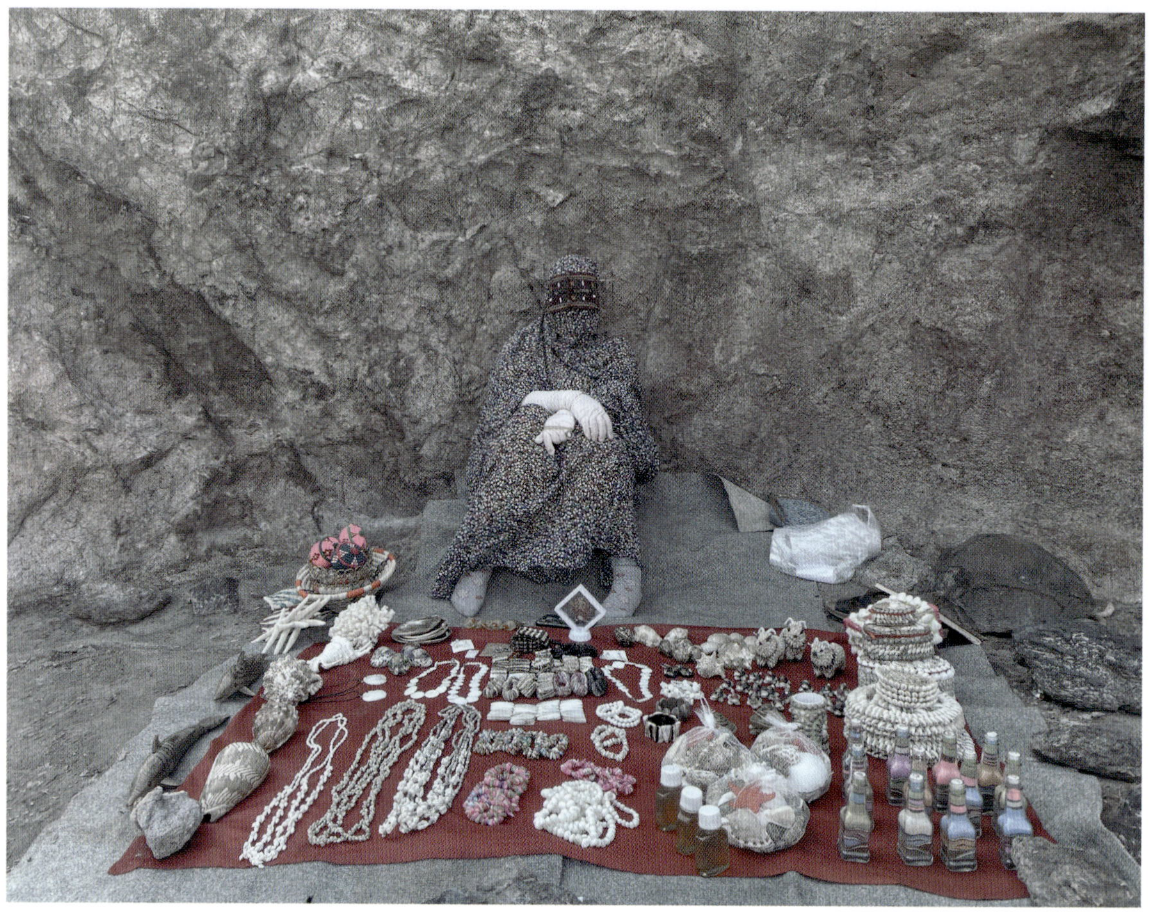

ABOVE: Sakina is a boat captain and goes fishing every day. Sometimes she goes with her daughter to catch food for them to eat. She has three children and, due to the bad economic conditions in their town, she also has to work as a vendor to earn a living. She is sitting on the rocks wearing a burqa in the hope that no one will recognize her. She was one of the toughest people I've ever communicated with.

'I like shooting on a smartphone because it's portable, so I take it everywhere. Also, it would seem weird to point professional cameras with big lenses at people here. My subjects would be intimidated and distracted by that. I find that I can capture their more honest feelings with a smartphone camera rather than with a big pro camera.'

BELOW: Some women in the south of Iran wear a battoulah. There are different tales about the origins of this piece of clothing. Some people say they were originally used to reduce the damaging effects of harsh sunlight on the face. Another story is that women wore them to prevent them being harassed by strangers, as the southern cities were historically invaded frequently by foreign tourists. Young unmarried girls don't wear them. Nowadays Iranian women mostly wear them as an adornment or out of habit.

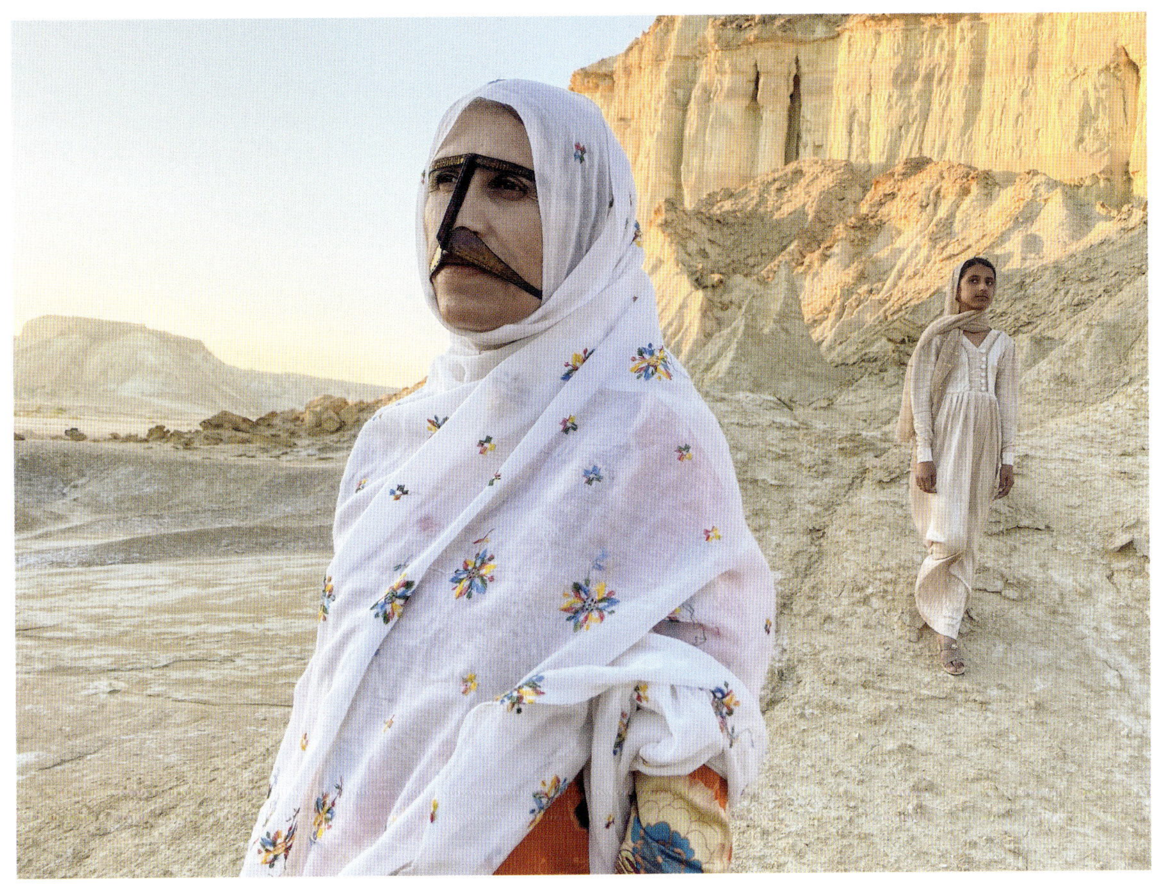

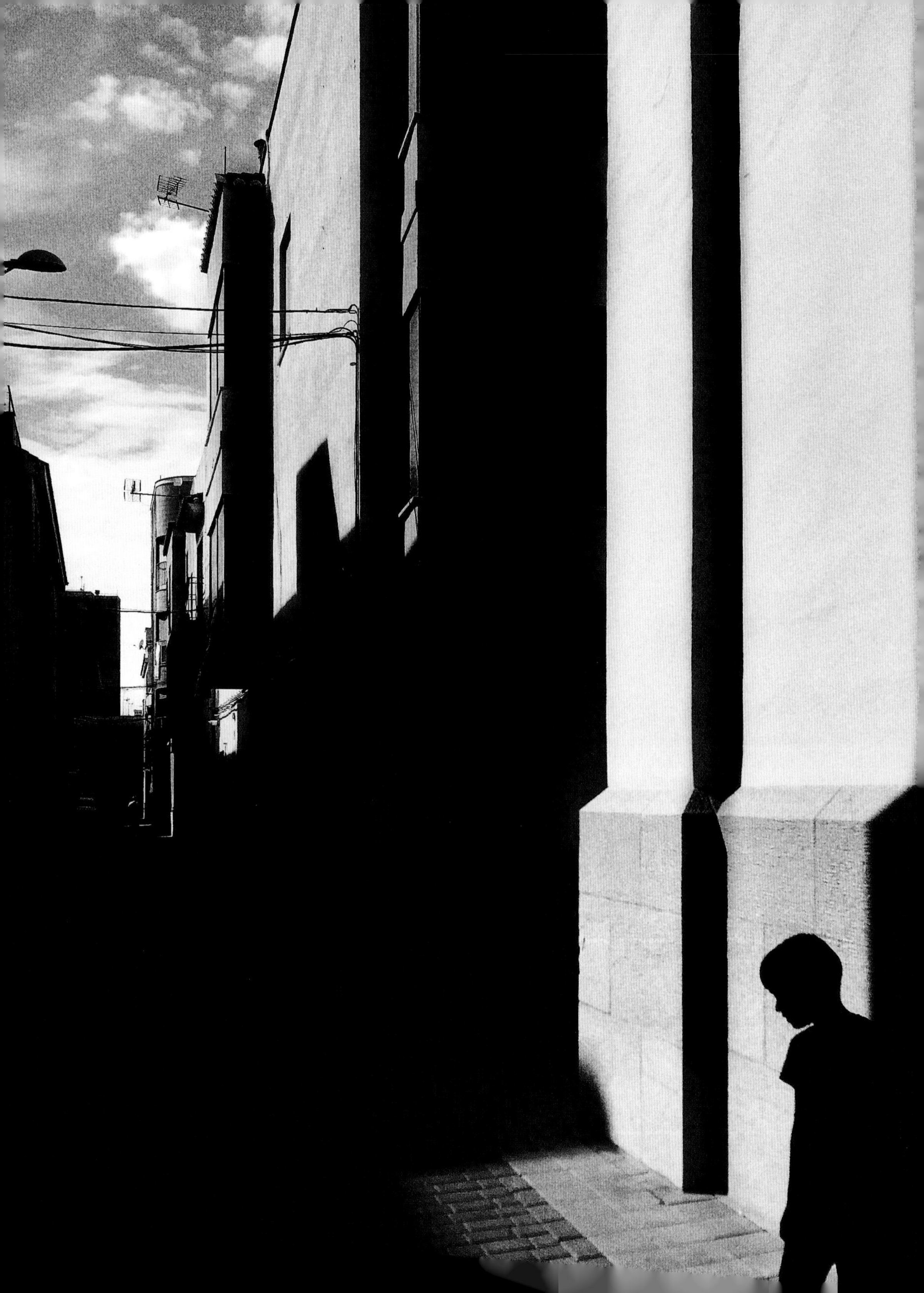

Franc Ortiz Rodrigo
Nules, Spain

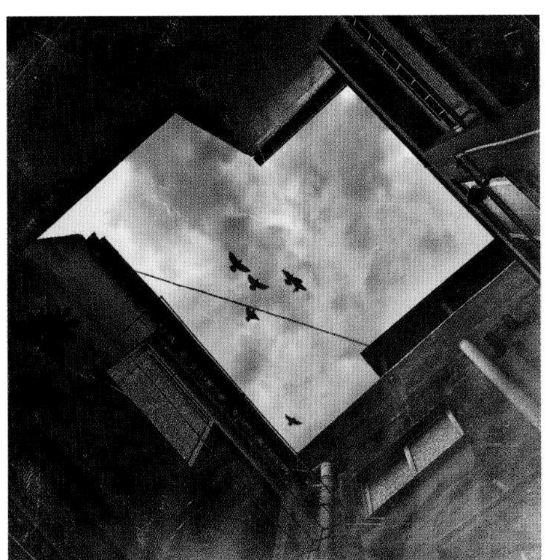

ABOVE: I like the architecture in the courtyard and the shape of the birds. I was lucky, I heard the fluttering of pigeons, framed the image and bingo!

LEFT: This photo of my son was taken as we walked back from his school in Nules. It shows my love for using shadows in my photography. I like the contrast of the shadowed lines and my son's silhouette.

Professional photographer and videographer Franc Ortiz Rodrigo uses an Apple iPhone – most recently an iPhone 13 – to capture fragments of everyday life. He is influenced by German expressionism and is a fan of the photographer Henri Cartier-Bresson. Ortiz Rodrigo had his own black-and-white darkroom laboratory, so he feels everything he does using his phone is embedded in what he did on paper in the lab. He always tries to create the texture of that authentic black-and-white look. He works with a mobile phone because, for street photography, the photographer has to be invisible. For Ortiz Rodrigo, the most important thing is to catch people being natural. He likes it best when the sun is lower, making long shadows, and so he shoots very little in the middle of the day. He plays a lot with shadows, as it's what he enjoys the most.

'I always work with light and shadow. My modus operandi has two stages. I walk down the street, I look for a background that I like and then I wait for a person to pass by, a suitable person, because they don't all work with the background...there are times when I have to be patient and wait.'

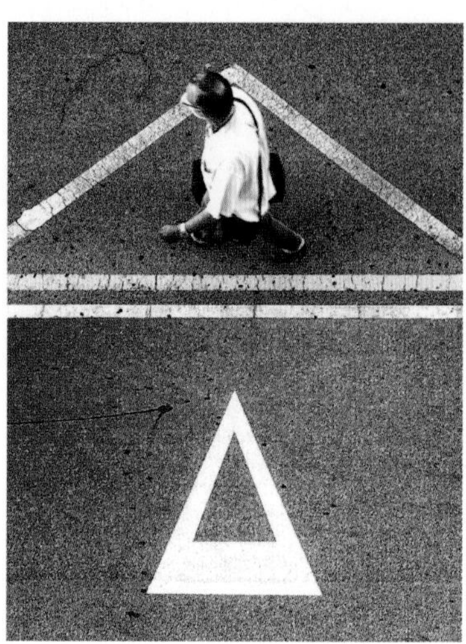

ABOVE: I was waiting at the
hospital when I saw these
triangles marked out on the
floor. I waited and waited for a
person to walk through to get
the perfect composition

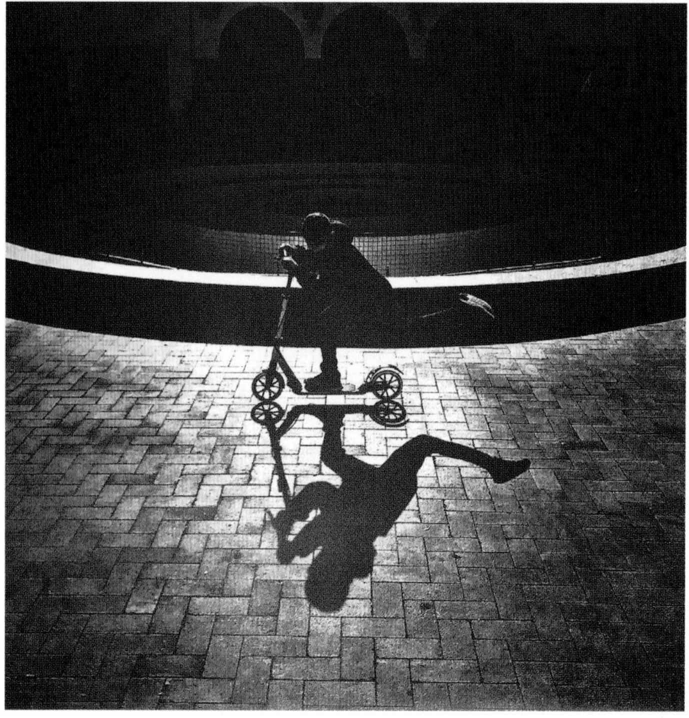

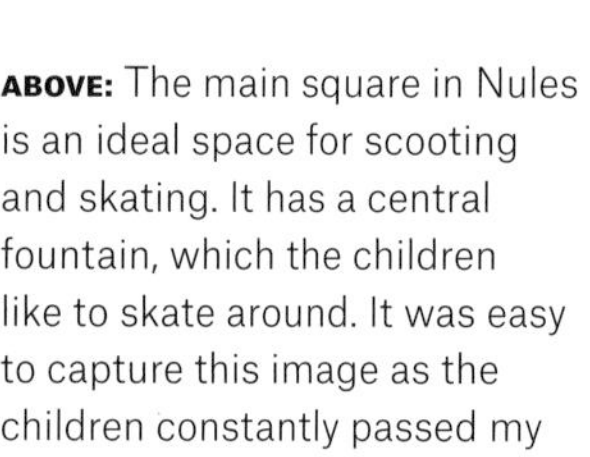

ABOVE: The main square in Nules
is an ideal space for scooting
and skating. It has a central
fountain, which the children
like to skate around. It was easy
to capture this image as the
children constantly passed my
viewpoint. I like the aesthetics
and the backlighting.

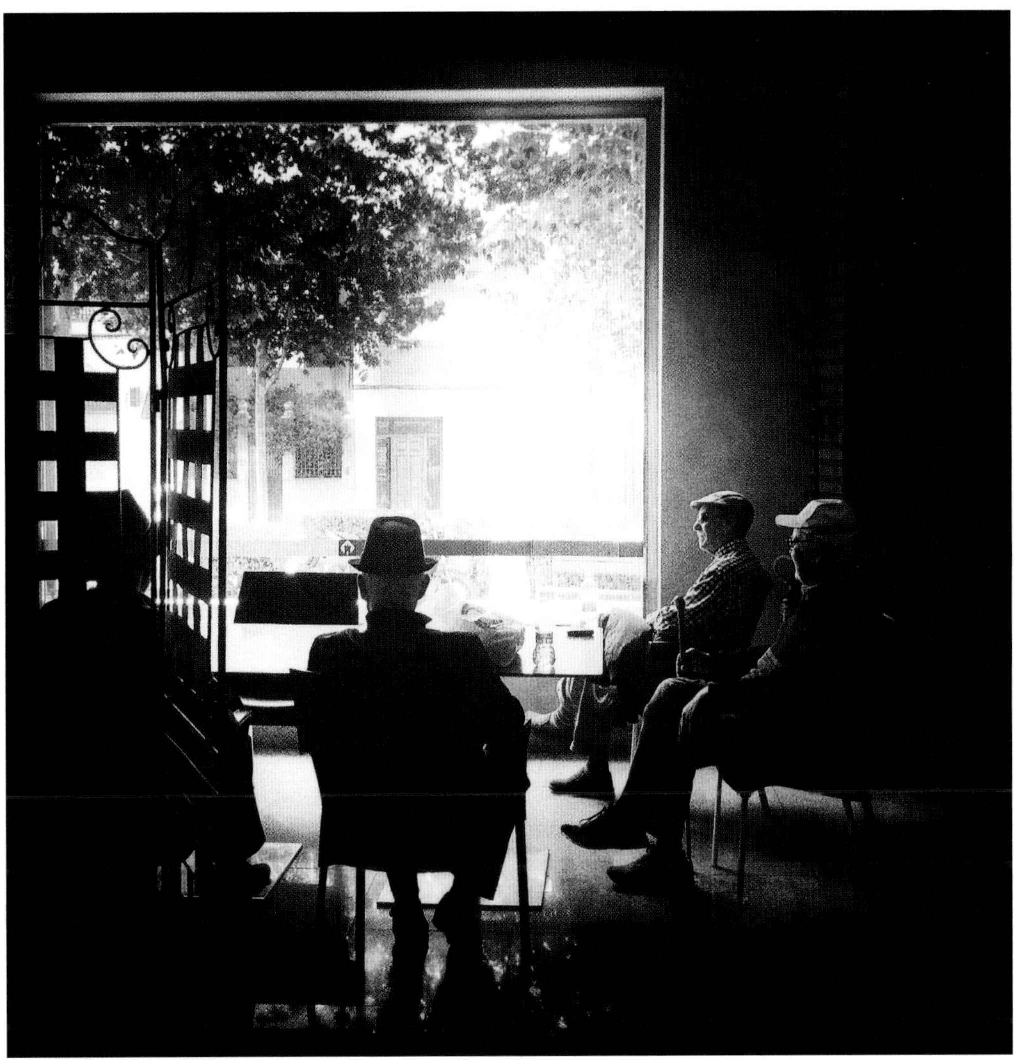

ABOVE: This photo was taken in the town of La Vall d'Uixó. A group of elderly people were sitting looking out of the window, having a coffee and watching life go by.

Glenn Homann
Brisbane, Australia

To pay the bills, Glenn Homann works in a large factory as a dispatcher, but photography with his iPhone is his great passion. It nourishes his soul and allows him to make the most of the creative opportunities that arise when the camera is always with him. His daily travels to and from work, by bus, train and occasionally by car, provide him with the opportunity to highlight the mundane beauty of the urban spaces around him and capture the essence of the city he calls home. Homann loves how light changes throughout the year can be dramatic and alter what might effectively be the same scene. He captures his images using the basic native camera function and does all his editing on his phone. He uses Snapseed to edit 99 per cent of the time. He occasionally uses Mextures to provide a specific aesthetic.

Through his photography, Homann explores colour, shape and texture, and often finds that industrial areas provide the scenarios that suit his aesthetic. He resets his viewpoint every now and then by capturing the natural environment at the edges of Brisbane, particularly at sunrise and sunset.

BELOW + RIGHT: As I move through the city, I often seek out scenes that are deliberately devoid of people. I feel that this creates a level of curiosity and lends itself to a slightly dystopian quality. Empty chairs can add to this feeling and become placeholders for the missing people. Like us, they have an infinite number of 'personalities', shaped by both their experiences and environments. We might also wonder about the people who have sat in them in the past, and who might do so again?

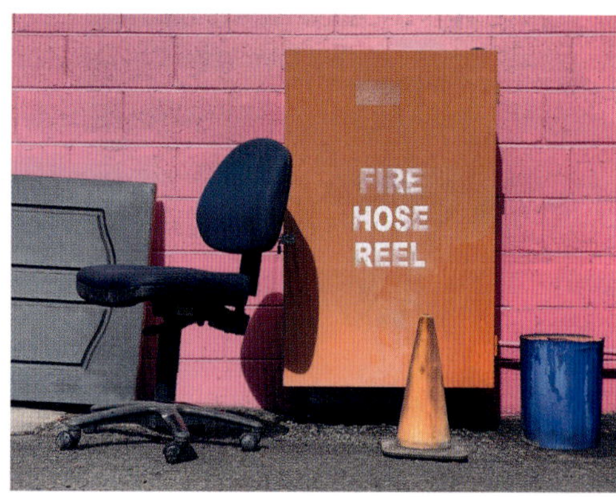

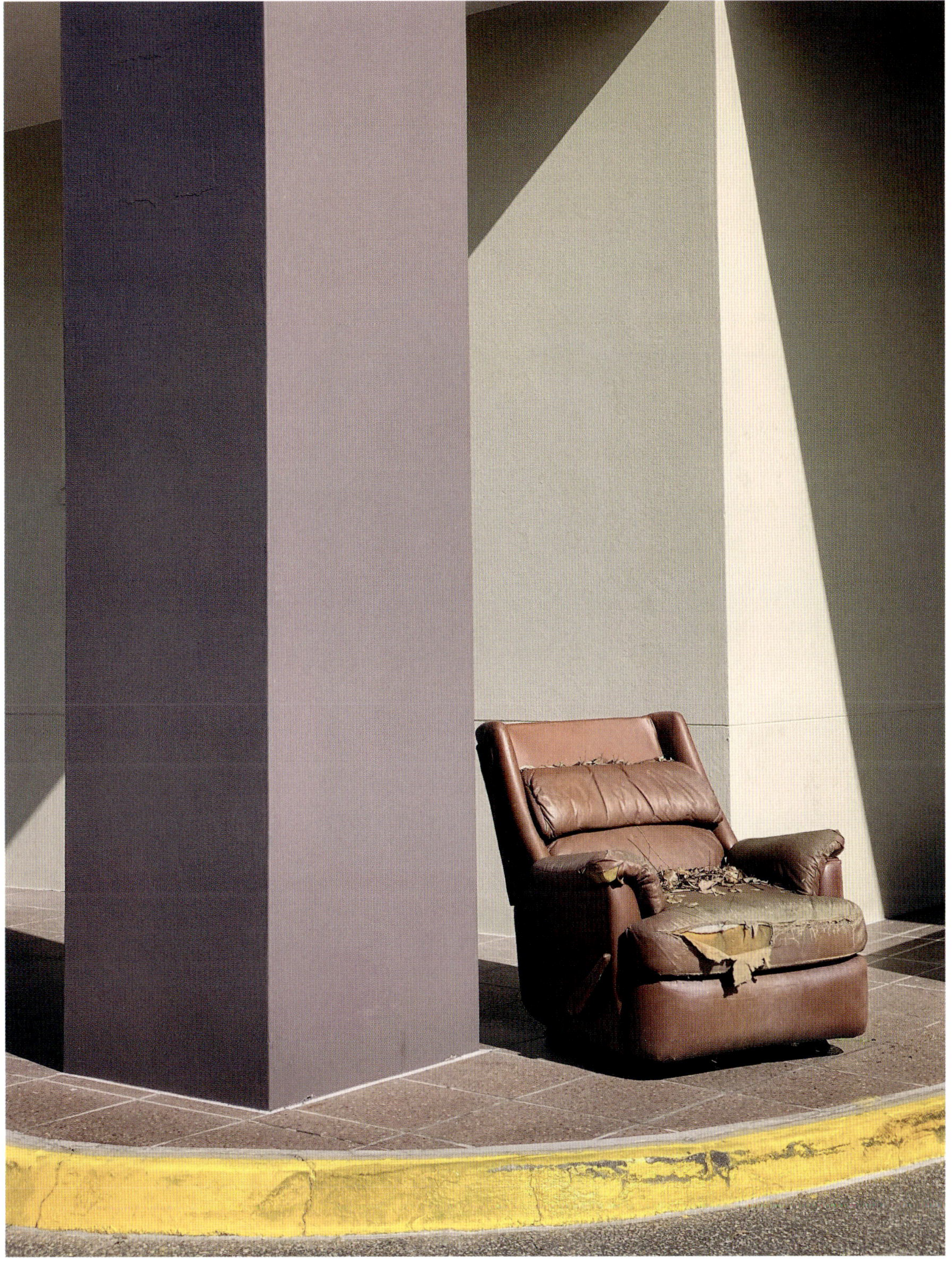

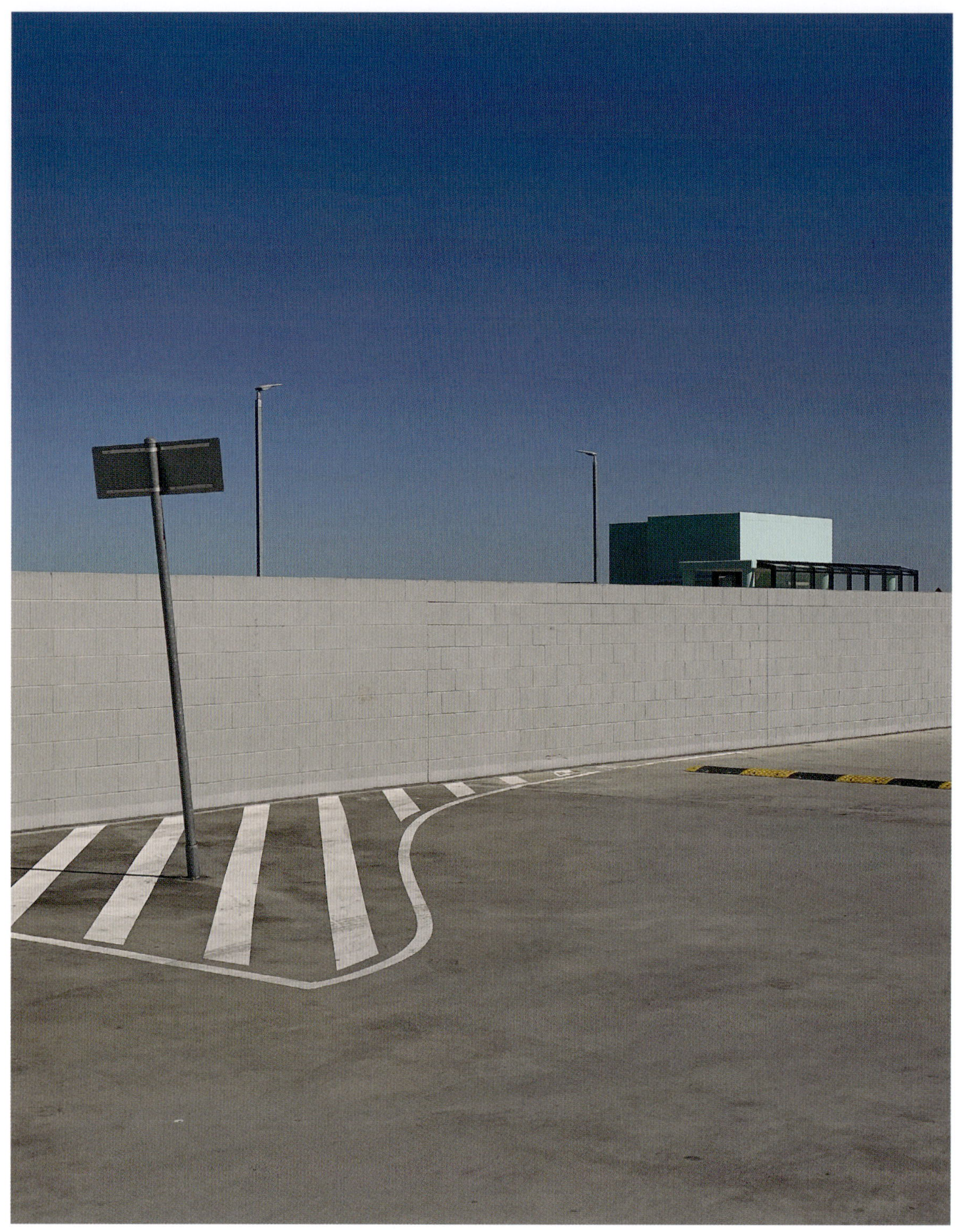

VIEWPOINT

It is imperative for a photographer living in a large modern city to find the interesting and beautiful in the built environment. Straight lines and stark colours will inevitably lend themselves to a minimal aesthetic. Spending time in a particular location will gradually unveil details and compositions that were not visible at first glance. Ultimately it becomes apparent that, while they were never intended to be seen in such a way, some of our urban structures could be perceived as grandiose modern sculptures; large-scale, three-dimensional works that invite exploration, examination and documentation.

'It is the contrasts and juxtapositions in life that make it endlessly enriching.'

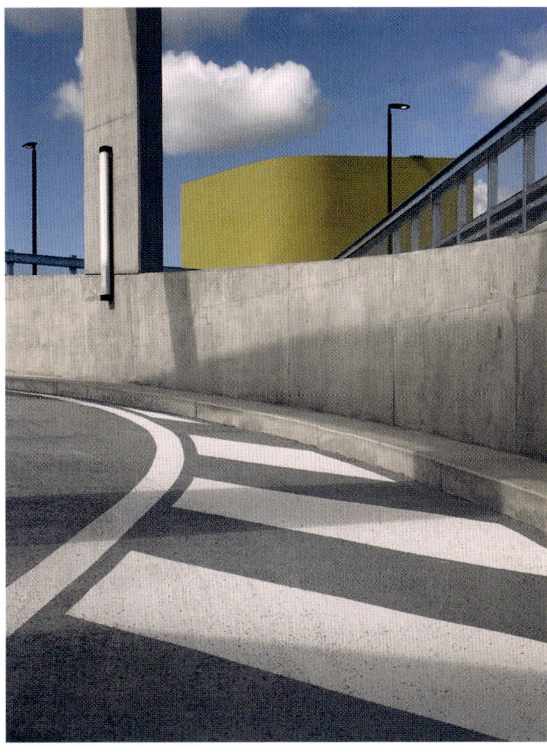

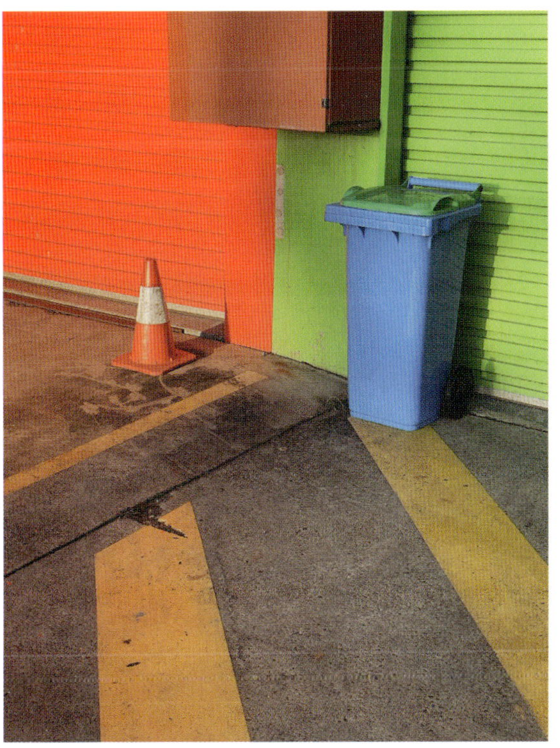

'Mobile photography is my great passion, a means of nourishing my soul and making the most of the creative opportunities that arise when the camera is always with you.'

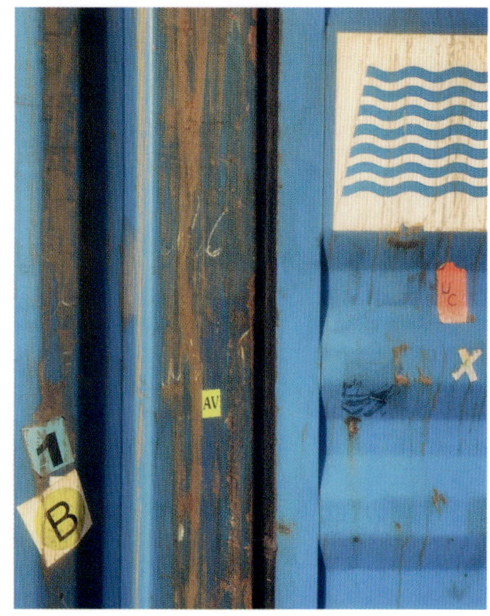

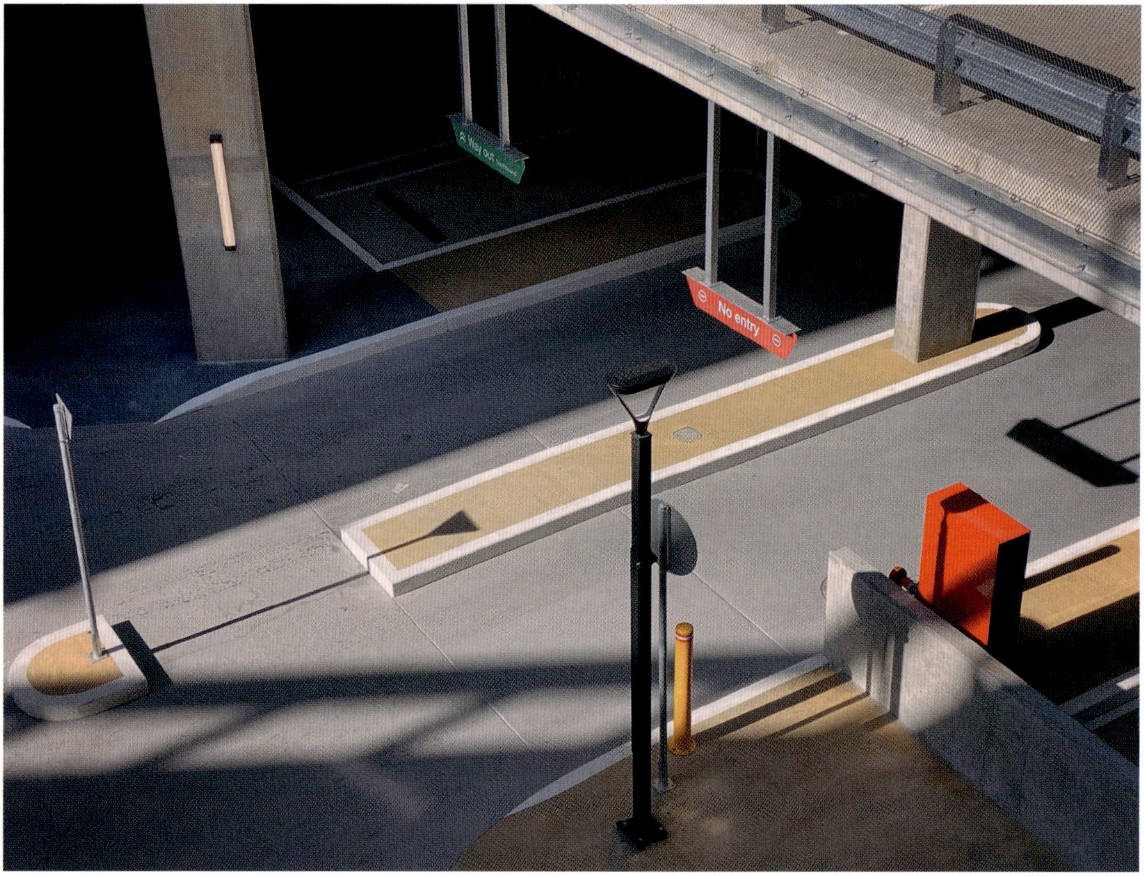

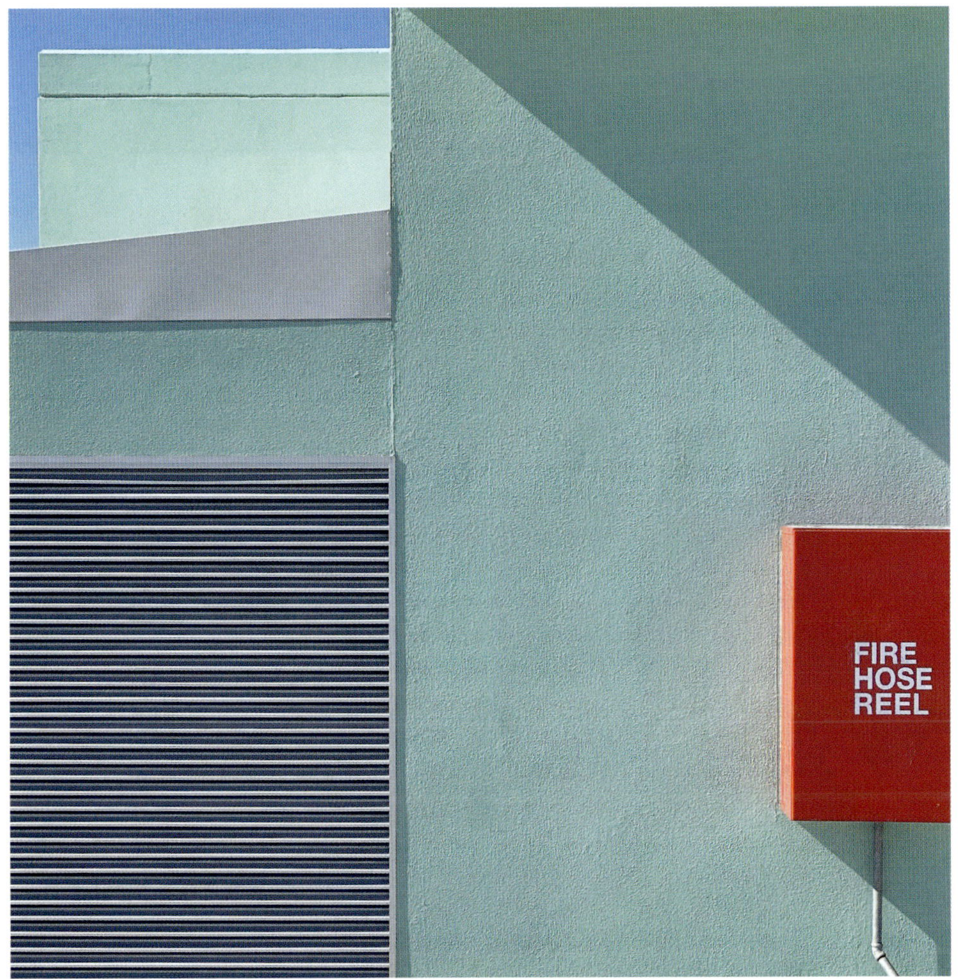

LEFT + ABOVE: City life can wear us down with endless straight lines, vistas of concrete and glass, roads and railways. The gentrification of huge swathes of our modern cities has meant that dust, dirt, grime and decay can be very hard to find. After a while it becomes natural and even necessary for a photographer to start to look beyond the relentless harshness and find the softness, the roundness, the humanity of the world that we have created. Perhaps we need to remind the viewer that it is the contrasts and juxtapositions in life that make it endlessly enriching.

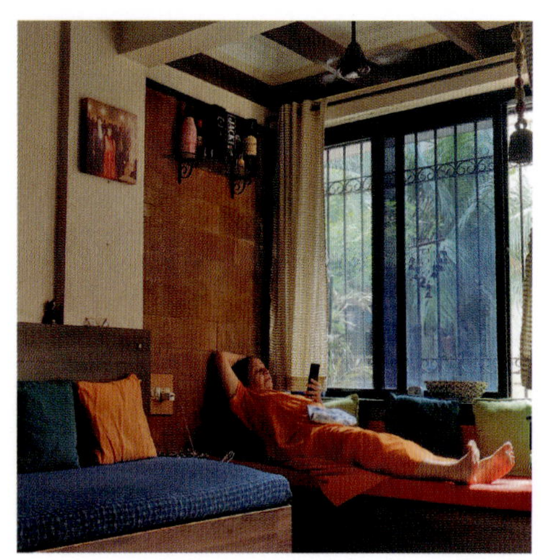

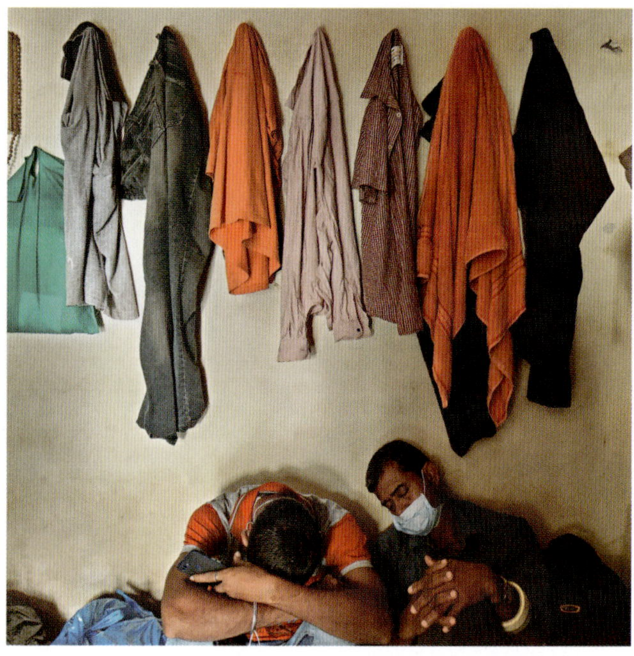

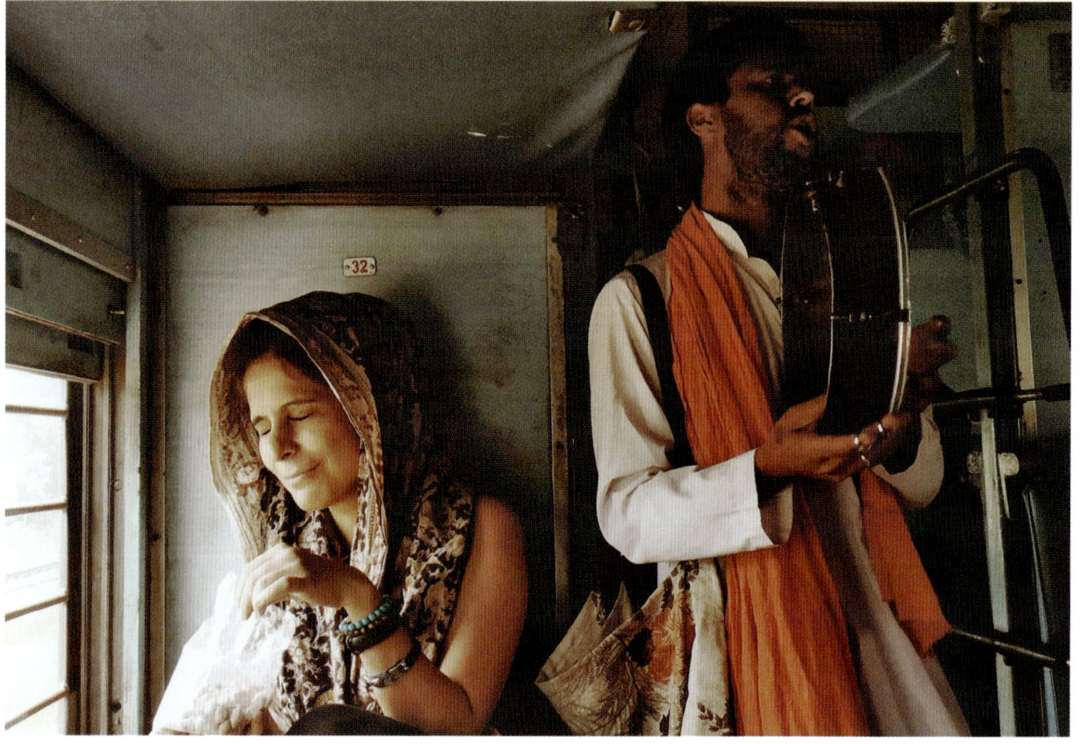

Harshita Sabnis
Mumbai, India

Harshita Sabnis is a creative producer for documentary films. When she started taking photos she used a 'point and shoot' camera, as that was all that she had, and her phone camera was not great. When she lost the DSLR her father bought for her just three months after receiving it, she didn't feel she could ask for another one, so she started using her phone camera. Now she only uses her smartphone to take photos. Sabnis enjoys contemplating a wide range of emotions through her photographs. She prefers to take candid shots rather than staged ones. She wants to show people the world as she sees it. Sabnis has recently started showing people the photos she takes of them, and enjoys the way they react to seeing their selves in a given moment.

On a personal level, Sabnis loves to look back at her pictures, enjoying what it means to be taken back to a specific point in time. She has been taking photos since she was in school and viewing her life through photos gives Sabnis an objectivity she wouldn't otherwise achieve. Some of her photos capture her father in hospital in the last week of his life after he suffered a stroke. The cathartic process of photographing the sights she encountered there offered her relief from the reality of her situation.

Sabnis currently uses an Apple iPhone 13 and Snapseed, and before that shot on a Sony OnePlus 7. She doesn't use any additional lenses, and prefers to use her phone camera as it allows her to focus on taking a photo in a moment rather than thinking about technicalities.

She takes photos everywhere and anywhere. She feels as though she is inseparable from her camera, but also that she would like to be more proactive and go out of her way to take photos.

'There is so much you can do with the mundane.'

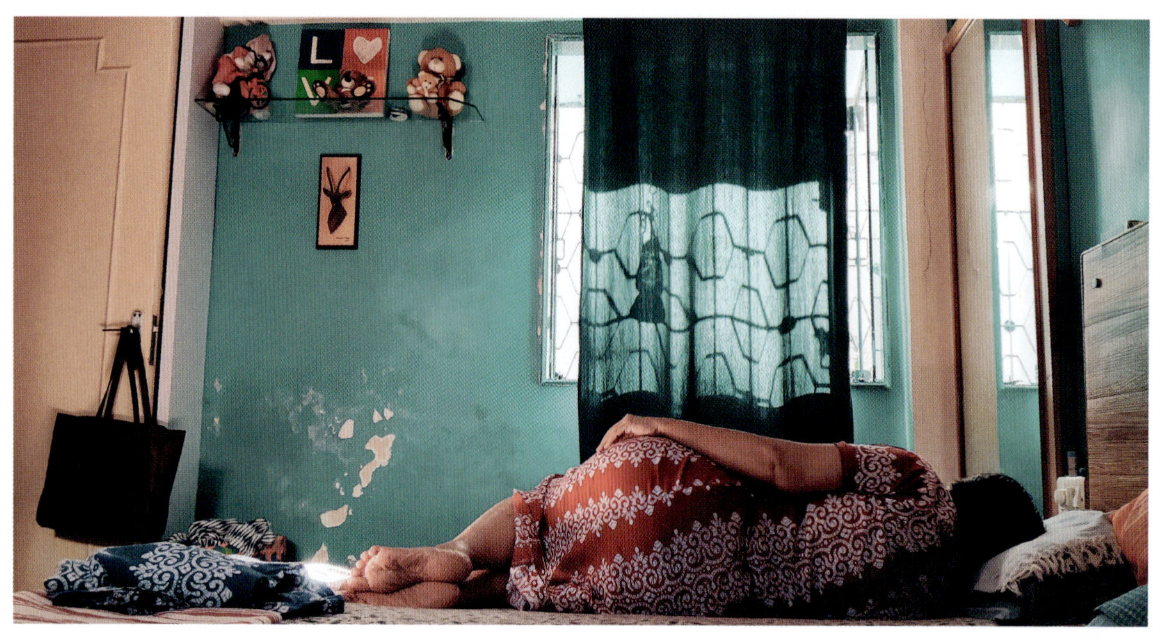

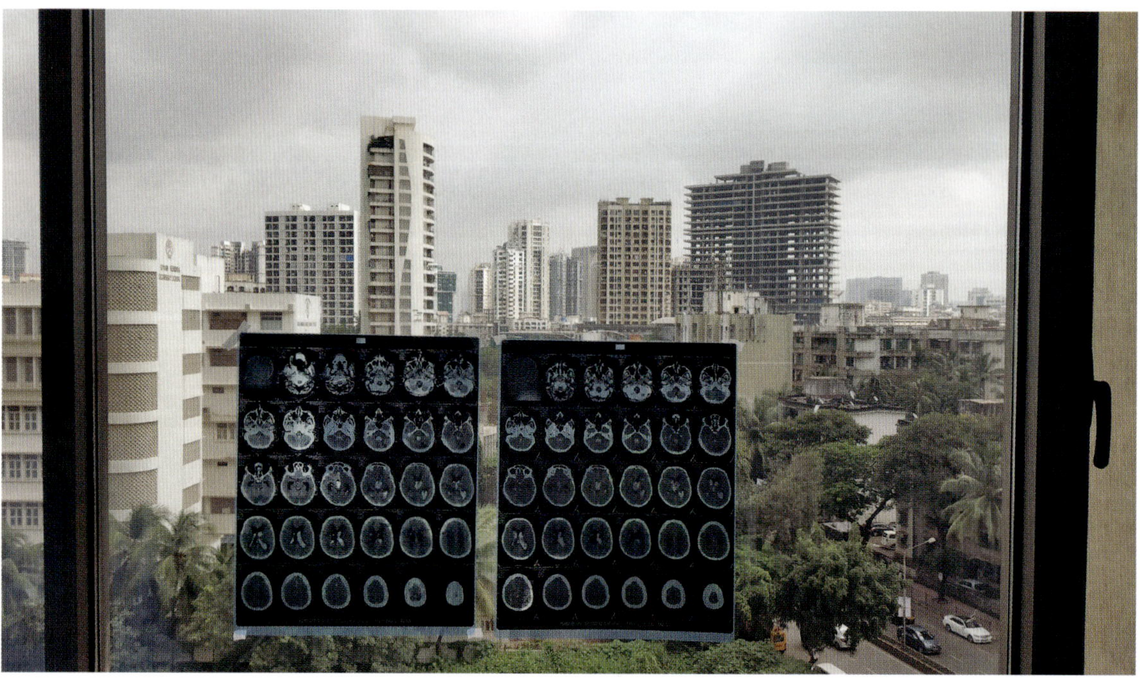

VIEWPOINT

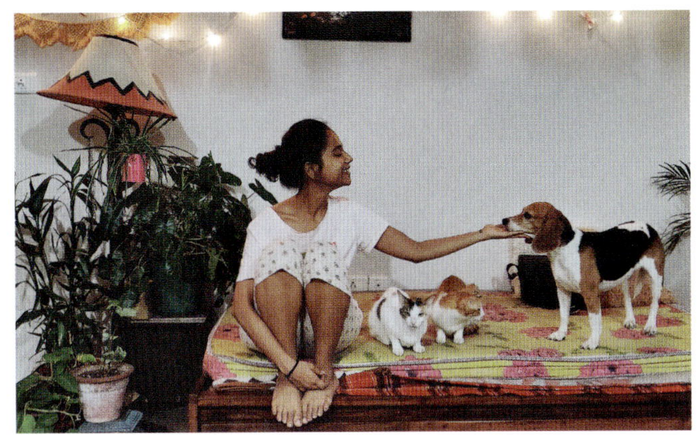

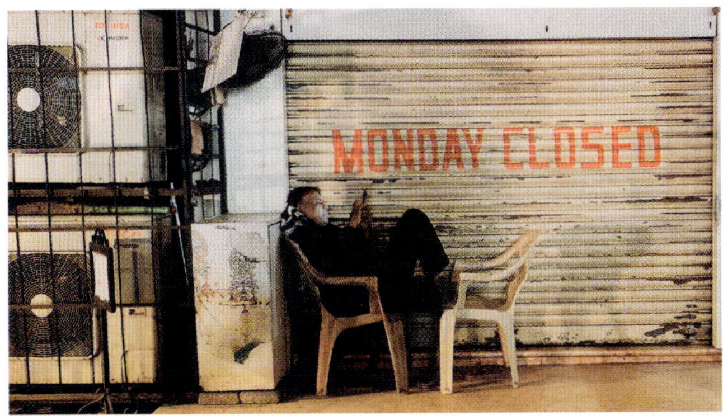

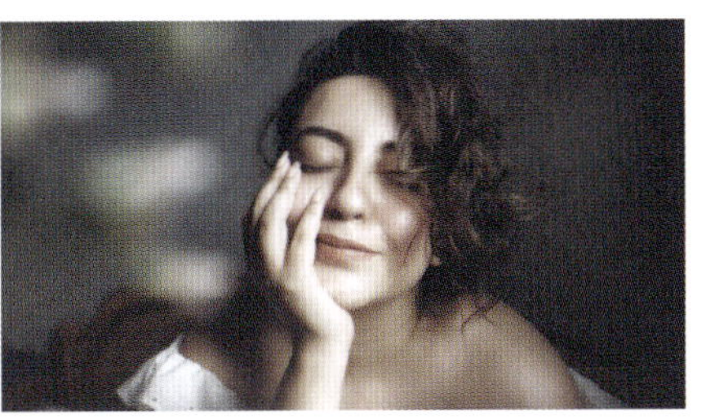

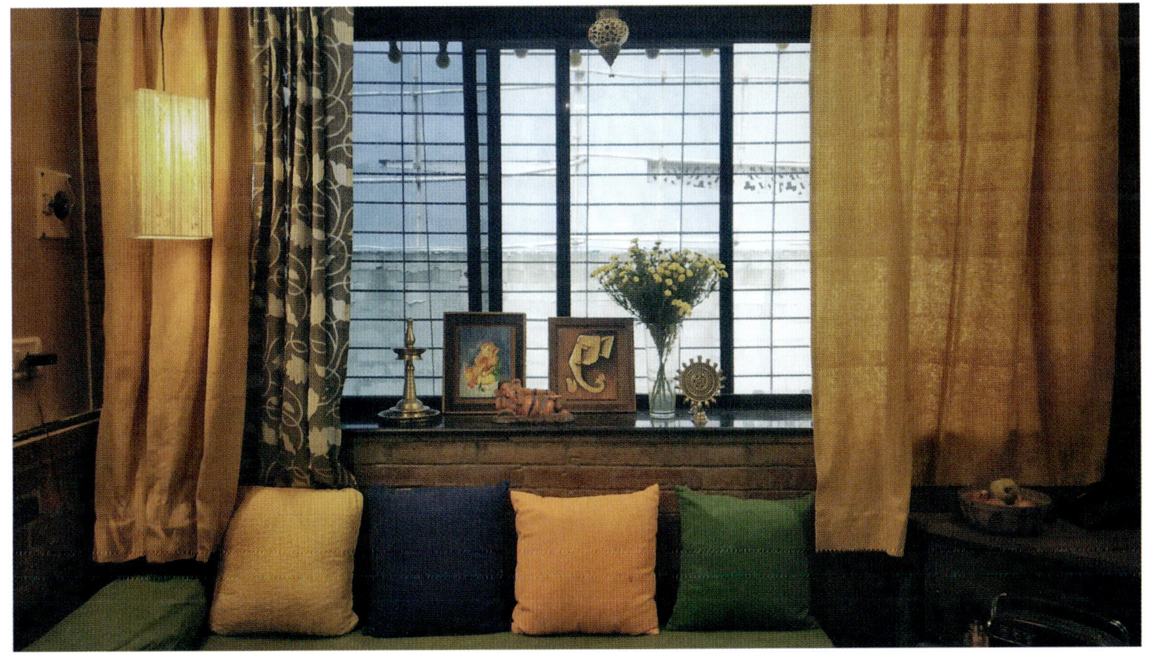

Hasan Belal
Damascus, Syria

Freelance photojournalist and economics graduate Hasan Belal is originally from the coastal city of Tartus. He moved to Damascus in 2017 for work. While he uses a camera for work, he finds great joy in using it to tell personal stories too. As well as being his main source of income, photography for Belal is a means of communication and a way to analyze daily life in Syria. He takes a visual anthropology approach to his art, seeking to understand the identity of his hometown as a place of ongoing conflict during ten years of war. He has worked with many local and international agencies and non-governmental organizations such as UNICEF to produce photo stories about life after the war in Syria. He hopes to be a war photographer and document other conflicts around the world.

Belal uses two different types of phone: an Apple iPhone 12 and a Huawei Nova 3i. He uses simple apps to edit his work: most is done using Snapseed, while some of the basic editing is done using the phone's native editing app.

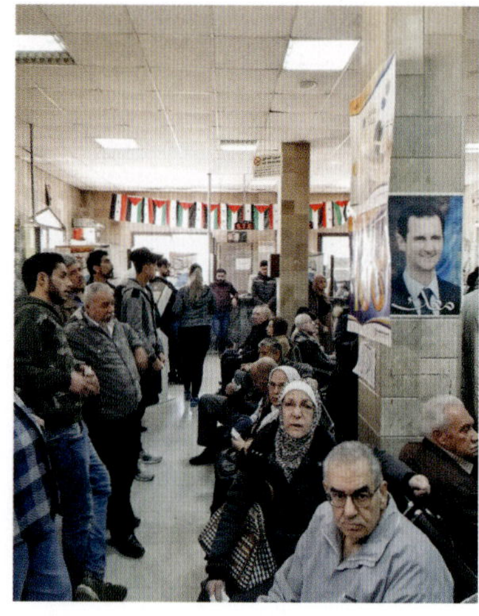

ABOVE: I took this photo stealthily in the post office in Damascus while I was waiting to pay my internet and phone bill. I waited for two hours because the system is so primitive. At this point I had lost patience. I turned around and saw all these people queuing, the frame filled with flags and the photo of President Bashar al-Assad, and couldn't resist this surreptitious capture. The daily tragedy of the Syrian government's institutions means that people are always waiting on foot for hours to pay their bills. There were a lot of older people, and seeing them next to the photo of the president made documenting it seem worthwhile.

RIGHT: Thieves Souq is a market in Damascus. There is a myth that many of the items for sale are stolen and so they can be bought for a lower price, hence the name. The market also sells a lot of antiques, but they are very expensive. It is a controversial market, but I love to go there to walk around and take photographs to try and understand it better. As there are potentially illegal goods, there are a lot of police on the streets, but they don't do anything. I often buy sunglasses there. I know an old man there who I usually have a coffee with before exploring this hidden area of Damascus. I like the spirit of freedom reflected in this photo. I saw the seller in his chair and loved how he had arranged his items so asked to take his photo.

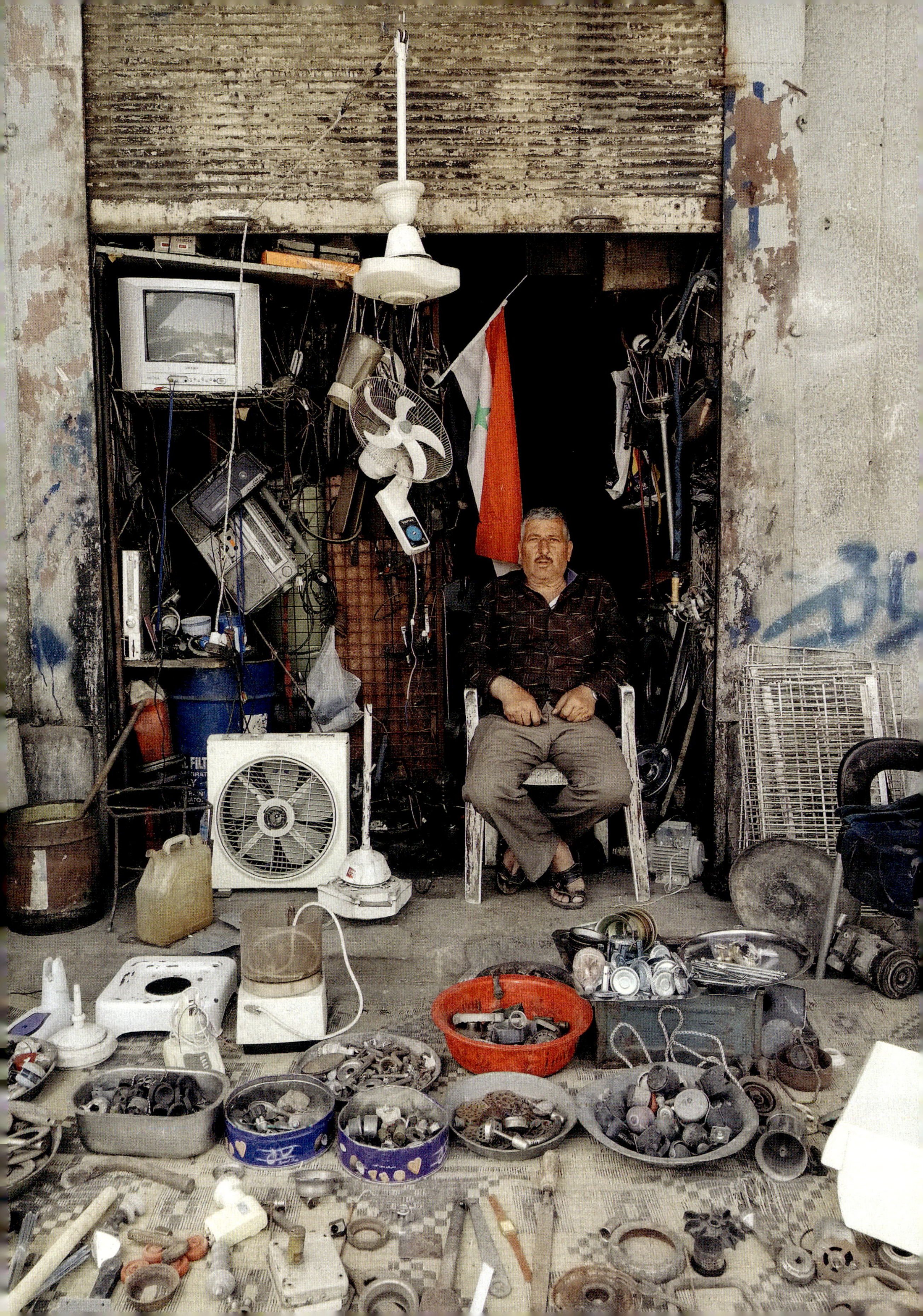

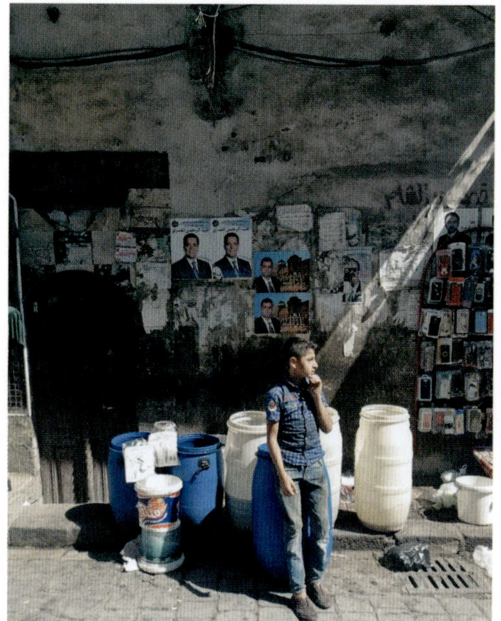

LEFT: This is another Damascan souq, called Bab Sreijeh. On one visit, I saw this kid; his posture, the wall and the lighting were enough to make me want to take his photo.

BELOW: In the Al Sayeda Zainab, southern Damascus, a sacrificial slaughter marks the anniversary of the death of Imam Hussain, known as Ashura. The sacrifice will be distributed to those attending the event. Many foreigners celebrate Ashura, and getting authorization to be there as a photographer is not easy thanks to rules that have been introduced since the war. From this angle we can see the huge number of people around the sacrifice, including young children. In my opinion it's not healthy for kids to watch the slaughter. I think the photo reflects the pressure and the mess that we live in.

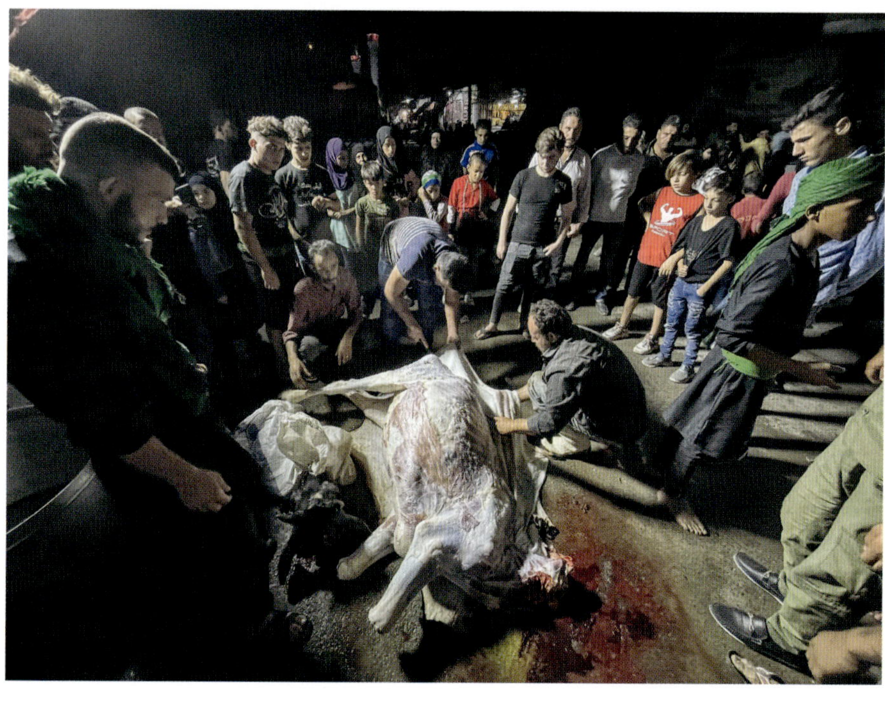

VIEWPOINT

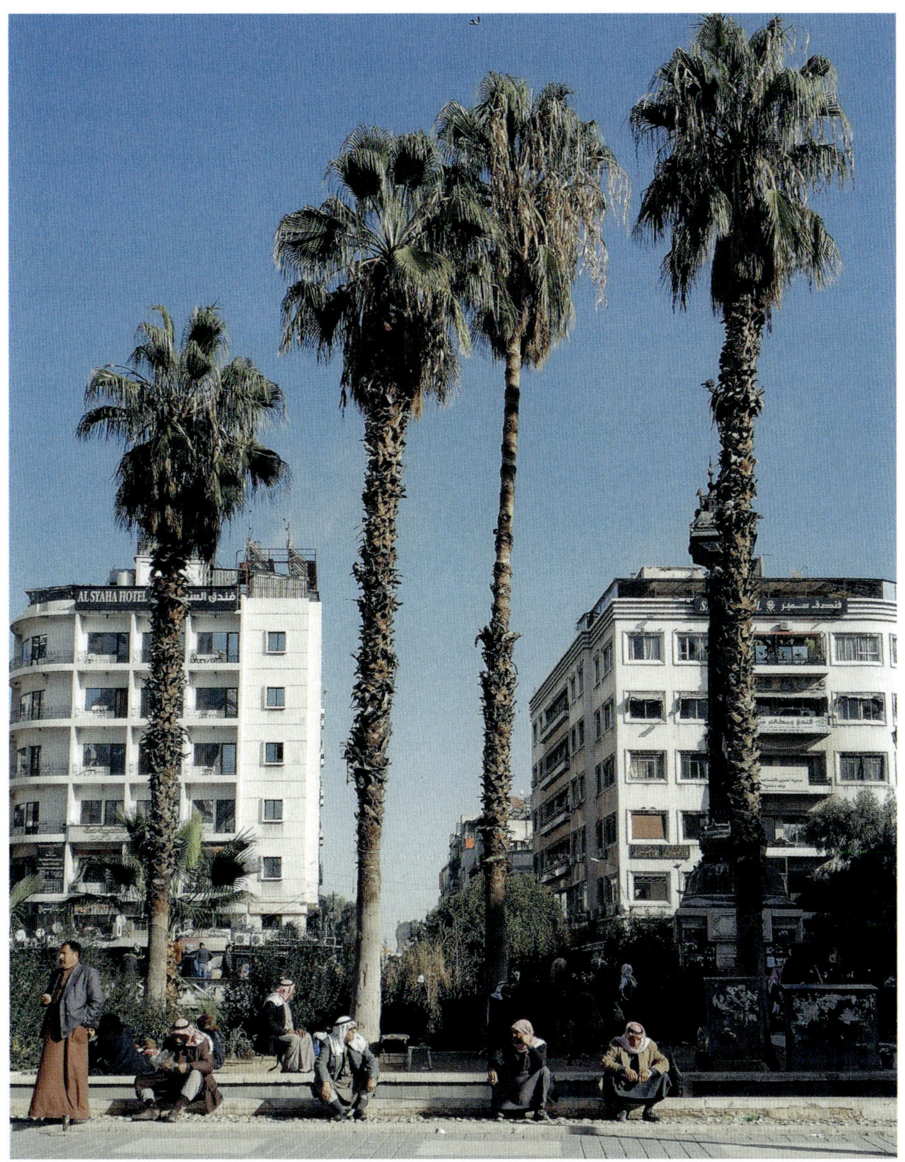

ABOVE: Al-Marja Square in the centre of Damascus dates back to the late 19th century. In May 1916 the Ottomans publicly executed seven Syrian national activists here and it became known as Martyrs' Square. Later, under French control, the square continued to be used for executions. I visit the area a lot to take photos; I like its size and history as well as the architecture. It gives a sense of what the city was like before the war. There are lots of hotels, which bring in many visitors from north and east Syria, and I have been working on an anthropological project about the relationship between these people and the square. I saw these men sitting on the side, echoing the palm trees, and thought it would help with my project, so took this photo to add to my analysis and research.

BELOW: This photo was taken in
downtown Damascus from a tower
called Al Ferdous. I was in the area
photographing a techno music event
for work and was taking a rest on
the rooftop when I saw the buildings
around me and was struck by how
they seem to reflect the pressure
we live with and the absurdity and
disorganization of our daily lives. Using
the wide lens of my iPhone 12, I was
able to distort the image and show the
buildings as a block combined with
each other.

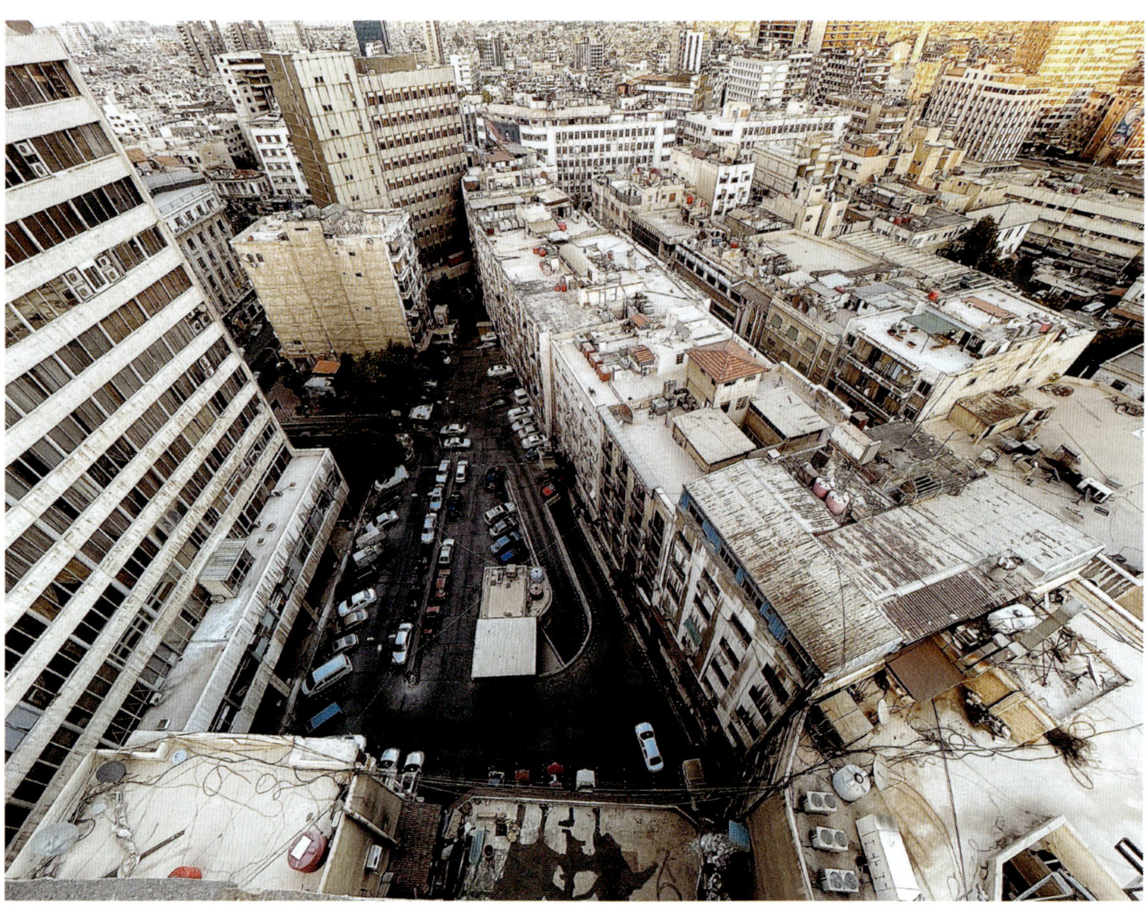

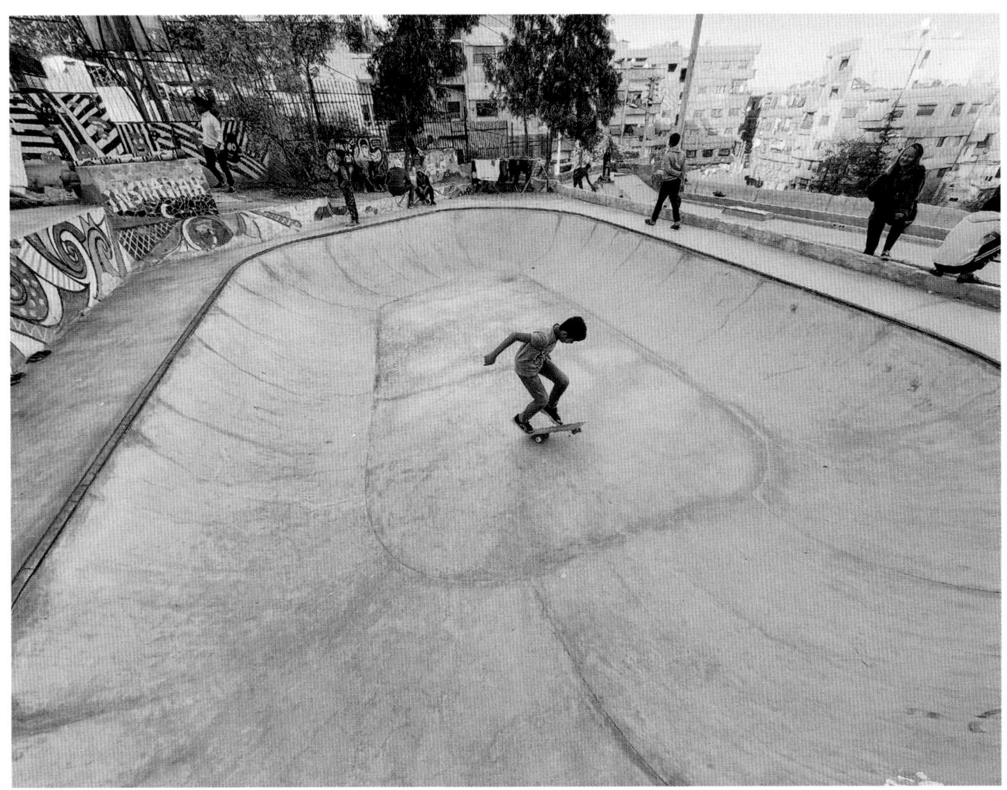

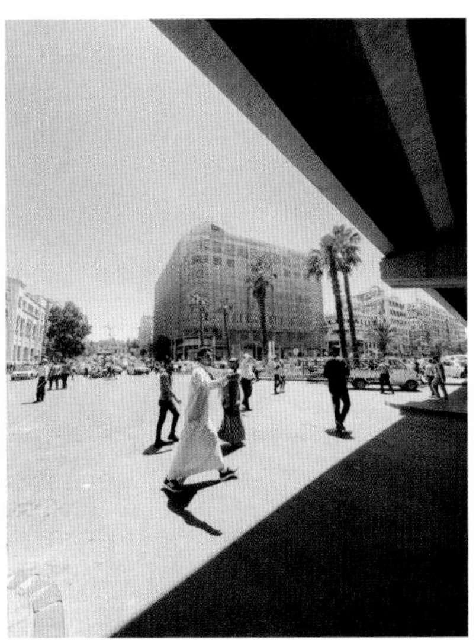

LEFT: For me, this spot under Victoria Bridge in the middle of Damascus is one of the best in the city for photography. I love the brilliant ancient architecture, and the great palm trees make me feel like I could be a rich man living in a rich city. I wish we could go back to the 1960s or '70s, before the war, when Damascus was a prosperous city with a strong, positive identity. This photo combines some of those things I dream of.

ABOVE: Damascus is home to the first designated skateboarding area in Syria. Funded by skate-aid international in 2018, the project aimed to help rebuild the community when the residents, who had relocated during the war, started to return. The skate park, together with recreational space and a playground, is in a remote area. Initially equipment was provided and volunteers taught the children how to skate. My first visit was to take photos and learn about the place and people, but I started skating there too. It is often crowded with children wanting to skate. I was taking a break when I noticed this boy had the park to himself. I waited for him to be in the centre of the frame and took my photo

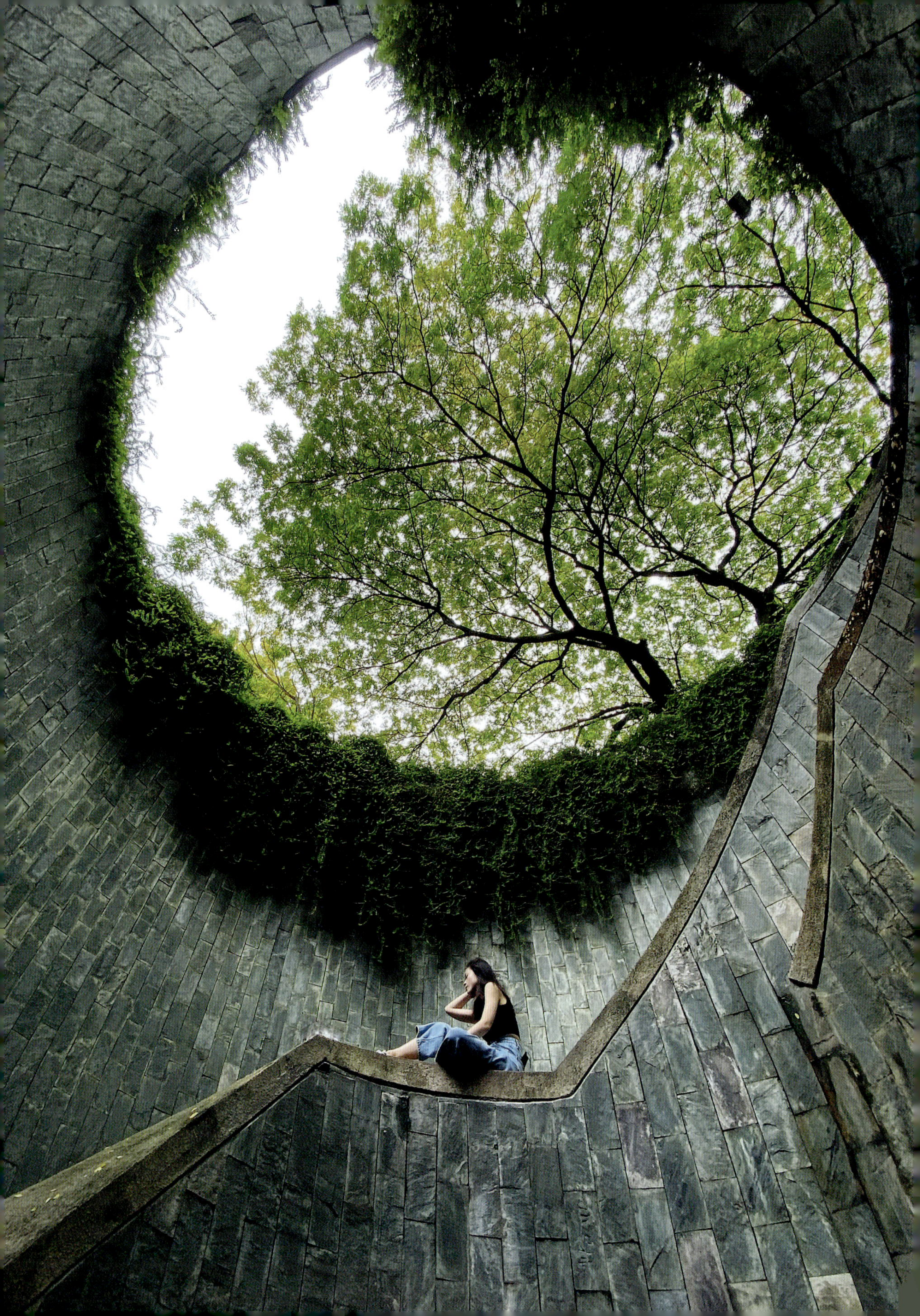

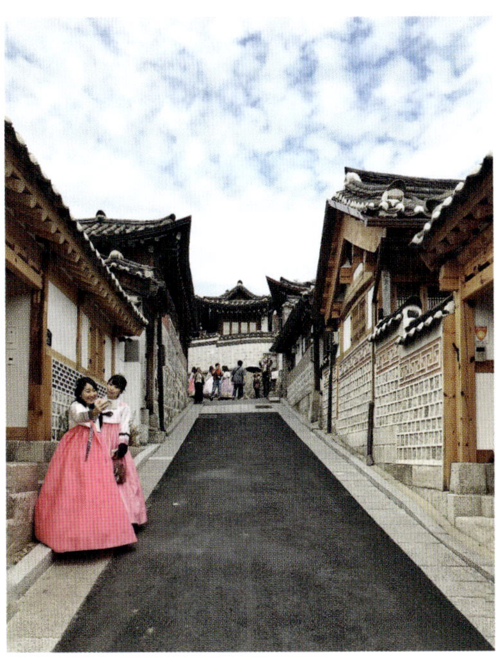

ABOVE: The traditional Bukchon Hanok village in Seoul, South Korea, is a favourite holiday destination for Singaporeans looking to immerse themselves in Korean culture. I couldn't resist this scene while I was working there.

LEFT: Fort Canning Park in Singapore is a popular leisure location with lots of history. This photo was taken during the Covid-19 pandemic when the borders were closed, and my wife and I took the opportunity to stay at home and explore the city-state in more depth.

Hezron Chen
Singapore

Hezron Chen works in the aviation industry and so he is constantly flying and on the move – for him, home is many places. He often travels with his wife, who he describes as his 'model and inspiration', and he enjoys capturing their 'backstories of love' through his lens. Chen was grounded during the Covid-19 pandemic, when all international travel was halted, but he enjoyed the opportunity to spend quality time with his family and friends.
He admits that he was glad to see the aviation industry returning to normal afterwards. Chen uses an Apple iPhone and edits with Snapseed and occasionally VSCO. He likes to shoot with his iPhone because it's convenient and easy to access from his pocket. Most of his photos have symmetrical lines and architectural themes, often with a human subject as the focus, because he feels that images of beautiful buildings and structures are made all the better by the presence of people.

Inga Dinga
Vilnius, Lithuania

Freelance photographer Inga Dinga was born and raised in Vilnius and, having travelled widely, still feels there is nowhere else she would rather live. Photography is her 'everyday joy', her lifestyle and her craft. Alongside her smartphone photography, Dinga plays with vintage analogue, instant and pinhole cameras to create mystical and atmospheric street-style photography. Her smartphone photos are a personal diary to capture the interesting things in her everyday life, sparked by her natural curiosity. She is drawn to the eerie.

Dinga uses a Huawei P30 Pro, but some of the pictures here were also taken with her previous phone, a Sony OnePlus 5. She occasionally uses the Huawei's built-in picture editor, and in rare cases ToolWiz Photos. If the picture is going to be printed in a larger format, she can't manage without Photoshop.

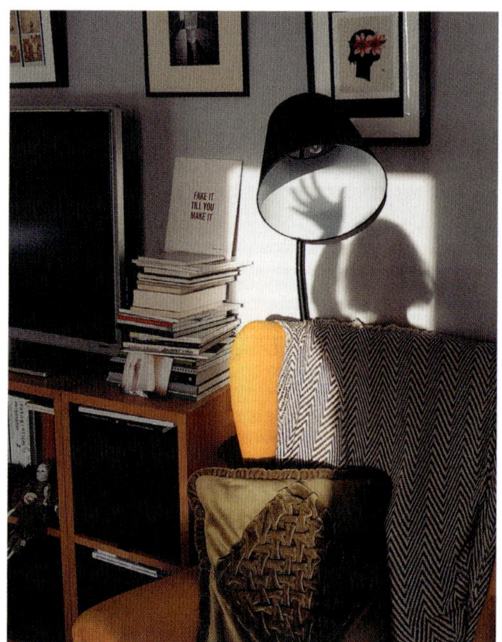

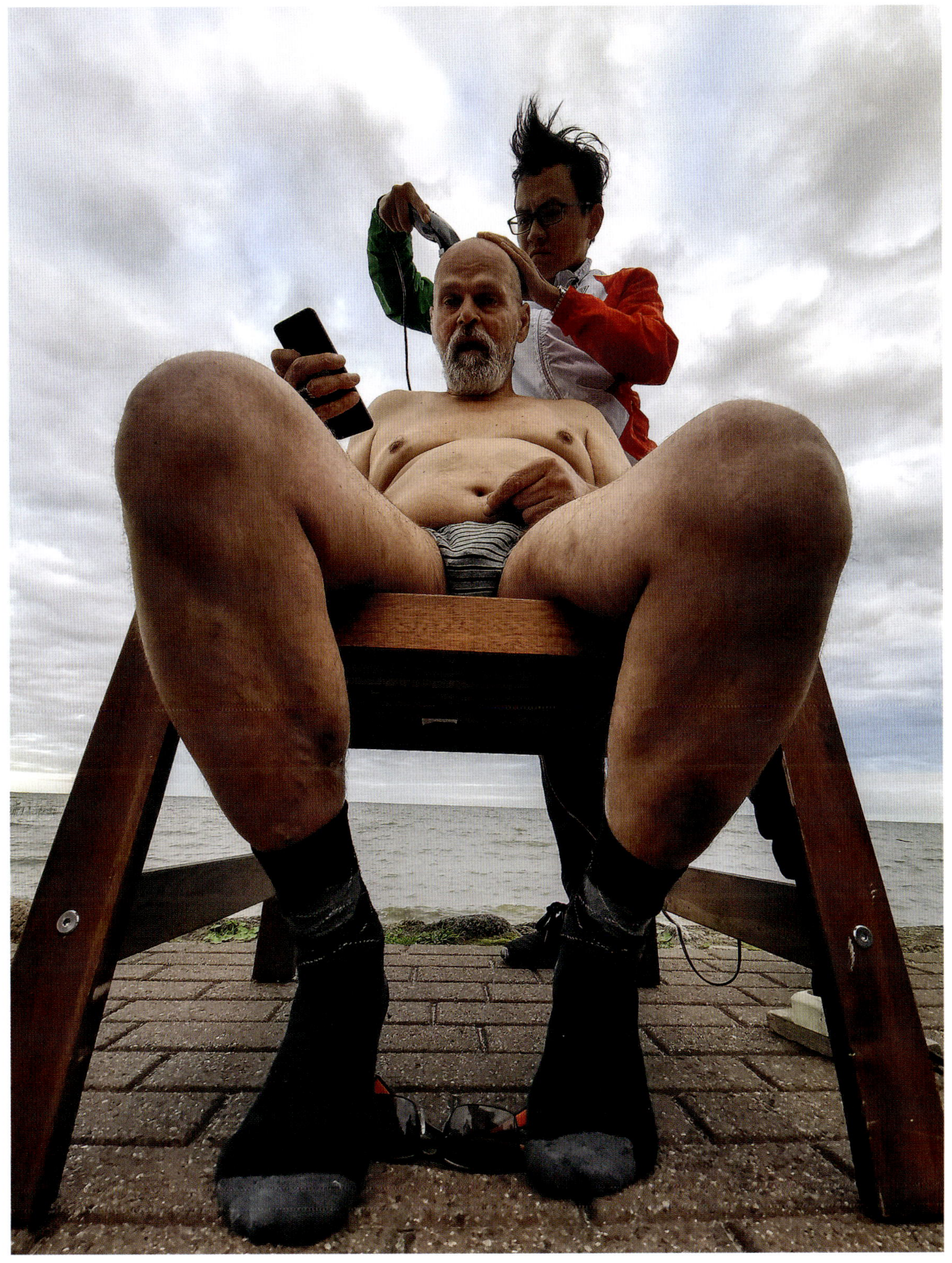

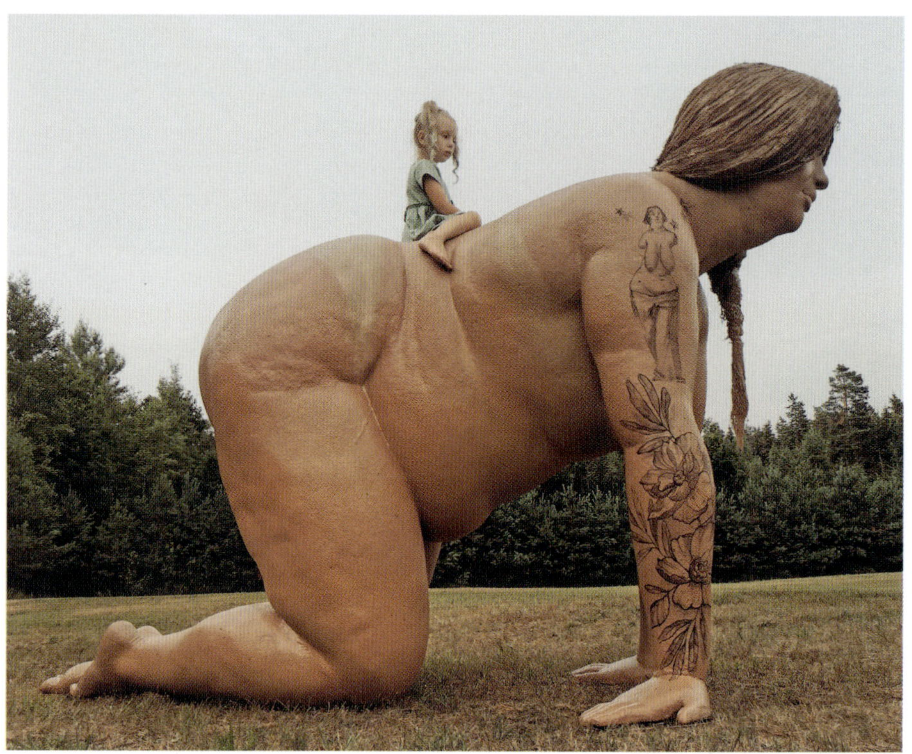

ABOVE: I was judging a photo competition in Kryžbarkas, 124 miles (200km) from Vilnius. The organizers had commissioned a sculptor, Martynas Gaubas, to produce a piece for the event. He delivered it at night and everyone was surprised to wake up and find this Lithuanian Girl coming out of the woods. She has sunburn marks, mosquito bites and acne, 'Lithuanian girl' tattooed on her back, and more tattoos on her arm. Someone sat their daughter on her back. I loved the contrast between the tiny girl and the massive woman. Also, both the sculpture and the little girl had tattoos (temporary ones on child's hands) and their hair colour matched; it looked like a secret connection or allegory about fragility and power.

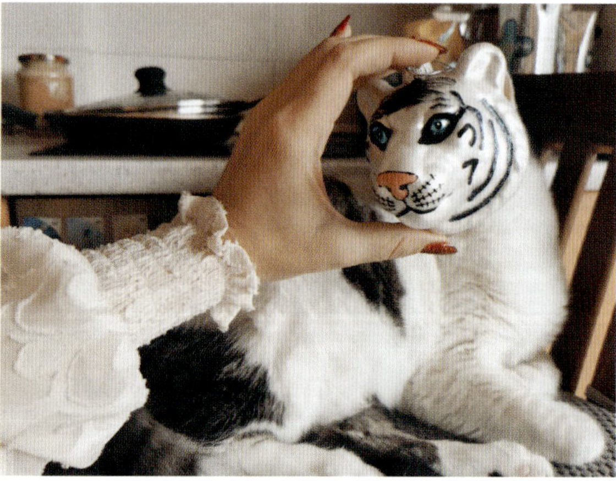

ABOVE: This is a tiger bauble for the Christmas tree. I got it as a present for my friend – that's why it wasn't on the tree. It was lying somewhere nearby, and I noticed the colour of the tiger is the same as that of my cat. So I held it up to compare them.

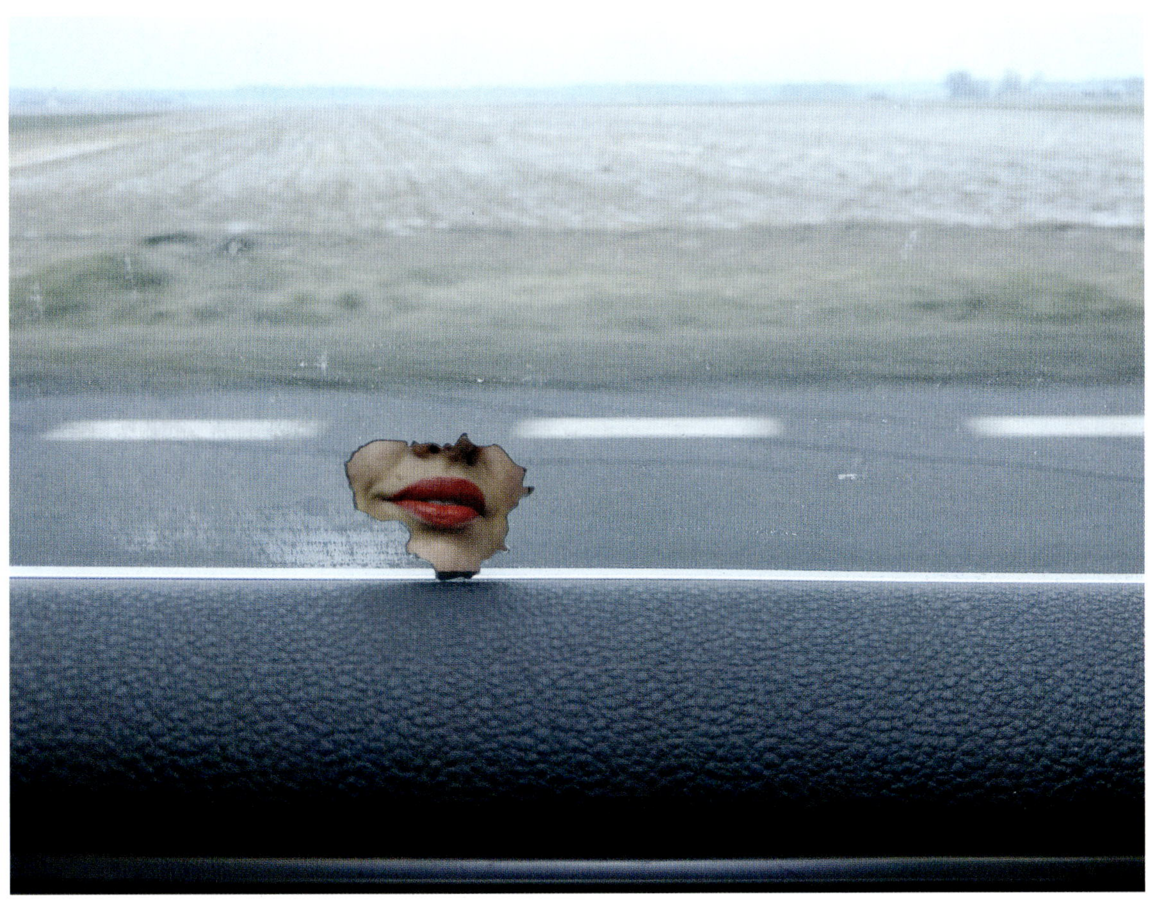

ABOVE: This photograph was taken on the 100th anniversary of the Act of Independence of Lithuania, which was signed on 16 February 1918. Lithuania later became the first of the 15 states of the Soviet Republic to declare independence from the Soviet Union. The mirror is shaped like Lithuania, and the reflection of my red lips is supposed to be understood as a kiss – which means love to my homeland.

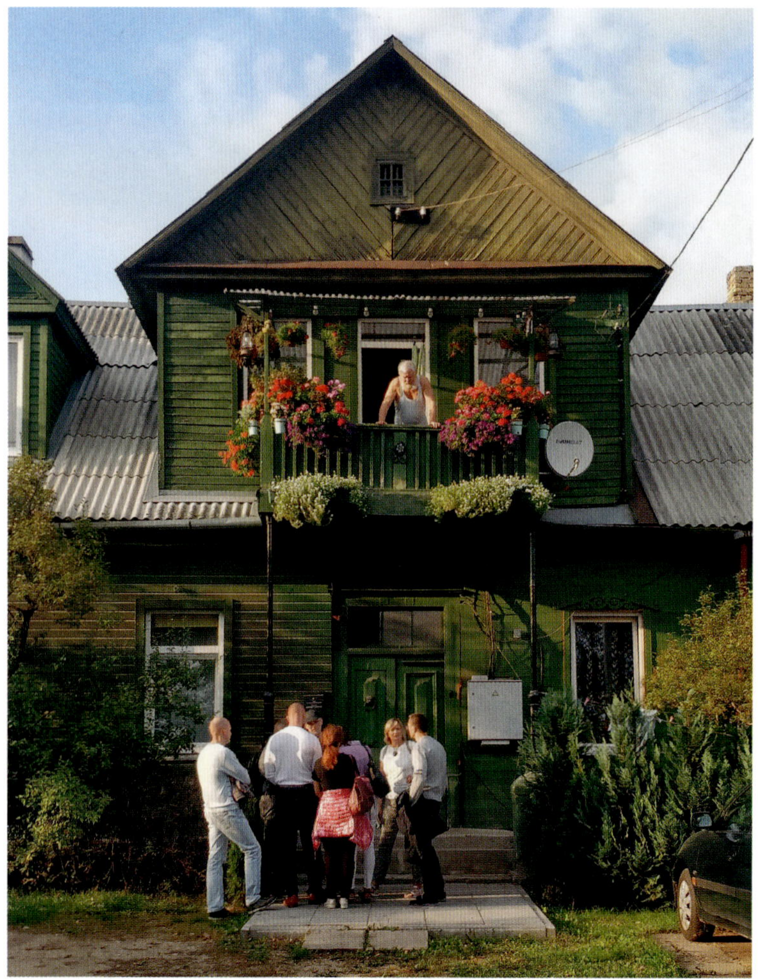

LEFT: The house in this photo
is in a historical central
neighbourhood of Vilnius called
Žvėrynas – which translates
as 'menagerie' or 'zoo'. Much
of the wooden architecture of
this neighbourhood has official
cultural heritage status. This
house was built around 1910–15,
and is famous because the
columns supporting the central
balcony are former gas street
lamp poles. Some locals are
meeting in front of the house
with an old man watching from
above. I live in a newer part
of Žvėrynas, where there are
modern houses. I noticed this
scene and couldn't pass by
without taking a shot, I like to
wonder what the people were
doing there.

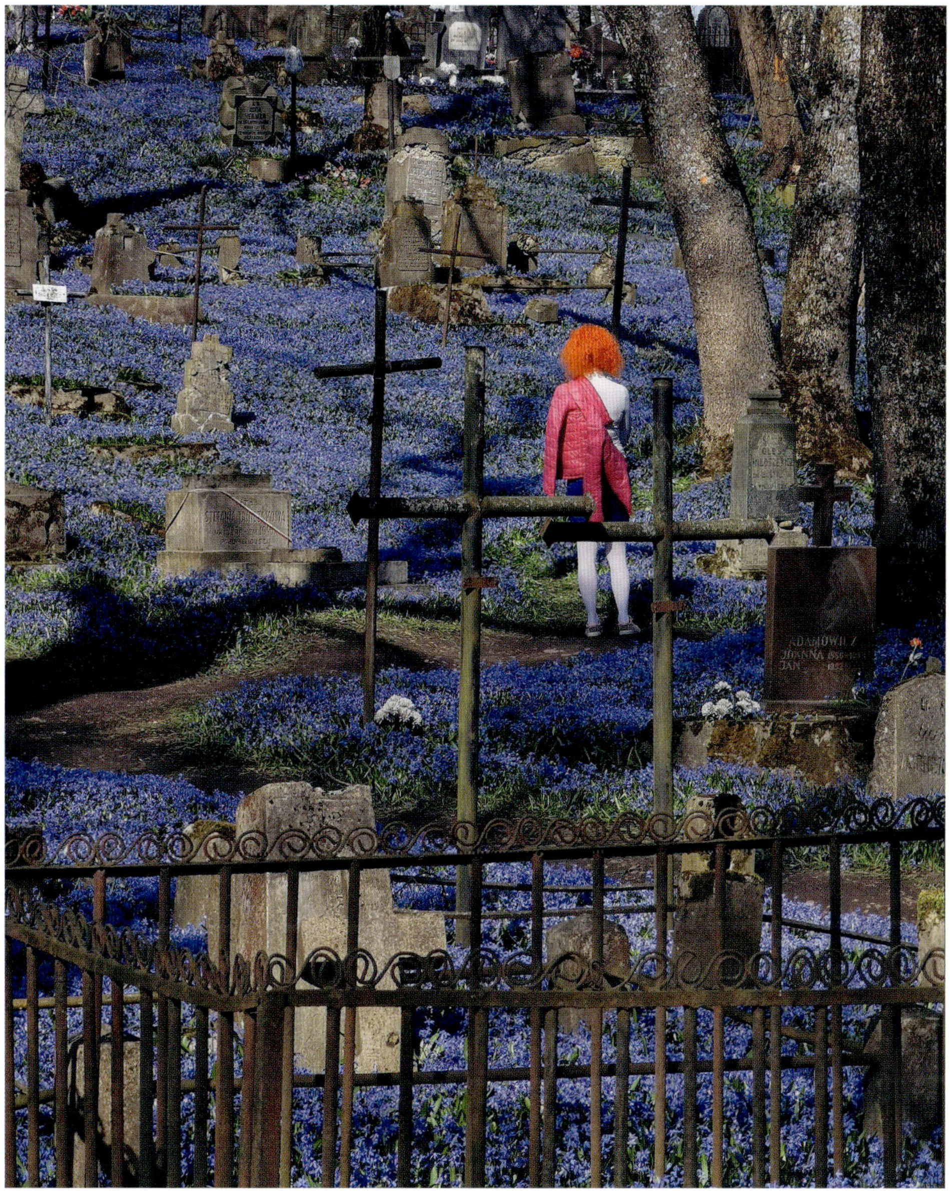

ABOVE: The Bernardine Cemetery is one of the oldest in Vilnius. It was established in 1810 when Lithuania was part of the Russian Empire and people were prohibited from burying the dead near churches. The St Benardine monks created this cemetery on the eastern outskirts of the city. Over the last two decades the city has grown around it and now it is close to the centre. Every spring tourists are drawn to see the *Scilla siberica* flowers, which grow in unusually high numbers here. I found myself in the cemetery at a quiet moment when I spotted this woman who is a famous Lithuanian television presenter.

Isaac West

New York and
Wyoming, USA

Isaac West was born in Liberia in West Africa. His Ghanaian father moved the family to America as refugees when he was about eight years old.

West was introduced to photography by his friend Steve, who encouraged him to get a Canon DSLR. He started making music videos with it, without really knowing how to use it. West continued using photographer friends to shoot his projects until, after an instance of artistic differences, he decided to ask his brother Darlington, a photography student, to teach him how to use a camera and edit his own images. When he annoyed his brother by asking too many questions, he turned to YouTube to learn more.

West didn't set out to photograph only people with dark skin tones, but says his lens fell in love with it. His images have drawn responses from people, especially older women, telling him that they have given them confidence in their own appearance. West sees himself as shining a light on people who aren't usually in the spotlight. After he posted his first picture of a South Sudanese girl in 2017, he got lots of messages from people from the country wanting to model for him. He keeps a mood board with ideas for projects and potential models and connects the two when the time is right.

In 2020, when Apple iPhone cameras became more advanced and offered the ability to shoot in RAW, West started to use his phone for photography. He likes the fact that, if you have an idea for an image, you can pull out your phone and shoot it there and then. His models are sometimes surprised, expecting big professional cameras, but then they're blown away by the results.

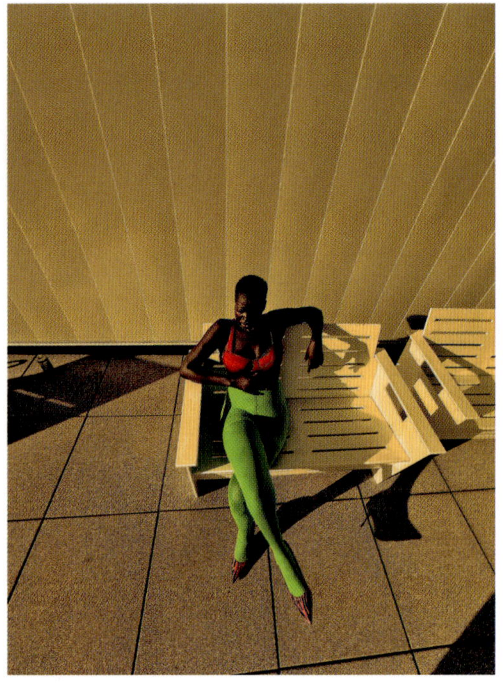

'I don't have time for racism...I don't really like to acknowledge it.'

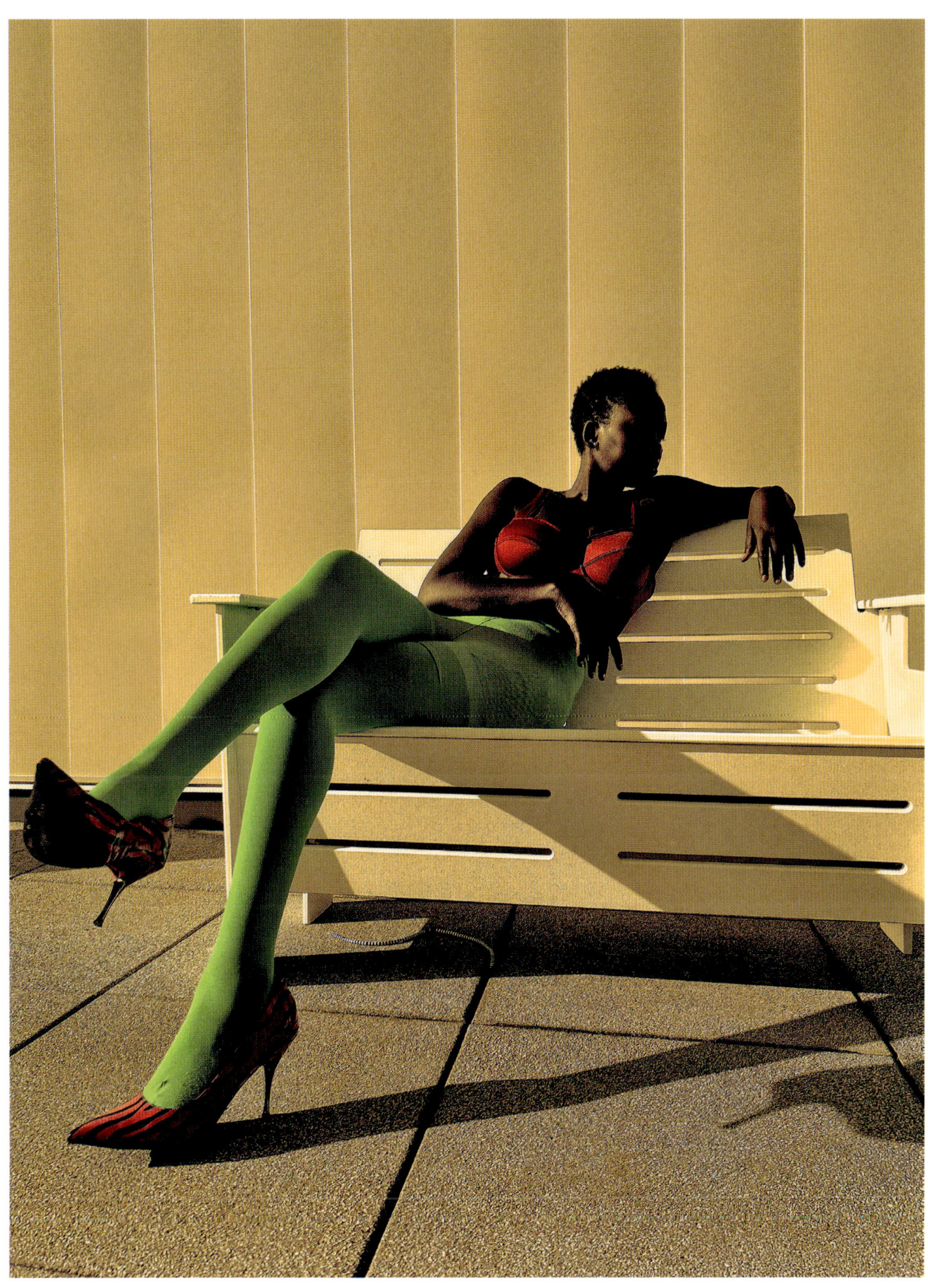

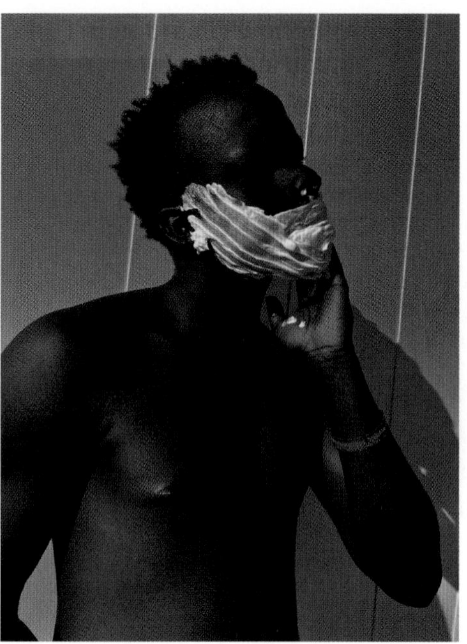

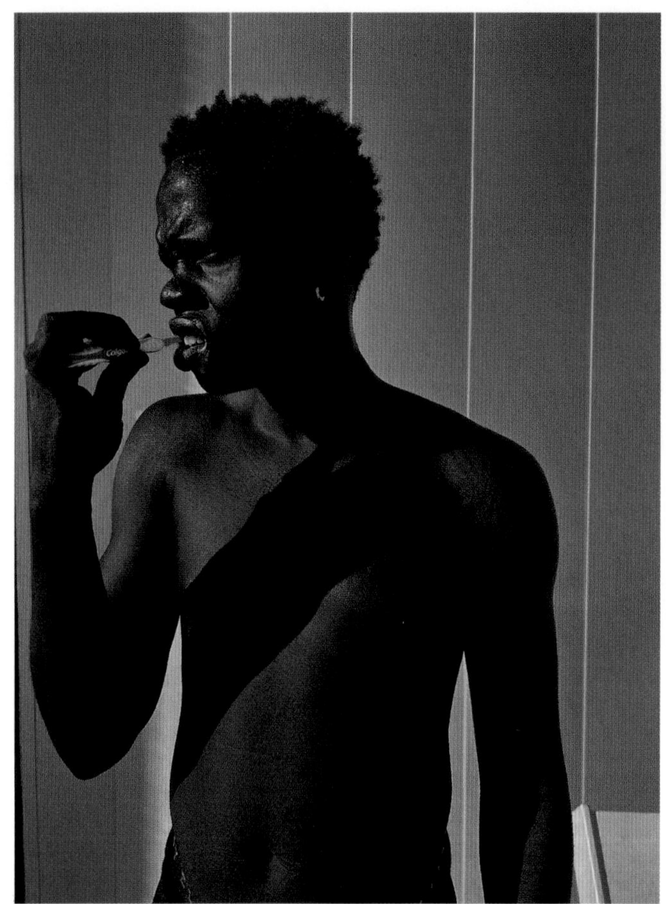

ABOVE + LEFT: I wanted to capture the fact that in America you don't see people doing things like shaving or brushing their teeth outside, whereas it is really common to see this in Africa. In the morning you often see someone shaving with a mirror in their hand outside their house. This man, originally from South Sudan, now lives in Iowa.

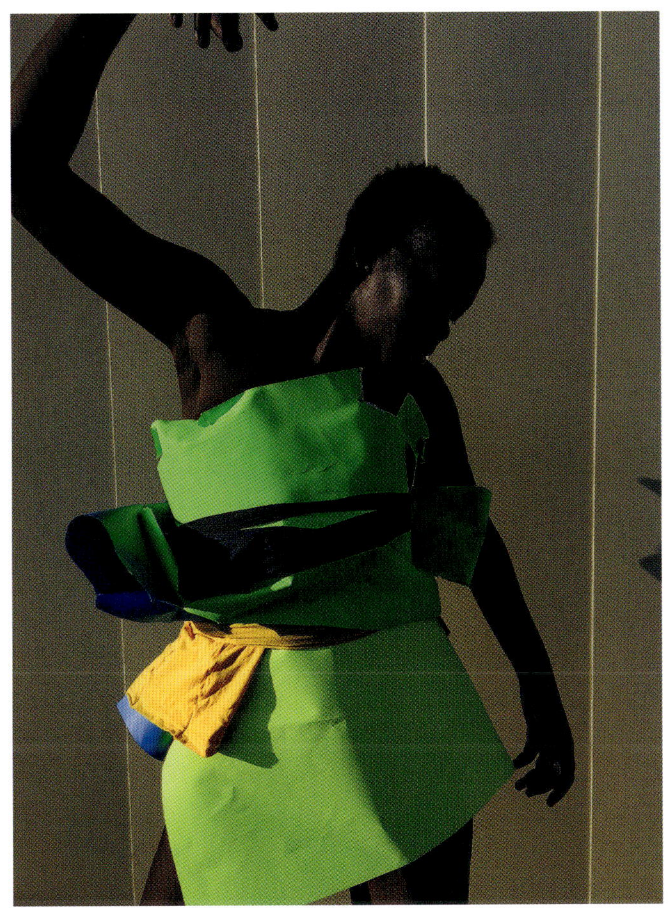

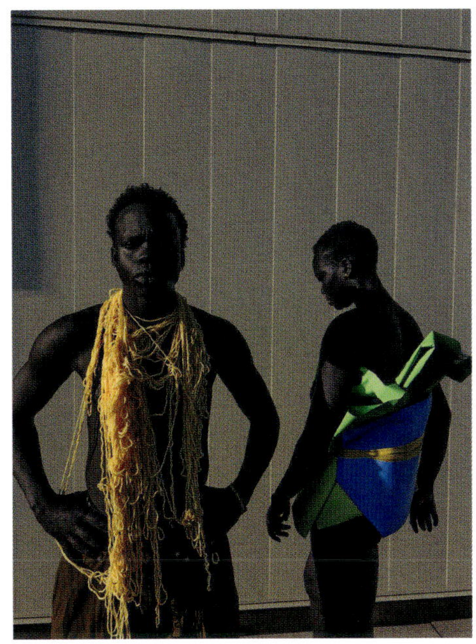

ABOVE + LEFT: I wanted to explore ideas of resourcefulness and the idea that clothes can be made out of anything. I used classroom supplies that are freely available in the US but are not available in African classrooms as a commentary on both the basic need for clothing and education in Africa. The dress is made from coloured card and I bought the yellow wool from a store and draped it over the man. The wool can be woven into textiles to create a clothing fabric.

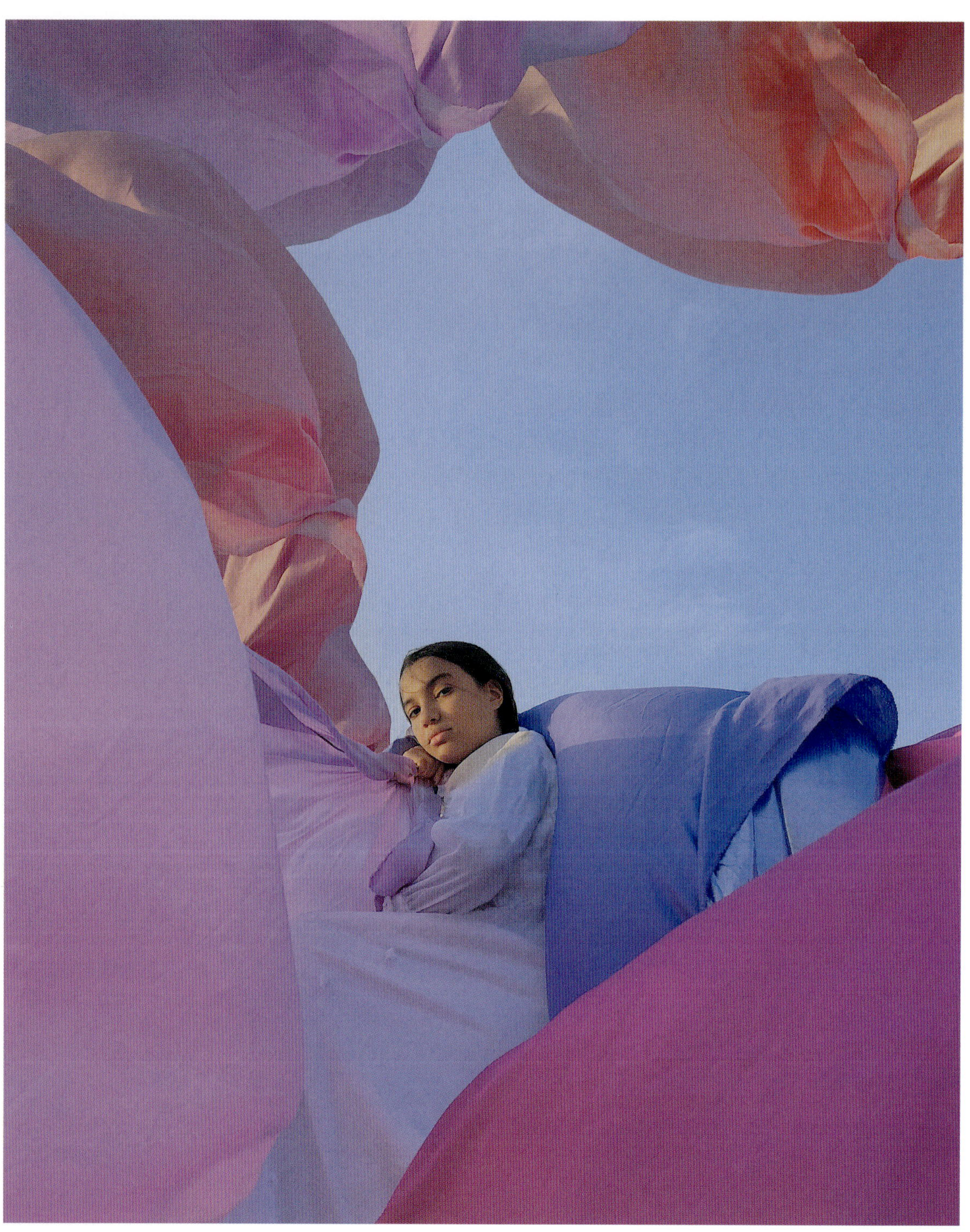

Ismail Zaidy
Marrakech, Morocco

'To begin with, I primarily focused on capturing my immediate surroundings in Morocco. As I grew more comfortable as an artist and a creative, I began to develop, and now my photographs have a more minimalistic, abstract and poetic style.'

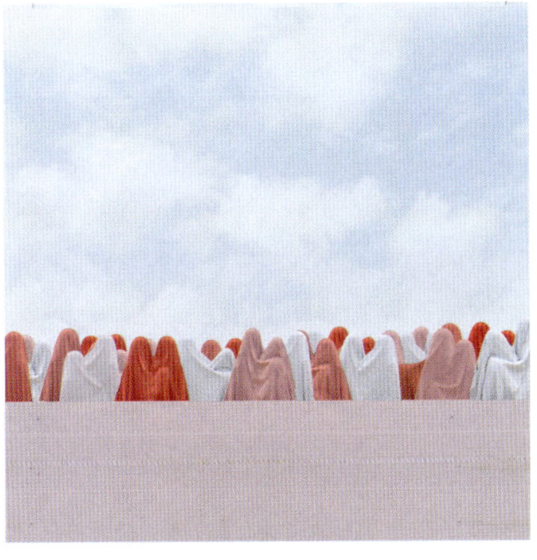

Photography is a shared passion for the family of full-time artist Ismail Zaidy. In 2018, he initiated a project named 3aila ('family' in English) with his younger brother Othmane and sister Fatimazohra. They are both creative and play a significant role in conceptualizing the ideas and stories behind his staged photographs. All of Zaidy's pictures are taken in and around Marrakech, where he lives with his family.

Zaidy explains that photography allows him to express his inner thoughts and perspectives on subjects that he may find difficult to convey through words. As a person who is not very talkative, photography and imagery have become the most effective way for him to express himself.

In the past, he used a Samsung S5, and now Zaidy enjoys shooting with an Apple iPhone 11 and editing with VSCO.

'I am particularly fond of pastel colours, but since they are not commonly found in our daily lives, I try to incorporate them into my photographs. I believe that playing with colours and tones enables me to communicate the issues faced by my family and society. Each colour has its own story, meaning and purpose, but sometimes the colours are chosen simply for the aesthetic impact they have on the image. The colour pink is often associated with feelings of hope and joy, and it can be used in various forms of creative work to evoke those emotions. For example, an artist may choose to use pink in a painting to convey a sense of optimism or happiness. A designer might incorporate pink into a logo or website to create a cheerful and uplifting atmosphere. By using the colour pink in your work, you are referencing these positive emotions and potentially evoking them in your audience.'

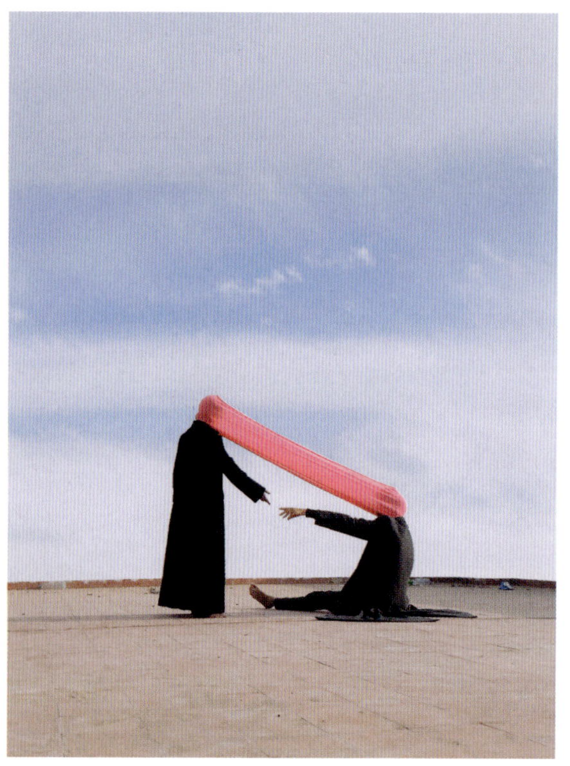

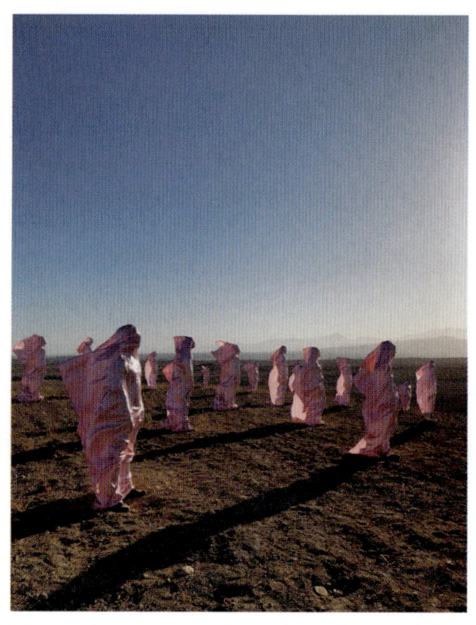

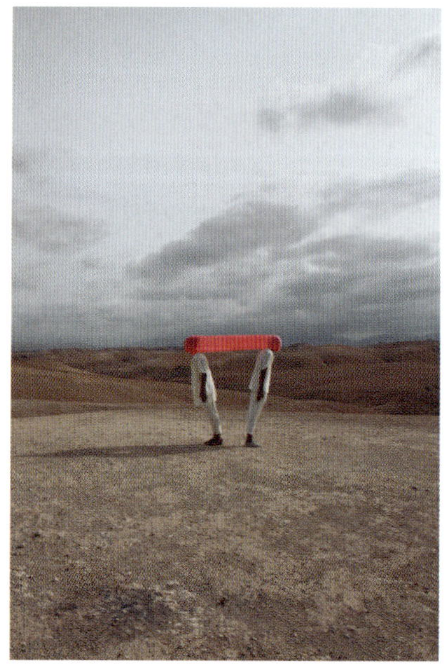

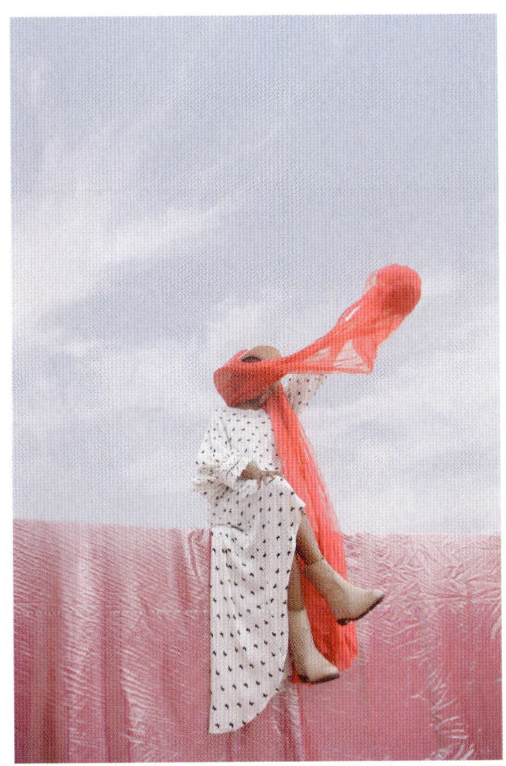

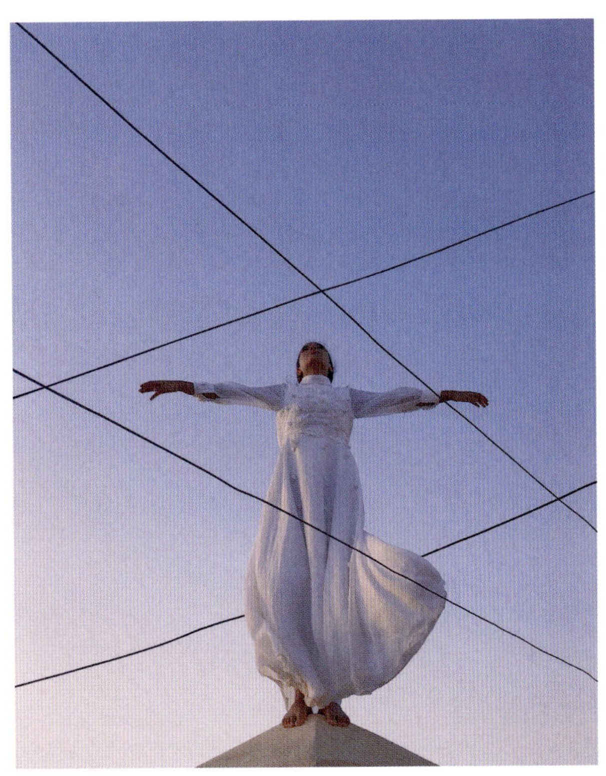

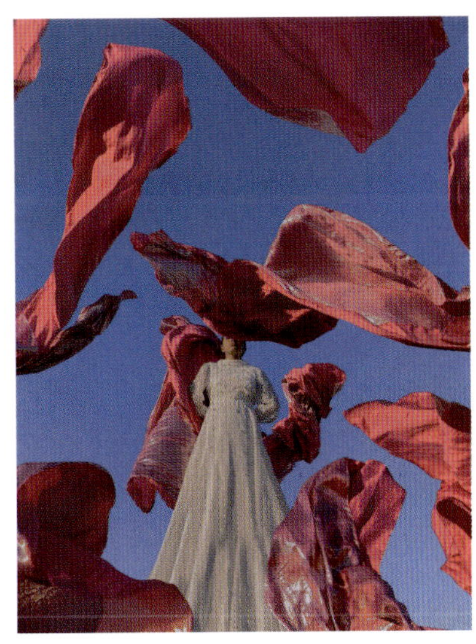

'I grew up in a modest neighbourhood in Marrakech, where women wear colourful fabrics, hijabs and djellabas. These women continue to be a major source of inspiration for me.'

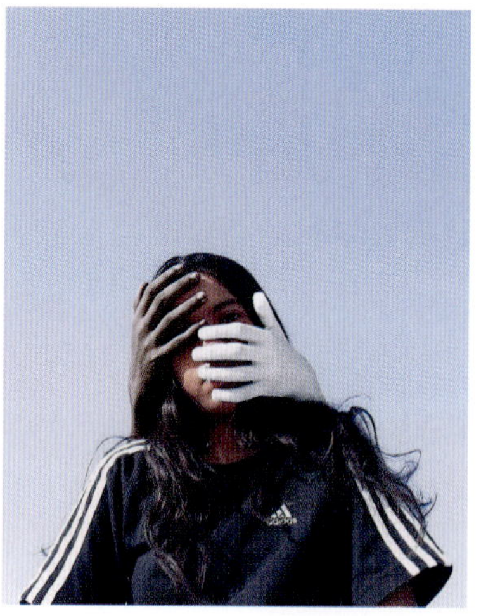

'My photographs describe the fight of young souls seeking to escape from old rituals in order to build their own story and future.'

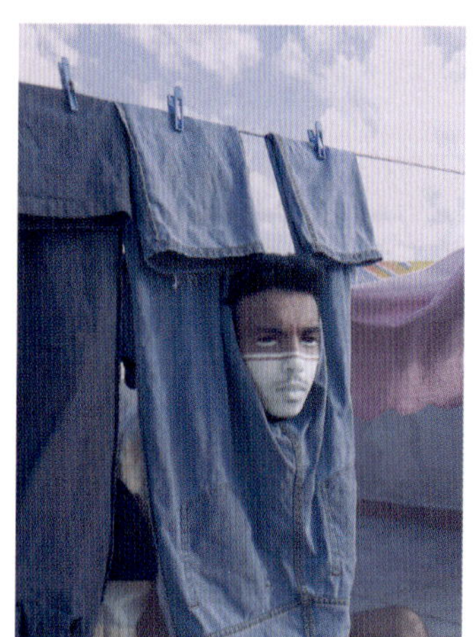

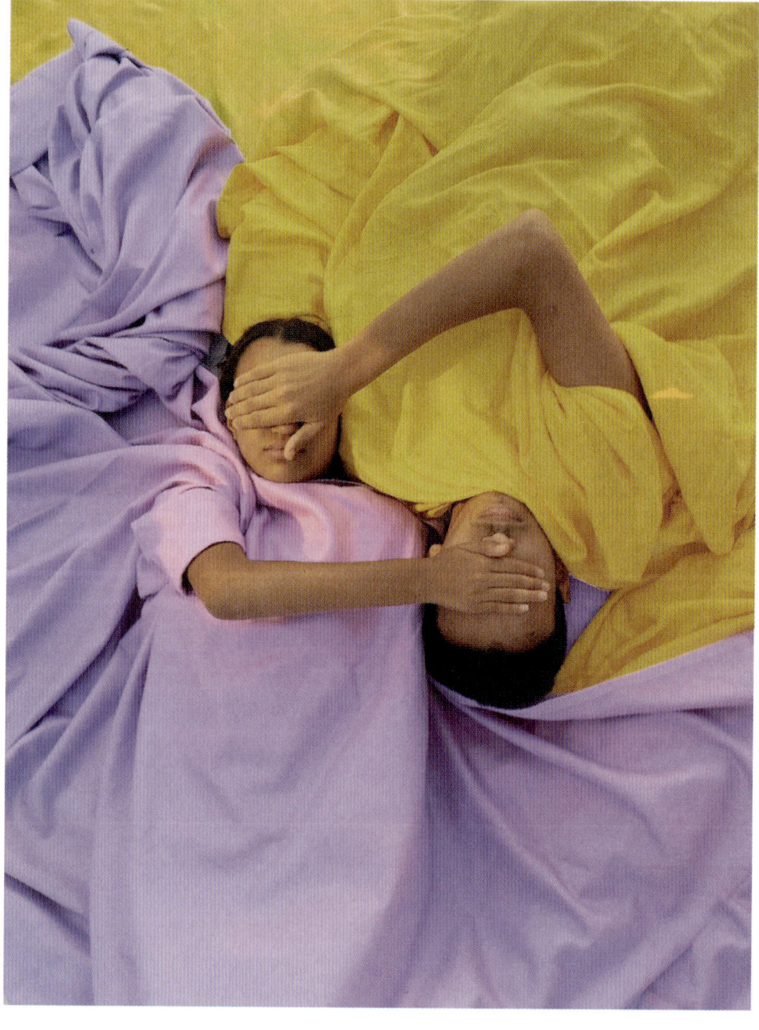

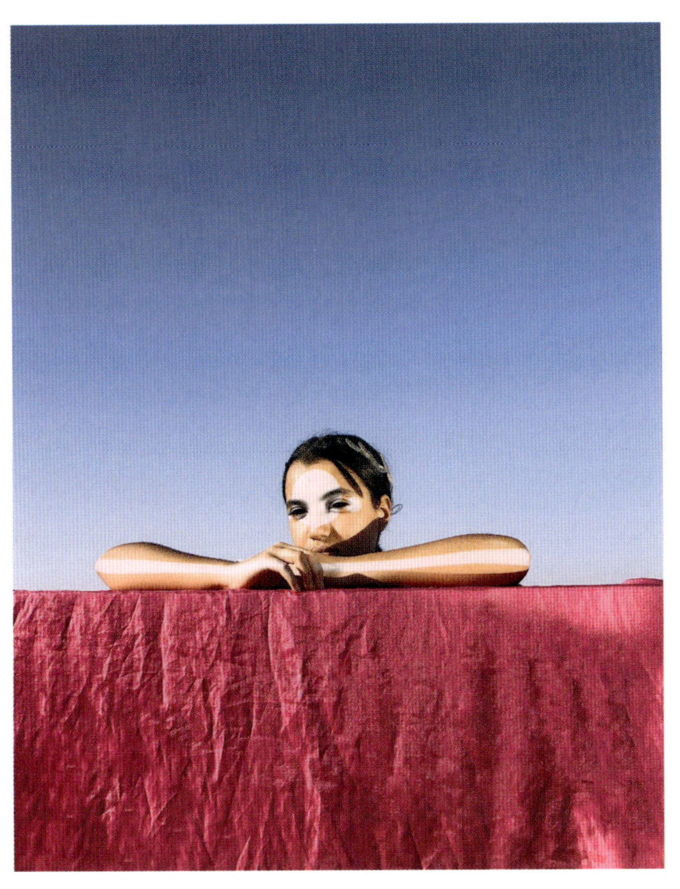

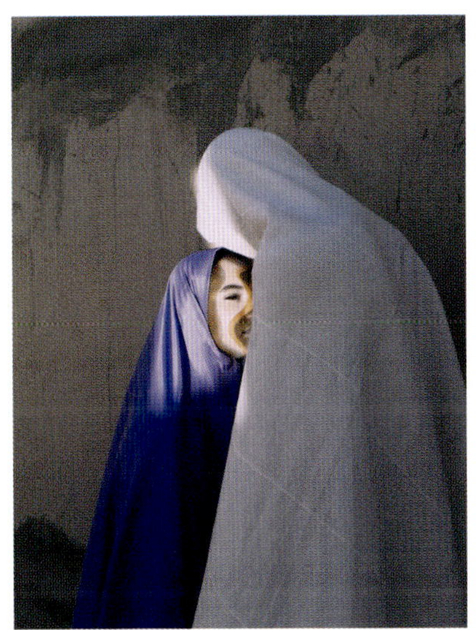

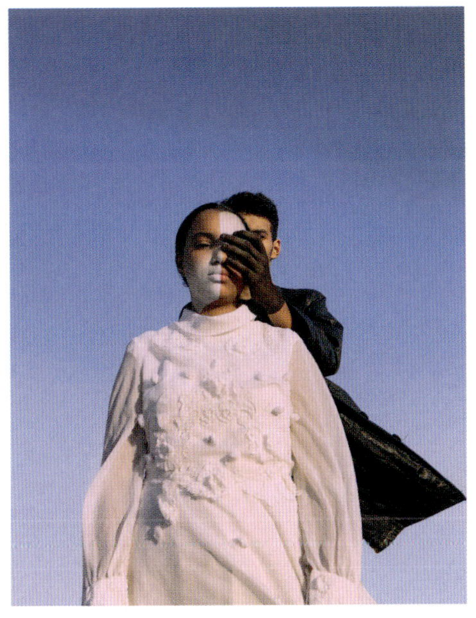

ISMAIL ZAIDY

Joyz Kwok
Hong Kong

Photography – and in particular street photography – is the favourite pastime of Joyz Kwok, who works in the service industry. She shoots on a Samsung phone and has used a Huawei in the past.

In her early days with her camera, Kwok found she was most often drawn to recording patterns, shapes and forms. More recently, her interest has shifted and she finds herself drawn to capturing fleeting moments of light and shadow. Over time she has developed a working method that is more akin to that of someone working with a large-format film camera. She has learned to be patient, to wait for the shot she wants, rather than to take vast numbers of photos in a random fashion and hope for the best. This patience, combined with her search for clarity of vision, fulfils her desire to create tiny perfect moments in her photos.

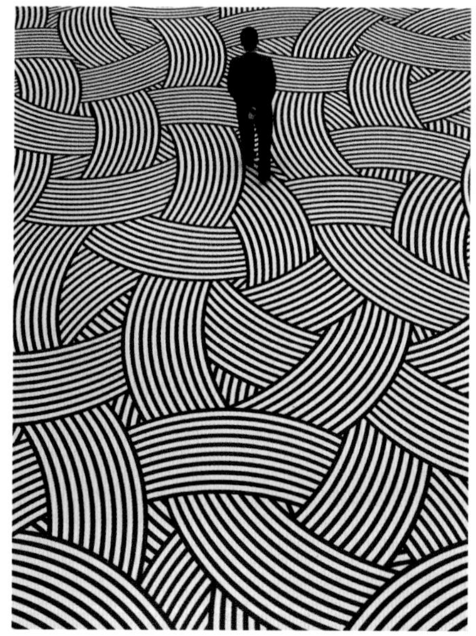

ABOVE + RIGHT: These photos of passers-by and fleeting moments were taken on the streets of Hong Kong.

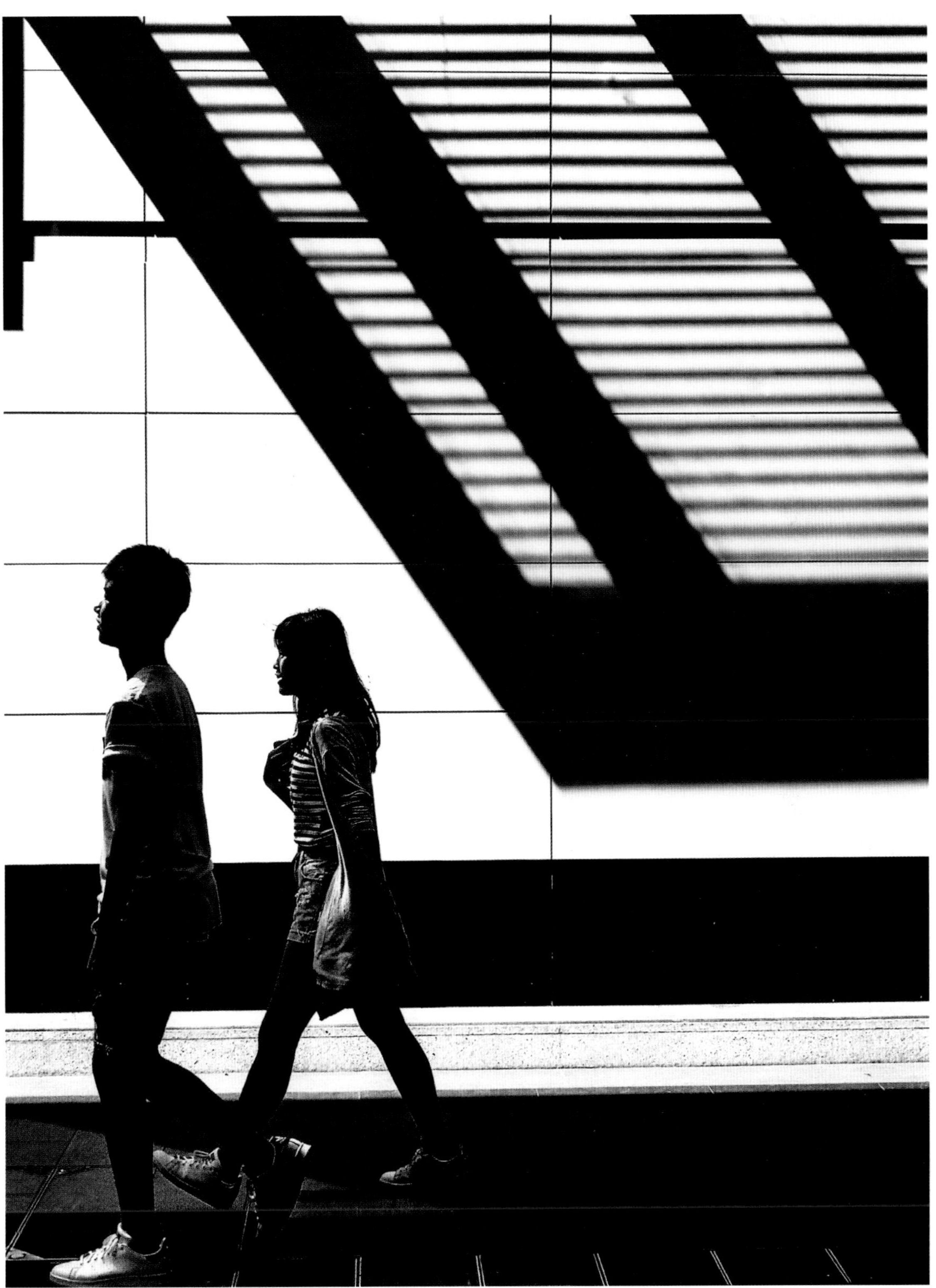

Julia Shatun
Belarus

Film director, screenwriter and editor Julia Shatun was born in Belarus, where most of these photographs were taken, and lived there for almost all of her life. But in 2020, mass protests against President Alexander Lukashenko and the falsification of elections resulted in the massive political repressions that continue there. Then, at the end of 2021, Shatun and her partner were forced to leave the country, and moved to Lviv, Ukraine. After Russia attacked Ukraine on February 24, 2022, and the war escalated, they moved to Poznań, Poland.

Shatun started taking pictures when she got a phone with a camera. She takes photos of the things around her that she finds beautiful and soulful: moments of life, people and places. For the last six years she has used an Apple iPhone. Now she uses an iPhone 12 mini. She mostly uses VSCO to edit the exposure, contrast, colour and brightness of her photos.

RIGHT: This photo was taken on a train from Minsk to Kalinkovichi in Belarus in May 2021. The woman was travelling in the same compartment as me. Covid-19 restrictions were in place and everyone had to wear masks. I found the image of the woman peacefully lying on a bed with the mask on to be an intriguing juxtaposition. I like that this photo combines something that is connected with the eternal, old – a train, a woman in a hat, her pose – and the disposable mask, which was starting to be worn during the pandemic and which is a little bit out of place, but accurately indicates the time in which this woman lives.

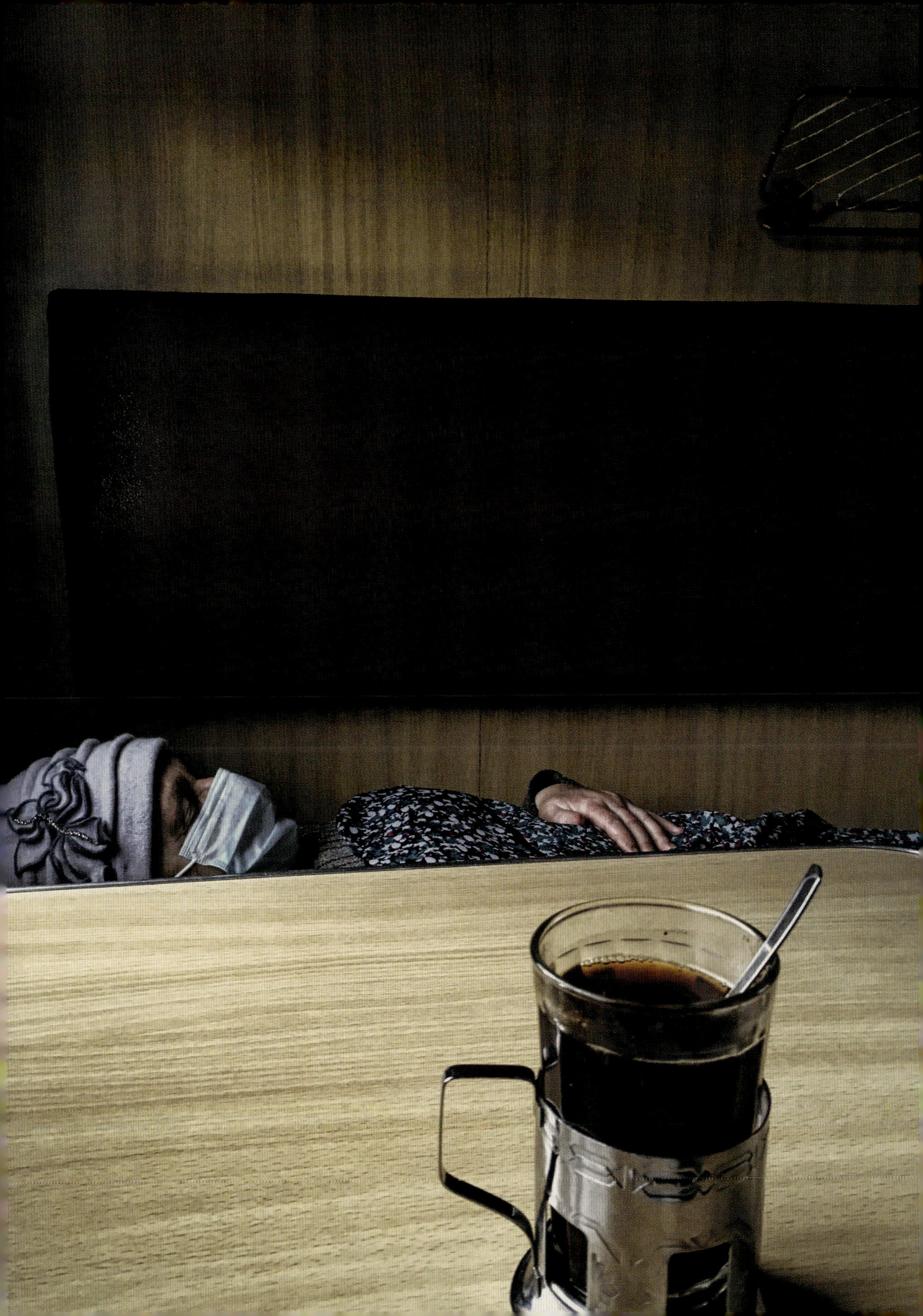

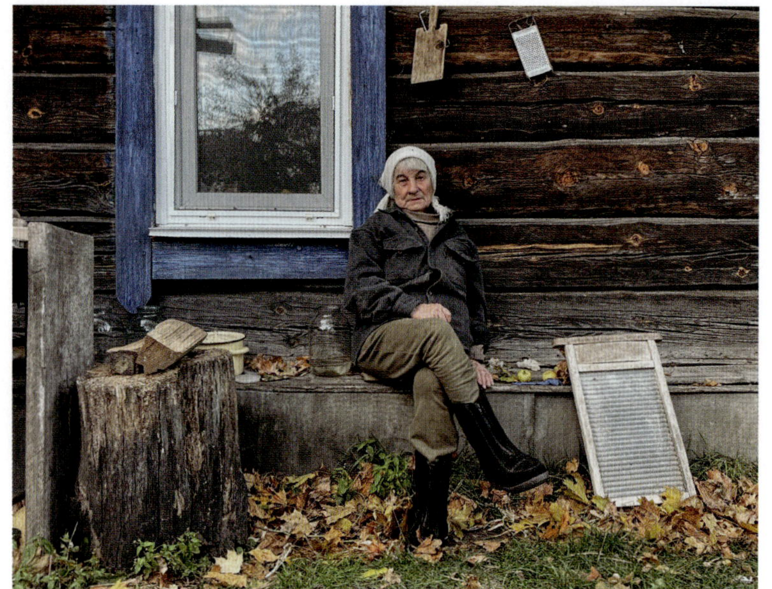

LEFT: My grandmother Svetlana is sitting outside her house in the village where she lives. My grandfather was raised there and, when his mother died, he and my grandmother spent most of the year there, growing crops for the entire family. My grandfather died eight years ago, but my grandmother still grows potatoes, vegetables, fruits, berries, nuts and flowers. She says that she is not as bored in the village as she was in the city. I like taking photos of my grandmother when I am visiting. Everything that surrounds her in the village has some history, and I really like photos that are composed of objects that have history.

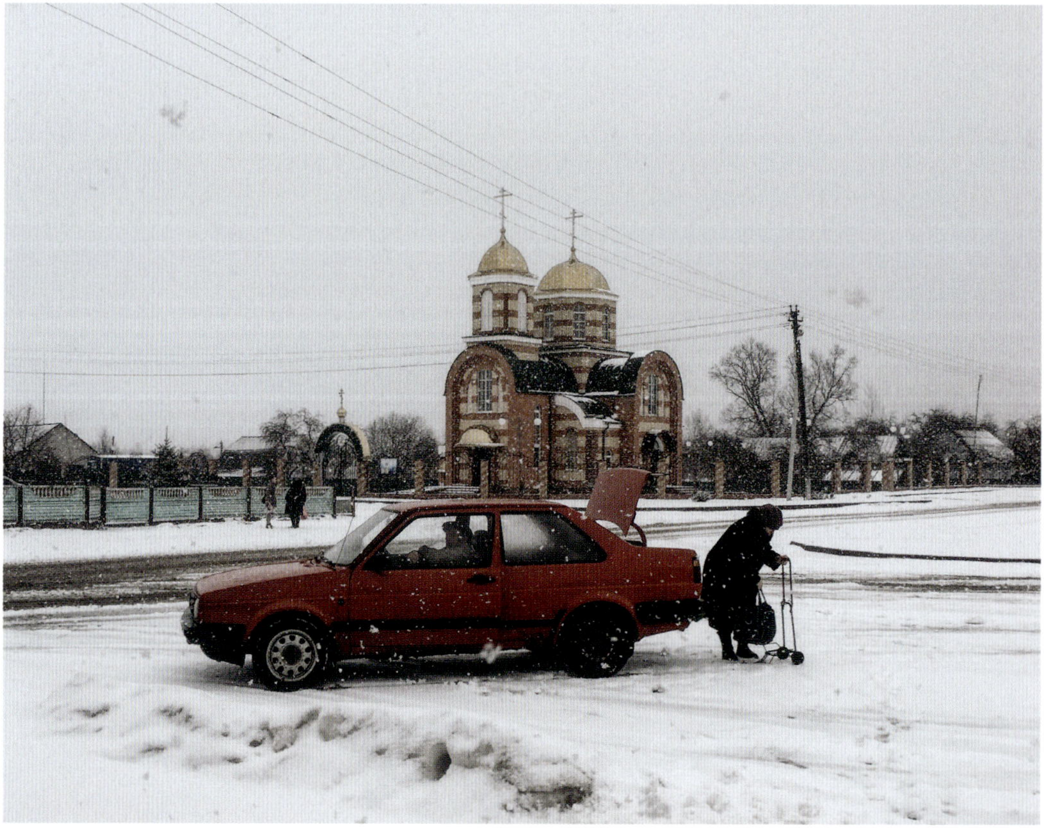

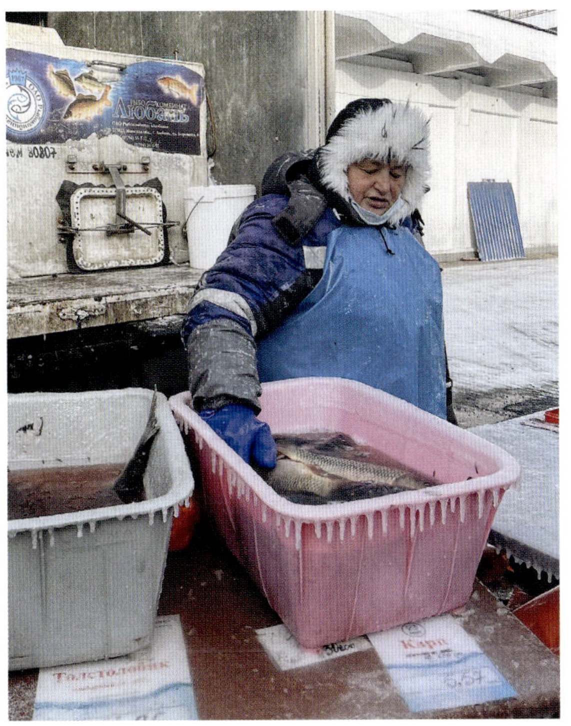

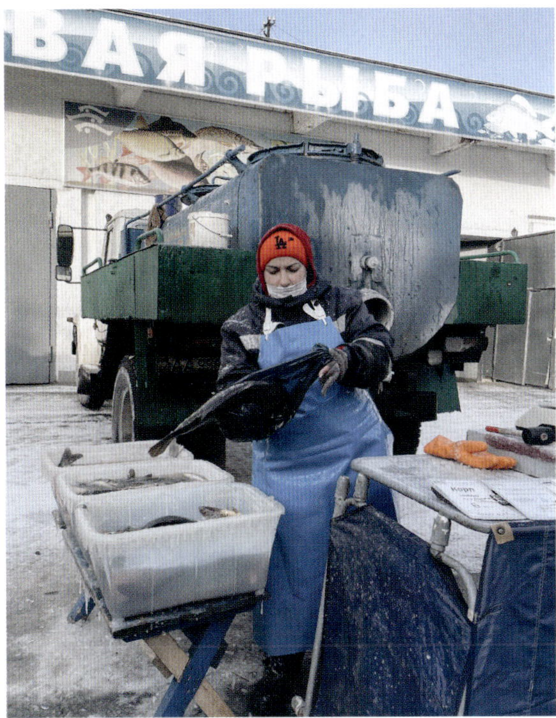

LEFT: When we lived in Belarus, we sometimes liked to go to different small towns and I was visiting Tolochin with friends to go for a walk. I liked the contrasting colours in the photo: the red car and church with the white snow and sky in the background. The scene also represents a fundamental truth about these people's lives: the way in which the man sits in the car daydreaming while the woman puts the heavy bags into the car on her own.

ABOVE LEFT + RIGHT: Kamaroŭski market is one of the most famous markets in Minsk. It is the largest district and is located in the middle of the city. The market has stalls for fresh vegetables, fruit, meat and fish that arrive daily from neighbouring farms.

BELOW: During my evening walk around the Eminönü district of Istanbul I saw this man sitting next to a hotel entrance. I liked the unusual atmosphere that was created by the combination of night lights and colours. It looked like a scene from a movie by my favourite film director, Apichatpong Weerasethakul.

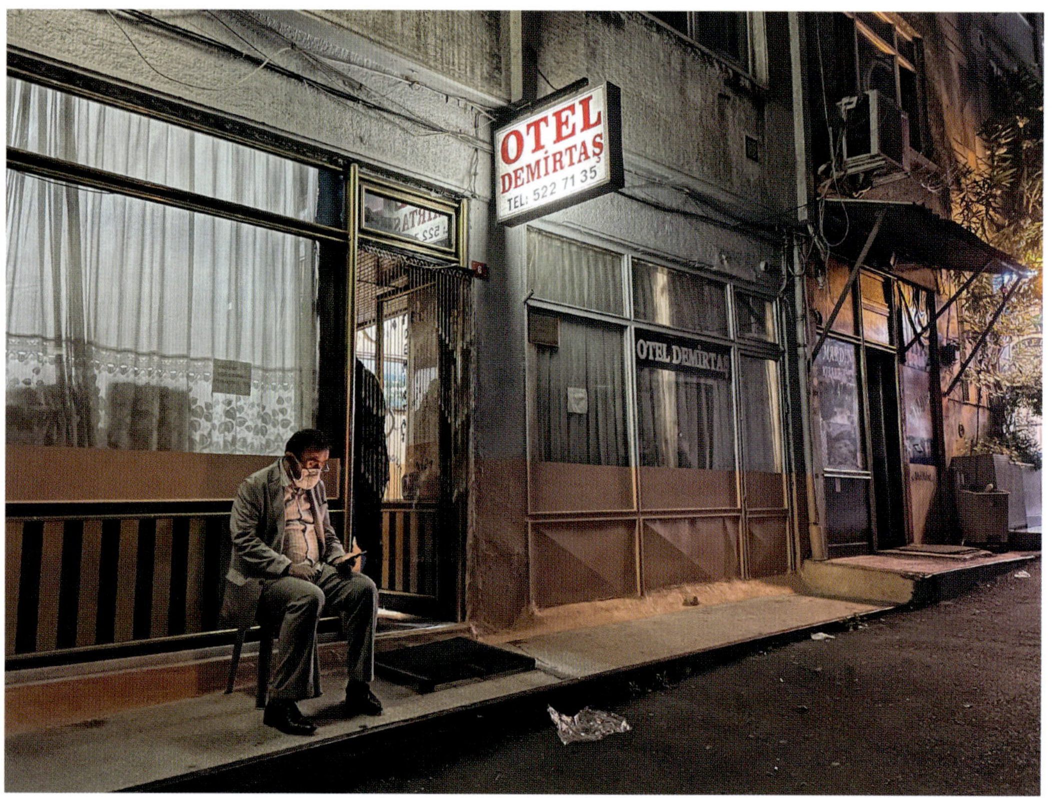

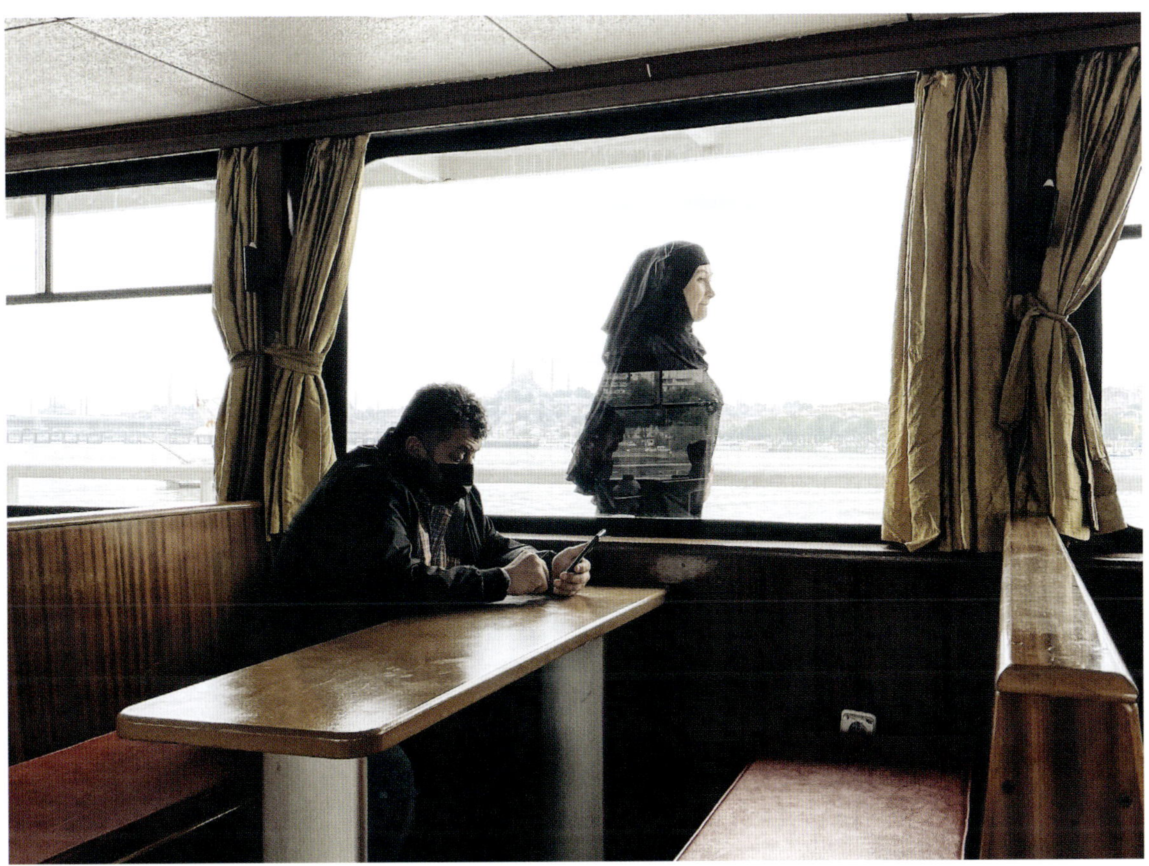

ABOVE: In cities, ferries are my favourite means of transportation. This photo was taken on a ferry crossing the Golden Horn of the Bosphorus in Istanbul. I like the colours and light, and the image of the woman on the other side of the window, who looks as if she has travelled from a different time or as if she is a ghost.

Juliet Cope
Hove, UK

Juliet Cope lives by the sea. She used to work as an assistant director on films sets but now she teaches photography. Cope photographs her family, mostly her two sons, to document their lives. She captures all the little things that may be missed or forgotten; ordinary moments rather than events like birthdays.

Cope is interested in boyhood in general, too, and is working on a project called 'Hot Dust and the Myth of Being a Man'. In the UK, since the 1950s, three quarters of suicides have been male. The project investigates why, and considers whether the archetypes fed to boys – the unwavering hero, the silent, the strong, the superhero – are as stifling and damaging as those fed to girls. She would like to create a database of boyhood that looks at what it means to be a boy and grow into a man across different cultures.

She says that photography is a positive addiction, an outlet. Cope is inspired by colour, and uses it almost as a character in each image. Her first photographic love was photojournalism, and she seeks to blend classic photojournalism and painting. She loves things that can be both beautiful and informative.

For Cope, smartphone photography is another means of telling a story, perhaps the best way, because her Apple iPhone is always with her and is a less invasive way of taking a picture. Getting children to cooperate to recreate things is difficult, so Cope finds she just has to be ready and hope for the best. She takes a photojournalistic approach, working around her subjects and not the other way around. She uses phone apps for editing: Snapseed for the main edits, then a combination of Lens Distortions and Afterlight, plus Carbon for black and white and Mextures for colour images.

'The spaces between the main events are the moments when real childhood happens.'

RIGHT: This photo was taken at the dentist. Casper had to have a tooth out, which was of course painful, but he had to leave school early, so he was in two minds whether it was good or bad! I am often drawn to photographing a close-up of the face, especially the eyes or mouth. Going to the dentist is a childhood milestone and I'm always looking to add to the collection of benchmark experiences, especially firsts. Here it's the first time he had a tooth out. I like the purple and the red in this photo. The colours are always the main driver and the story.

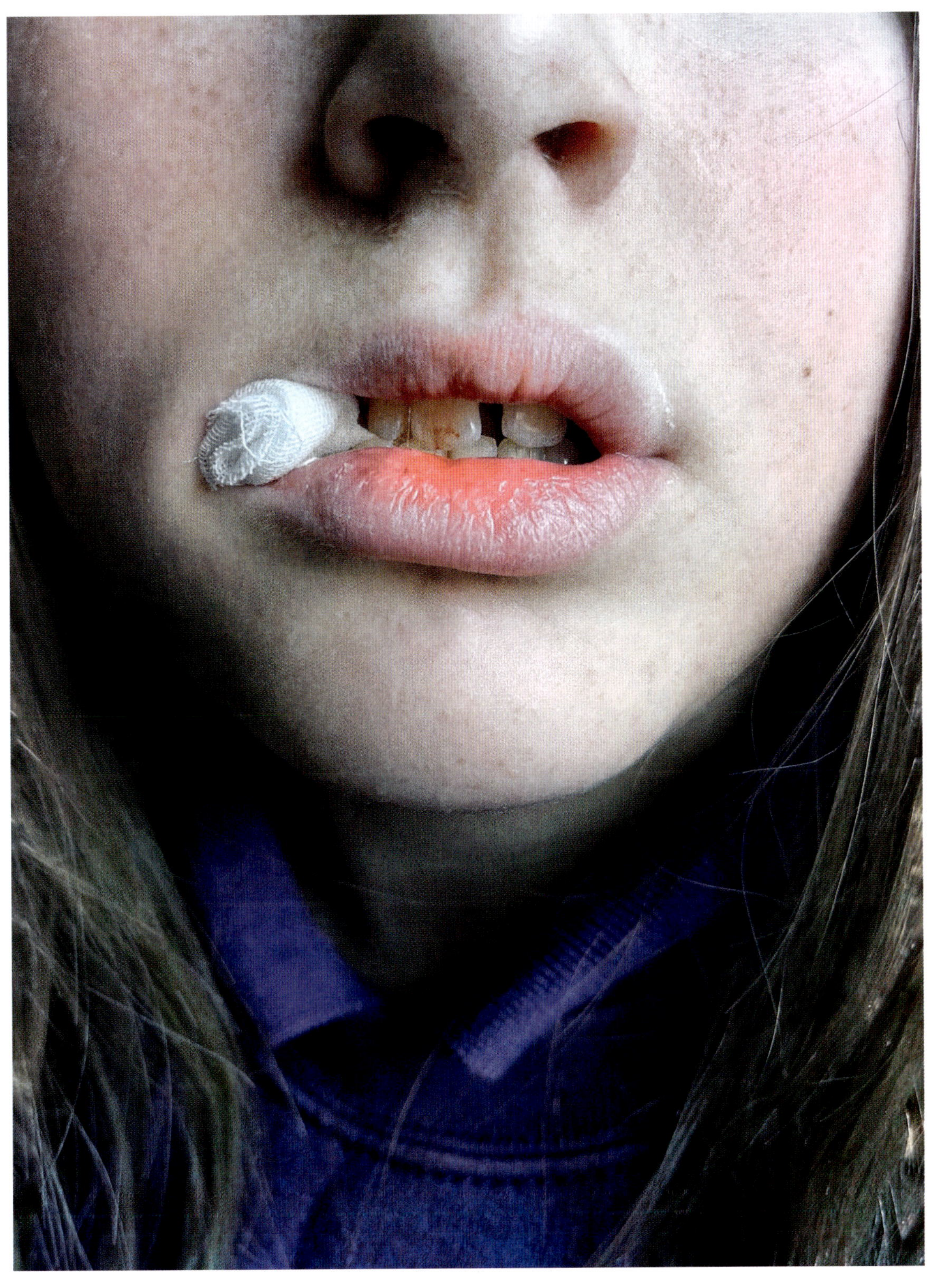

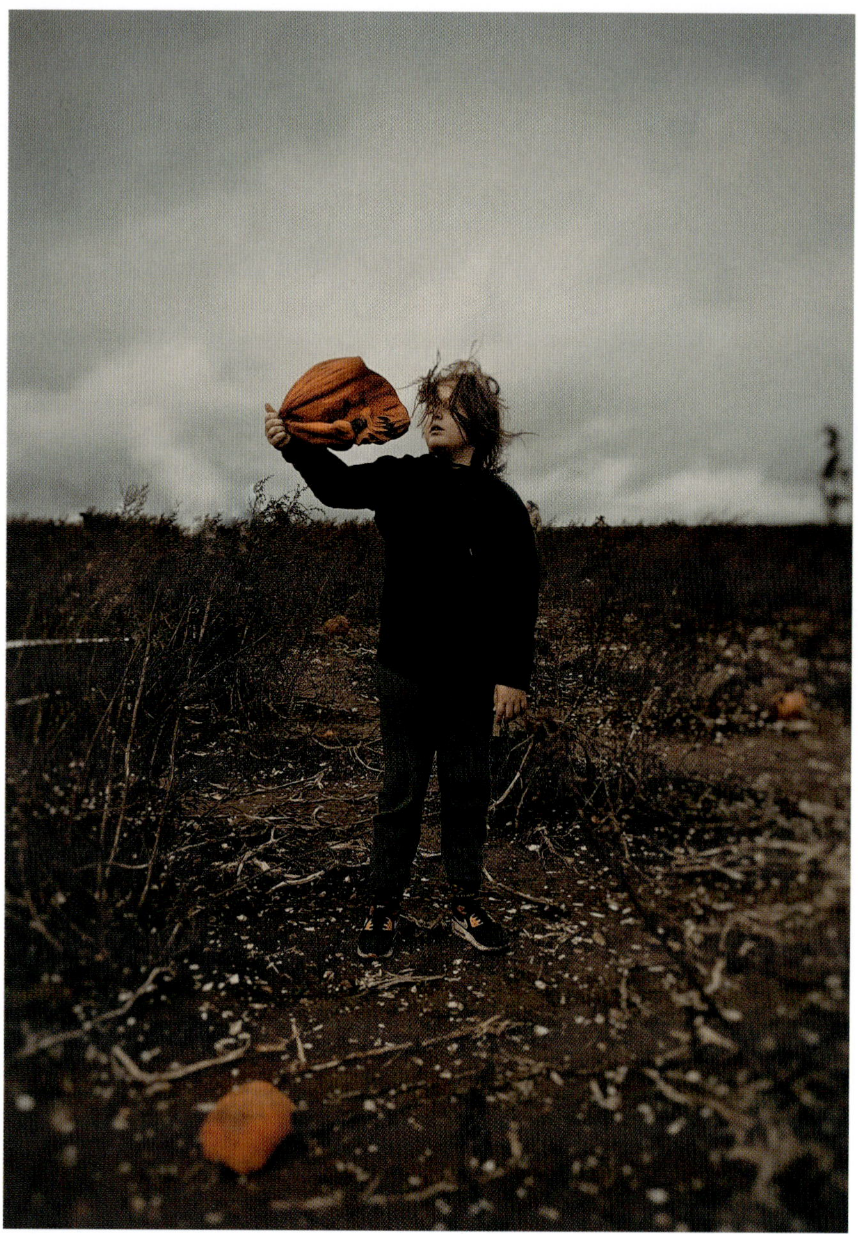

ABOVE: This was taken at the pumpkin patch we go to every year in Sompting. Casper's brother had brought a mask for trick or treating, and we happened to bring it that day. Of course, the boys were walking around wearing it trying to scare people. I thought it was kind of cool to be a pumpkin in a pumpkin patch. This is a good example of how little time you have to shoot kids – after about 3 seconds he pulled the mask off! But it always shows me that you do need to go with the flow, as these moments often make for the best images.

RIGHT: I take a lot of pictures in the car on the way home from school. I love photos taken in a moving car or on a train. The car becomes a dark box and the flash of light coming in as the sun goes in and out between buildings creates a light I love. It's the kind of light you see in a Renaissance painting. I love the writing on Casper's hand. Those hand doodles speak to me of childhood. I think that was what I was trying to get initially. I always look for the hero in the photo, the main character. It may be a colour or an element. The hand doodle was my hero here.

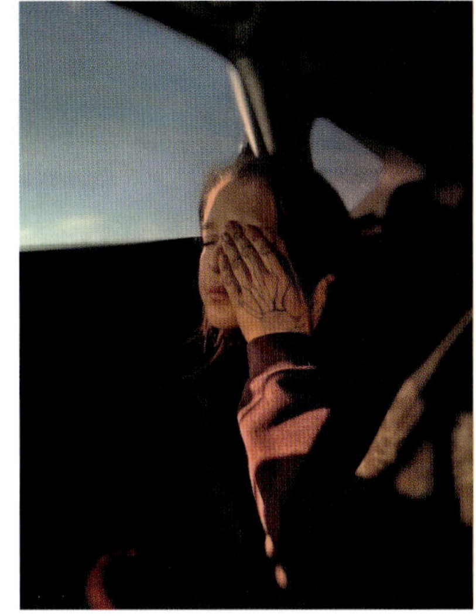

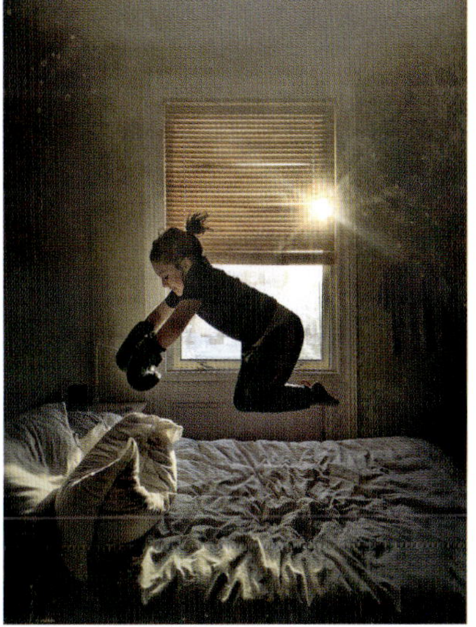

'Photography has become the thing that fits in the space between everything else, it's kind of the seams of our life.'

ABOVE: This photo of my sons was taken on the way to Greece. I like the colour and the light. I'm also attracted to nostalgia and pop culture. It's traditional for us to let the boys get one of those oversized airport sweets. (I always regret letting them eat that much sugar on the plane!). Aeroplane light is always great too. I love it when ordinary moments get lifted up and become a little more magical. I was attracted to the surreal ordinary moment of the sun hitting the red of the big lollipop.

Jun Imaizumi
Tokyo, Japan

Architect Jun Imaizumi works in the city where he grew up. His architectural design work focuses on private houses as well as museums, music halls and other public buildings. Perhaps unsurprisingly, given his line of work, his photographs are often inspired by architecture and the notion of space. He tends to explore the way these principal features are used in harmony, and how they can be elevated by their interaction with nature.

Imaizumi takes great pleasure in photographing the ordinary, everyday life that unfolds around him. The images he makes often have a soft, whimsical and undeniably poetic beauty about them. He often points his camera lens at his family, capturing their daily moments in a way that awakens a pang of familiarity, perhaps harking back to our own hazy memories of distant childhood experiences. When his eye looks beyond family life, he sees interesting strangers and passers-by on the streets and parks near his home. Imaizumi always includes a human-interest perspective in his photos because, as an architect, it's necessary to think about providing a sense of scale to his work. This thinking has influenced the way he takes photos as well. On a personal level, he charmingly believes that 'when a person enters the photo, kindness and a story are born.'

He uses his Apple iPhone to edit as well as shoot. His go-to apps for editing are Snapseed and VSCO. Imaizumi values his iPhone as a camera, for the freedom it gives him to choose unusual angles and alternative compositions, and for its unique ability to deliver rapid, off-the-cuff photography.

'Photographs can be a part of life. What I felt, how I interpreted and remembered the moment I shot an image can be told to others with a photograph.'

RIGHT: This scene is along the river bank at the Gongendo Tsutsumi, a park in the beautiful Japanese city of Satte. It comes alive in the spring, as it is the most famous Sakura cherry blossom viewing spot in the prefecture. Cherry blossom season is also the time when Japanese students graduate from school. Although I don't know the woman in this picture, I suspect she was dressed in a traditional kimono as part of a graduation celebration. She was engrossed in talking into her smartphone camera, and I wanted to capture the intensity combined with the ordinariness, and explore the story I felt from her presence in this setting.

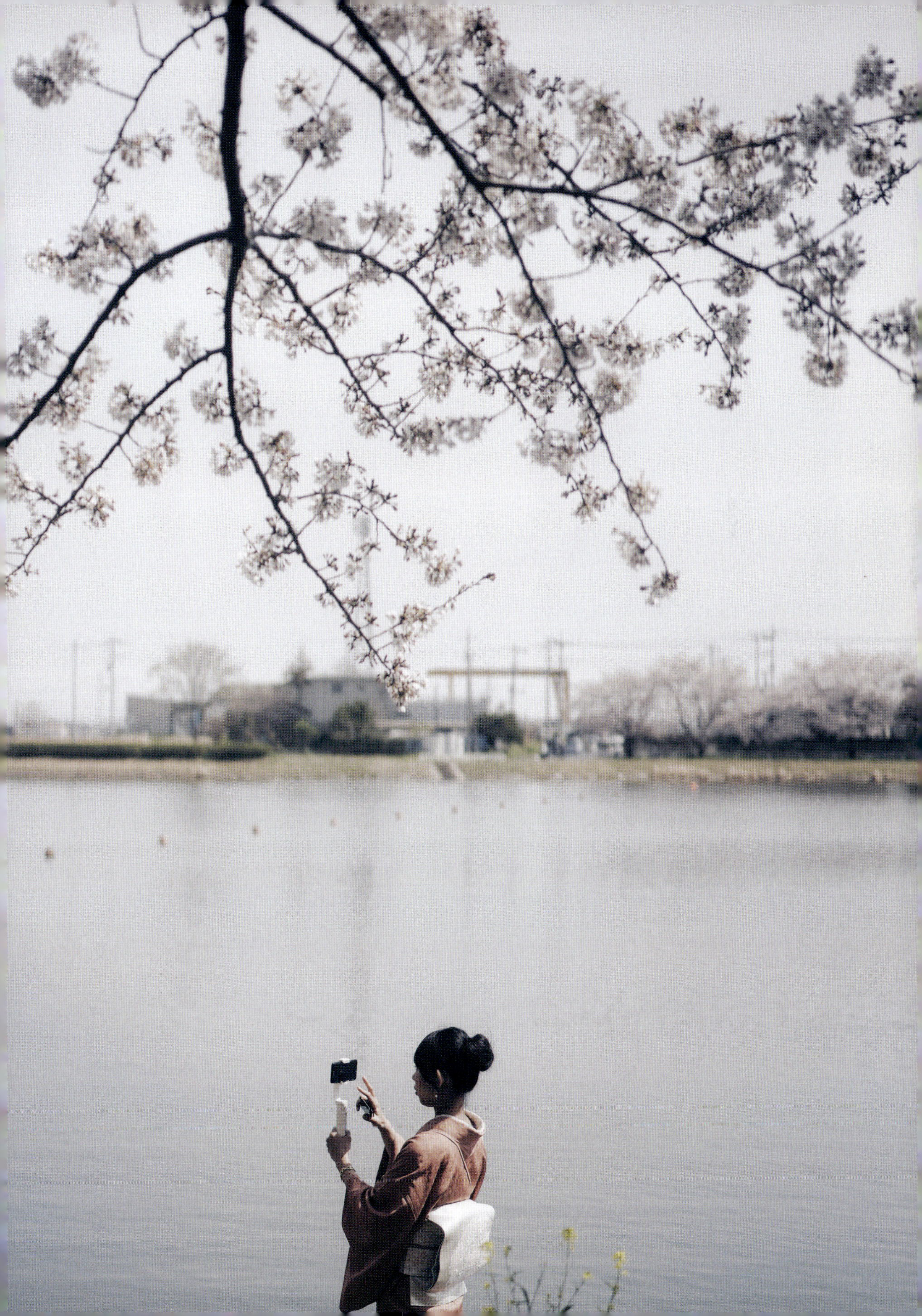

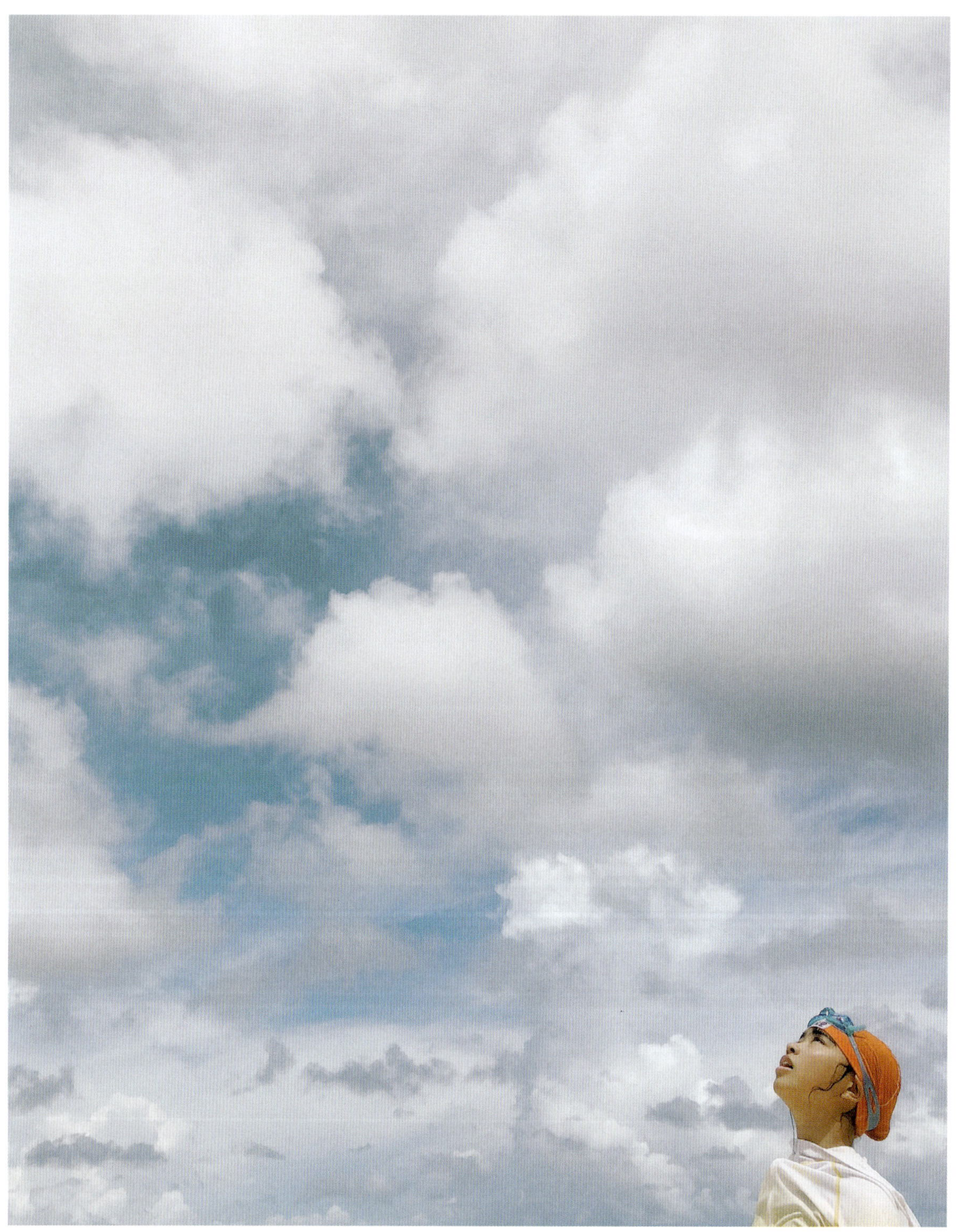

VIEWPOINT

'I always value everyday ordinariness, which tells the relationships of things more naturally, unconsciously.'

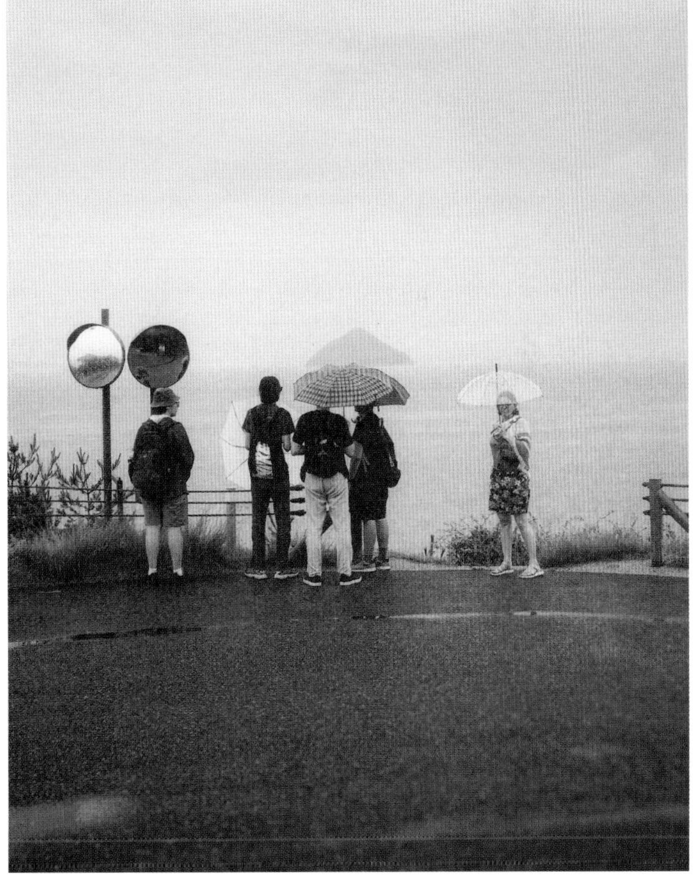

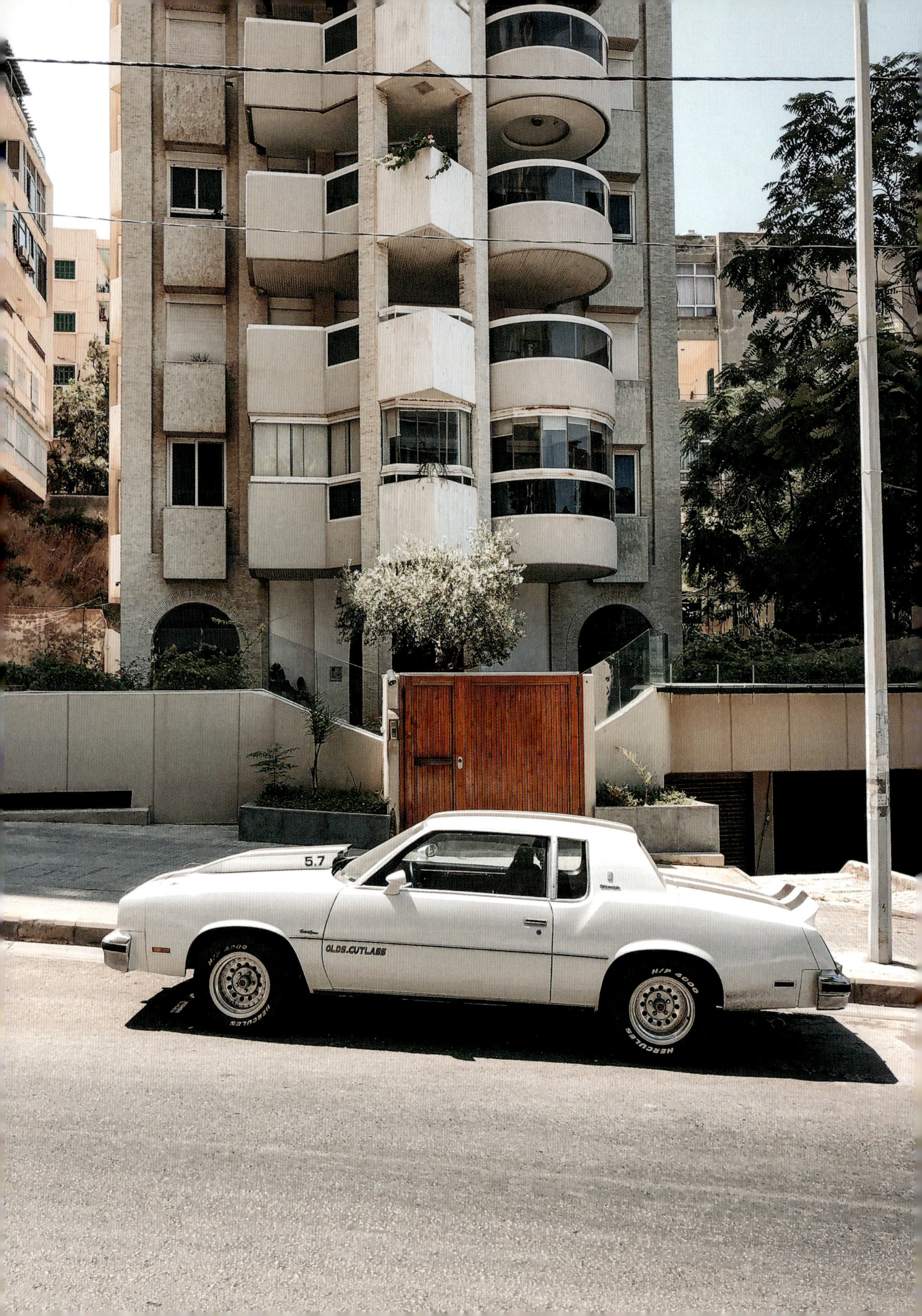

5.7
OLDS.CUTLASS
H/P 4000
HERCULES

Karl Mansour
Beirut, Lebanon

Architect and urban planning specialist Karl Mansour works as a consultant for a company in Jounieh. He has a particular interest in street photography, and he always finds himself drawn to the beauty of old buildings, street shots, vintage cars and old people on the street. He started taking photos in his own time for the love of it, and now it's almost a part-time job. He is currently using an Apple iPhone 14 Pro Max, and usually edits with Snapseed, VSCO and Lightroom mobile. He is most often motivated to take his photos out of a desire to share the authentic beauty of Lebanon – especially its architecture – with others.

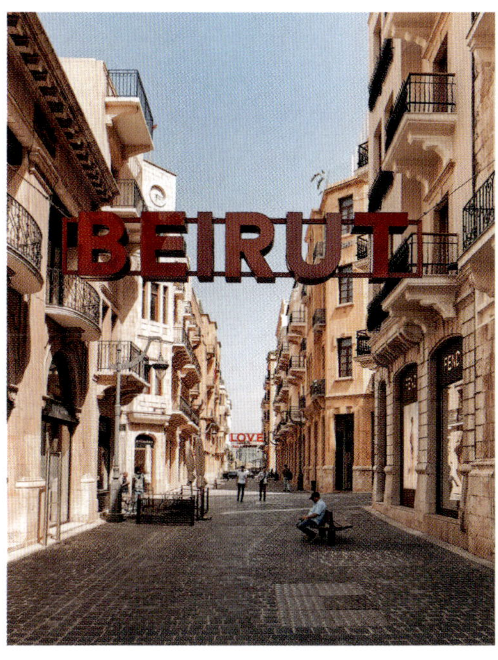

ABOVE: Downtown, there is this street with Beirut written over it. It feels like Beirut is calling you to come and explore.

LEFT: I just loved the way the car was parked on the street in the Ras Beirut area.

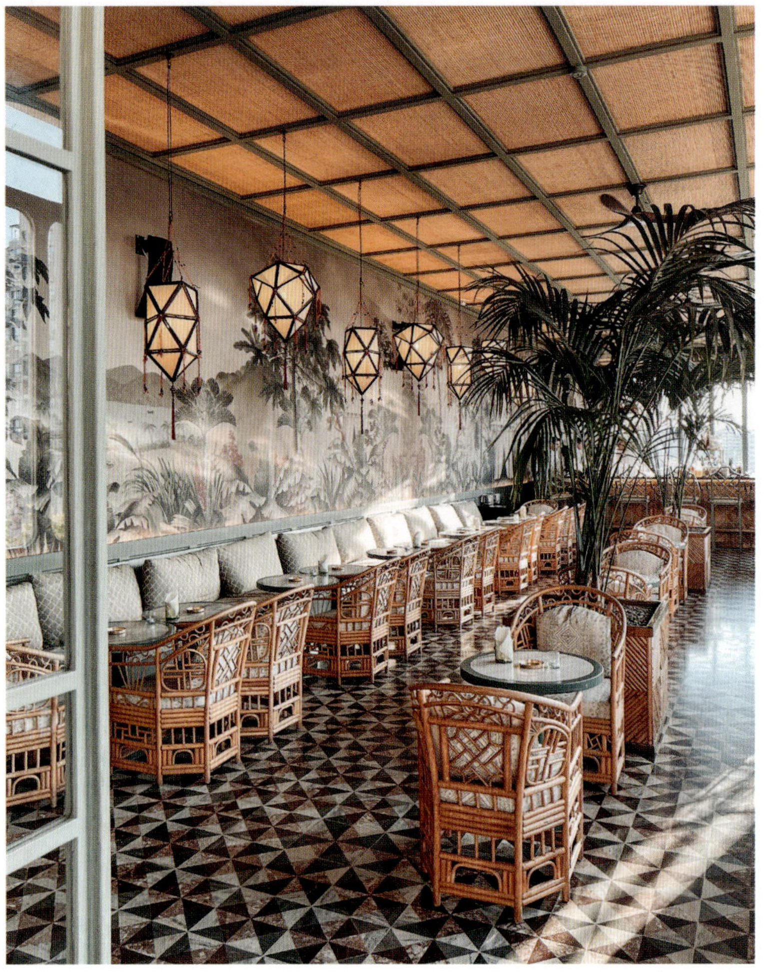

ABOVE: I couldn't resist taking a photo of the Hotel Albergo because the interior is so beautiful.

RIGHT: These typically colourful Lebanese houses in the Achrafieh neighbourhood bring joy to the city.

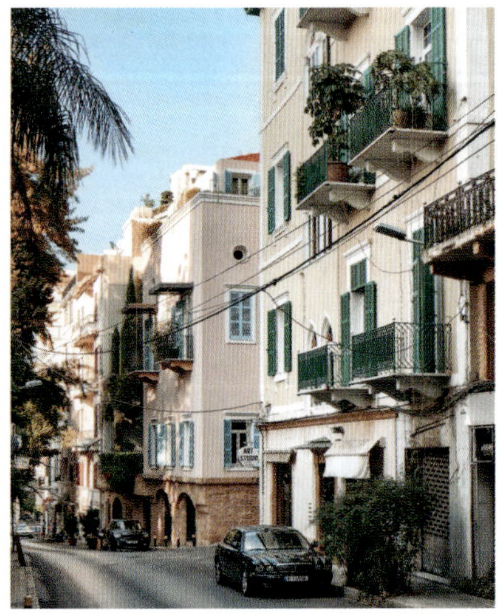

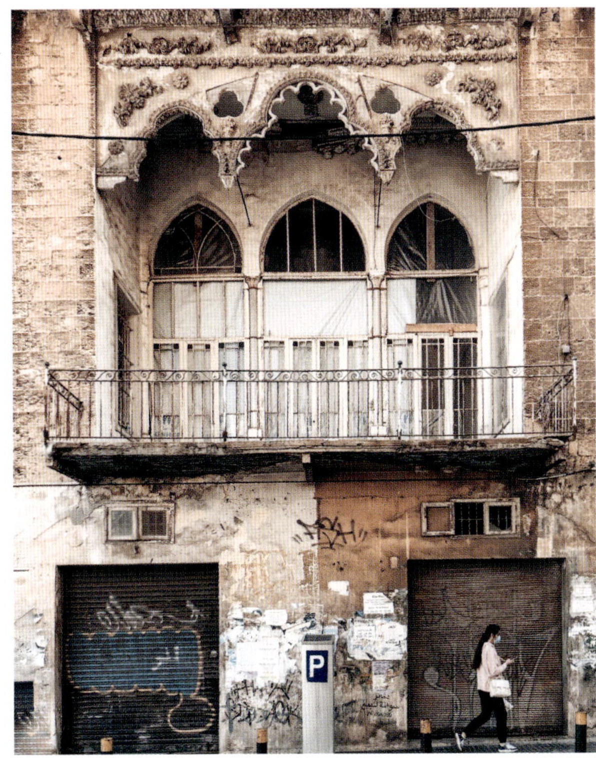

ABOVE: Bliss Street, near the American University of Beirut. The ornaments on the triple arches are different to the ones I see every day.

RIGHT: I found these doorsteps that looked so welcoming with the plants and a beautiful door in the Hamra district of Beirut.

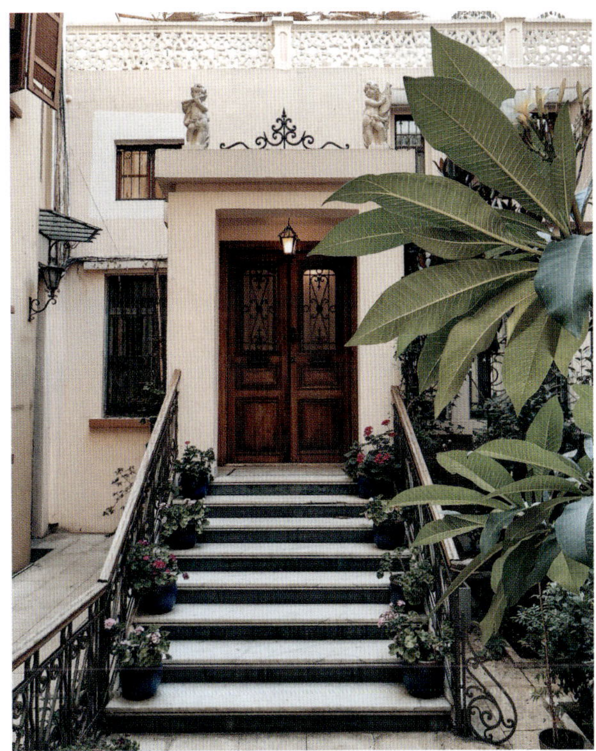

'The iPhone is so democratic…it's awesome when you travel because people do not get scared away by getting their picture taken on an iPhone. They often don't realize the skill level of the photographer behind the lens.'

Kelley Dallas
Denver, USA

Medical sales representative Kelley Dallas works for a company that produces medicines for heart failure and to lower cholesterol. An avid traveller, she started documenting her trips on film in her early 20s and continues to do so, taking her young daughter with her. As the daughter of an artist and an accountant, Dallas says she has inherited a very business-like artistic brain. Her photography ranges from documentary-style work capturing her daughter and the people she meets on her travels, to a more fine-art aesthetic of nature and the landscape. Photographing her daughter at home led Dallas to use her Apple iPhone camera more and more, and this spread into her other photography. She edits in Snapseed.

ABOVE: My mum at the Denver Art Museum. I loved the shaft of light highlighting her face while she sat down to take a break.

RIGHT: I loved the low, soft light on her face as my daughter played with her hair in my bedroom. I feel like it is a foreshadowing of her preteen years and an obsession with her hair.

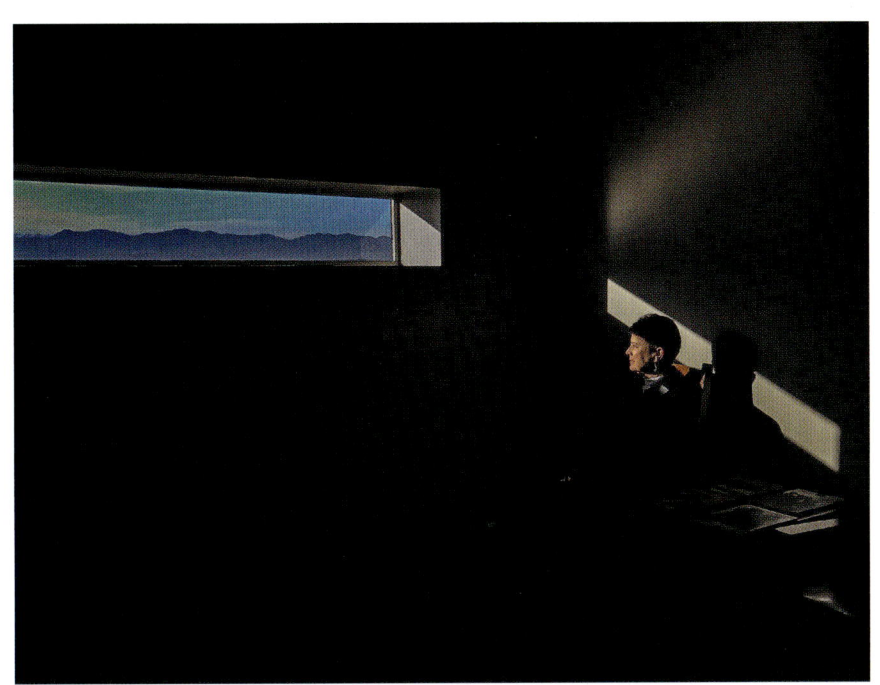

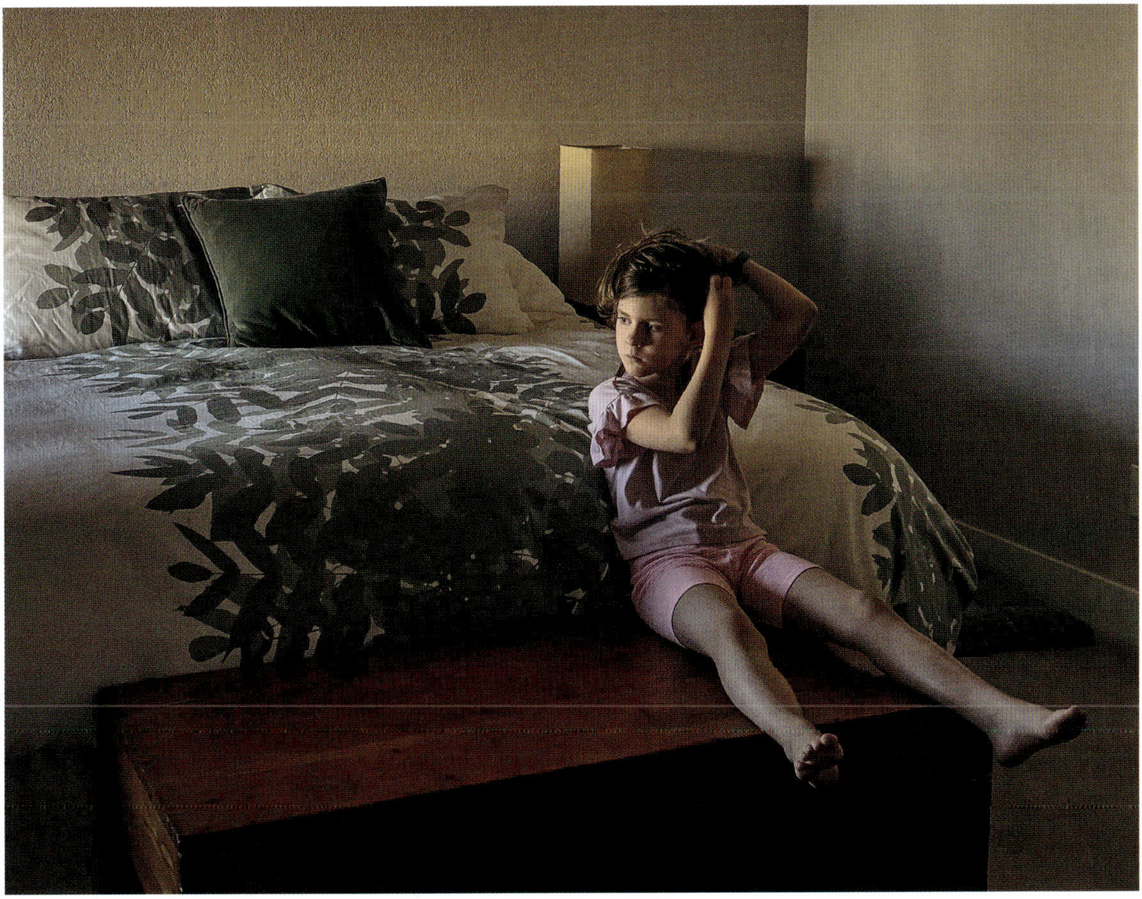

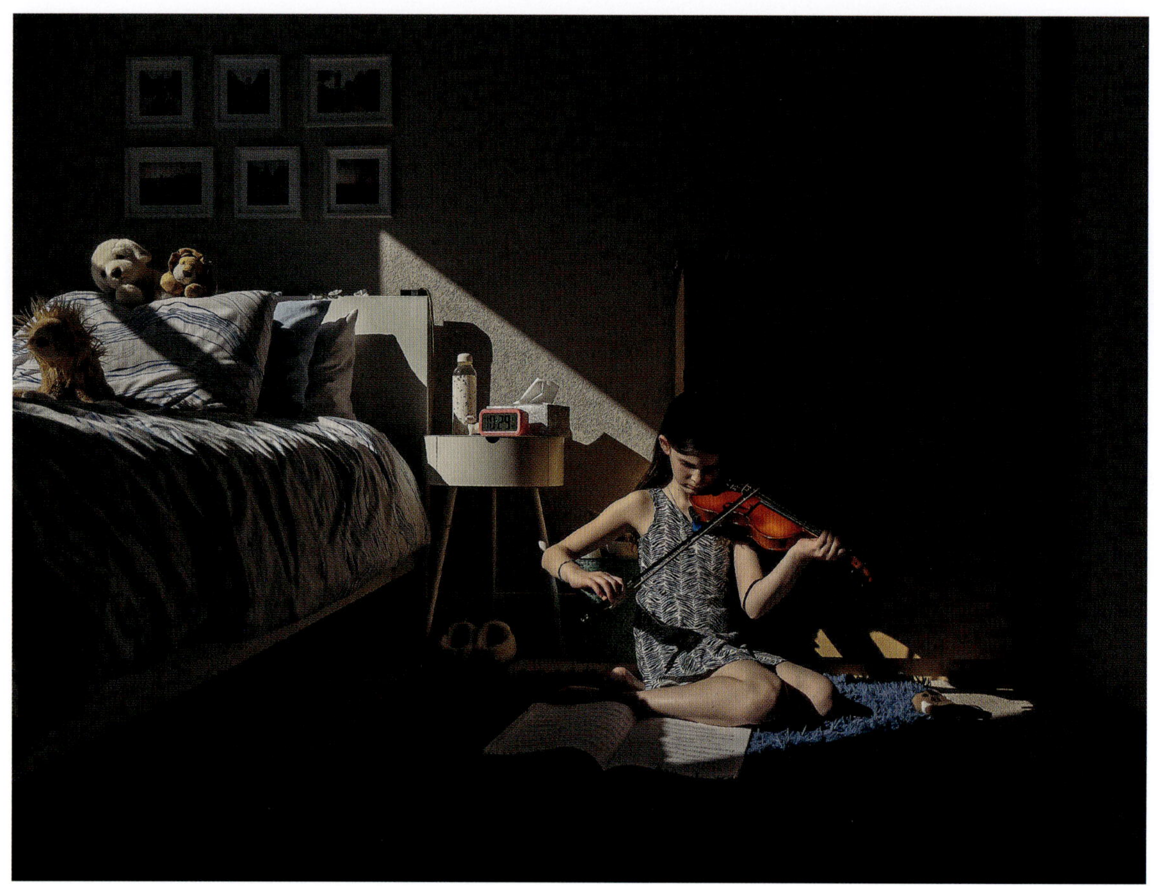

ABOVE: My daughter in her bedroom practising her violin. I loved the way the shaft of light highlights her concentration on the music.

RIGHT: I was picking my
daughter up from a playdate
with her best friend and
could not resist capturing
the beautiful light streaming
through the window as it
highlighted the two of them
attempting to play the piano.

BELOW: My daughter playing
a game on the floor with her
half-sister. It was during the
Covid-19 pandemic lockdown
when they hung out a lot more.
I loved the light highlighting
the game, the dog and her half-
sister's face.

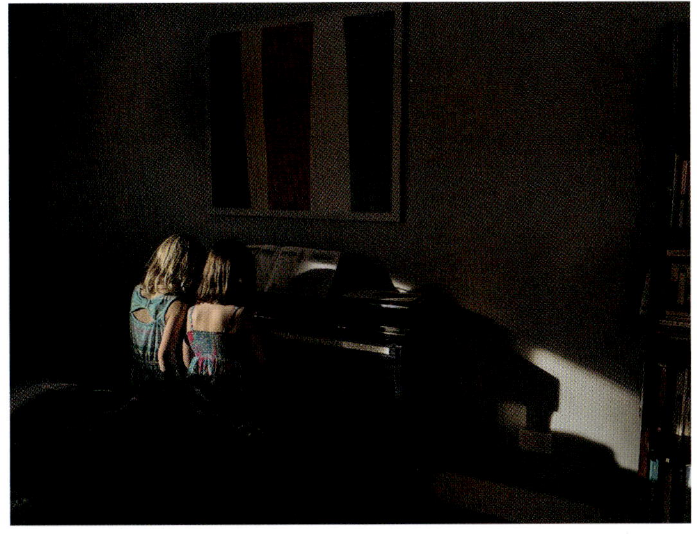

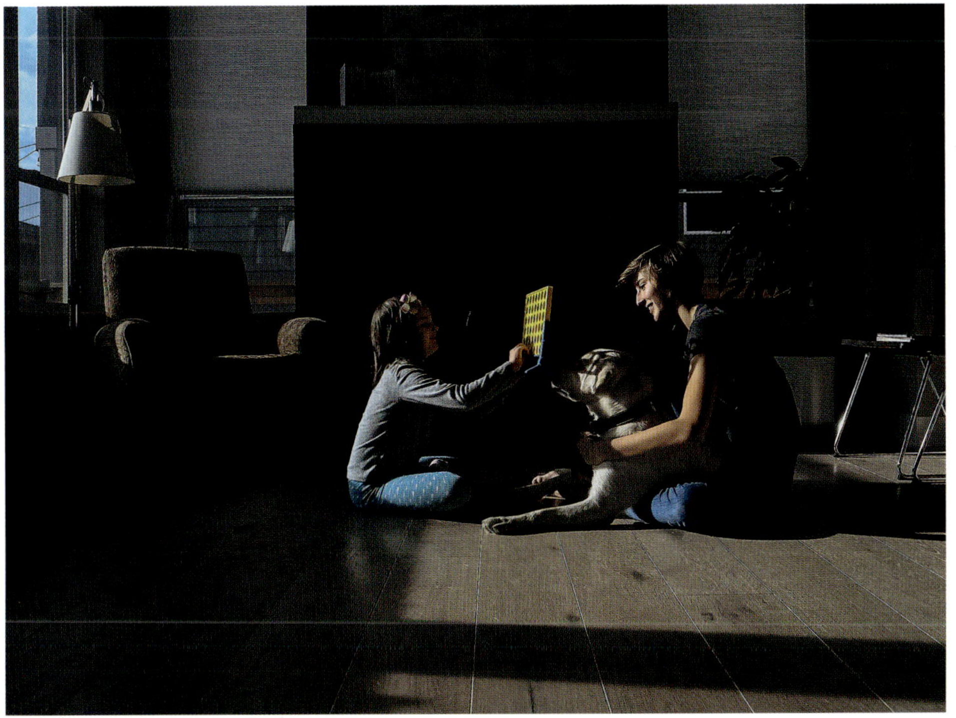

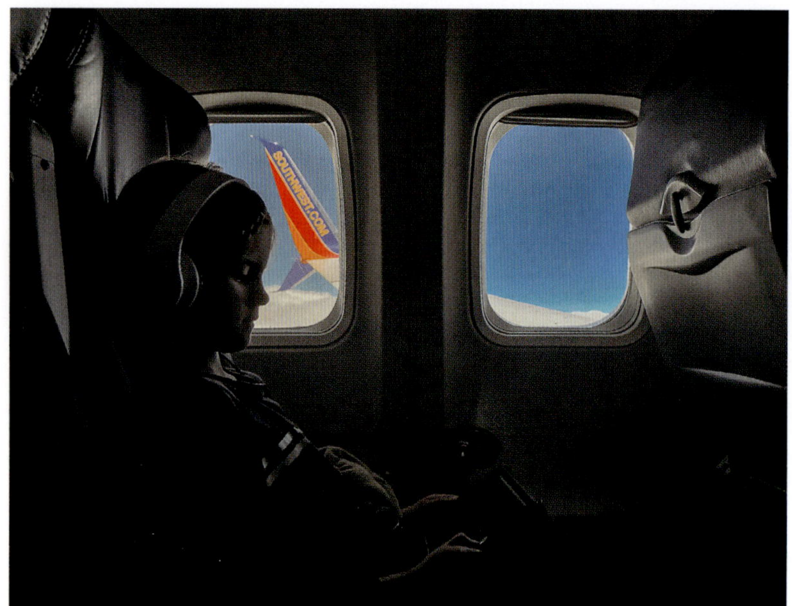

LEFT: My daughter and I were flying to visit her Nana and Poppy. I wanted to show the Southwest Airlines logo on the wing, the clear separation of her face and the wing, and capture her profile as a little girl.

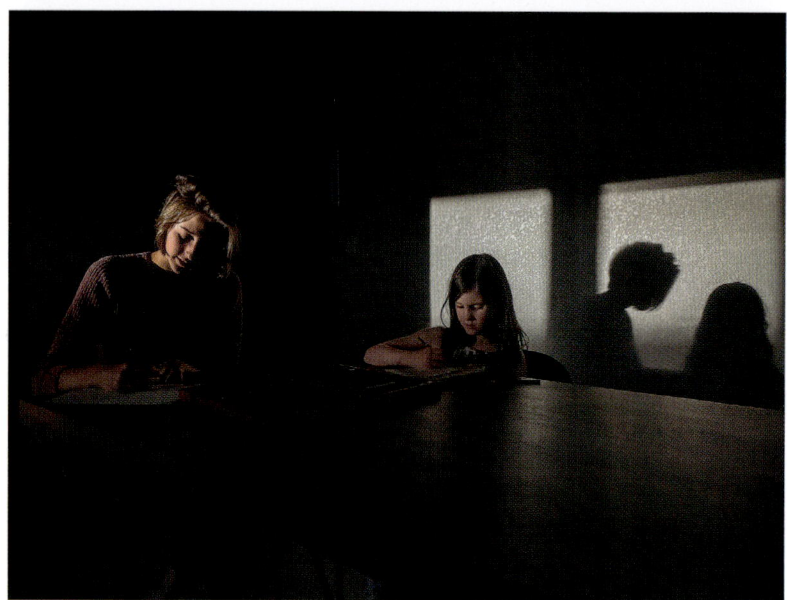

LEFT: My daughter and her half-sister during lockdown. This time they were drawing together. Again, I love the way their faces are highlighted.

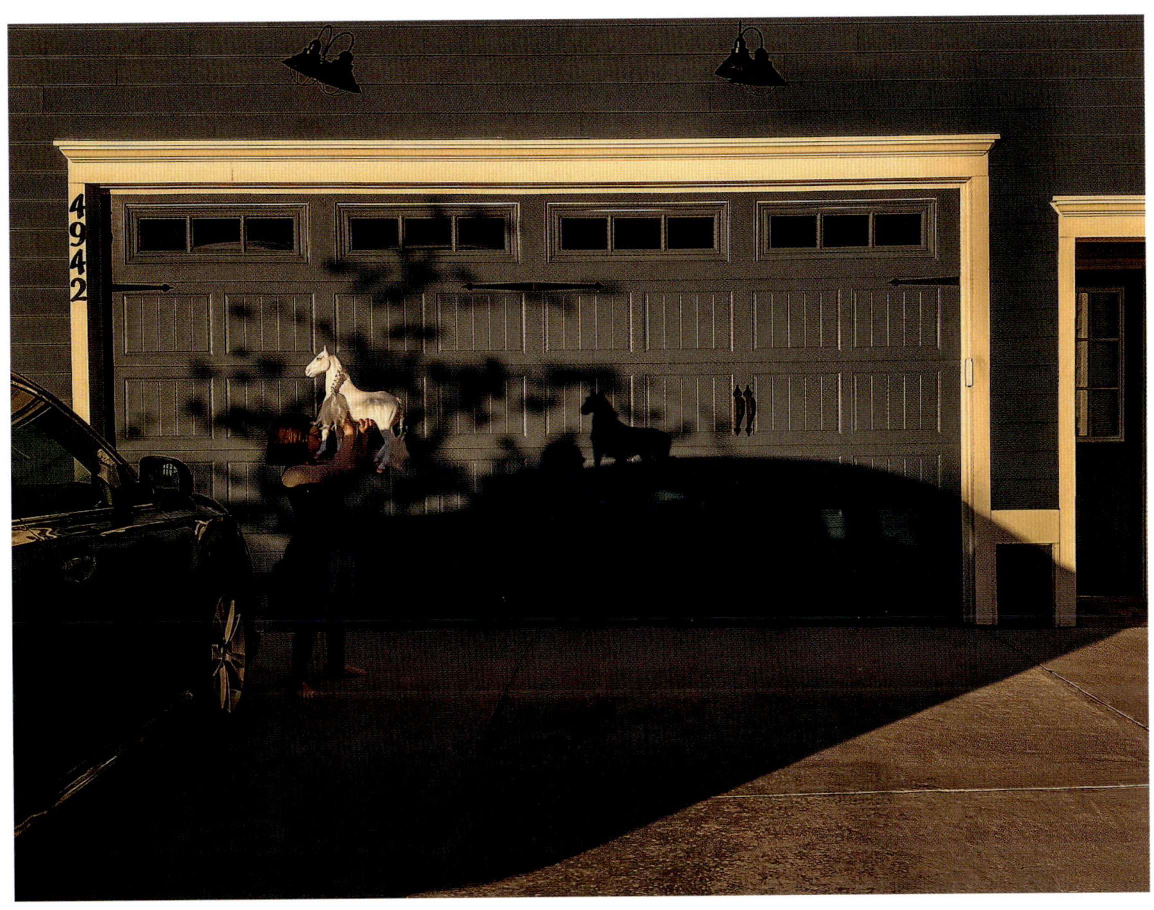

ABOVE: A socially distanced playdate during Covid-19. My daughter and her friend played together with a definite distance between them. The afternoon light hit the toy horse and created a perfect shadow on the garage door.

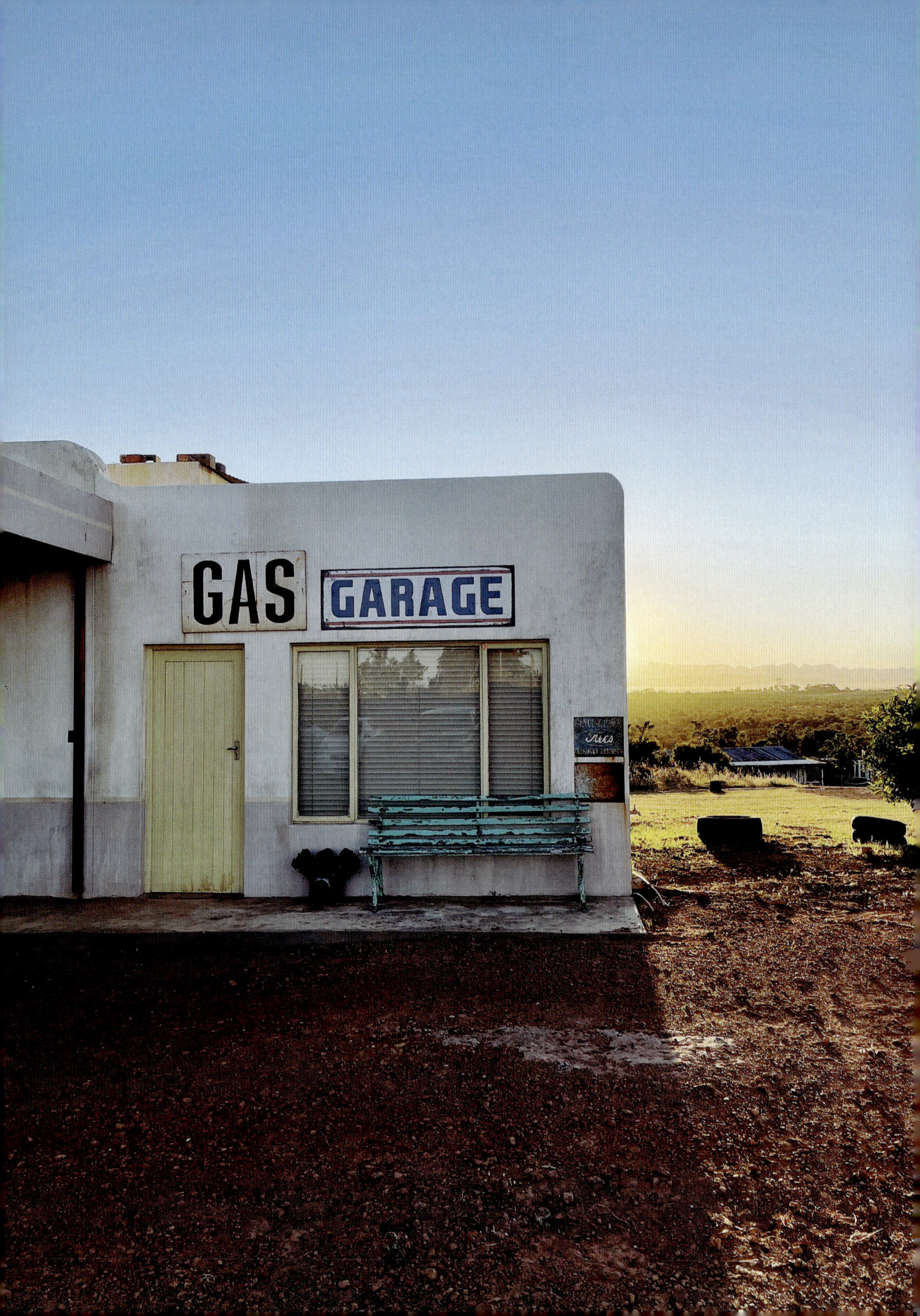

GAS
GARAGE

Kgomotso Neto Tleane

Johannesburg,
South Africa

Kgomotso Neto Tleane is a full-time portrait
and commercial photographer. He uses an Apple
iPhone alongside DSLRs. His personal photography
includes street work. He lives with his partner and
their daughter.

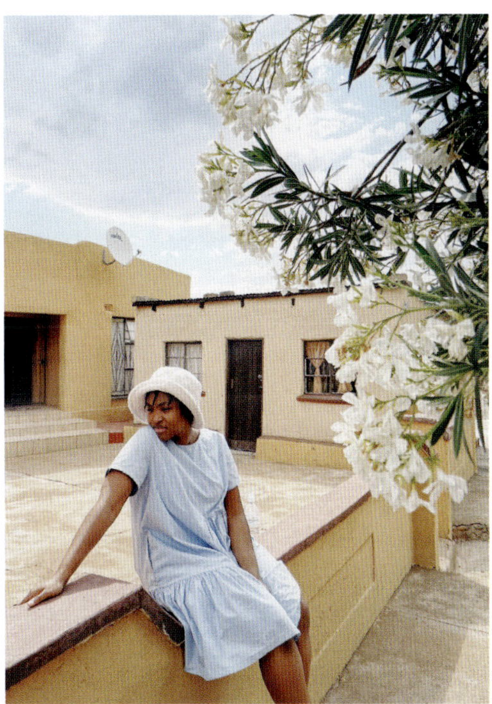

RIGHT: My grandmother's house in Ga-Maja, Limpopo, where I grew up. It was the first time I had taken my partner, Lerato, to the area where I grew up and the first time she had met my grandparents. I always shoot lots when I am home, but I liked how Lerato was dressed and the way the colours of her dress complemented the surroundings. It's everything about my life, it's taken in the place that made me who I am today, and the person who's in the picture is my partner and the mother of my child.

LEFT: In the Western Cape on a commercial shoot. It was early in the morning when we arrived, and I loved the beautiful sunrise behind the building.

'Photography is all I know at this point in terms of work, but it also functions as a tool for me to navigate the world I live in.'

BELOW: I was born in Alexandra township, Johannesburg. My grandfather worked in the city. I was visiting my cousin and took this photo of a street barber and his customer. I love street barbers, there's a certain feeling and look about them. I grew up getting my hair cut on the streets around where this photo was taken.

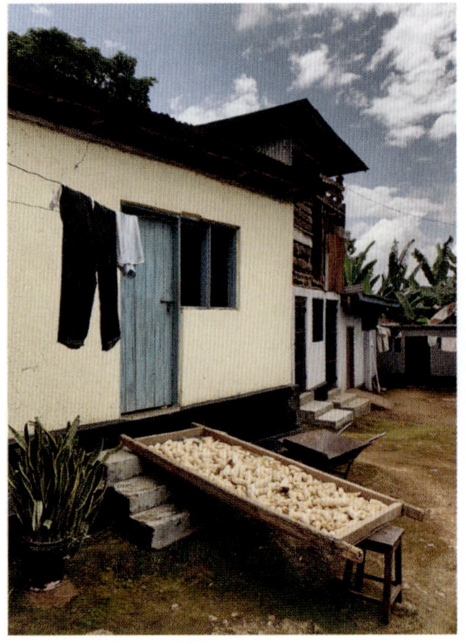

ABOVE: I was in Tanzania for work. This village is next to Mount Kilimanjaro and the photo represents a very normal sight and part of life in that area. I grew up in a rural village like this one, and we also used to dry maize in this way.

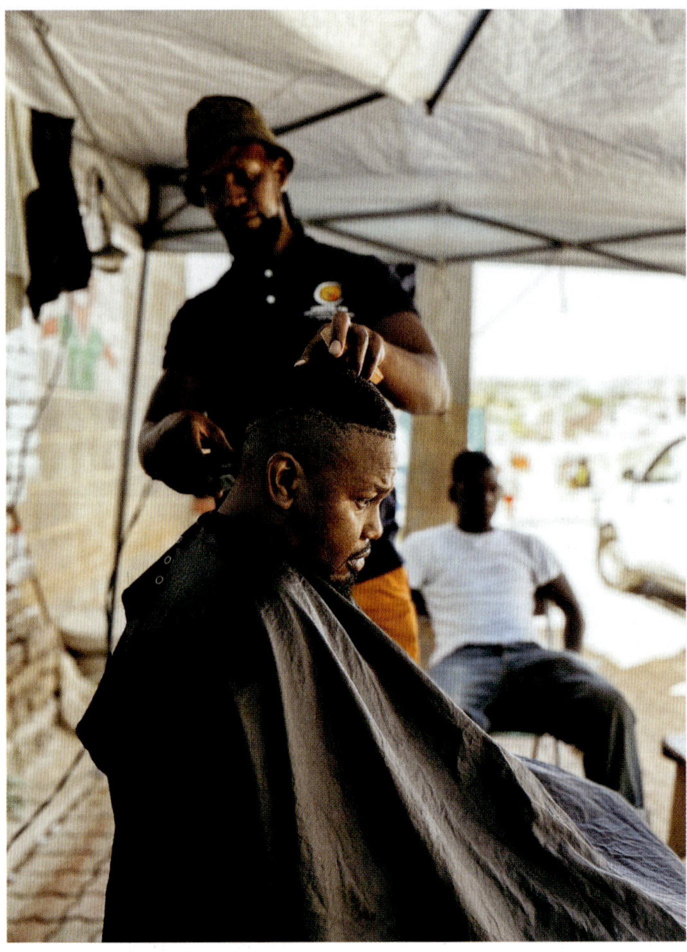

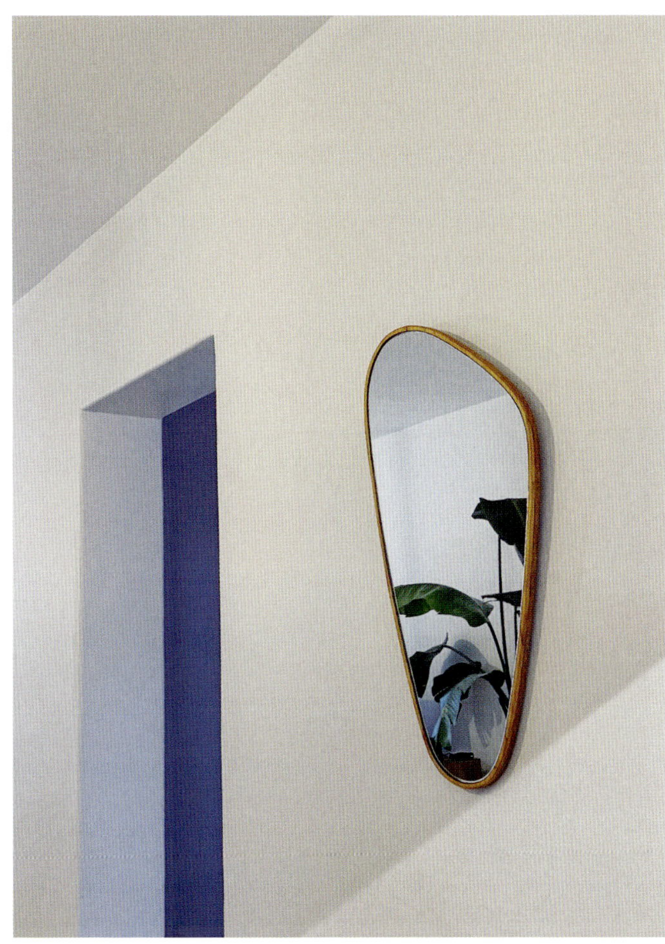

BELOW: At De Peak, a tavern in Newtown, Johannesburg. I lived in the heart of the city at the time, meeting lots of different and interesting people. I was there for a drink with this man. I loved the light from the match when he lit a cigarette.

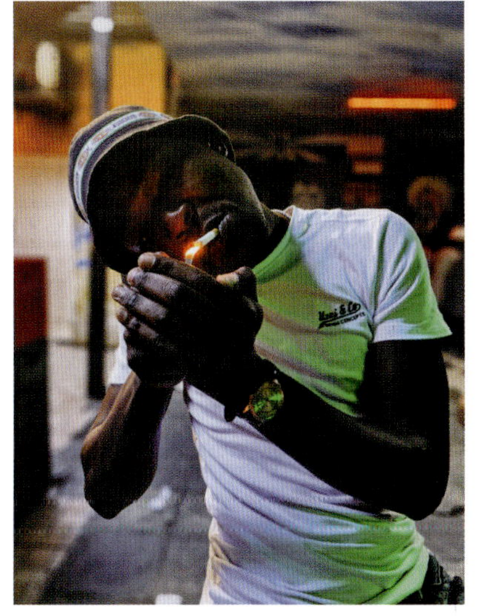

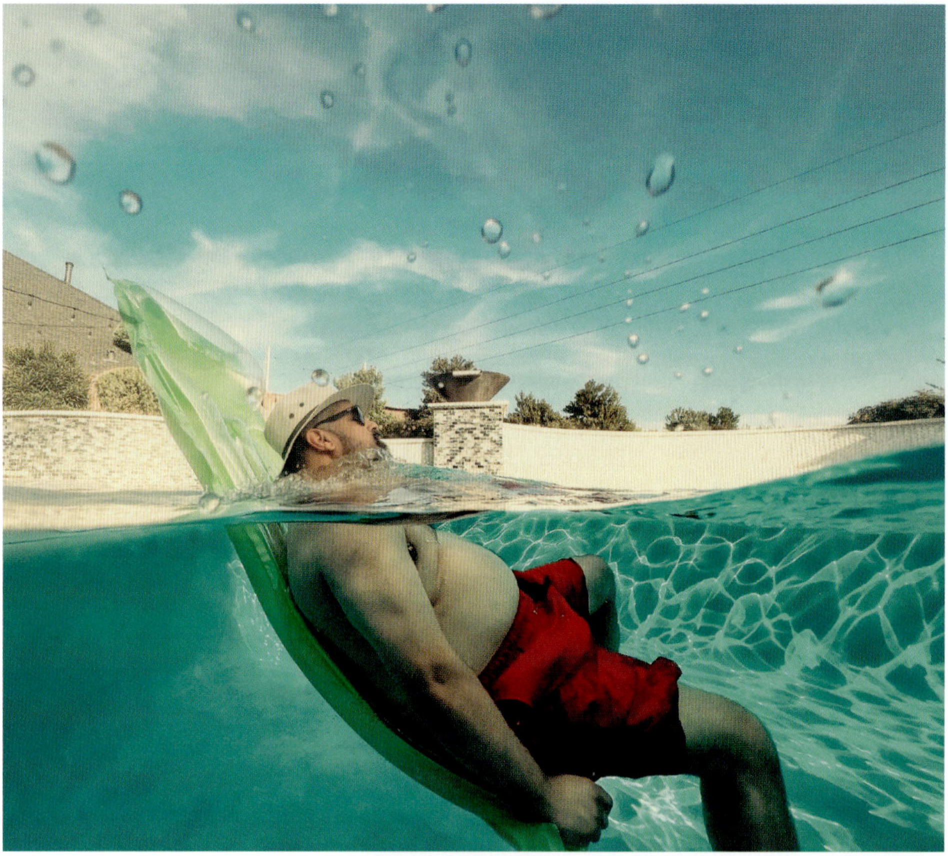

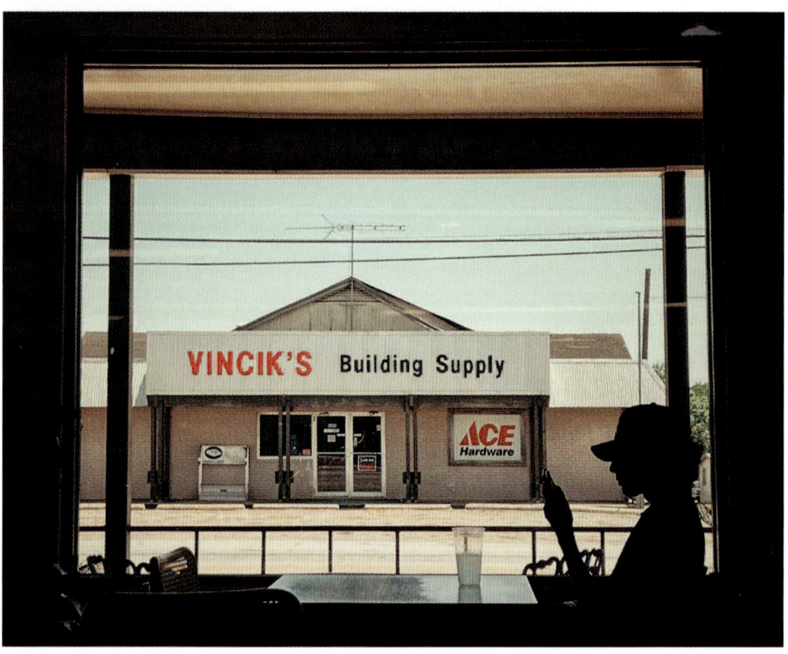

VINCIK'S Building Supply
ACE
Hardware

'An important part of my love for photography is my desire to connect with others through storytelling.'

Kim Abbas
Katy, Houston, USA

Kim Abbas is the social media manager and business development manager for her husband's finance business. She admits to not being a numbers person, but is pleased to have found a creative role that still allows her to support the business.

Abbas says that photography, her true love, is part of her DNA. At college she majored in fine art photography for a year before switching her major to journalism. She felt drawn to explore the voices of people through their words. She has since realized that this is much the same as the way photography allows her to explore 'voices' through her photographic images. After graduating, Abbas worked as a desk production assistant at a news radio station and then as a local news reporter. A naturally interested and curious person, she takes smartphone images daily, on an Apple iPhone 13 Pro, using a DSLR when she needs better lens performance. She mostly edits in Snapseed and Lightroom.

'I think it's important to take an interest in cultures and people different from one's own. I find a great satisfaction in understanding what makes us unique, but also what brings us together. Every culture has value, and I like to leave room to showcase those voices through my photos.'

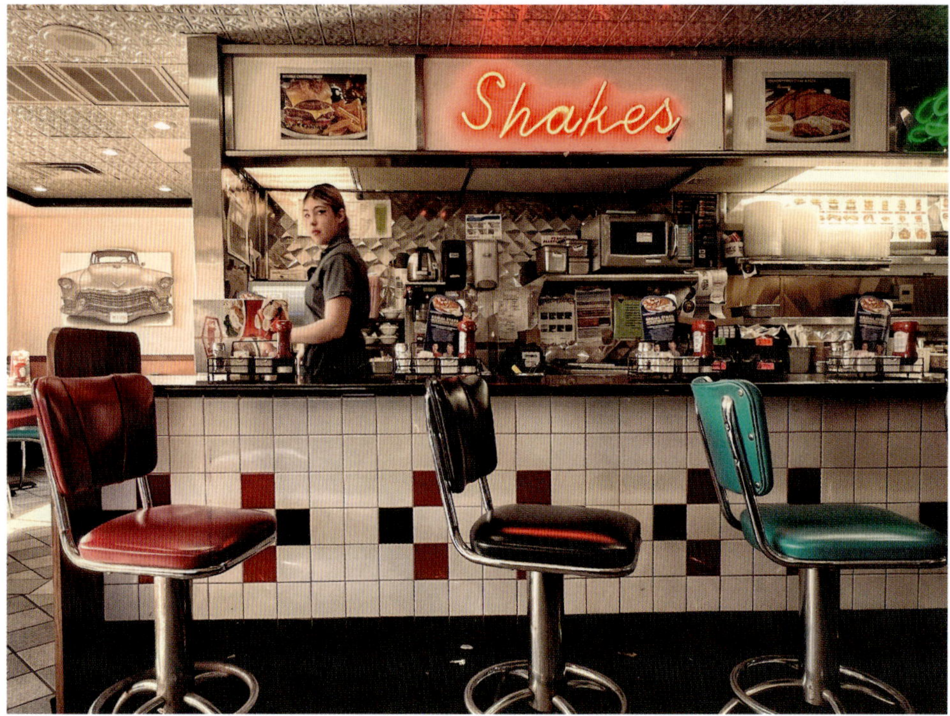

ABOVE: This is one of the servers at my local diner. I don't know her name, but she is always kind. She works hard for what I presume is modest pay. I love the casual vibe; I don't feel like I have to put on airs and graces when I go there. Like me, it doesn't pretend to be anything it isn't; it is easy going and friendly. I like her expression as she glances my way. It's not rehearsed. For that moment, she puts away her customer 'smile' as she completes her tasks. I took a wide shot to include the environment and give a sense of place. Diners have a nostalgia that many of us gravitate towards.

BELOW: I was at a small outside performance of young Mexican folkorico dancers at a Cinco De Mayo event in Houston. My eyes were drawn to what was going behind the performance. I love the background story, but wanted to ground the picture, so made the dancer the main focus in the foreground. It helped to anchor the shot, which is quite busy, not usually something I like. You have someone applying make-up, another dancer appears to be looking at someone or something with disdain, and of course, the spectators and other dancers are watching. I like the spectrum of moments occurring at the same time. There is always a story behind the story. There is what we choose to put out into the world, and there is the reality beneath.

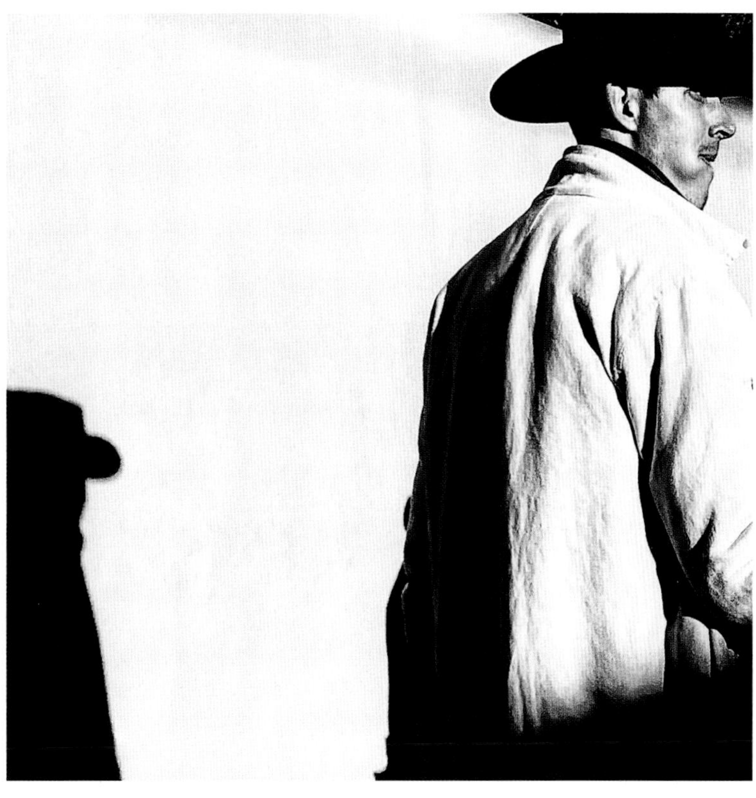

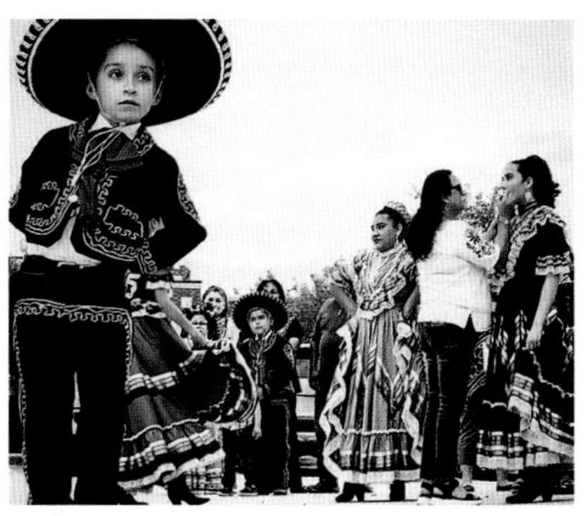

ABOVE: We were en route to the Grand Canyon and staying at a ranch in Arizona when I saw this man who seemed to have the look of a quintessential cowboy. I was attracted to his intense gaze as he looks to the side, and it might be cliché, but the 'cowboy chew' (chewing tobacco) in his lower gum made his appearance all the more iconic. I take a lot of inspiration from film, and when I converted this shot to black and white it came alive and really looked and felt like a frame out of an old Western movie.

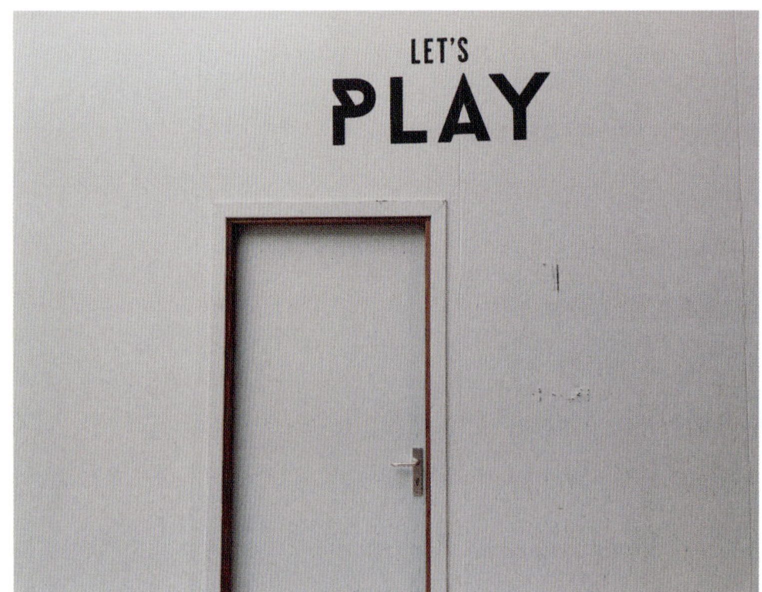

LEFT: I found a wonderful book shop in Utrecht, in the Netherlands. I walked around the shop and I saw the words 'Let's Play', which really made me smile.

BELOW: While visiting my mother in France, I saw the word 'Joy' written in English on a big gate – a wonderfully simple and beautiful word in whatever language.

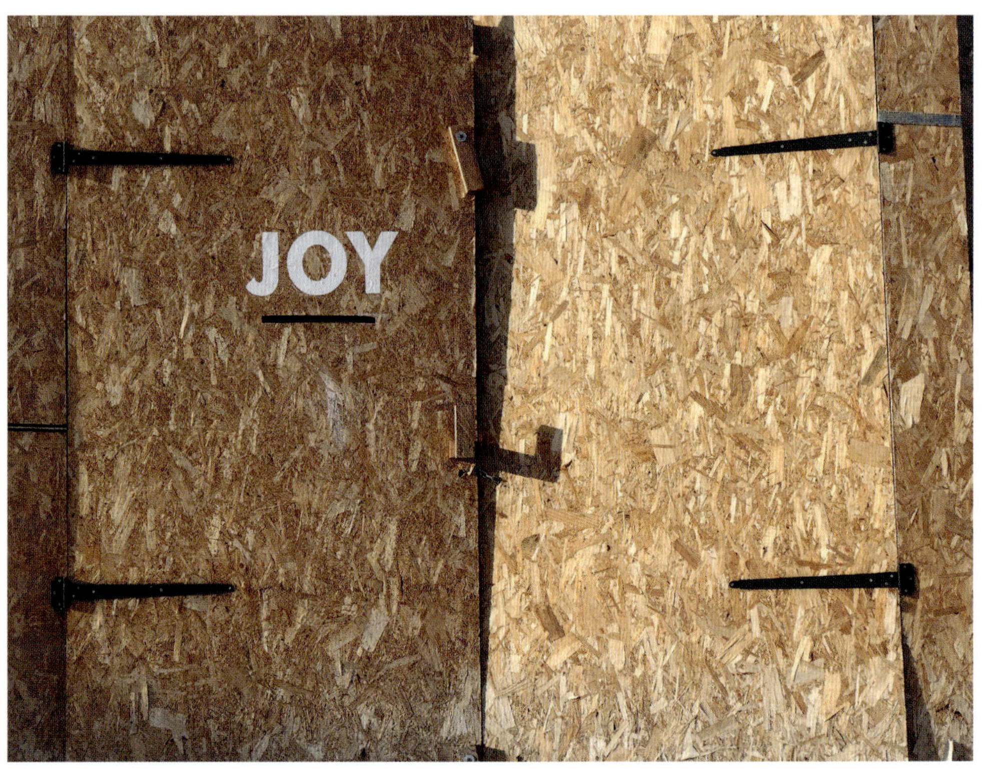

Laura Gorun
Brașov, Romania

Freelance photographer Laura Gorun was born with perfect hearing, but she became ill with a high fever when she was 1½ years old and unfortunately the doctor gave her the wrong injection, causing her to become profoundly deaf. She says that her eyes hear for her by lip-reading when people speak. Gorun travels internationally to events for the deaf community and this gives her the opportunity to visit friends and family. She says she is an open person, and a proud member of the LGBTQI+ community. She wonders if perhaps in the future she may identify as non-binary.

Gorun is interested in books, interior design, artists and creativity. She is inspired by words, typography and text, murals, architecture and beautiful people, but also loves uncomplicated, down-to-earth people. She photographs all kinds of subjects. Gorun studied fashion design at a school for arts and crafts, but gave up on fashion in favour of a photography course in 2004. At first she didn't understand how to use her film camera but quickly learned how it worked and, as she discovered her unique style, she became more interested in photography.

Although she now works as a freelance photographer, Gorun says she is still learning. She has had many cameras – digital, 35mm film and polaroid – but gave up her digital camera a few years ago because she did not use it. She likes to use the newest Apple iPhone when it is released. She edits direct from the iPhone rather than using other apps. Many things catch her eye, but she particularly likes minimalism, words and finding typography out on the streets.

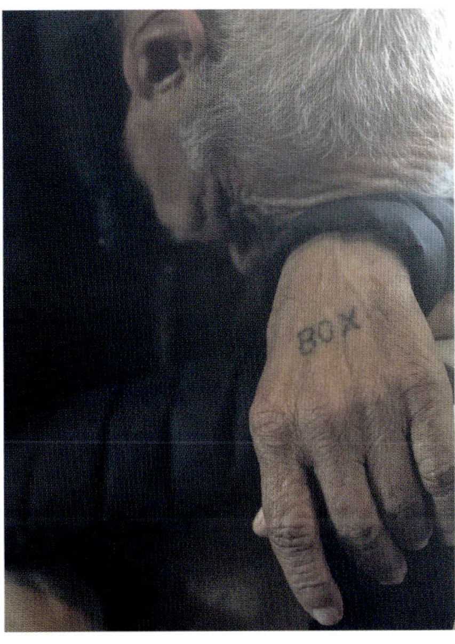

ABOVE: I travelled by train to visit friends in Bucharest for a few days. I saw an old man sleeping and noticed that he had a tattoo that said 'BOX' on his hand. I wondered if he had tattooed it there, as it means 'fighting with fists' in both Romanian and English.

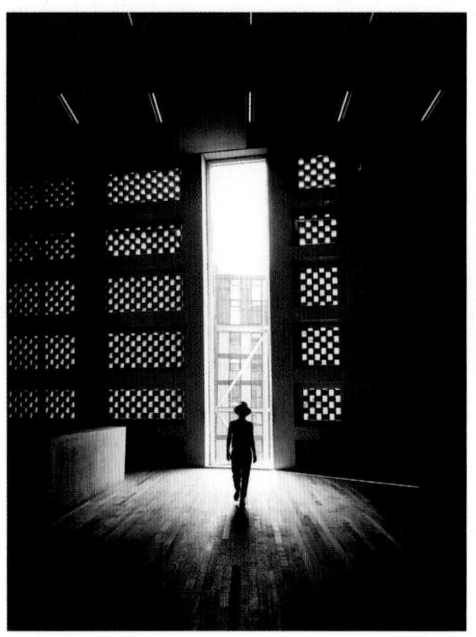

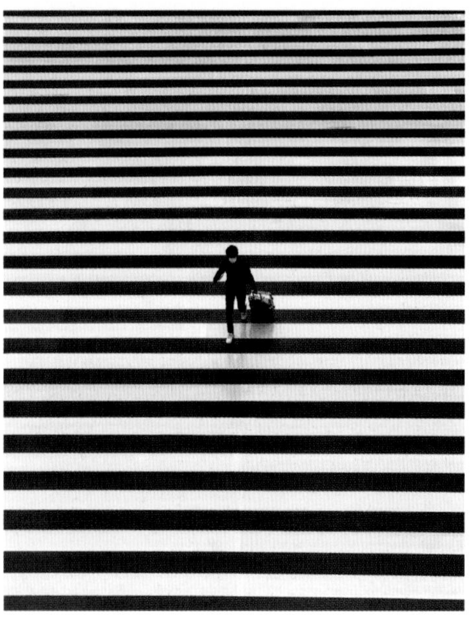

Laurence Bouchard
Tokyo, Japan

British-born Laurence Bouchard moved to Japan 13 years ago after meeting his Japanese wife while working in London. He works as an English teacher and taught photography workshops before the Covid-19 pandemic.

Bouchard shoots on an Apple iPhone 13 Pro Max and a Sony Ar7ii and edits with Snapseed. His main interests are street and travel photography. He finds he has to consciously make time for his photography; he checks the weather forecast and squeezes in creative time when the conditions are favourable. His family photography is undertaken in a more random fashion, capturing scenes as they unfold, and he says he has a long list of portraiture ideas he would like to pursue when he has the time.

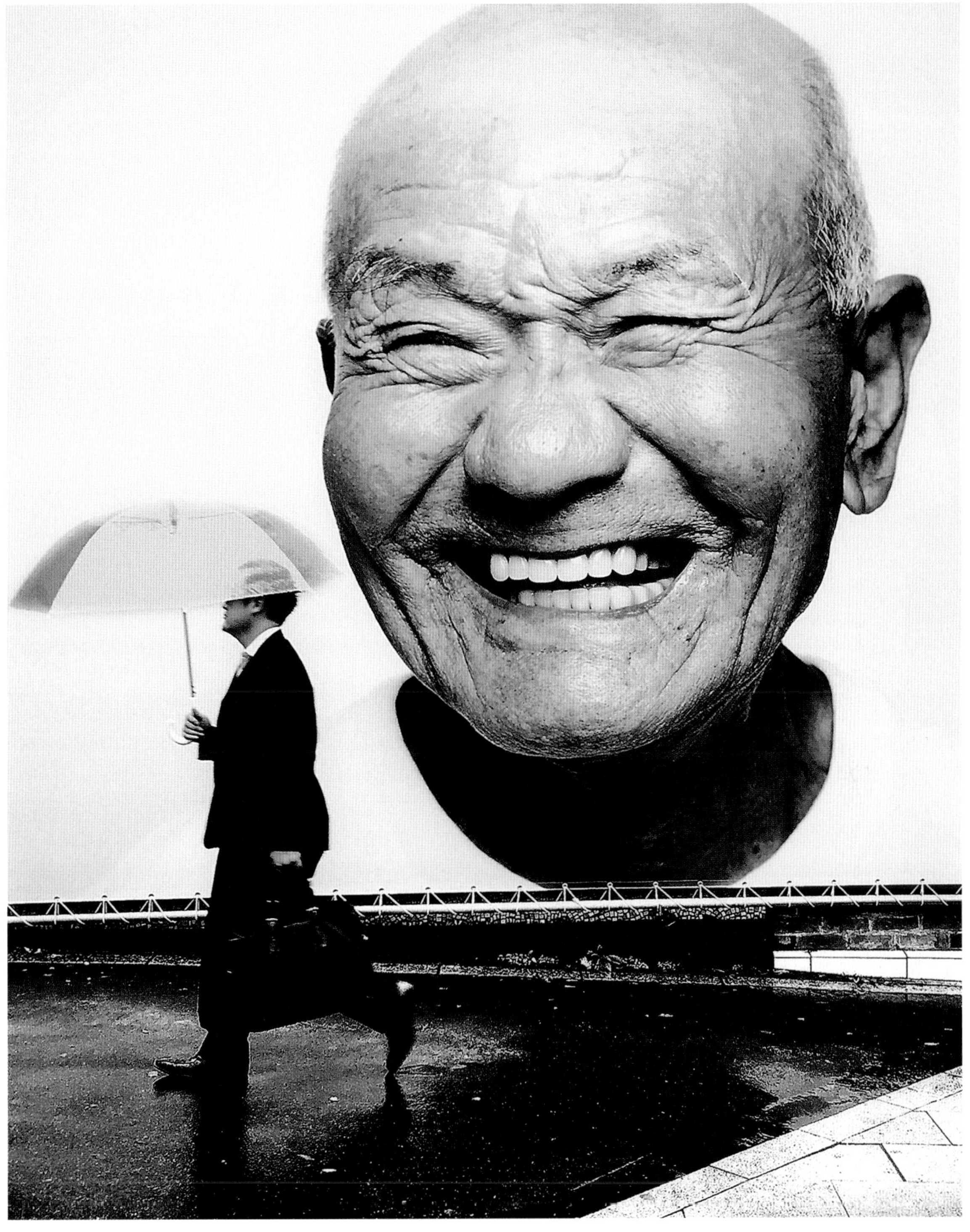

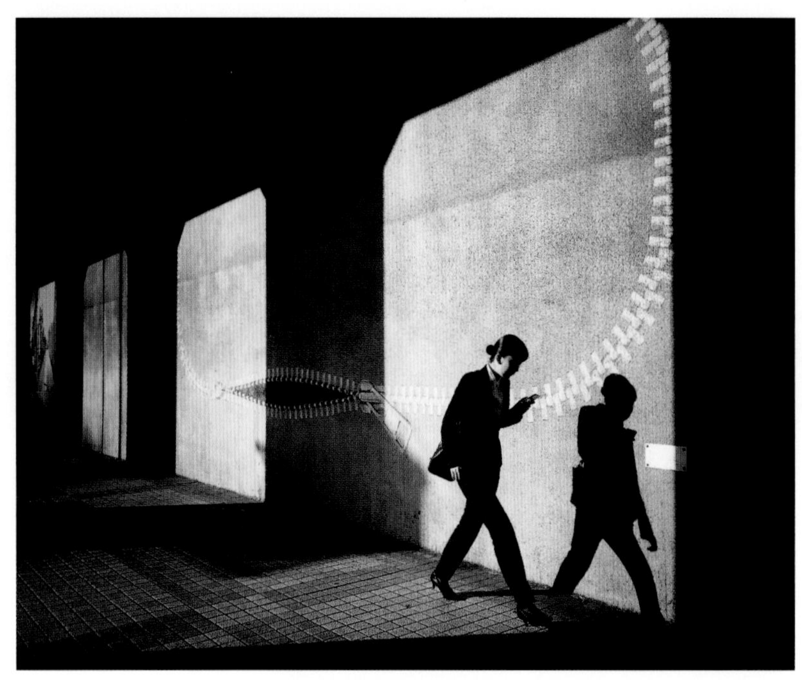

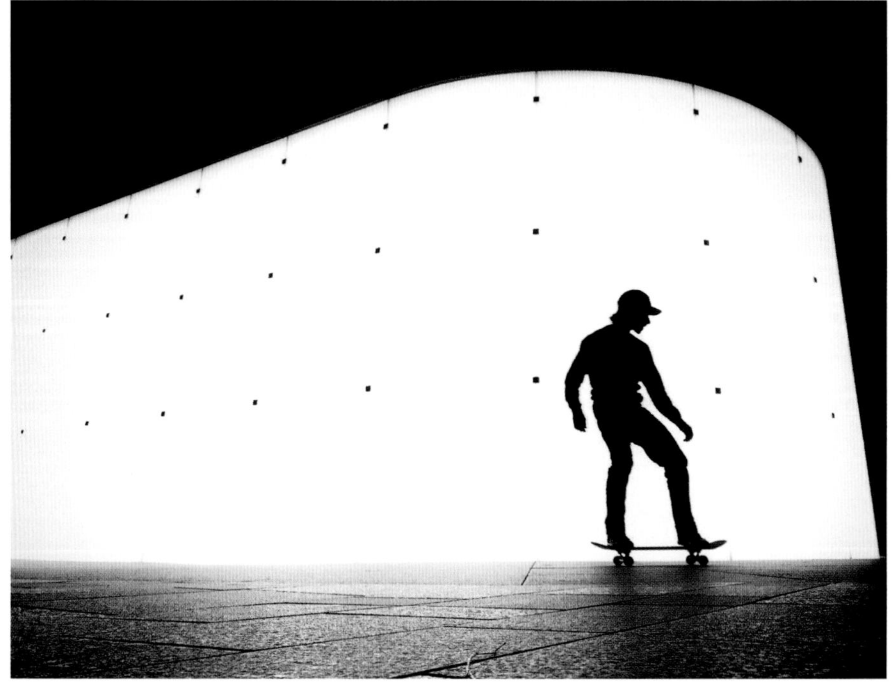

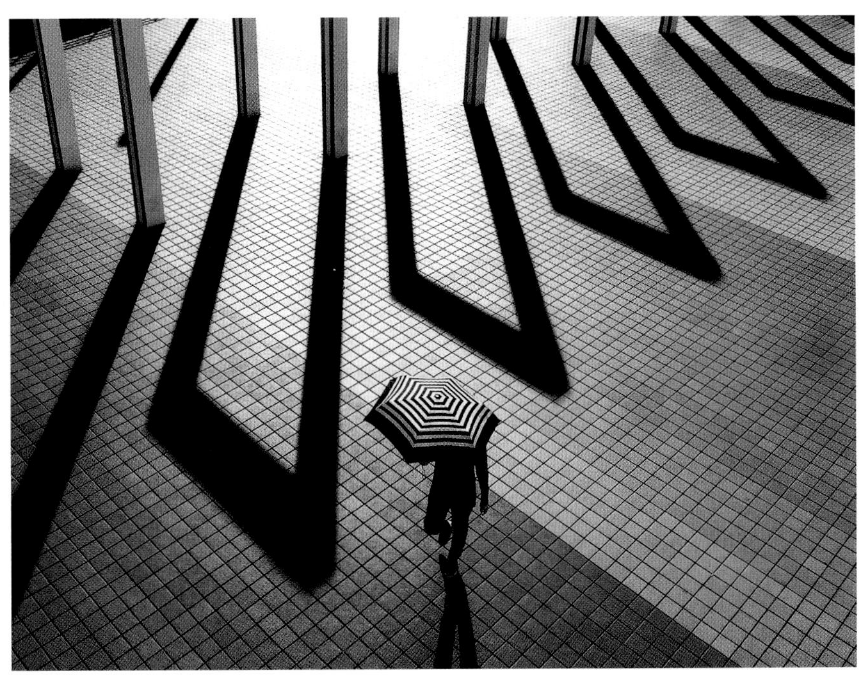

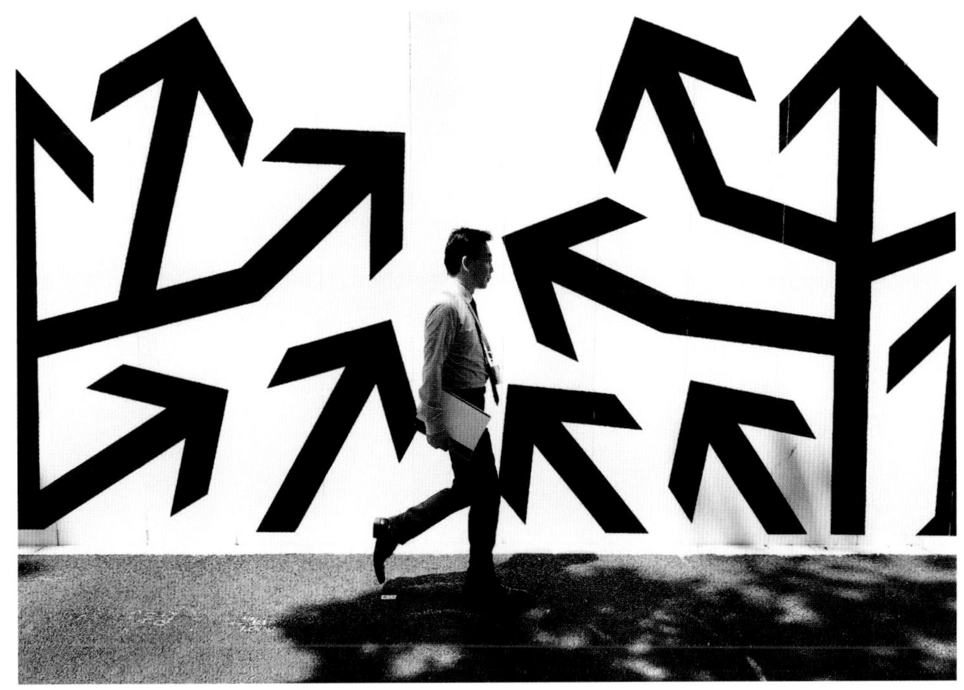

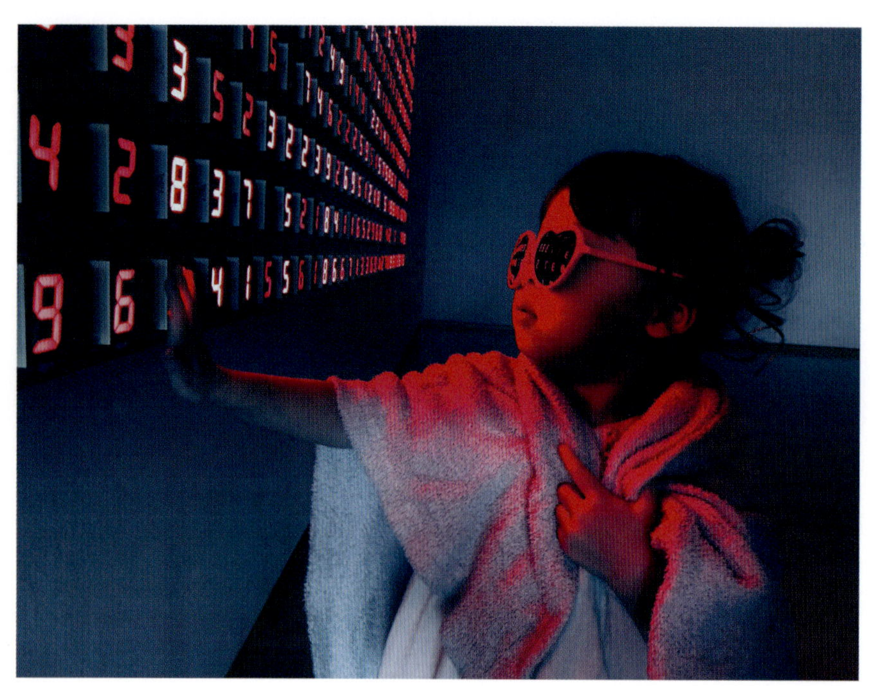

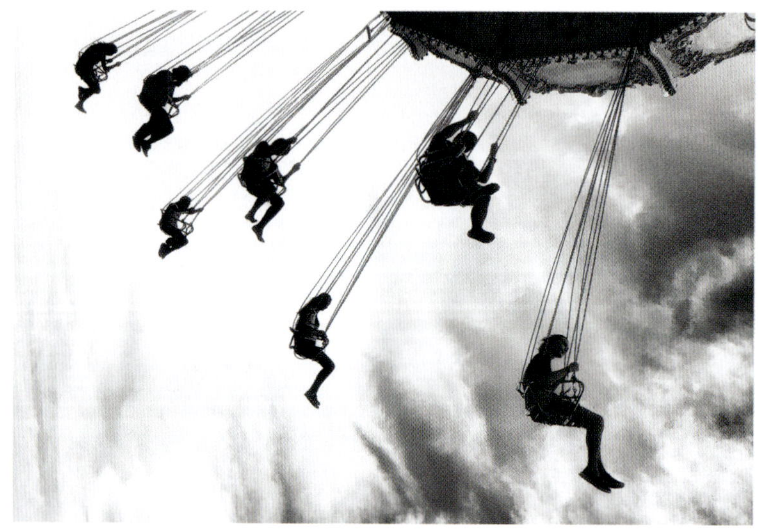

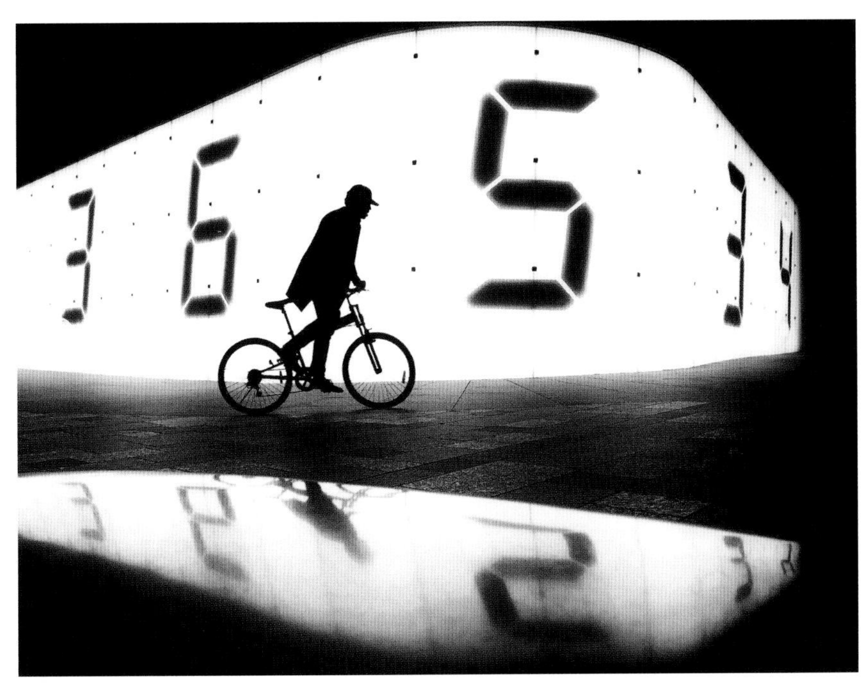

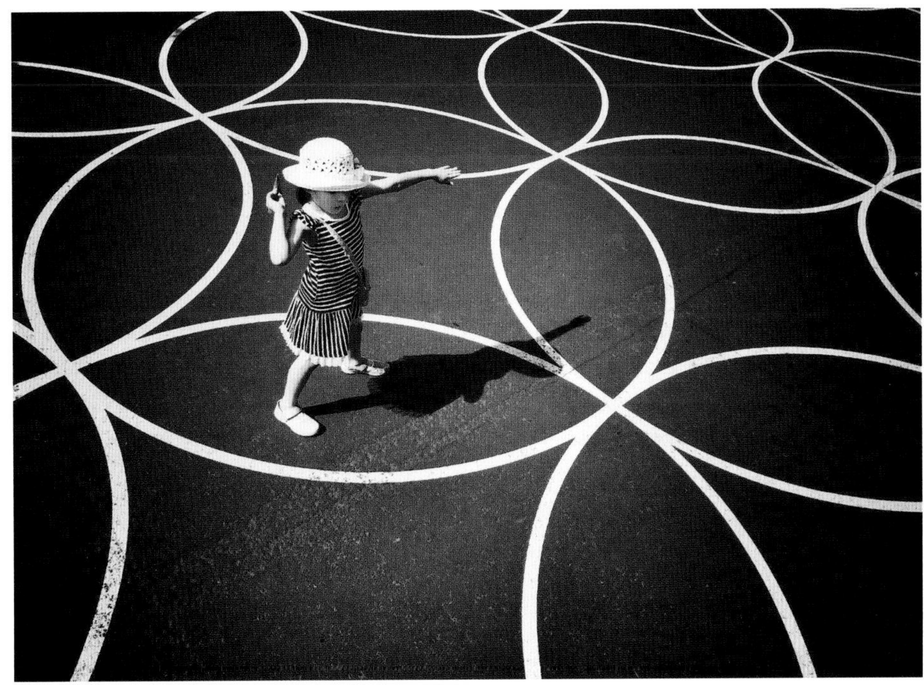

LAURENCE BOUCHARD

Leonid Pryadko
Norilsk, Russia

Miner Leonid Pryadko says that as well as being his hobby, photography helps him to survive. Pryadko takes photos with his Samsung S21 Ultra and edits using Snapseed.

His photographs record life in Siberia – Norilsk is 190 miles (300km) north of the Arctic Circle and 1,500 miles (2,400km) from the North Pole. It is one of the most remote cities on the planet, the second-largest city inside the Arctic Circle, and one of only two large cities inside the continuous permafrost zone. Norilsk also sits on top of one of the largest nickel deposits on Earth, so the major industries there are mining and smelting ore. It is accessible only by air – there is no road or passenger rail connection to the rest of the world – and Norilsk is a closed city, meaning that foreigners cannot visit. The city's 175,000-strong population endures the harshest of winters. It is covered with snow for at least 270 days a year, there are snowstorms one day in every three, and the sun doesn't rise above the horizon from late November to the middle of January. The average high temperature in January is -24°C (-11°F).

A significant proportion of the residents of Norilsk are descended from the Siberian prisoners who were held here and laboured to build much of the city.

'Like all residents of Norilsk, I really hope to leave here before I turn 40, but my heart will forever belong to the north. Life in the far north is not different from that in any other city. The inhabitants of the city have become adapted to the far north. It is also small and so I often see my friends because we live so close to each other. The living conditions are difficult but they unite the town's people like a bad adventure.'

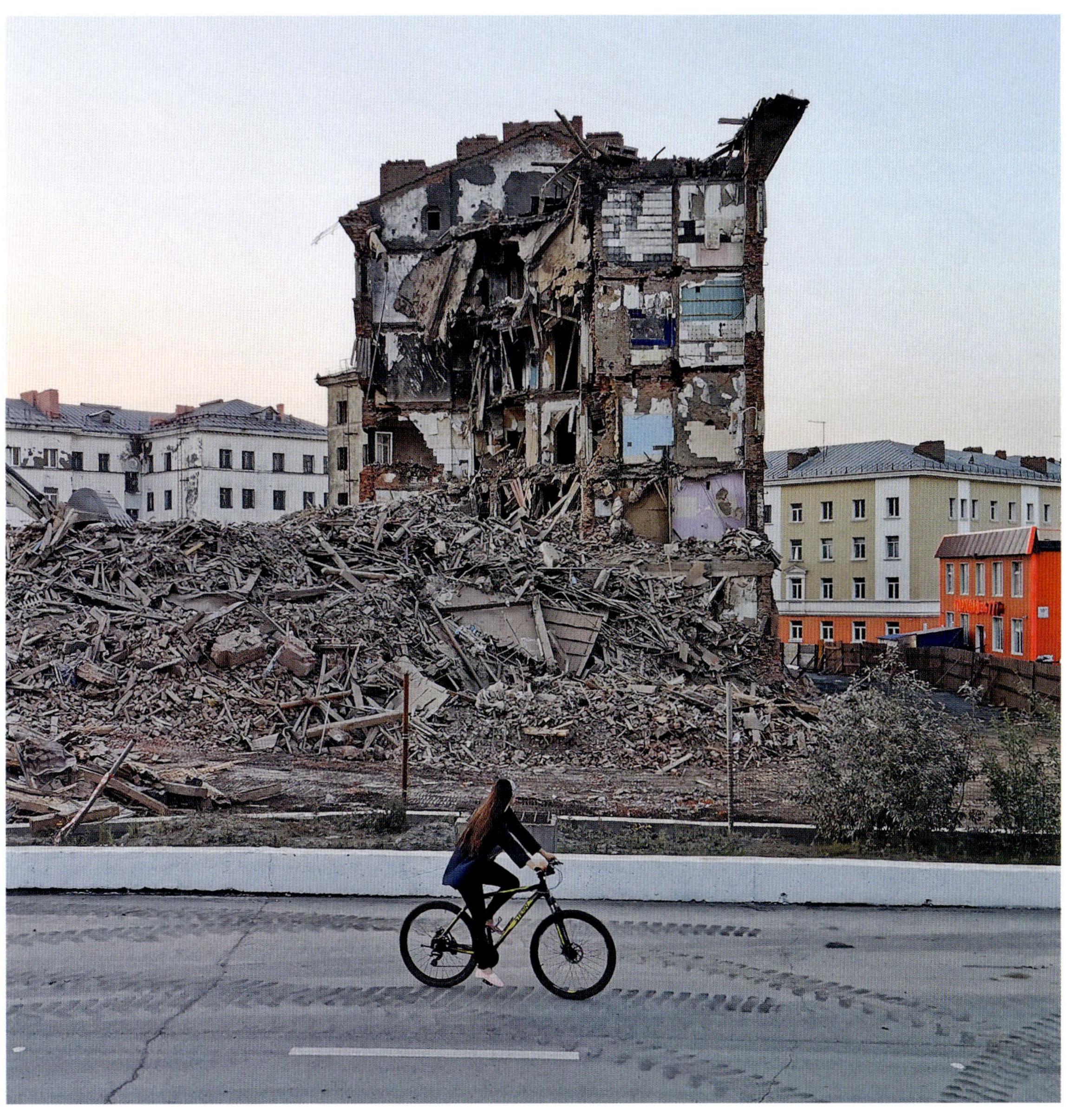

ABOVE: A dilapidated house. Some of the houses in Norilsk are in a critical condition. I often take walks around the city and could not pass by this semi-demolished building without taking a photo.

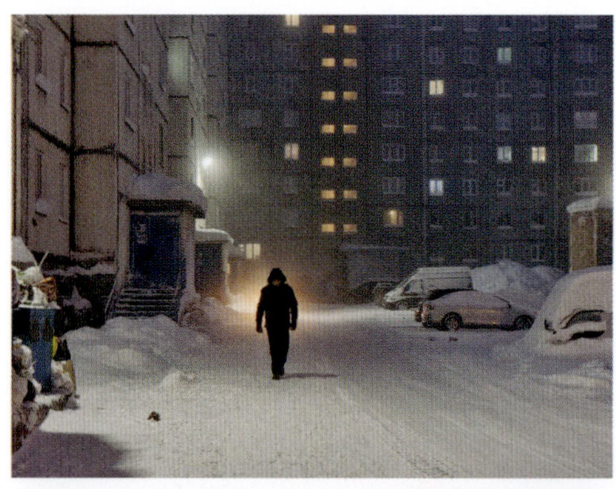

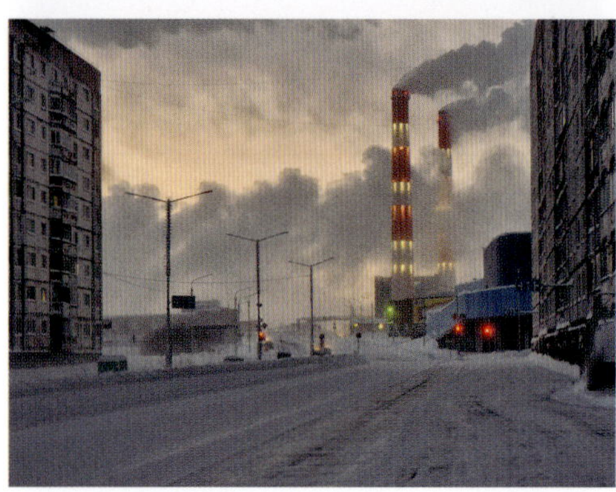

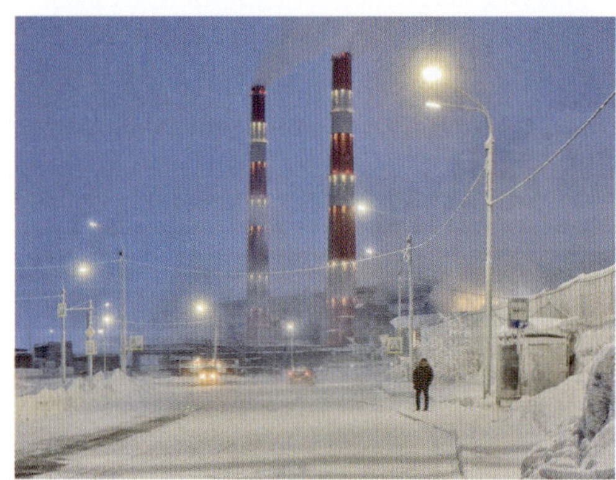

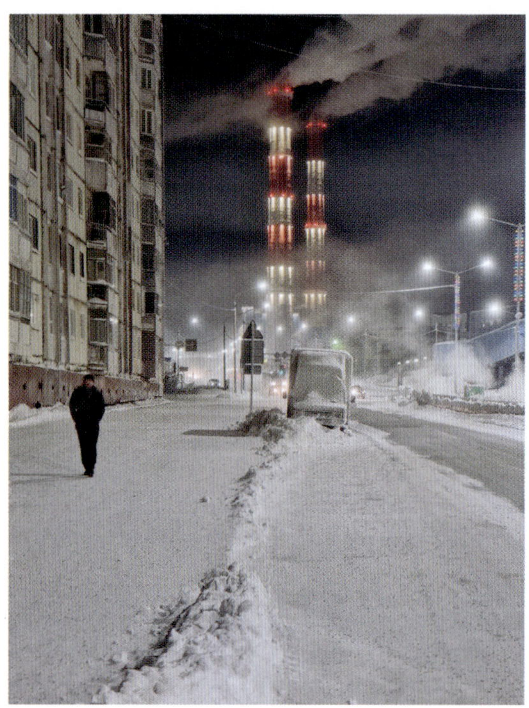

TOP LEFT: 10.45 a.m. 9 January 2023 – the sun doesn't rise.

CENTRE LEFT: 11.41 a.m. 14 December 2022.

BOTTOM LEFT: 11.30 a.m. 21 December 2022.

BELOW: 7.43 p.m. on New Year's Day 2023.

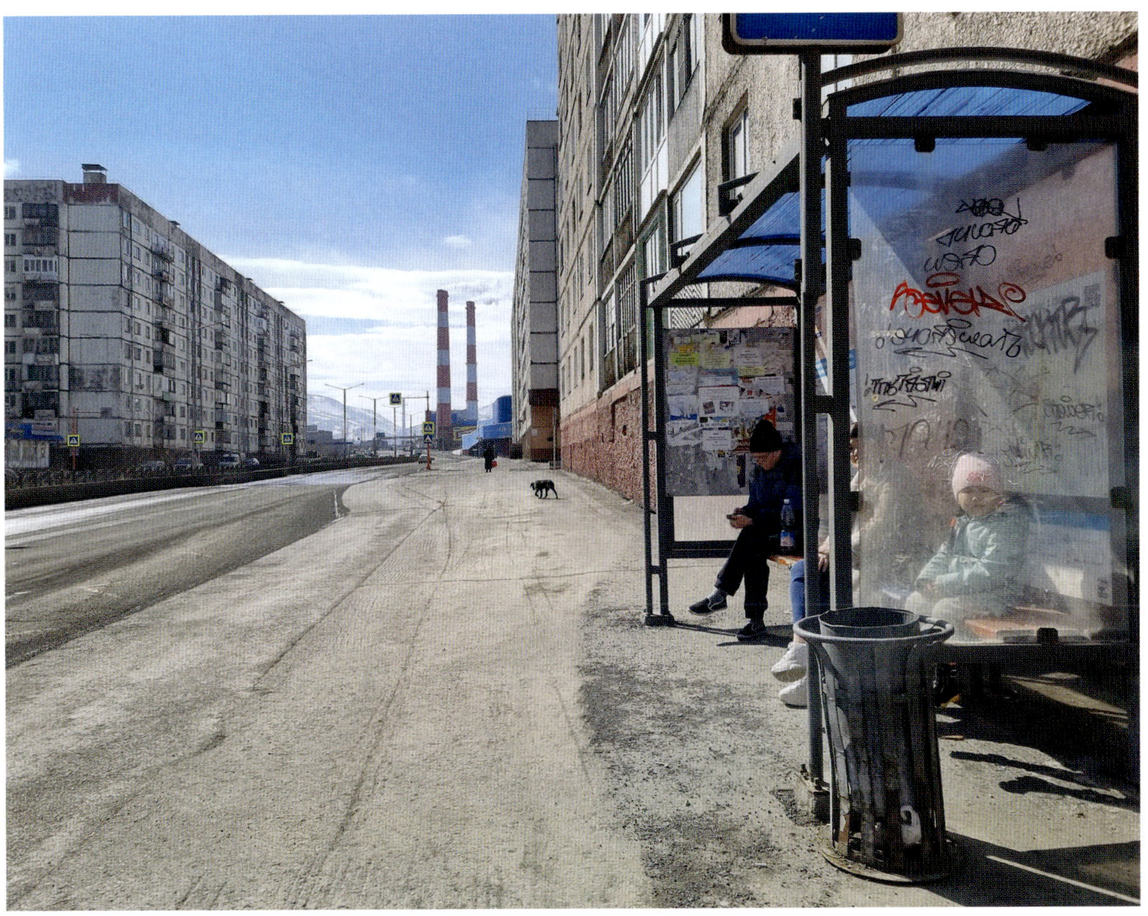

ABOVE: A bus stop. I don't have a dog, but sometimes friends leave their dog with me when they go away. One day I was walking the dog on our usual route. I didn't have my professional camera with me, so took this photo on my phone.

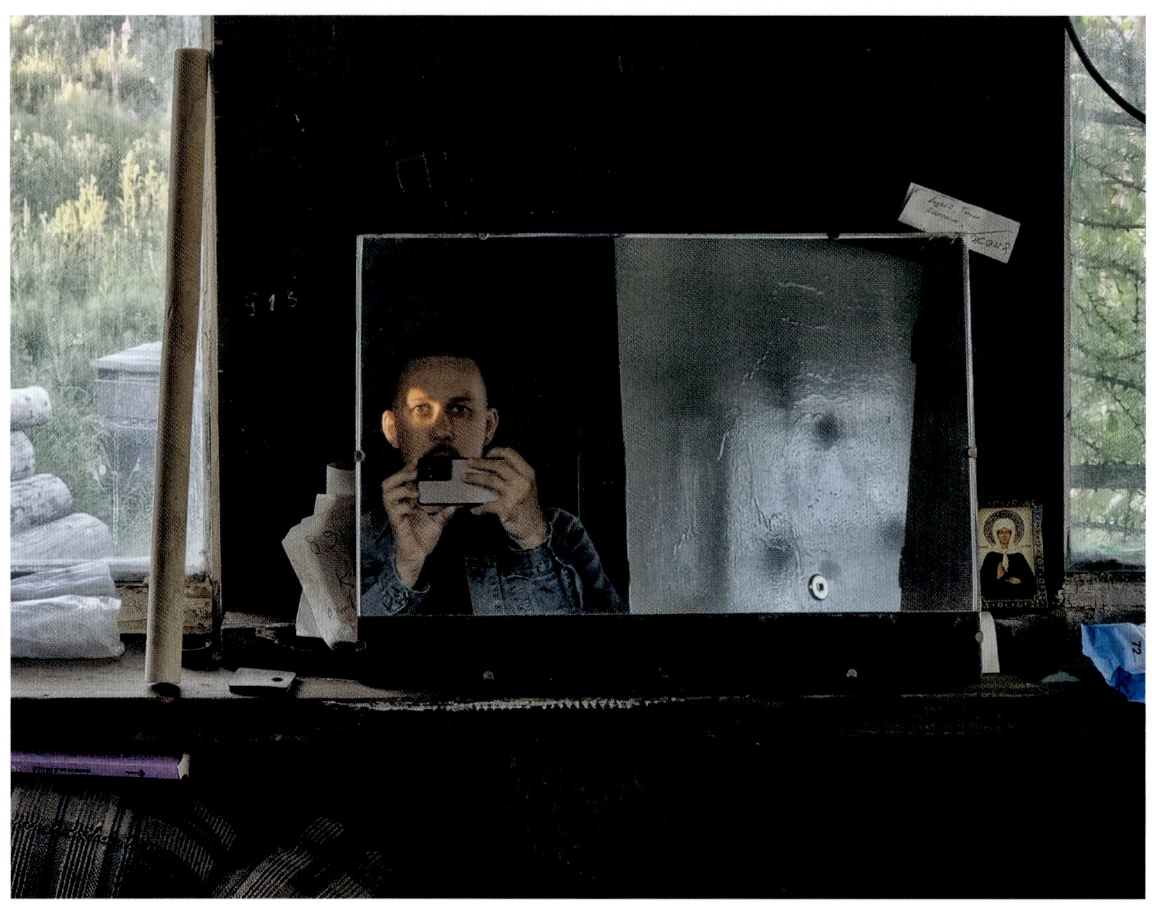

ABOVE: Selfie in a house in the country. It's a little difficult to call it a house, but it is very cosy. It belongs to my wife's parents. It was the first time I had visited it and couldn't pass by this mirror without taking a photo.

'I was born and raised in Norilsk. Children who were born in maternity hospitals in Norilsk were given a medal for being born in the far north.'

RIGHT: Unloading the goods. I was on my way to check on my wife who was at work when I saw a poster on a truck. I thought that it was interesting, yet not interesting enough for me to take my camera out of my backpack, so I took a photo with my phone. I regretted not taking it with the camera, because I saw a person working in the back. But he noticed me immediately, so I hurried away.

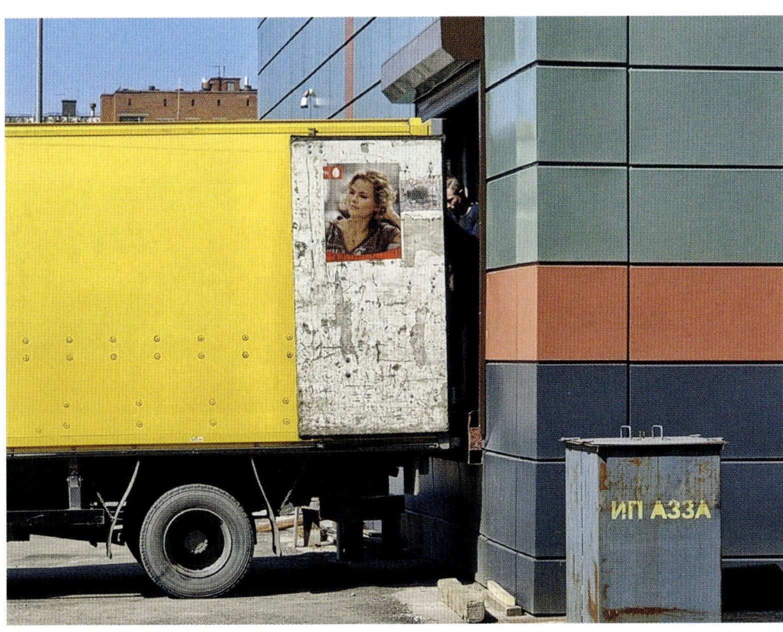

ИП АЗЗА

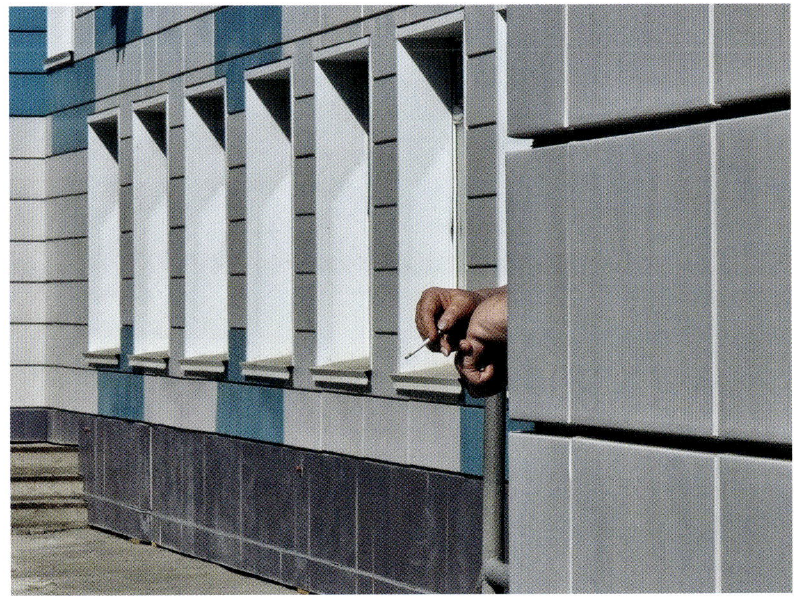

LEFT: My colleague's hands. My colleague smokes before each shift. As I was getting closer to the changing room building I noticed his hands. I found this detail very telling.

LianYu Lu
Chaozhou, China

Photographer and short video director LianYu Lu worked as a freelancer for a number of years but now has his own company. For him, mobile phone photography is the most convenient way to record his life. He shoots daily using an Apple iPhone 11 Pro and a Huawei P40 Pro. Lu mostly photographs scenes of life and humanity he encounters around him, but has been developing an eye for more abstract, quiet moments. He has recently started seeking out empty landscapes to try out new styles of composition, making work that carries within their frame a more artistic vision.

RIGHT: I attended a lantern festival in Meizhou to shoot the fire dragon performance for work. This traditional dance is often performed at festive celebrations, particularly at lantern festivals to mark the Lunar New Year. The giant dragon puppet is held on poles and skilled dancers move it to mimic a dragon's movements. Dragons are a symbol of good luck in China, and the longer it dances the more luck it will bring. Afterwards, as I was packing up, the fire dragon ran towards me. I pulled out my phone and quickly shot this photo. I was amazed by what an iPhone could do at night.

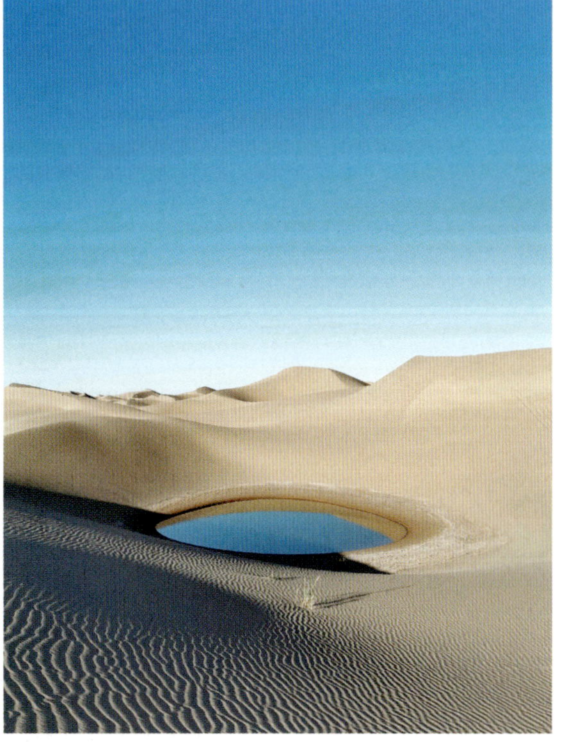

LEFT: The Inner Mongolian desert in the spring of 2018. I was surprised to find a pool of water in the endless desert.

'The longer the dragon dances the more luck it brings.'

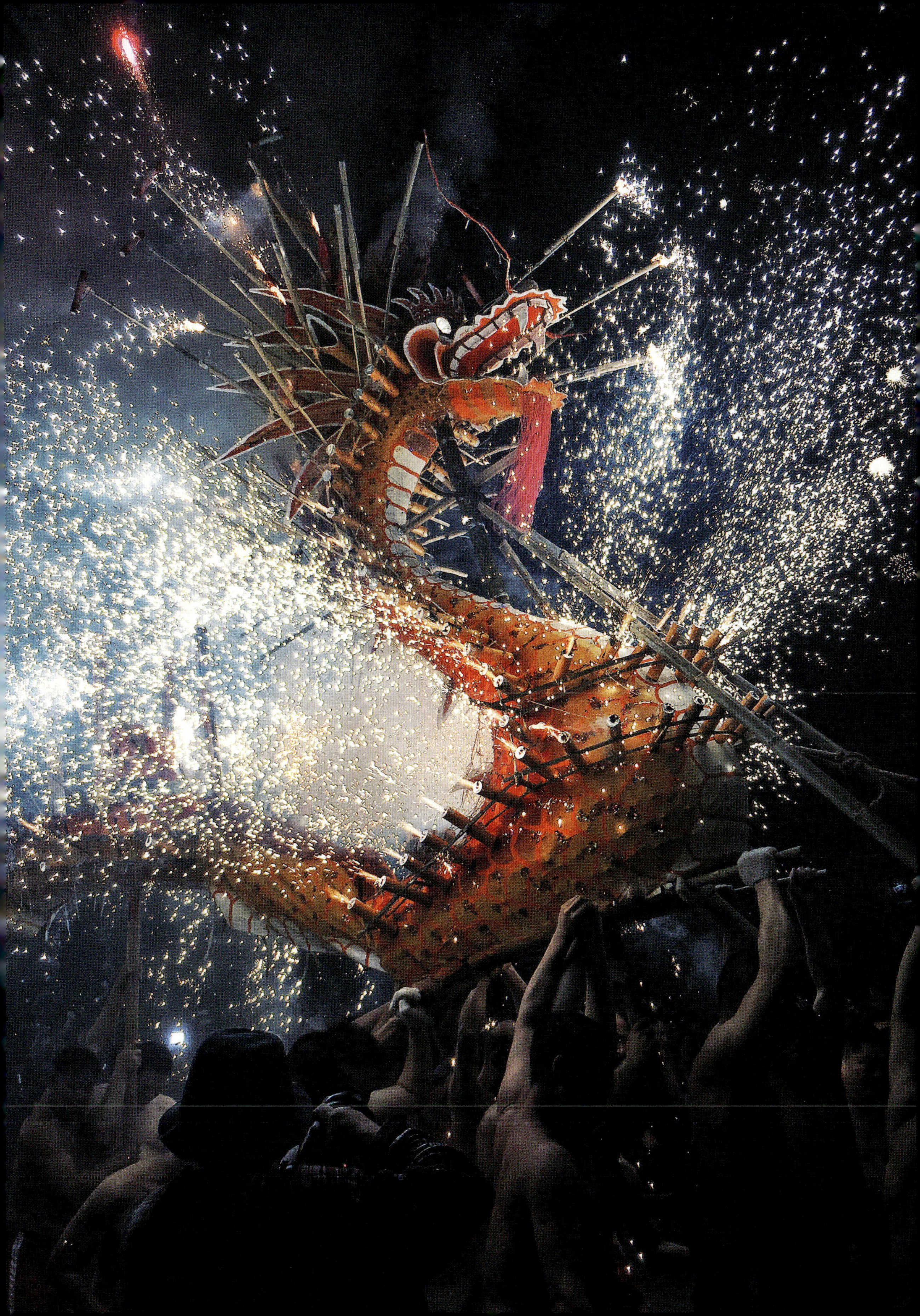

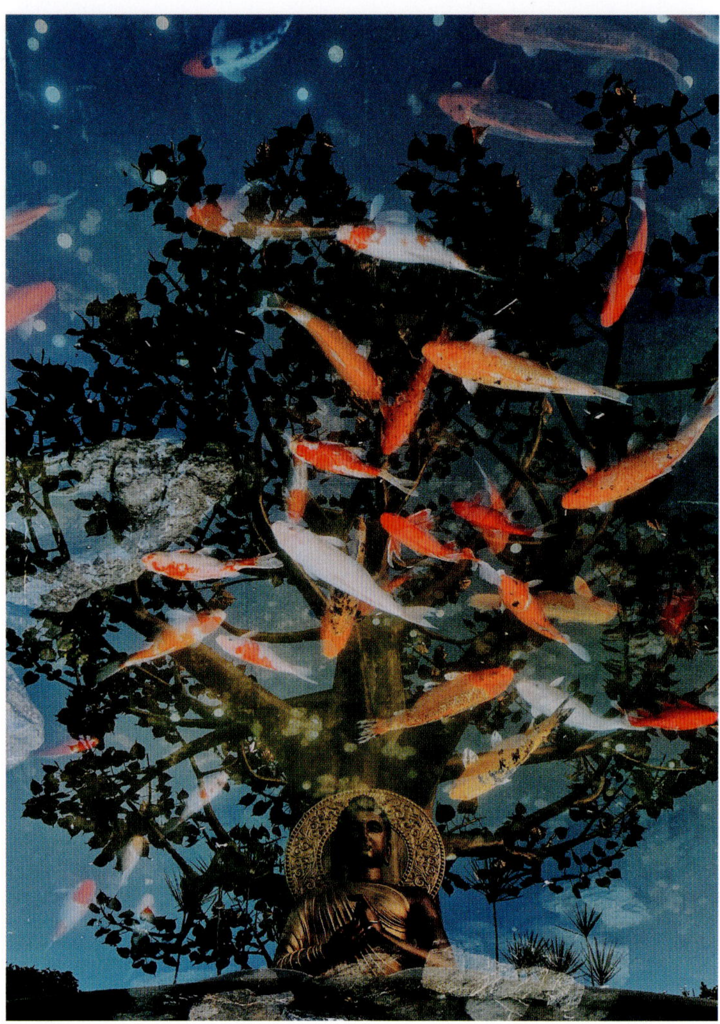

 At a temple in Heyuan City, Guangdong Province, I spotted a pond and decided to take a closer look. Buddha statues and trees were reflected in the pond and fish were swimming in the crystal-clear water. Later on I rotated the photo through 180 degrees so that the fish appear to be swimming in the tree.

BELOW: This photo taken at my parent's home shows a fleeting moment full of rich coincidence. The sun shines on a pot plant while its shadow falls onto an empty pot.

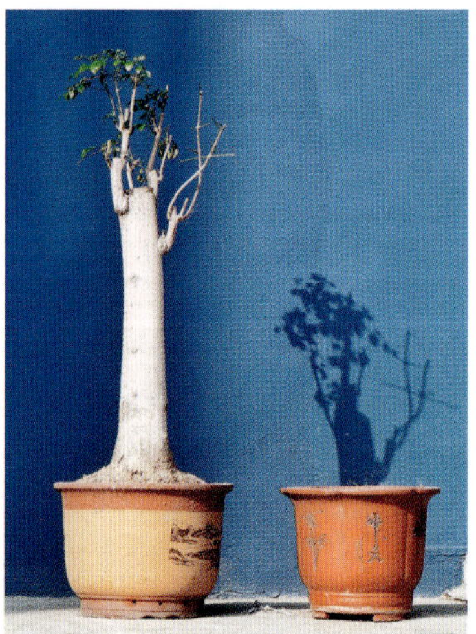

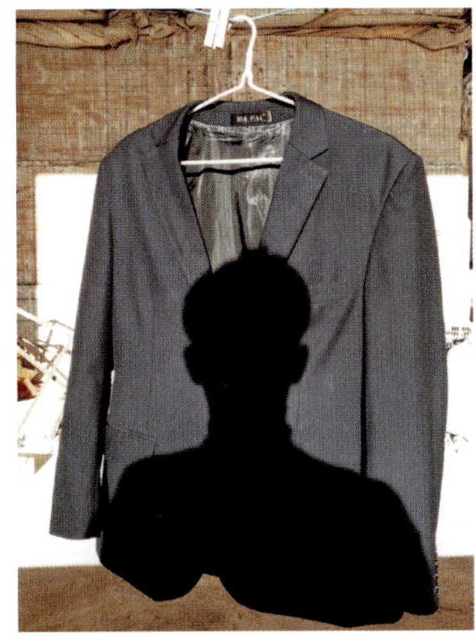

ABOVE: My shadow hangs over a suit jacket. I spotted laundry drying on the side of the road and liked the way my shadow appeared as I got closer to it.

BELOW: At an expressway toll station in Tibet, the neat arrangement of the red-and-white railings of the toll booth create a visual impact with the trees behind.

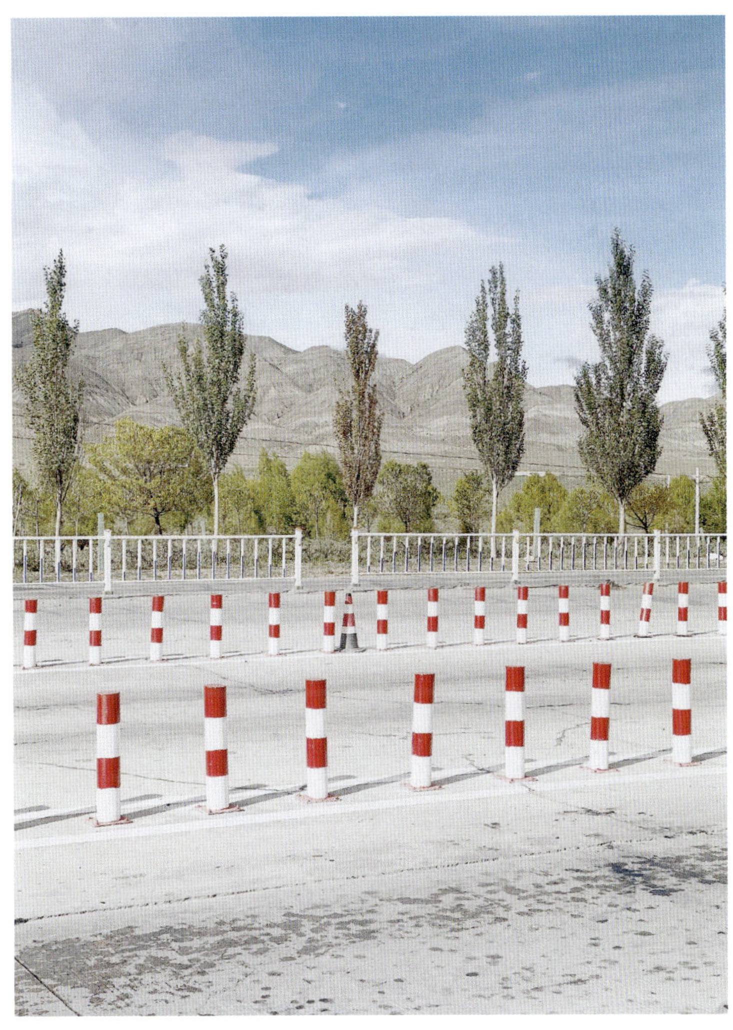

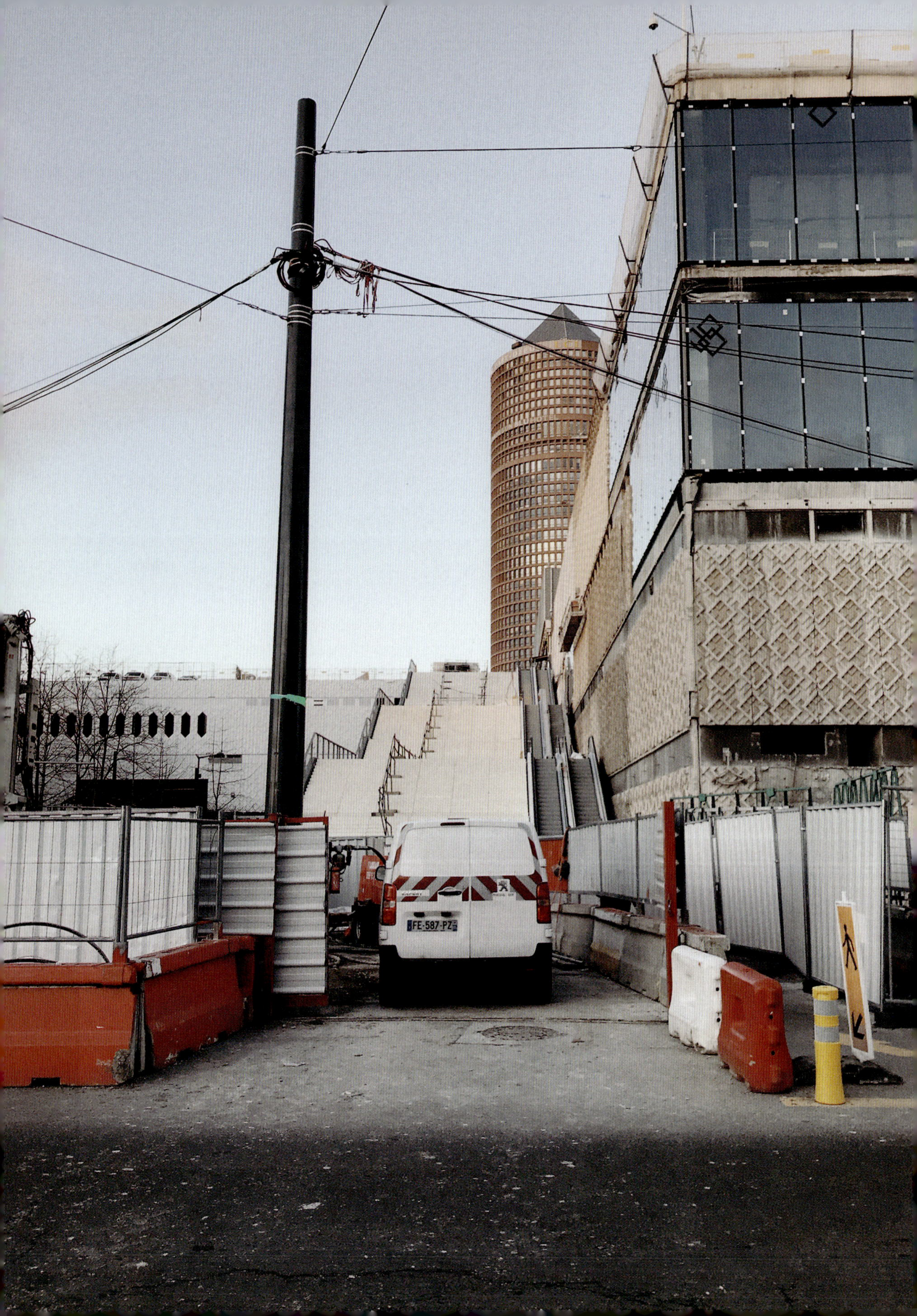

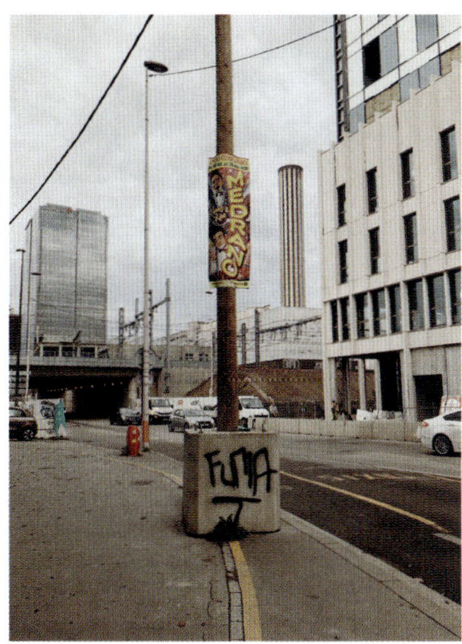

Ludovic Broquereau
Lyon, France

Ludovic Broquereau is an executive manager for a group of creative and digital marketing agencies. He discovered photography when he was young and his parents gave him his first camera – at that time there were only film cameras. Like most people, he started out taking pictures of his family, friends and places he visited.

Broquereau started to use photography as a means of artistic expression in 2010 when he realized what a powerful tool his smartphone camera was. Since that realization, taking photos with his phone camera has become a daily activity – in fact it's almost a routine. He has used an Apple iPhone SE, and now uses an iPhone 7 and Snapseed.

His approach to photography is very intuitive. He uses his phone camera like a point-and-shoot camera, and it works perfectly for this as it is always in his pocket or his hands. His work encompasses urban landscapes, street scenes, daily life, trips and holidays.

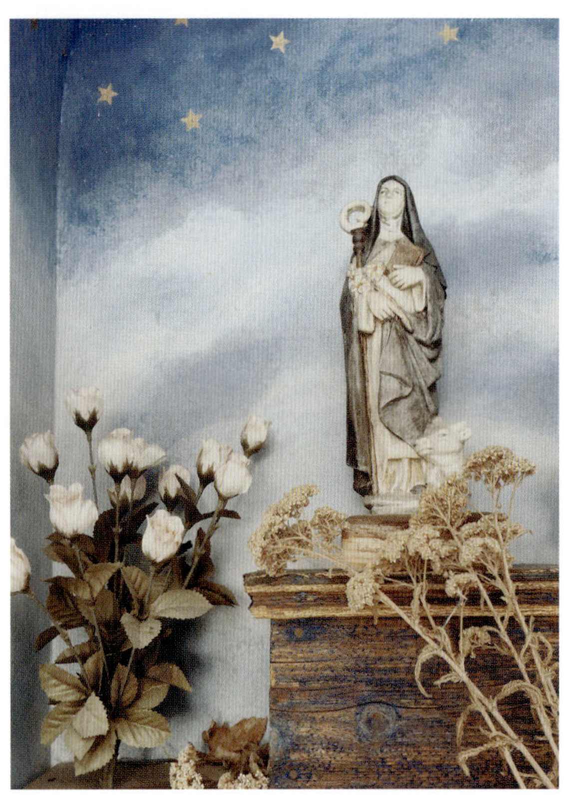

LEFT, BELOW + RIGHT: The crucifix seems to be lost or floating on the surface of the colourful wall. The faded colours, old wallpaper and crucifixes are typical of 1970s French middle-class interiors and I like to document popular faith objects in their environment in a simple way. At first glance you could see them as kitsch, but there is more than that. That's what I'm trying to show with the way the images are framed.

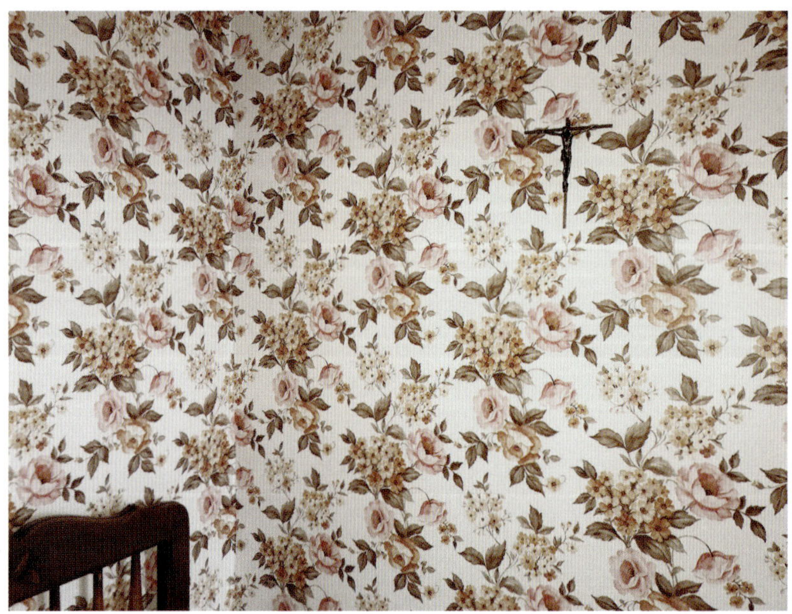

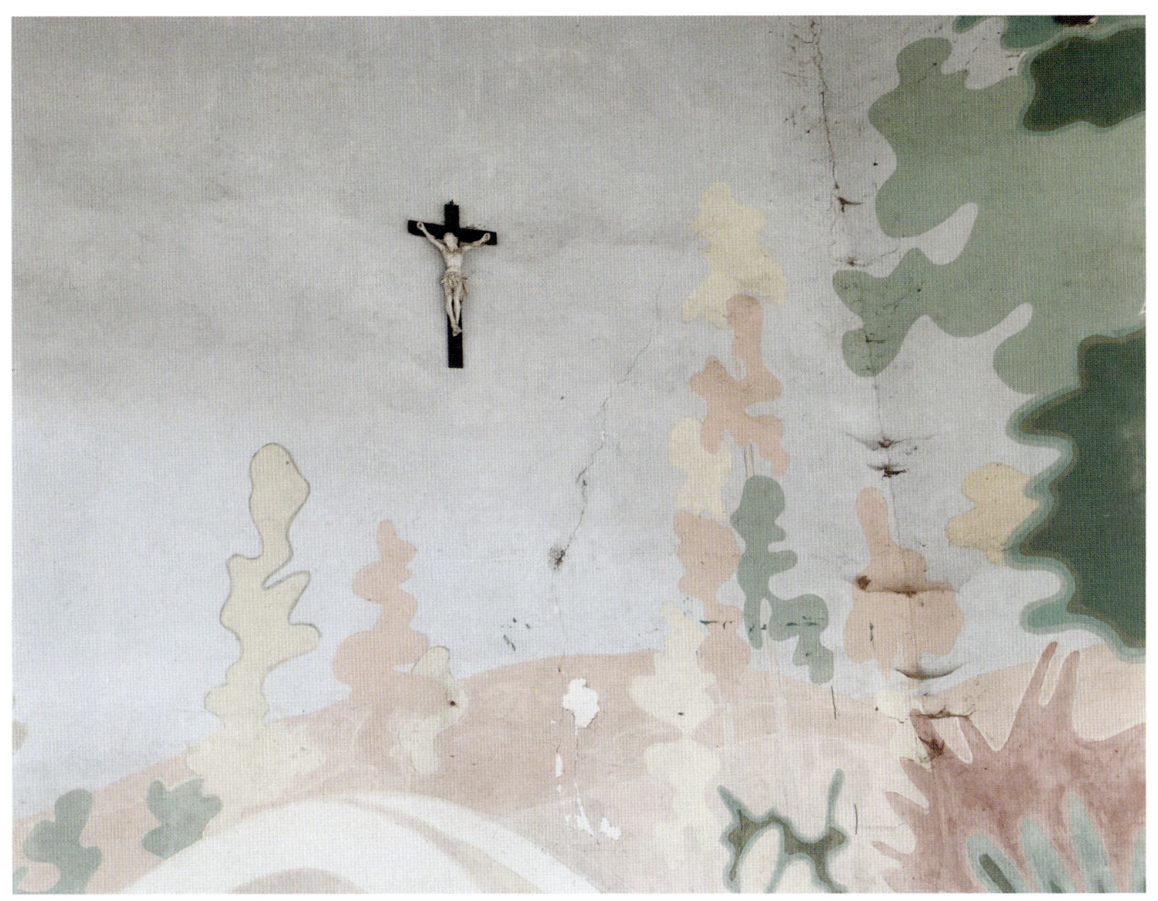

'I like the constraints generated by the smartphone. They push me to be more creative and rigorous in the selection of the subject, the framing and the mix of colours.'

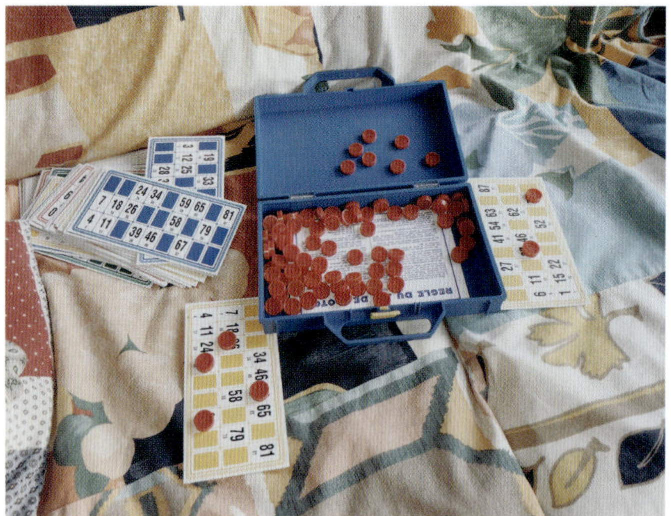

ABOVE: During the summer months at my parents-in-laws' home. It makes me think of an image by Stephen Shore. He is one of my favourite photographers and a great source of inspiration. It's a kind of tribute to his work.

RIGHT: I was in this restaurant near Flaine, a ski resort in the French Alps, after a full day outside in the snow. I appreciated the contrast between the outside, where a snowstorm was raging, and the cosy interior. I like the warm colours and the nostalgic view composed by all the postcards and flyers.

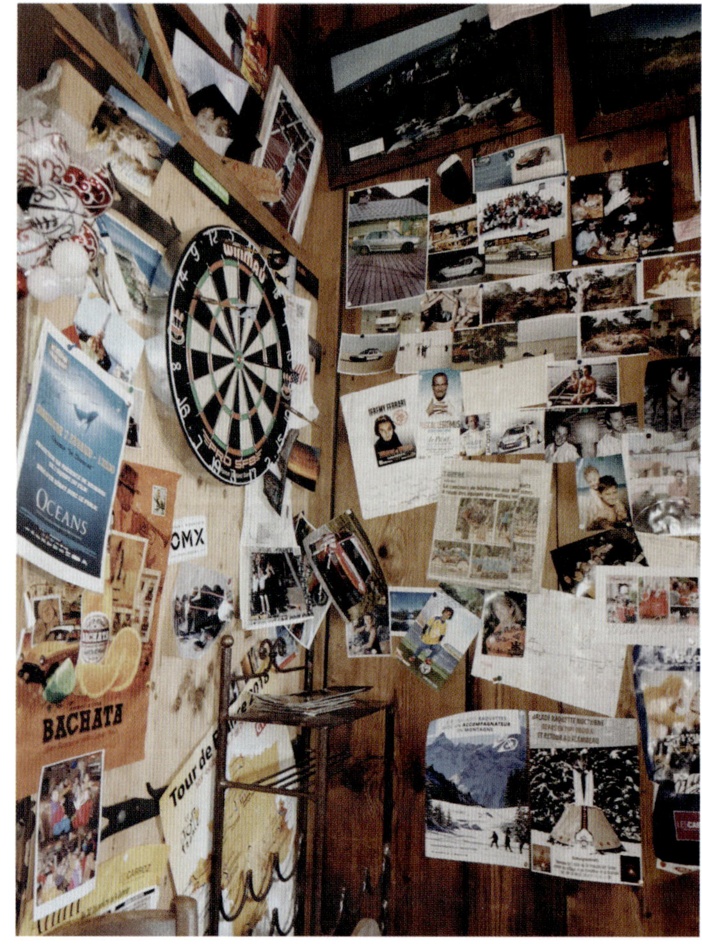

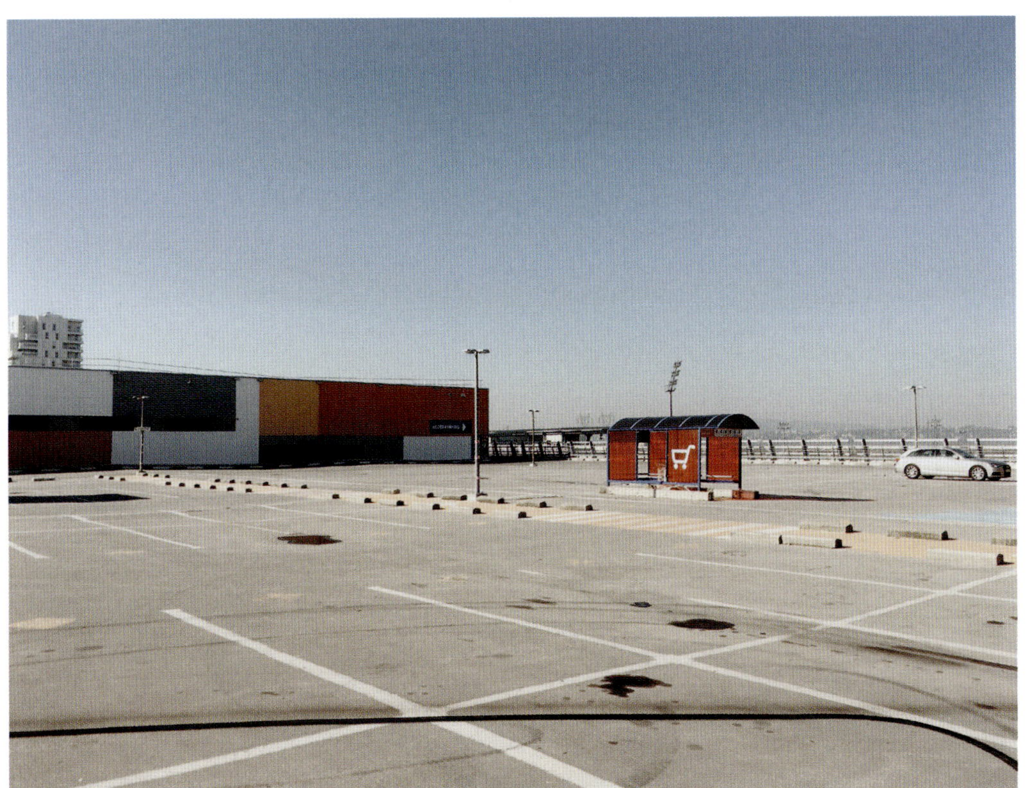

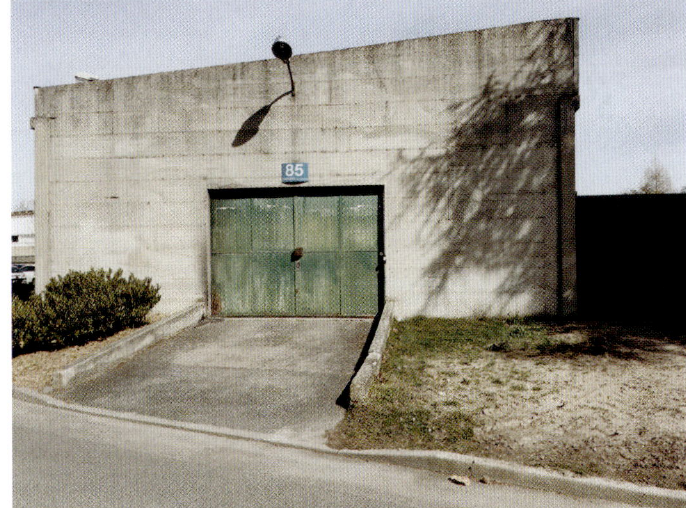

ABOVE: A shopping centre car park in the Lyon suburbs. The perspective and the strong colour blocking caught my eye. There's an impression of emptiness with traces of human activities at the foreground thanks to the tyre mark and the isolated car in the background.

RIGHT: This image was taken on one of the university campuses in Lyon where my office was located. The beauty of the green colours (the faded grass, the metal door) and the lines of the architecture appealed to me. It's a simple contemplation on the mundane beauty of the place.

RIGHT: We woke up at 3 a.m. and by 4 a.m. we were at the riverbank ready to take photos at sunrise. There is the most beautiful light, and silence and nature all around. At first, Lina and I took pictures near the water, but then I had the idea of taking a picture in the water. I saw the boat, climbed to the top of a tree and took this picture as she swam below me. It is a beautiful riverbank. I used to go jogging there. I am very happy with the colour, the light, the symmetry and the tranquillity.

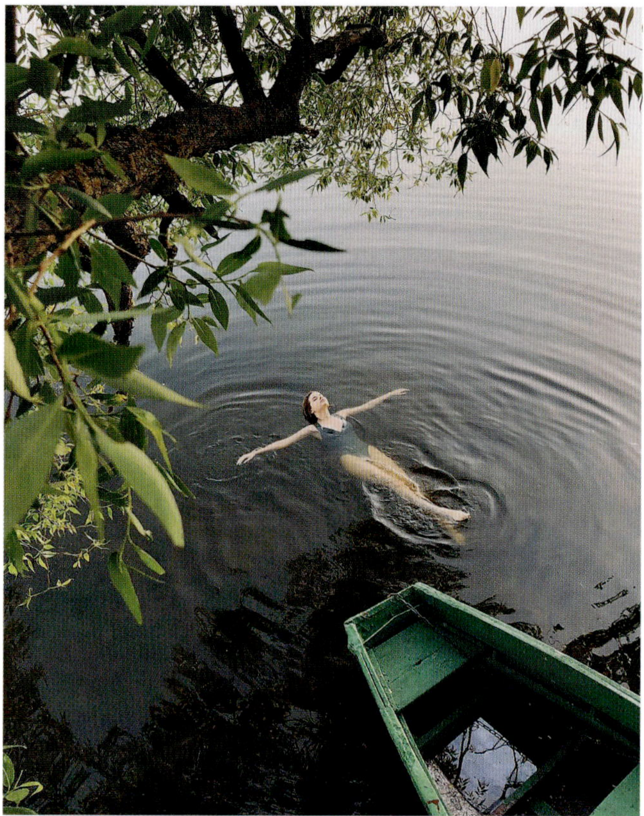

RIGHT: I already had this shot planned in my head. We were in a Minsk park and I asked Anastasia, Ulyana, Artem and Andrey to walk across the field so that I could take a few photos as they moved away from me.

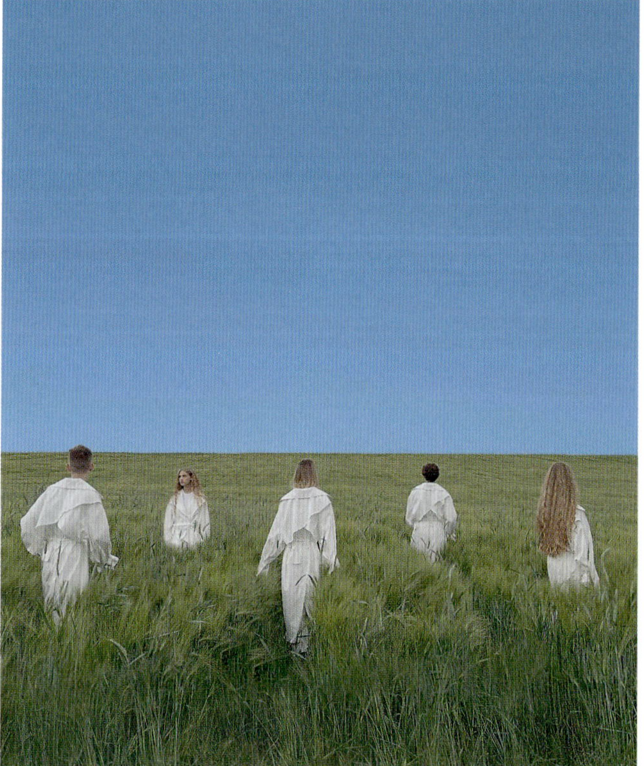

Maksim Goncharenok
Minsk, Belarus

Taking photos is Maksim Goncharenok's main source of income and he has been doing it for about ten years. He uses an Apple iPhone 12 Pro and he also shoots with a Canon EOS R digital camera. His main photo-processing applications are Photoshop and Lightroom, although he occasionally uses apps such as UNION, Visual Studio Code and RNI films. Lately he's been trying to use minimal processing on his photos.

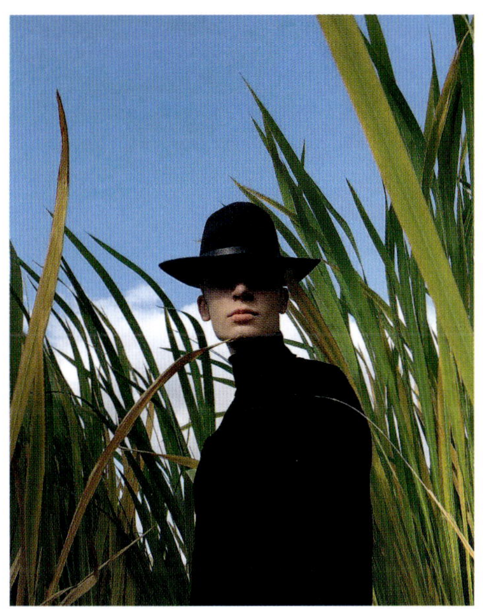

ABOVE: On the shore of the Minsk Sea. I saw these leaves growing so tall in the marsh. The day had such a clear sky, that I knew that these colours and shapes would be very harmonious with the figure, dressed all in black in the frame. We were both knee-deep in the swamp by the time we took this shot, but that didn't stop us working until we got the shot you see now.

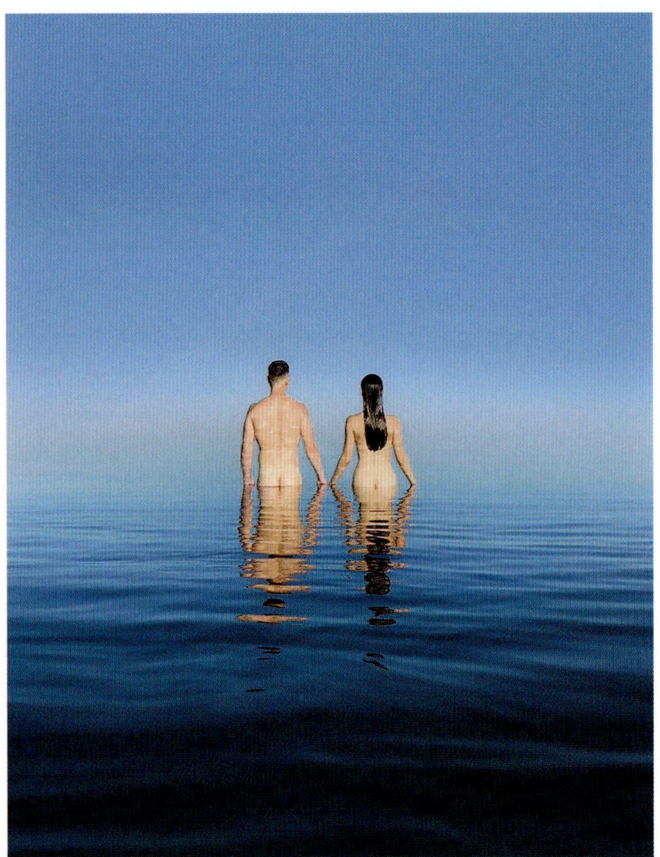

 Ilya, Tanya and I cycled all night to get to the Minsk Sea, which was over 60 miles (100km) away. It was on a summer morning at dawn and we swam and took photos. This is the result. I really loved the gradient of the early morning sky.

RIGHT: I took this picture in a field, lying on the ground between Anastasia and Ulyana who were both wearing white cloaks. It was a staged photo, as I already had a version of how I saw the finished photo in my head. It's one of my favourite pictures, and I'm also very happy that it was noticed and highlighted by Apple.

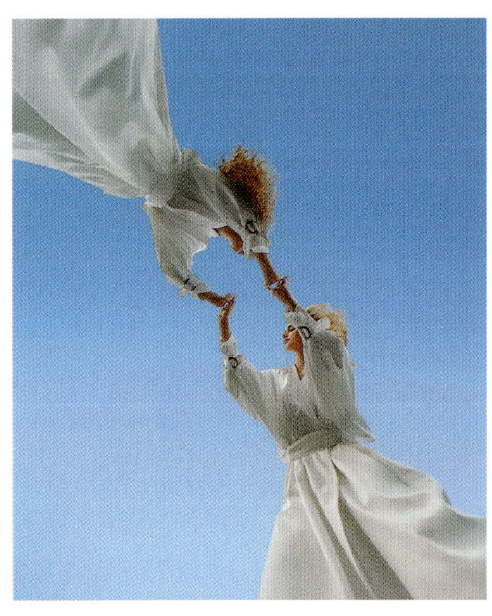

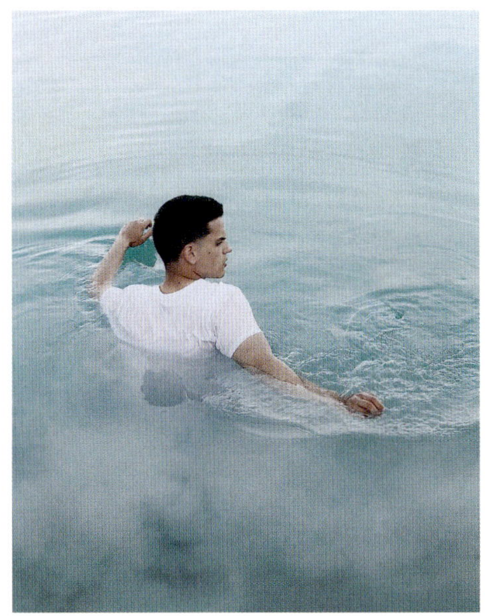

LEFT: The water at this chalk quarry is an incredibly beautiful colour. When I got there I immediately set up this self-portrait. I was travelling to different cities with friends, and this was one of the points on our itinerary.

RIGHT: This was one of my first meetings with Dasha. We met in Minsk and we agreed to take some beautiful photos together. We decided to experiment with a large piece of white cloth in the fields nearby. I didn't rate this photo at first but rediscovered it and it grew on me.

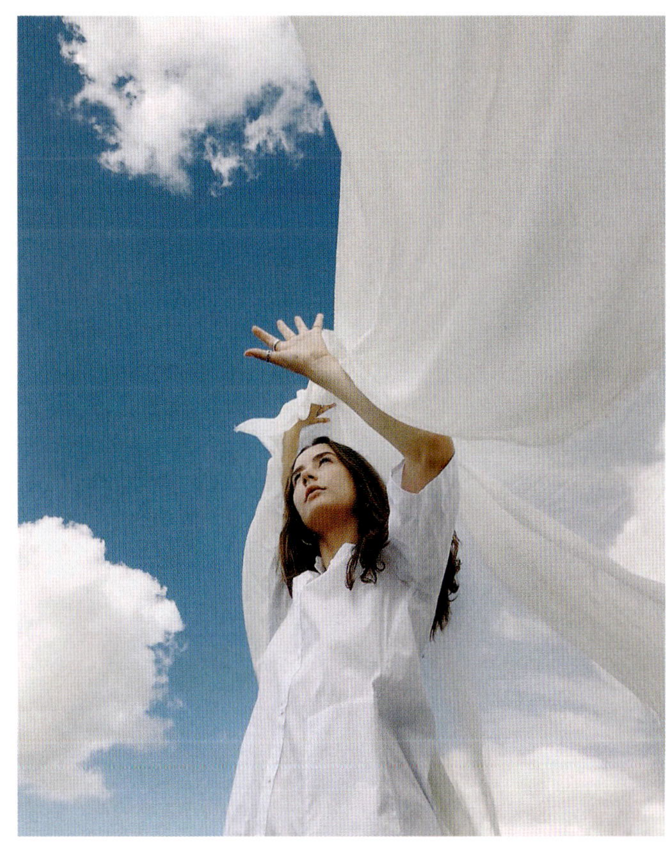

Marcello Raggini
San Marino

Italian-born Marcello Raggini lives in the smallest country in the world. His nearest large city is Bologna, over the border in Italy. He works as a radiology technician in San Marino's only hospital and is a keen musician, playing guitar in two rock bands. The Covid-19 lockdowns meant he was unable to perform with his bands and they have since disbanded. Aged 50 and looking for an alternative creative output, Raggini turned to photography. He took online courses, attended some one-to-one workshops and read photography books constantly. Although he normally uses a full-frame mirrorless camera, he started using his Apple iPhone to take more artistic and creative shots and realized that the equipment is less important than creativity. He uses an iPhone 11 Pro and Lightroom mobile for editing.

RIGHT: This is one of my favourite photos. It was taken in a shopping centre playground and shows the shadow of a child clinging to a rope and twirling off the ground. The diagonals are the fence around the playground. I was inspired by looking at the shadows out of context – it was like seeing a bird flying out of a cage. The Covid lockdown had recently been lifted and seeing children play freely was cathartic. I like the composition of circular and diagonal lines accompanied by the contrast of yellow and green, both colours linked to joy and hope. The fact that the child's silhouette is entirely contained by the yellow band seemed a good omen.

'I discovered photography consciously, not even two years ago, at the age of 50.'

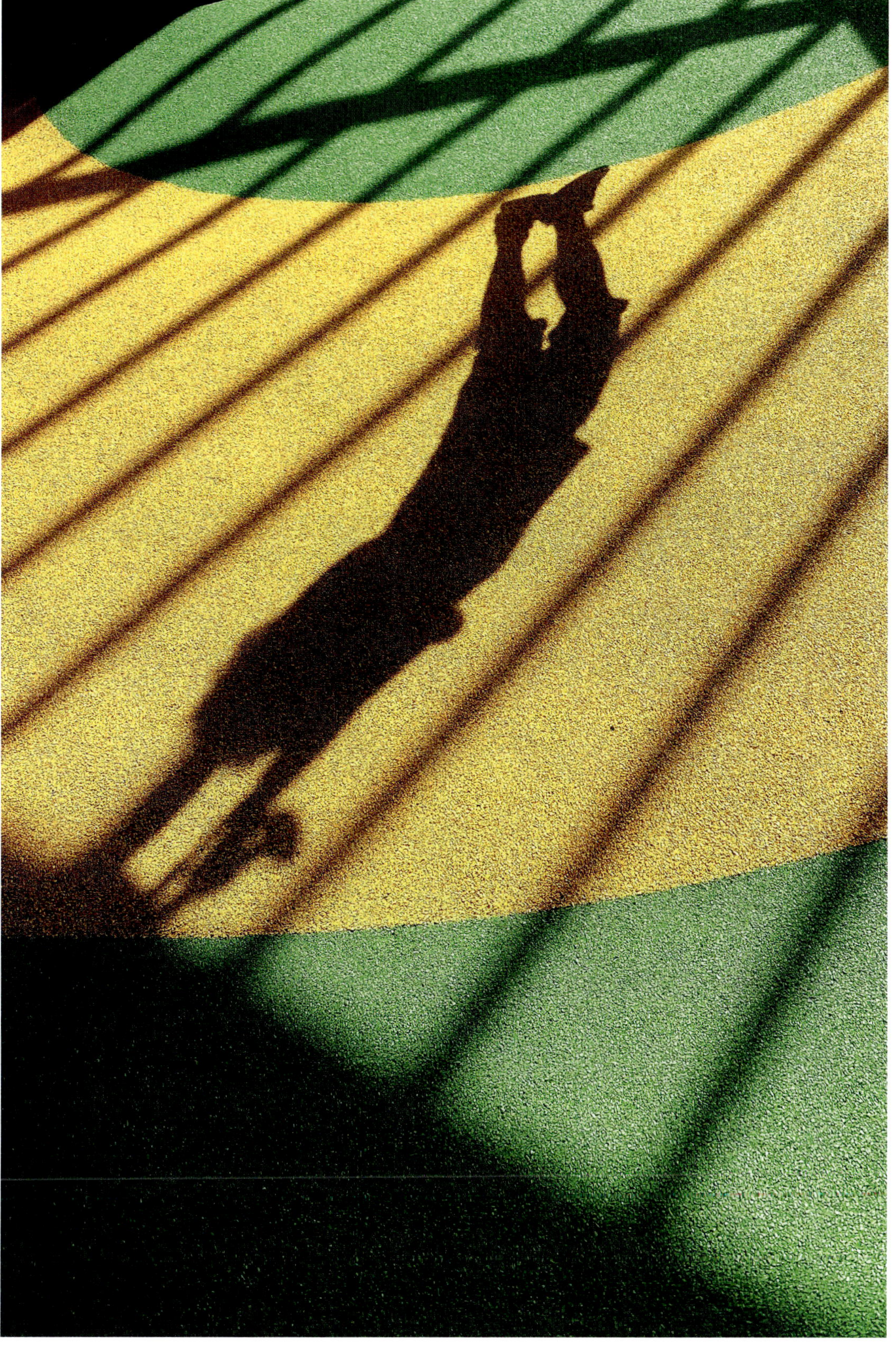

RIGHT: During a hike in the Puez-Odle National Park, in the Italian Dolomites, I found these sheets drying outside an isolated high-altitude shelter. I was immediately prompted to photograph them by the impact of the red on the green of the grass. It seemed so strange to see them hanging there in such a wild place as if they were flags. I like the contrast of the colours and the idea of the human against the natural world. This photo is a testament to how humans have adapted to even the most adverse conditions. Outside the shelter there were nets for transporting food and other items by helicopter. In such an inaccessible place, seeing such a human sign was inspiring.

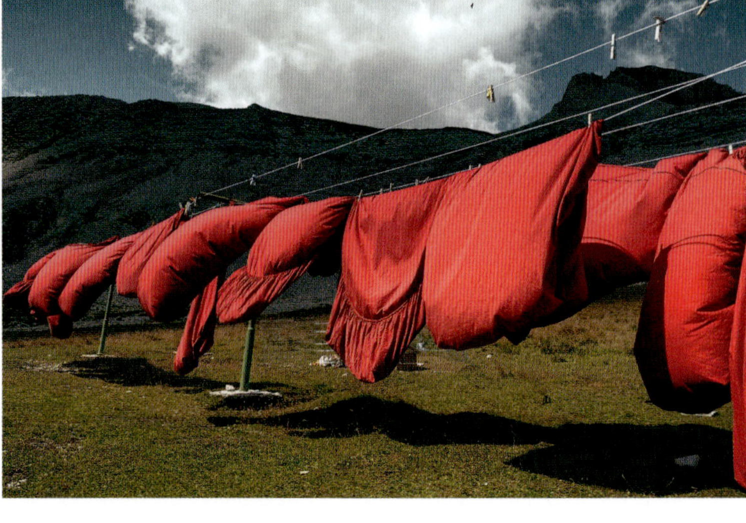

RIGHT: This photo shows the difficulty of living at altitude. It is strange to see washing drying in such a remote place. Perhaps it was because it was not sunny, or at over 2,000m (6,500ft) above sea level there is no lawn where you can stick the poles for the clothesline. The contrast between the yellow tablecloths and the blue trousers prompted me to take the photo. Somehow it makes me happy. Perhaps the bright colours are there on purpose to soften the hard conditions of people who work in an environment that is dominated by grey rock. On the right you can see the Austrian flag and this reminded me of the bloody events that took place here during World War I.

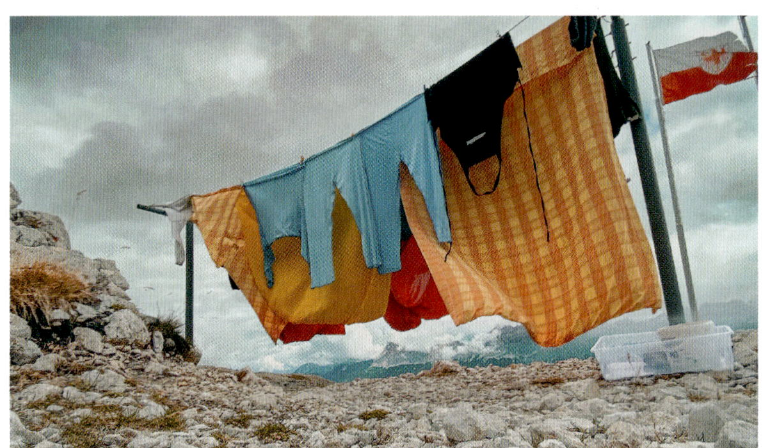

'I get a lot of satisfaction from using my iPhone to express myself.'

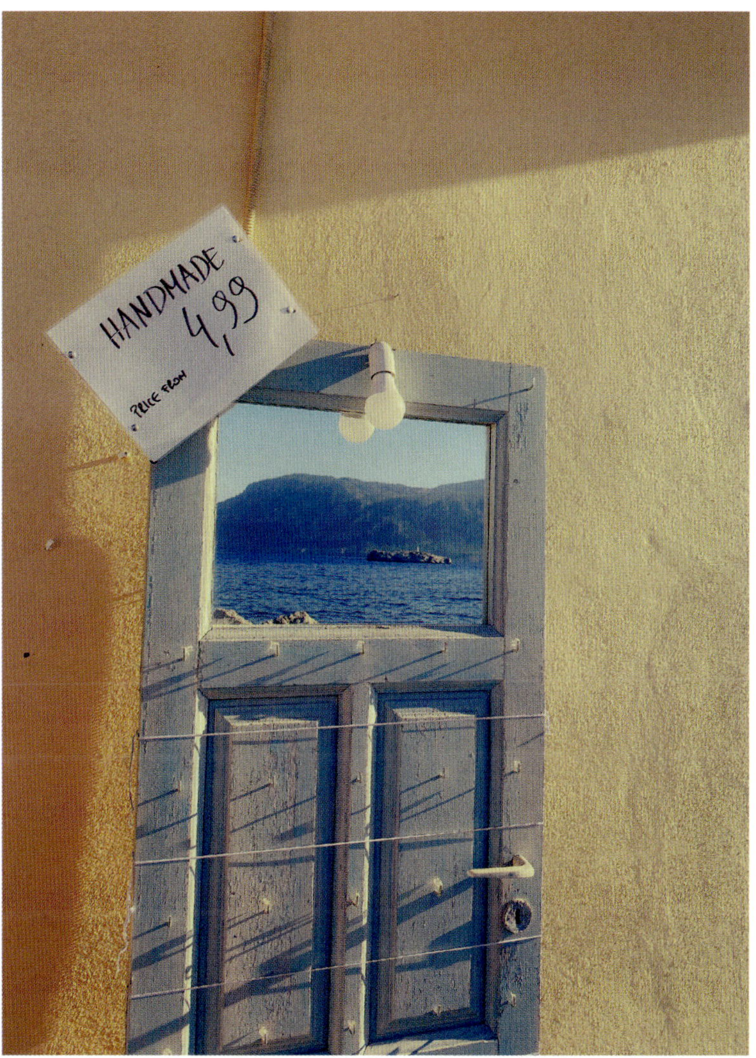

ABOVE: Many people were selling handicrafts here, and I was initially struck by the contrast between the blue door and the orange wall, amplified by the light of the setting sun. At the last minute I noticed the mirror above the door, reflecting a small island a few hundred metres away. I searched for a harmonious composition and was aided by the pipe on the wall and the geometry of the door itself.

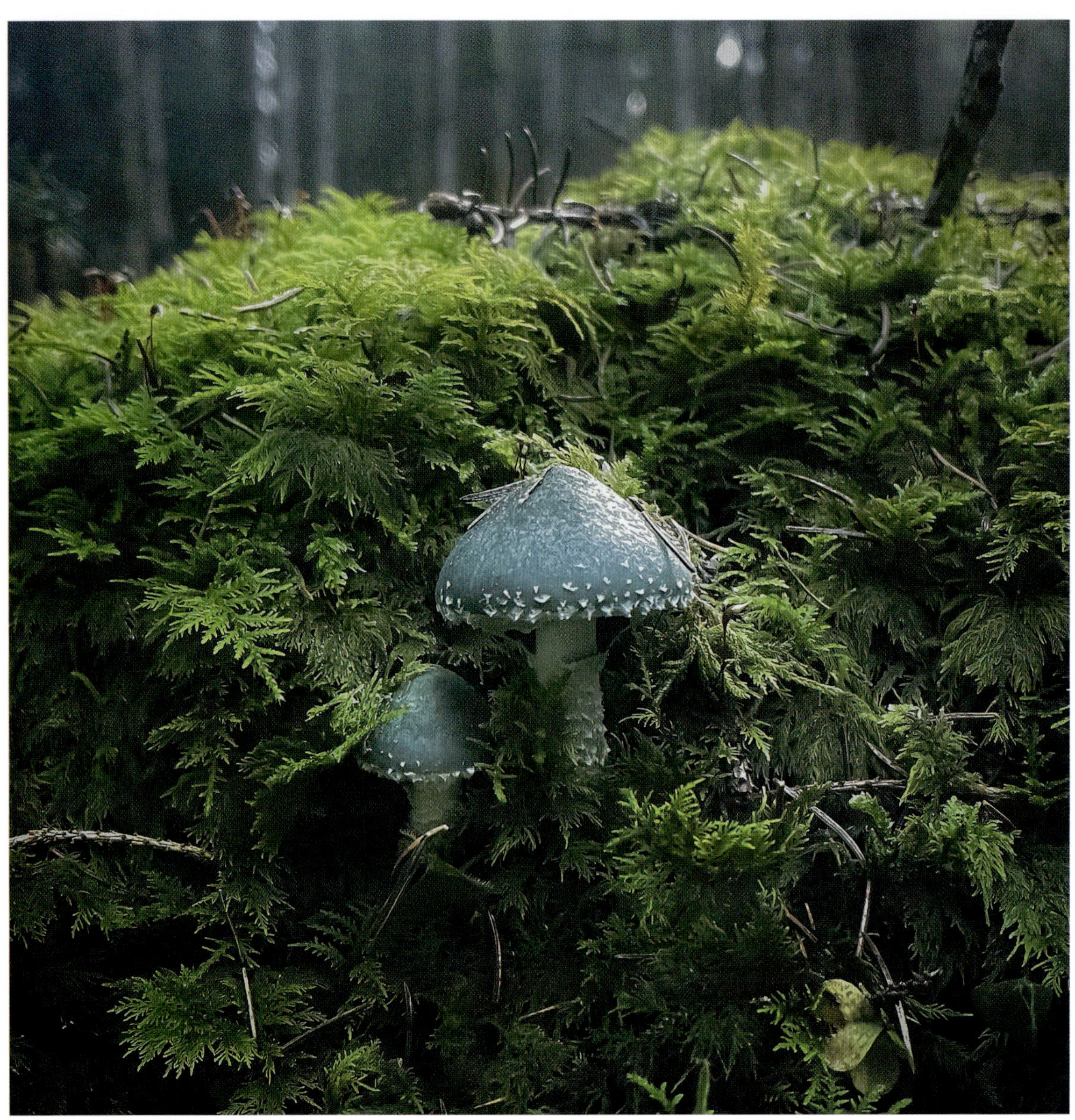

ABOVE: In autumn, when the
mushrooms are growing, I often go
for walks in the forest. I find looking
for mushrooms exciting as there
is such a great variety of shape
and colour. I found this pair of blue
mushrooms (verdigris agaric) in
a forest near Hörlkofen. I've never
seen mushrooms like these and
was fascinated by the turquoise
colour. I almost laid flat on the
ground to capture these beauties
nestled in the soft green moss.

Mariko Klug
Erding, Germany

ABOVE: I discovered this tree in the middle of a field in Niederwörth a few years ago. Since then I have visited it regularly. The night before I took this photo it was cold and very foggy. Being a fog lover, it was obvious that I had to visit the tree the next morning. When I arrived, the fog had lifted and the sky was blue. There it stood, my favourite tree, covered in hoar frost, a really otherworldly appearance. The blue sky made the perfect contrast.

Mariko Klug works part-time for a German airline at Munich Airport. She spends a lot of time outside in nature with her husband and her dog. Luckily, this combines well with her passion for photography. She started with an Apple iPhone 4 in 2011, and currently uses an iPhone 12 Pro Max.

Klug takes pictures using the native camera app or, in difficult lighting conditions, the ProCamera app. For basic editing (to adjust brightness, contrast, temperature, saturation and so on) she starts with Snapseed or Photoshop Express. To remove blemishes and small objects she uses TouchRetouch; to add or enhance light she uses Lens Distortions or LensLight; and for filters and textures, Picfx and Mextures. Her editing style has changed over the years. She used to edit a lot more than she does now, adding objects and applying textures. Nowadays she only uses a few apps for more or less basic editing.

All her pictures are square-format landscape and nature photos. This started years ago because she often used Hipstamatic to take pictures and, at that time, it was a square-format photo app. She also chases after the moody atmosphere of weather conditions such as fog, storm, frost and snow and at the golden hours (sunrise or sunset).

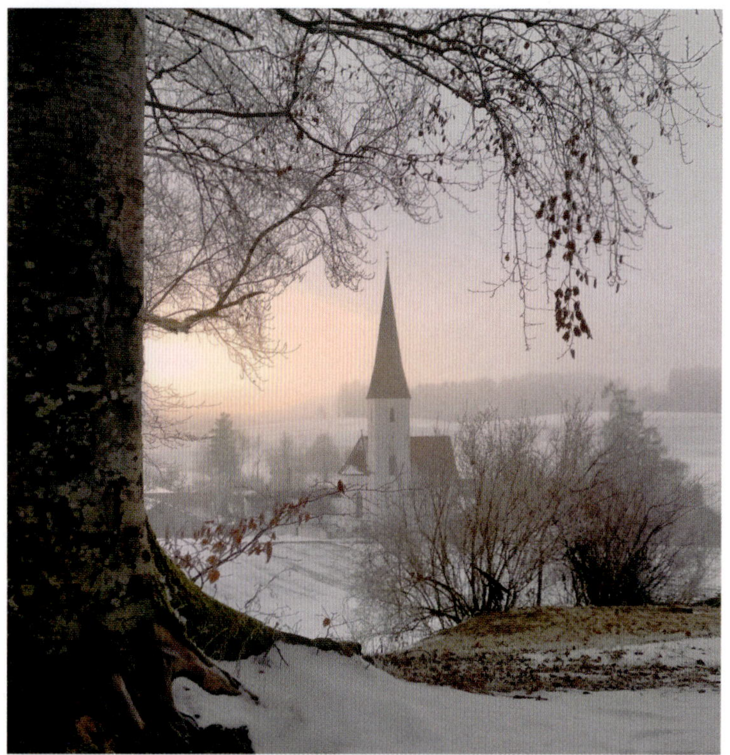

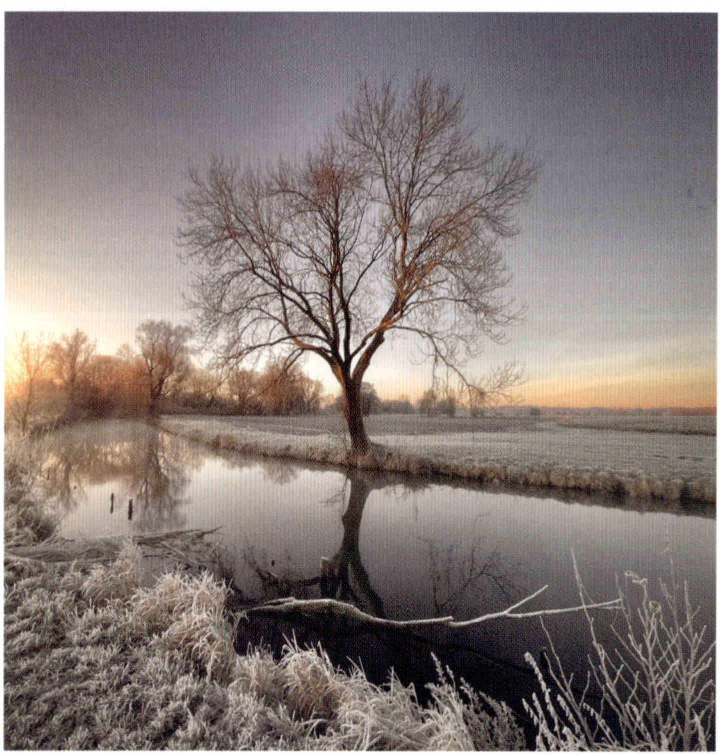

'Great photography is about depth of feeling, not depth of field.'

RIGHT: I love to capture the beauty of swans, they are so graceful and elegant. Sometimes I go to Lake Kronthaler in Erding to visit a pair of swans, which is what I did on this beautiful winter's morning. It was a very calm day, the fog was lifting and the sun beginning to rise. The swans noticed me on the shore and swam straight towards me, hoping to get something to eat. This was the moment I took the picture.

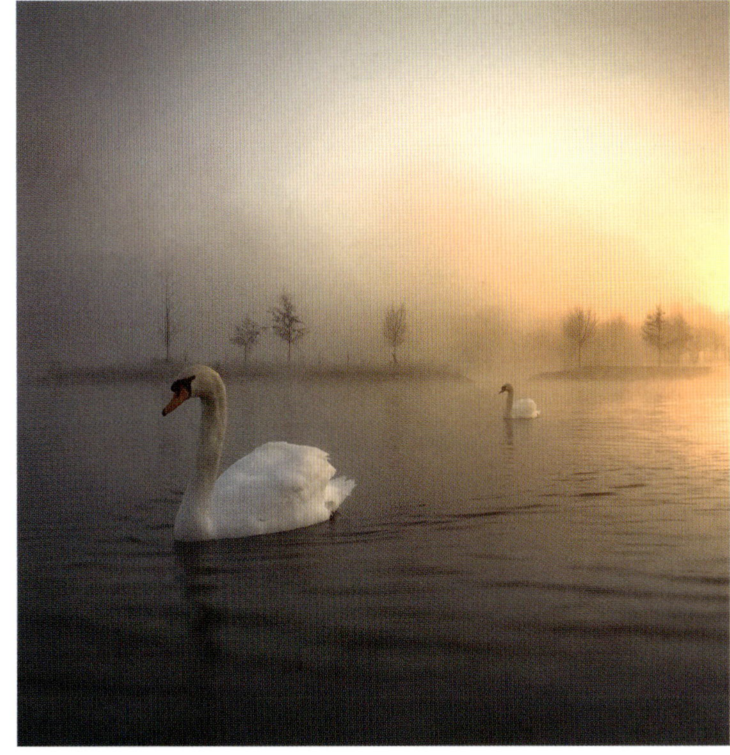

RIGHT: This path in Ebersberg passes an old linden tree with an inviting wooden bench beneath it. I love the peacefulness of this place. There are two old trees on a hill in the distance. The tree with its branches in the foreground creates a perfect natural frame for the hill and the trees. This photo is quite old, but it is still one of my favourites. It was taken in 2015 with an iPhone 5s.

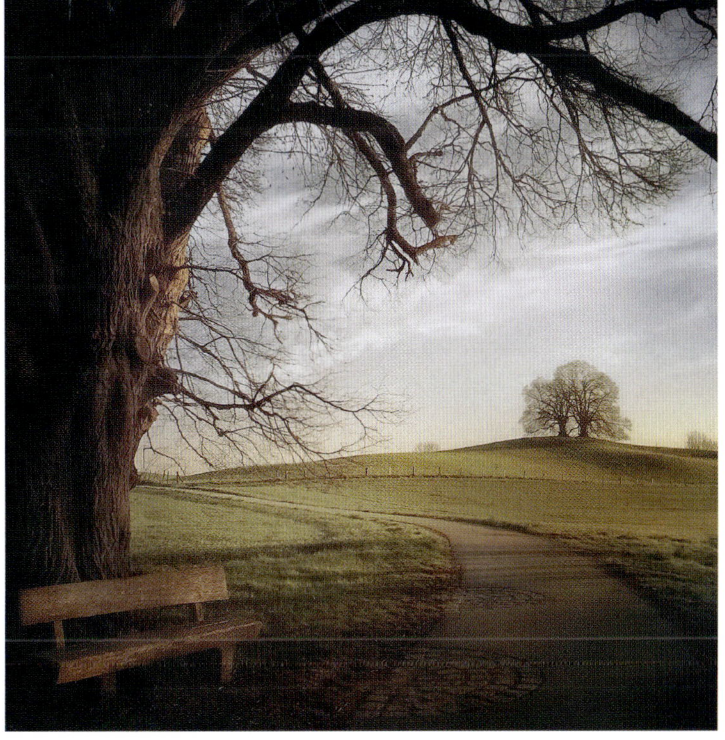

RIGHT: I passed this bench
while walking up the hill to the
chapel in Salmendingen. The
fog was dense on that autumn
day, softening and muting the
intense colours of the leaves.
I loved the lonesome mood of
the wooden bench under the
beech tree. I stood there for a
while, taking pictures until I
managed to catch some
falling leaves.

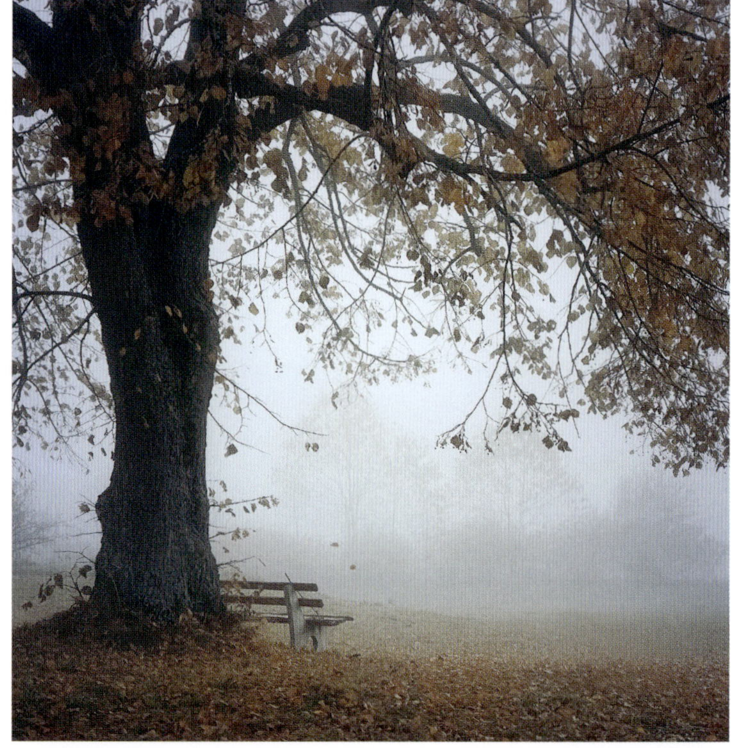

RIGHT: This avenue of old oak
trees is one of many beautiful
spots around Lake Egglburg in
Ebersberg. For the best light
conditions I went there in the
early morning. I was not only
rewarded with the beautiful
autumn colours, but there
were also soft sun rays shining
through the trees. It was almost
magical.

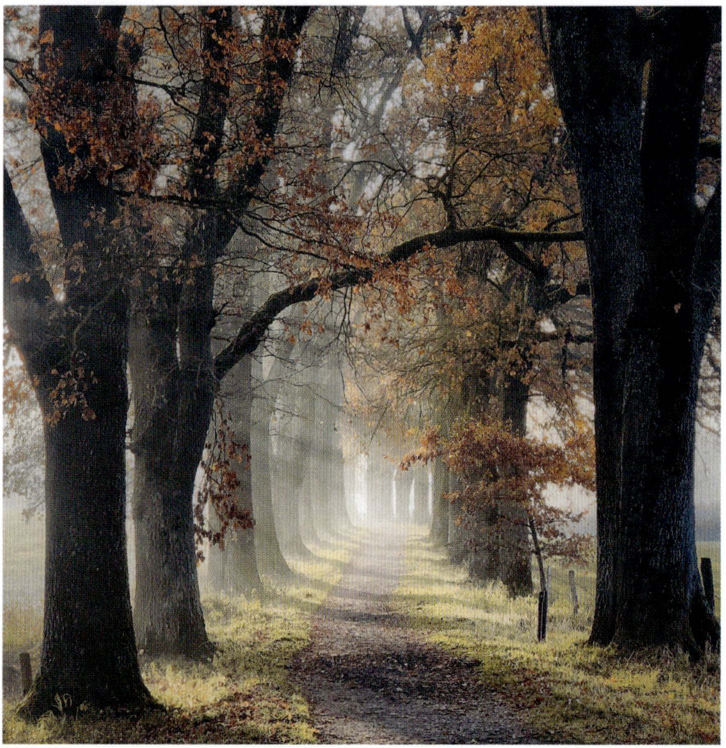

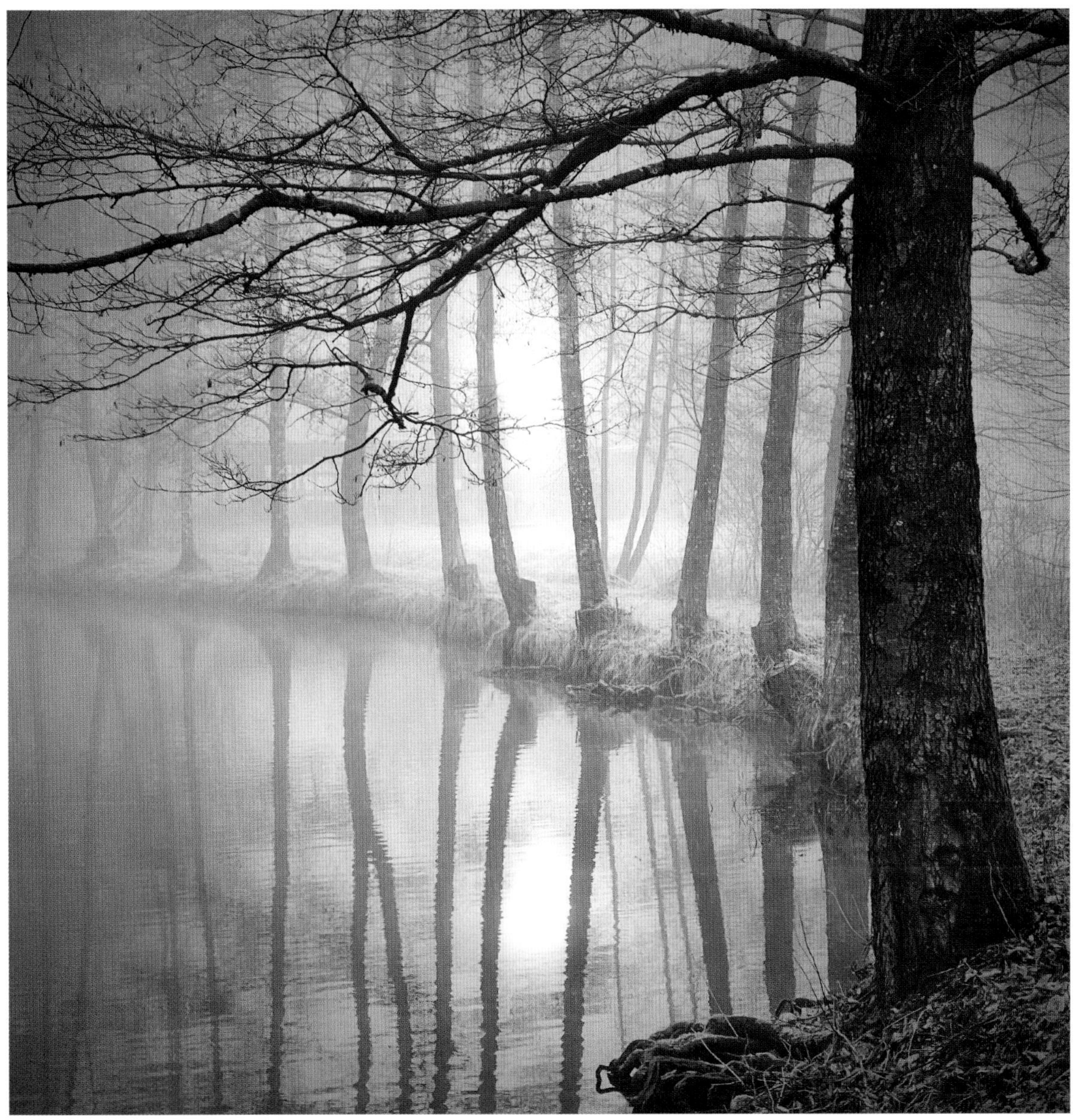

'Photography is not about the gear you use.
An image has to tell a story and evoke emotions.
Expensive equipment is not necessary for this.'

ABOVE: This is a fishpond near Forstinning, close to the source of the River Sempt. Because of the high water quality, trout are bred everywhere in this area. On this cold winter morning I was watching the trout in the clear water, when I noticed the reflection of the trees surrounding the pond. The sun broke through the mist and created a beautiful surreal atmosphere.

MARIKO KLUG

Martina Loiola
Lecce, Italy

Freelance photographer, videographer and art director Martina Loiola lives on the 'heel of the boot' on the Italian map. She feels lucky because photography is both her passion and her job. She mostly shoots on an Apple iPhone 13 and edits with VSCO, often using pre-sets she has created for her own unique look and style. Drawn to scenes of ordinary life, Loiola looks for perfect geometry and symmetry, light, muted pastel colours, and unusual subjects.

RIGHT: I love weird things located in the middle of nowhere. This shot of a petrol station made me go back in time. Its vintage vibes and colours are what made me capture it.

RIGHT: I spent all my childhood summers in the seaside town of Torre Chianca. I go there on winter Sundays to take a refreshing walk, and this photo was taken during one of those walks. I simply saw this sweet lady sitting by the shore and I was drawn to the contrasting colours of her outfit and the sea, and the simplicity of that moment.

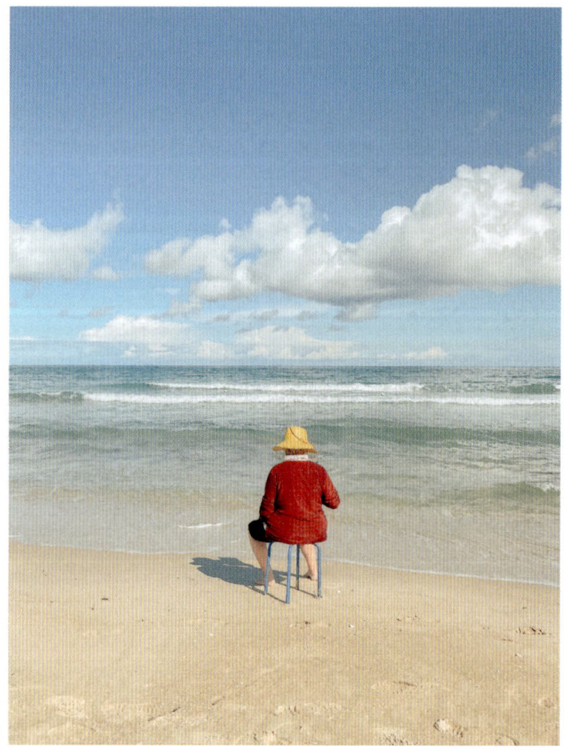

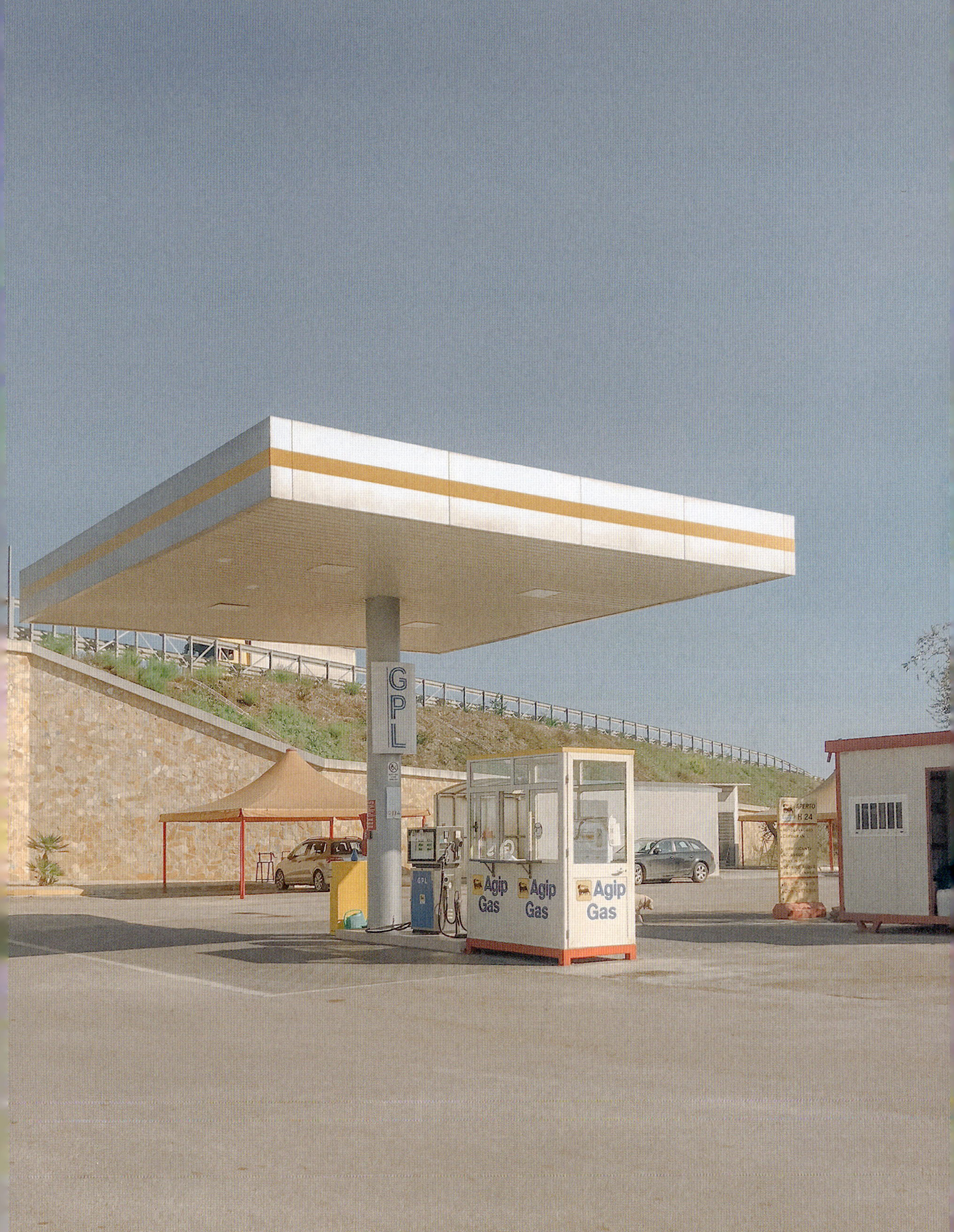
GPL
Agip
Gas
Agip
Gas
Agip
Gas
GPL
APERTO
H 24

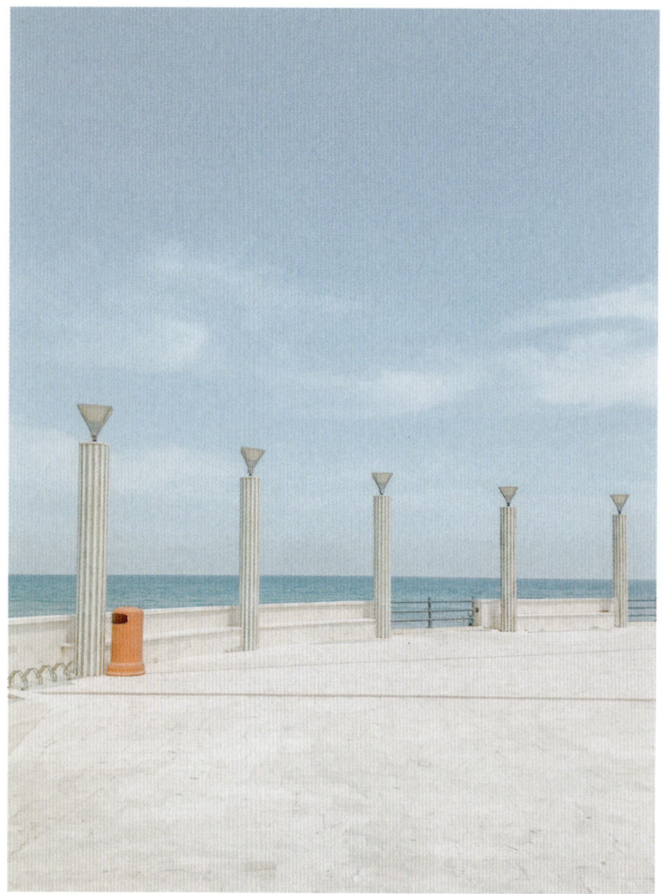

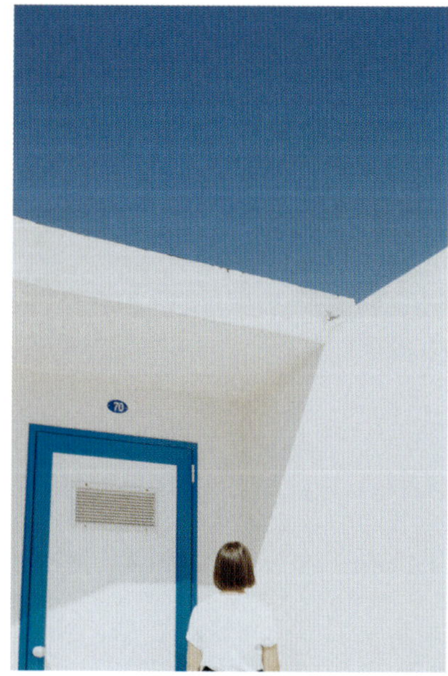

'I mostly shoot my photos with my iPhone
13. It only takes one minute to find
inspiration wherever I am, and I always
feel free to shoot what I like.'

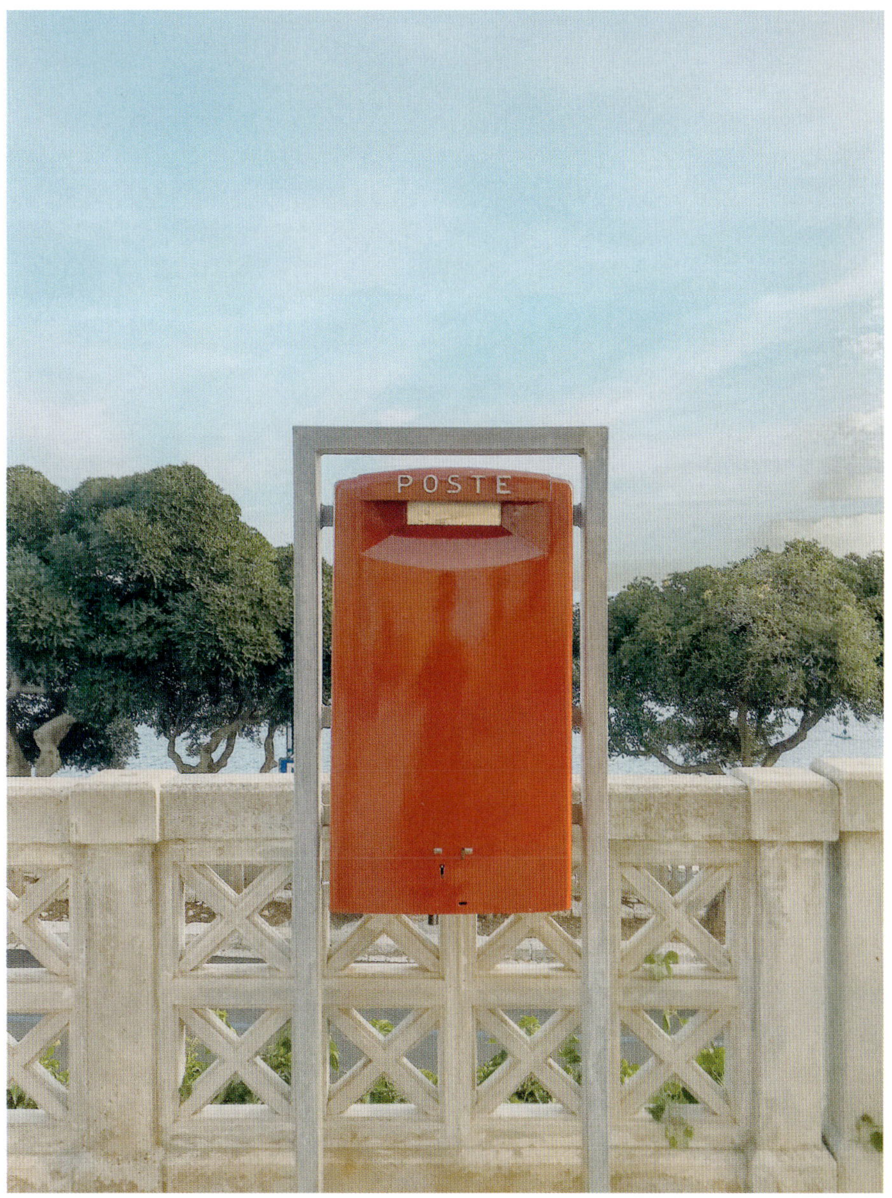

ABOVE: Wes Anderson is my favourite film director. I feel I have his same taste for colour, atypical scenery and symmetrical designs. Today, a public post box is a very rare find. Therefore, when I saw one in Santa Cesarea Terme I couldn't resist taking this photo – a reminder of the past that needs to be preserved.

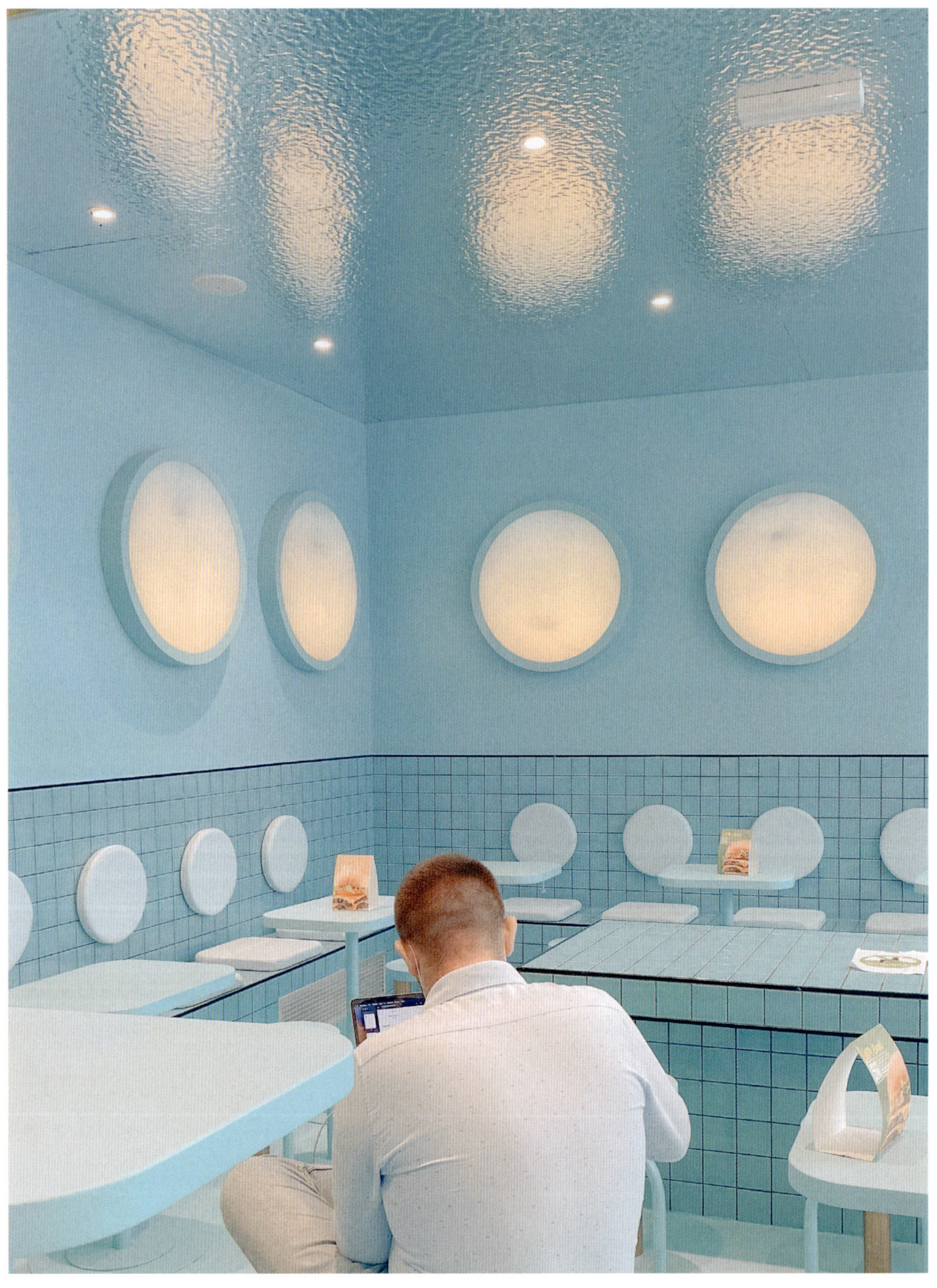

LEFT: I lived in Turin for a year, and this pool-like bar is one of my favourite places in the city. When I saw this man with a shirt which matched the walls, and the perfect geometry of the circular windows, I had to take this photo.

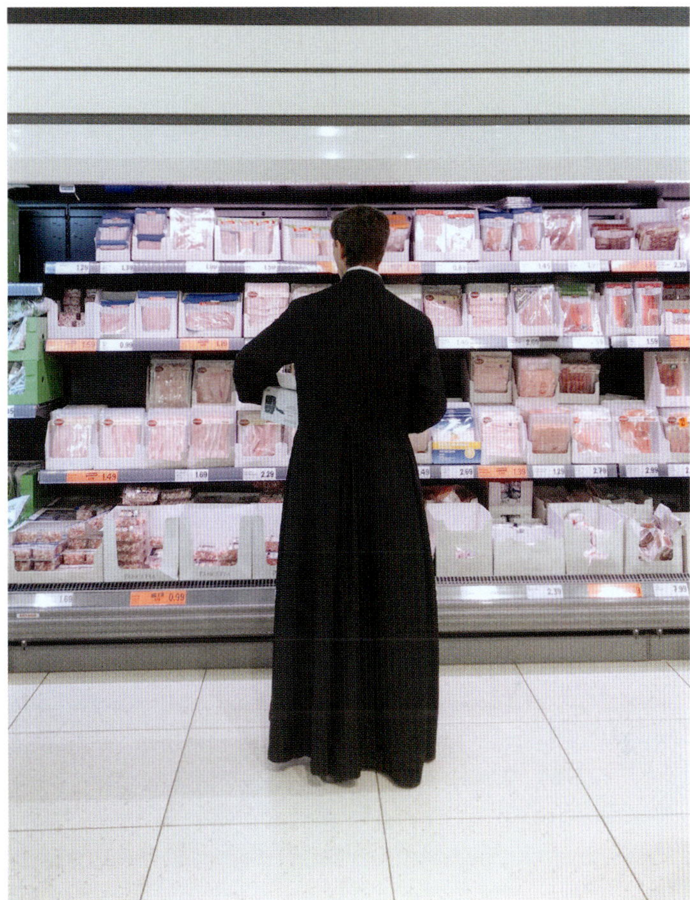

ABOVE: I love to shoot people and objects in places where you wouldn't usually find them. A priest buying prosciutto; a toy's leg in the middle of the beach; a Virgin Mary statue near a switchboard. It seems like something that needs to be documented.

BELOW: I always look at this spot in Torre Chianca, where I spent my childhood summers. I felt really sad during the winter when the traffic mirror was surrounded by the pruned empty branches. Finally, one spring I was there at the perfect moment to capture this scene full of life and colour.

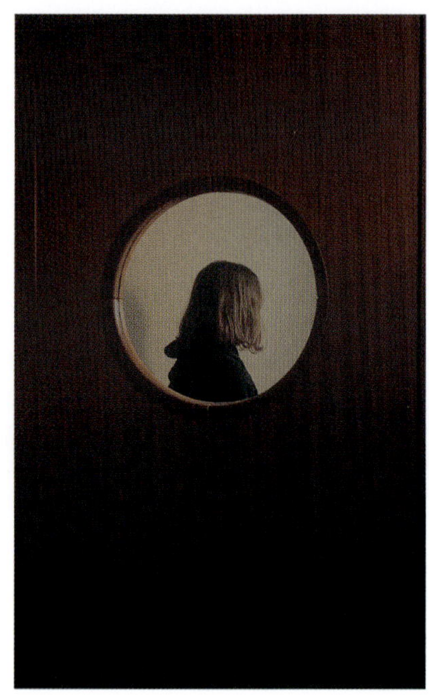

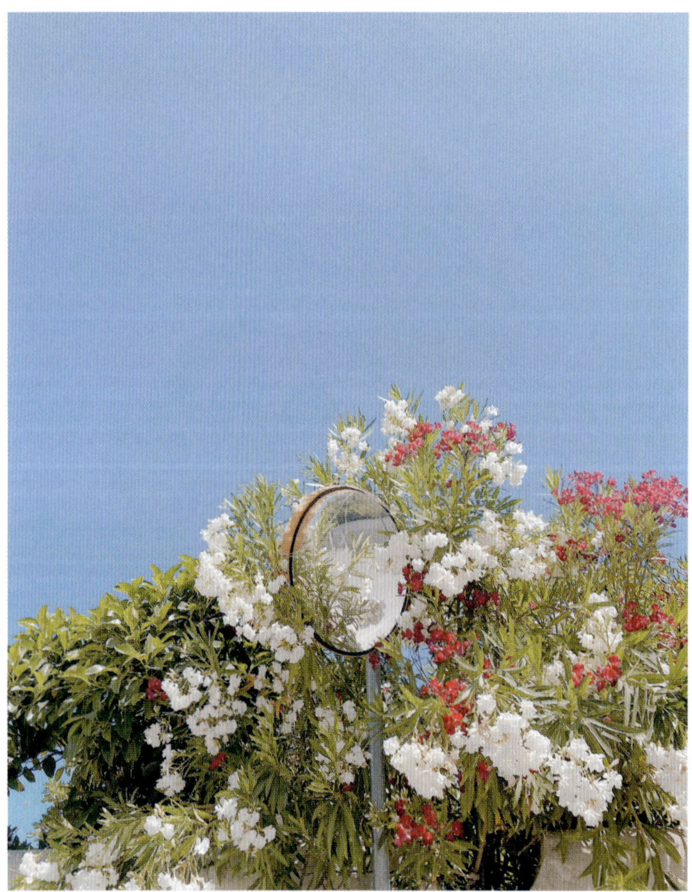

ABOVE: This may look like the door of a cruise ship, but it is actually the door of a cinema, the DB d'Essai, in my home city, Lecce. The owner of the cinema is pictured in the shot and I feel it is a very intimate and mysterious shot, just like the atmosphere there.

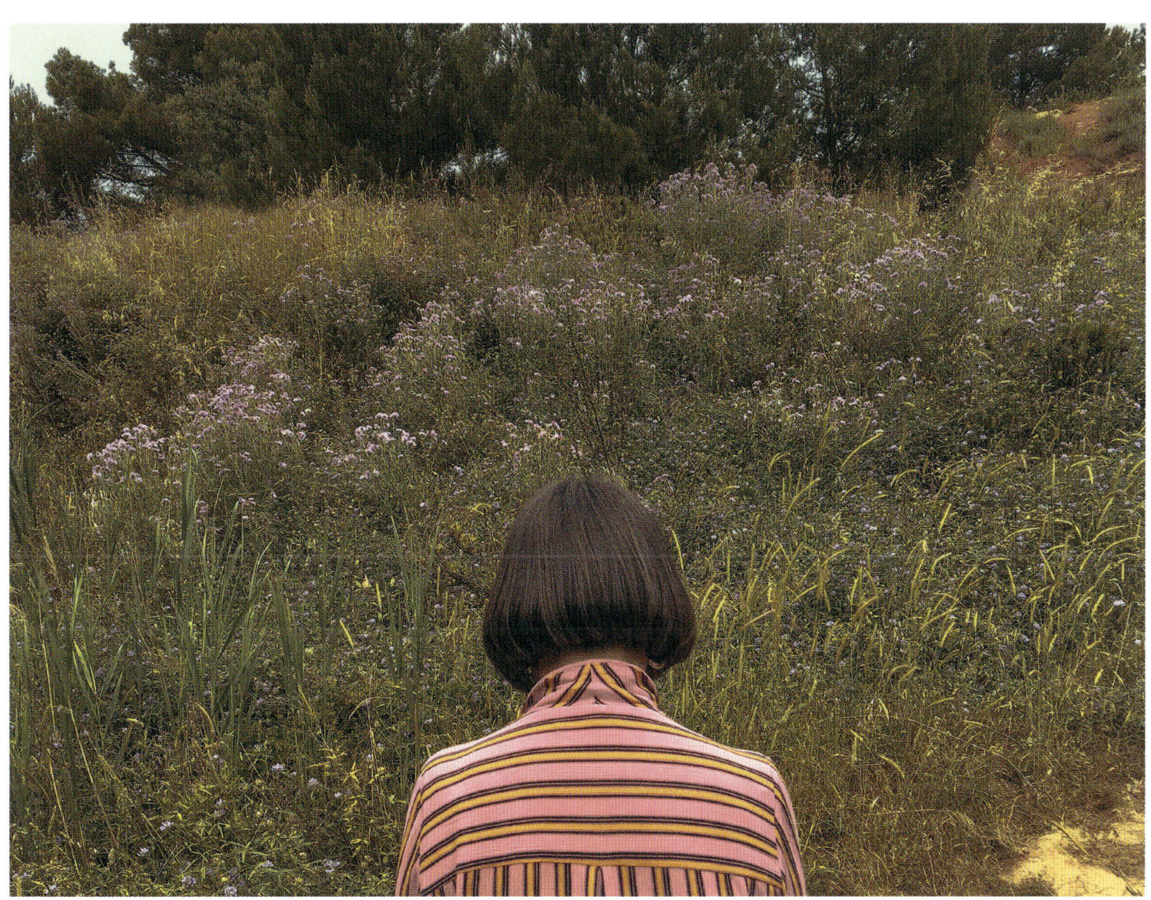

ABOVE: My best friend Chiara is one of my most common subjects. I often shoot her from behind when she is looking at a pretty landscape so that the view she is looking at forms the background of the photo. This is at the Bauxite Cave of Otranto.

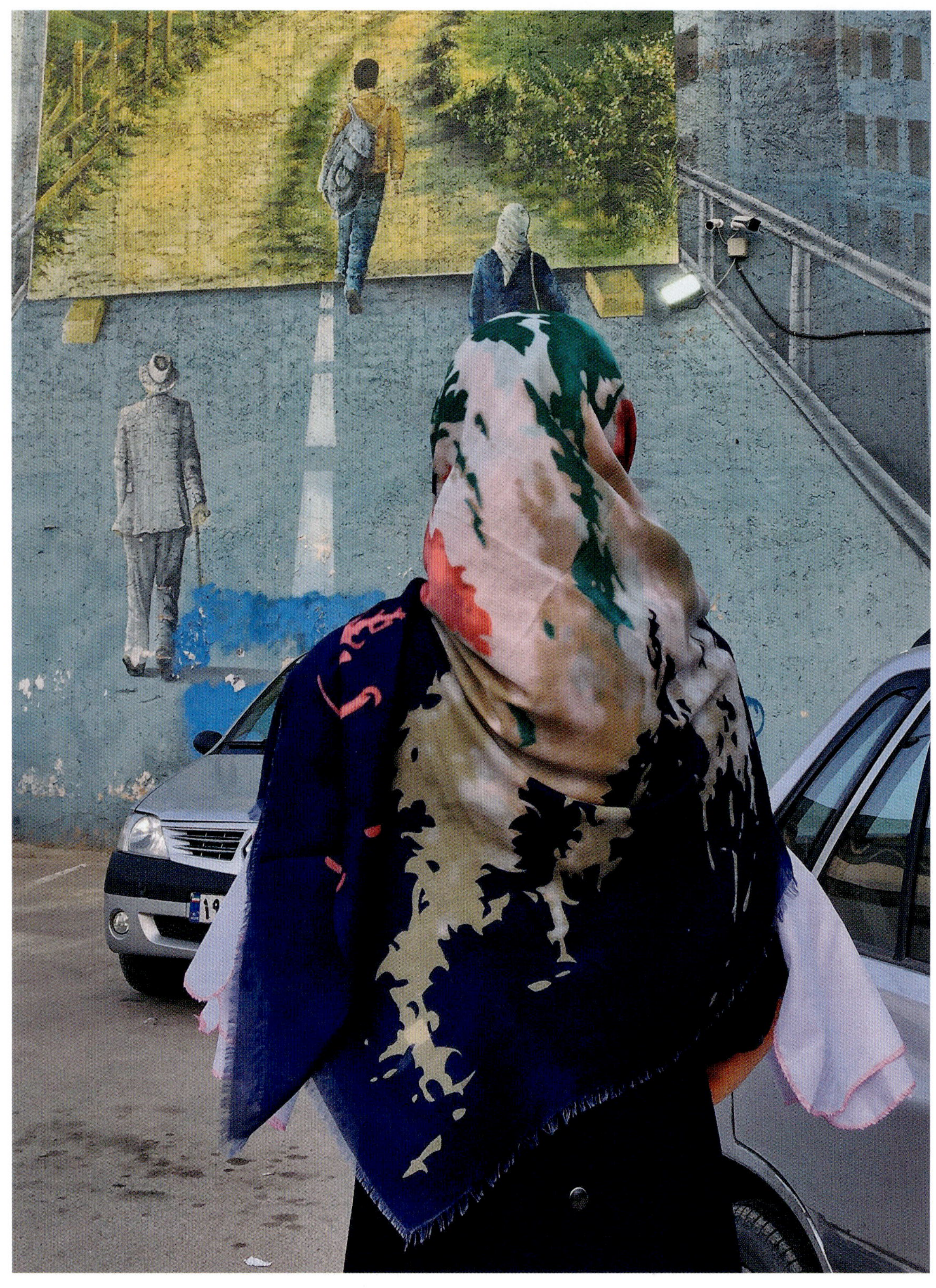

Mehrnoush Negahdari
Shiraz, Iran

Mehrnoush Negahdari works in Shiraz's free public library. It is part of the Shiraz Art House, which consists of a gallery, library and café. The goal of its founder is to promote art and culture and people have the opportunity to spend time in the gallery looking at art and visit the library and café too. Negahdari habitually walks around the city, roaming the streets, and finds that photography complements this activity. She enjoys the environment and the people she sees on her photographic walks.

Negahdari shoots with an Apple iPhone 6s with a 12 megapixel camera, and is interested in social documentary photography. She says that in the photographic process, regardless of the type of tool used, seeing and experiencing an event, and capturing it faithfully in that particular moment is important to her. Negahdari edits in Lightroom, Snapseed and Photoshop Express.

LEFT: I had almost got home after work when I saw this person. I don't know her, but I felt she was going into the world shown in the wall painting. I really liked that it got my imagination going. I took the picture so I could share my experience of seeing it with others. Shiraz has many examples of wall art like this. Most of the paintings are created at the request of the city authorities. They are usually signed at the bottom by the artist, but most of them are not well-known enough to be recognized.

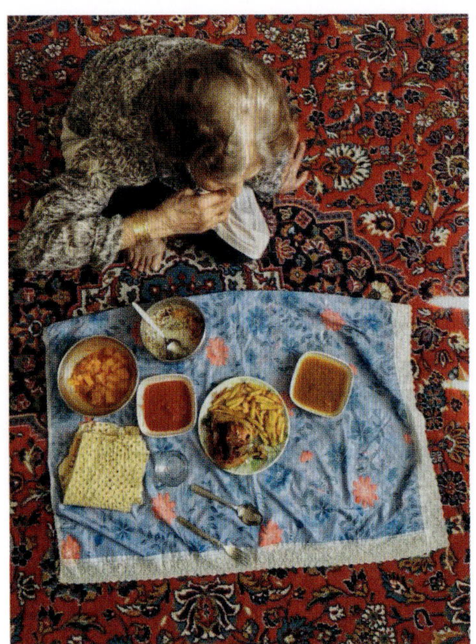

LEFT: This is my grandmother at her house. She is 87 years old. I was there to have lunch with her. I am frightened of losing her and being deprived of her presence, so I have decided to take pictures of her and the moments we spend together. I love the feeling that my grandmother is waiting for me to join her. I eat lunch with her once week. That day we ate barberry rice with chicken.

RIGHT: On Zand Street in Shiraz this man makes money by weighing people. Seeing his creative way of making a living, I decided to weigh myself to help him on the path he has chosen. When I got on the scale, I decided to take a picture of the deal. There is no set rate for this kind of service, the money received depends on the customer. I don't usually weigh myself, and my weight has always been consistent, so I wasn't surprised by the result but I was glad to be his customer.

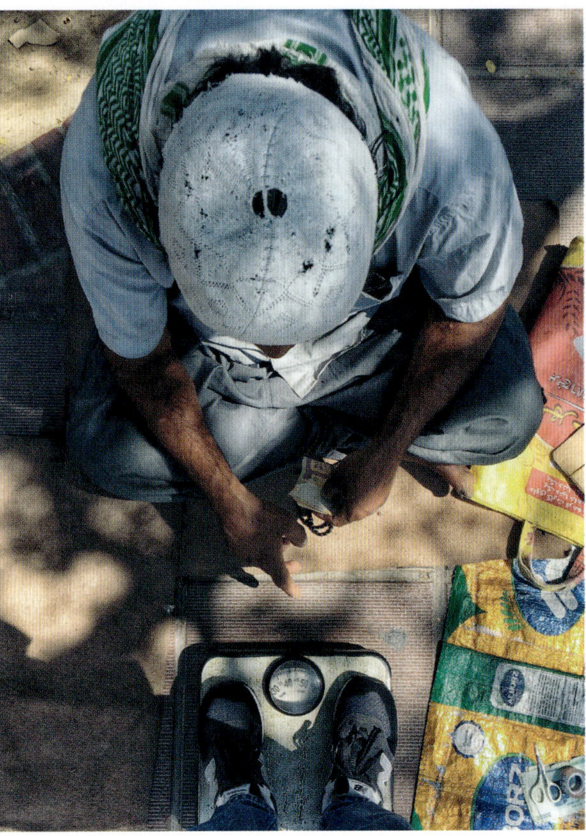

OPPOSITE: Close to home on my return from work, this stranger's interesting style made me want to take a photo of her. I love the sense of movement in this picture.

VIEWPOINT

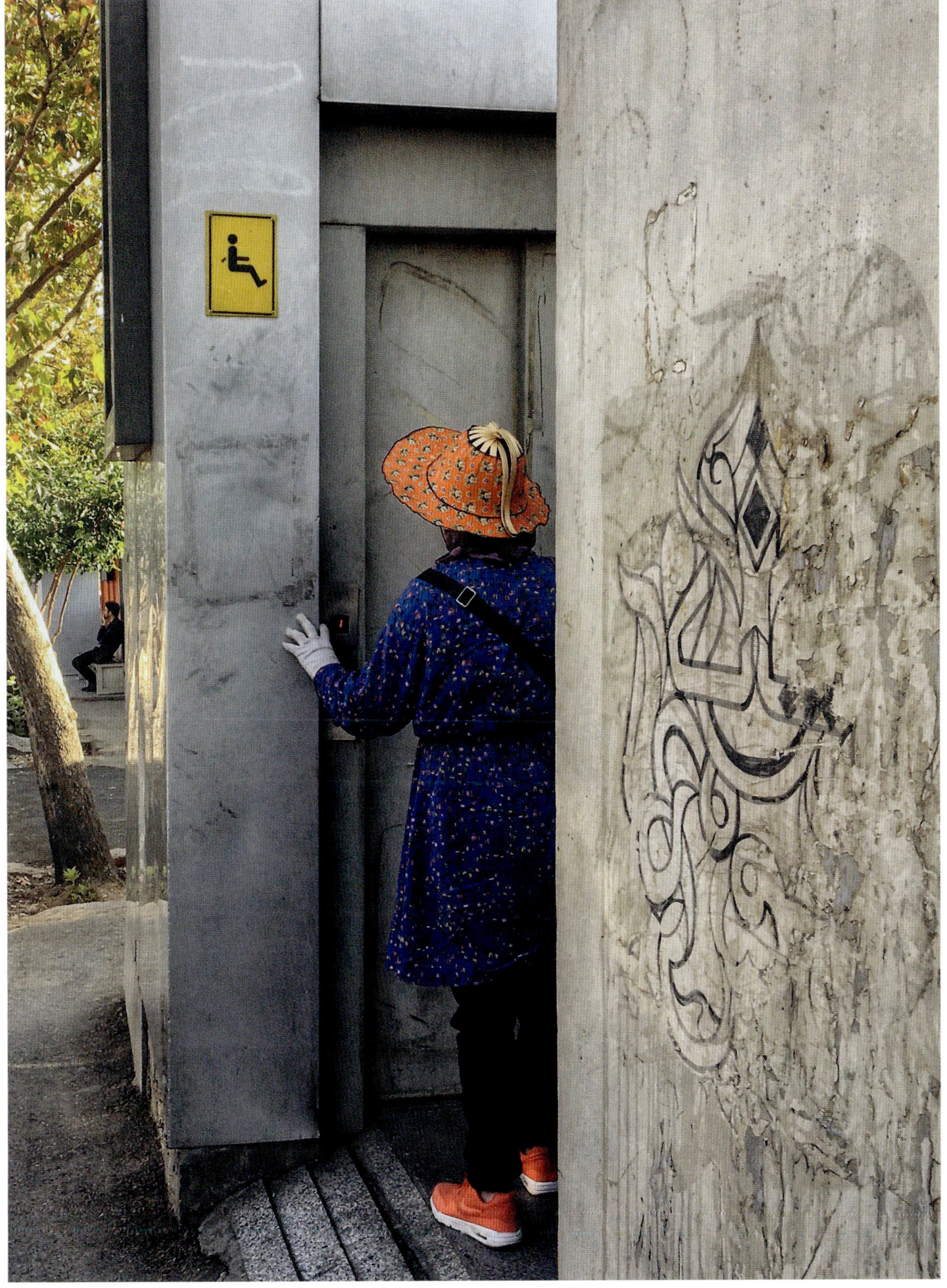

MEHRNOUSH NEGAHDARI

 A recess in a wall where a dead duckling has been placed. The wall belongs to a pet shop in the centre of Shiraz, where birds and animals are kept in large numbers in a small space with insufficient food. Every creature that dies due to these unfavourable conditions is separated from the other animals and birds. Seeing this scene reminded me that we no longer fear nature and have come to dominate it, and that this has gone beyond the stage of exploitation for our basic needs, leading to the indiscriminate use of natural resources in the form of silent violence.

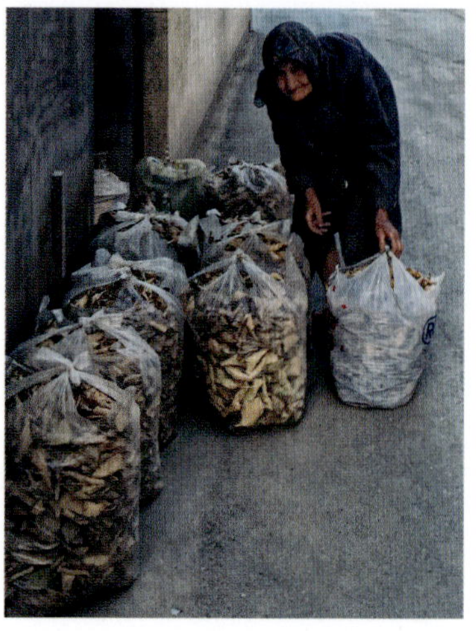

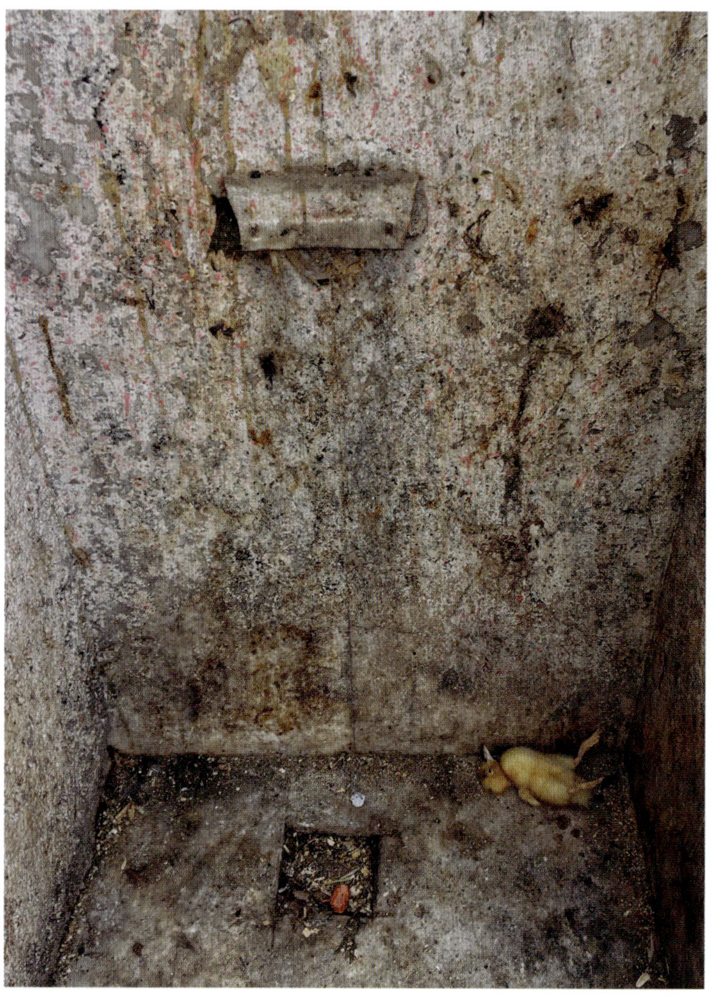

ABOVE: I was exploring the streets of Shiraz when I saw this lady and the quantity of dry leaves she had collected. In Iran, there are old houses with large yards and gardens planted with orange trees. In the autumn, the dry leaves are collected so that the plants can breathe better. Seeing the bags of leaves made me think about how much time the lady had spent on the work and how the volume of leaves seemed to be a symbol of the time spent. It was valuable for me to see a clear example of someone who understood nature. Unfortunately, due to the amount of new construction, the number of these houses with gardens has decreased.

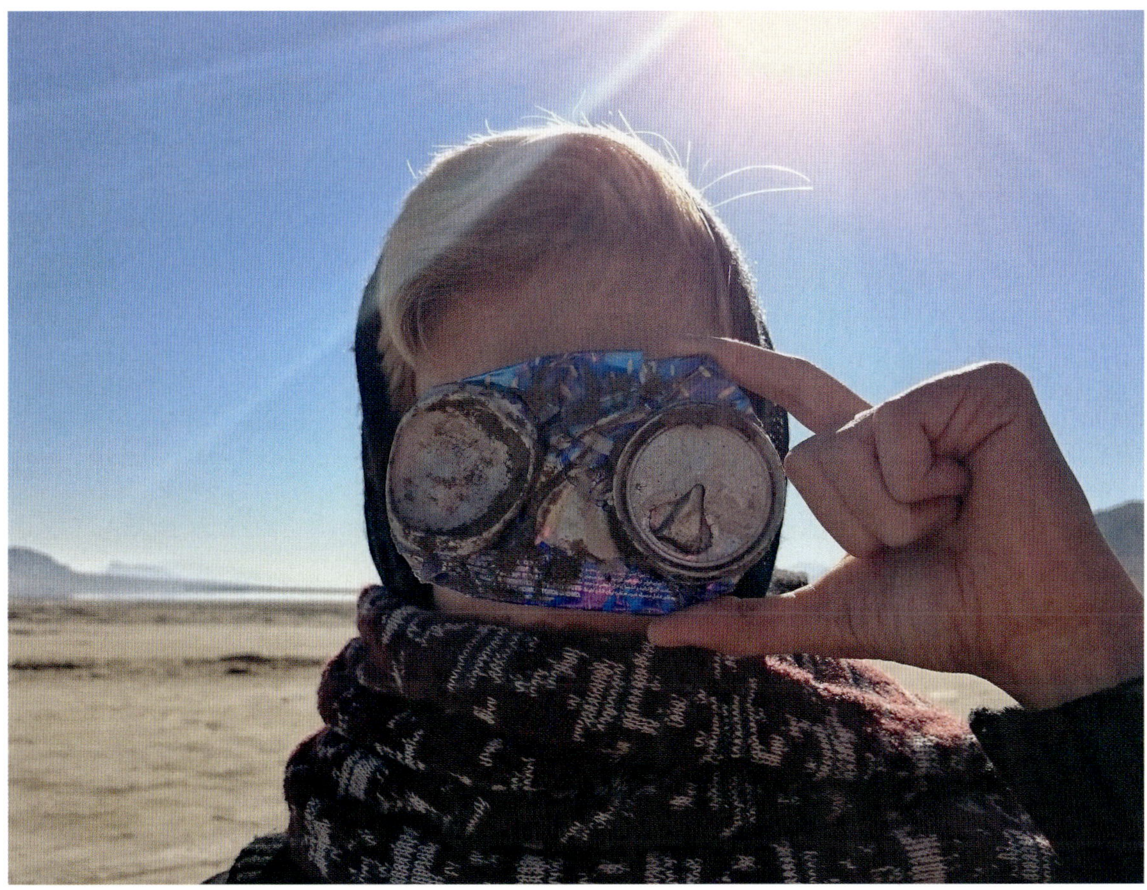

ABOVE: I was visiting this salt lake near Shiraz one weekend for pleasure. There was so much rubbish lying around that I decided to take this selfie with a crushed drink can that looked like goggles. I like it because it is really different to any selfie I have ever taken before.

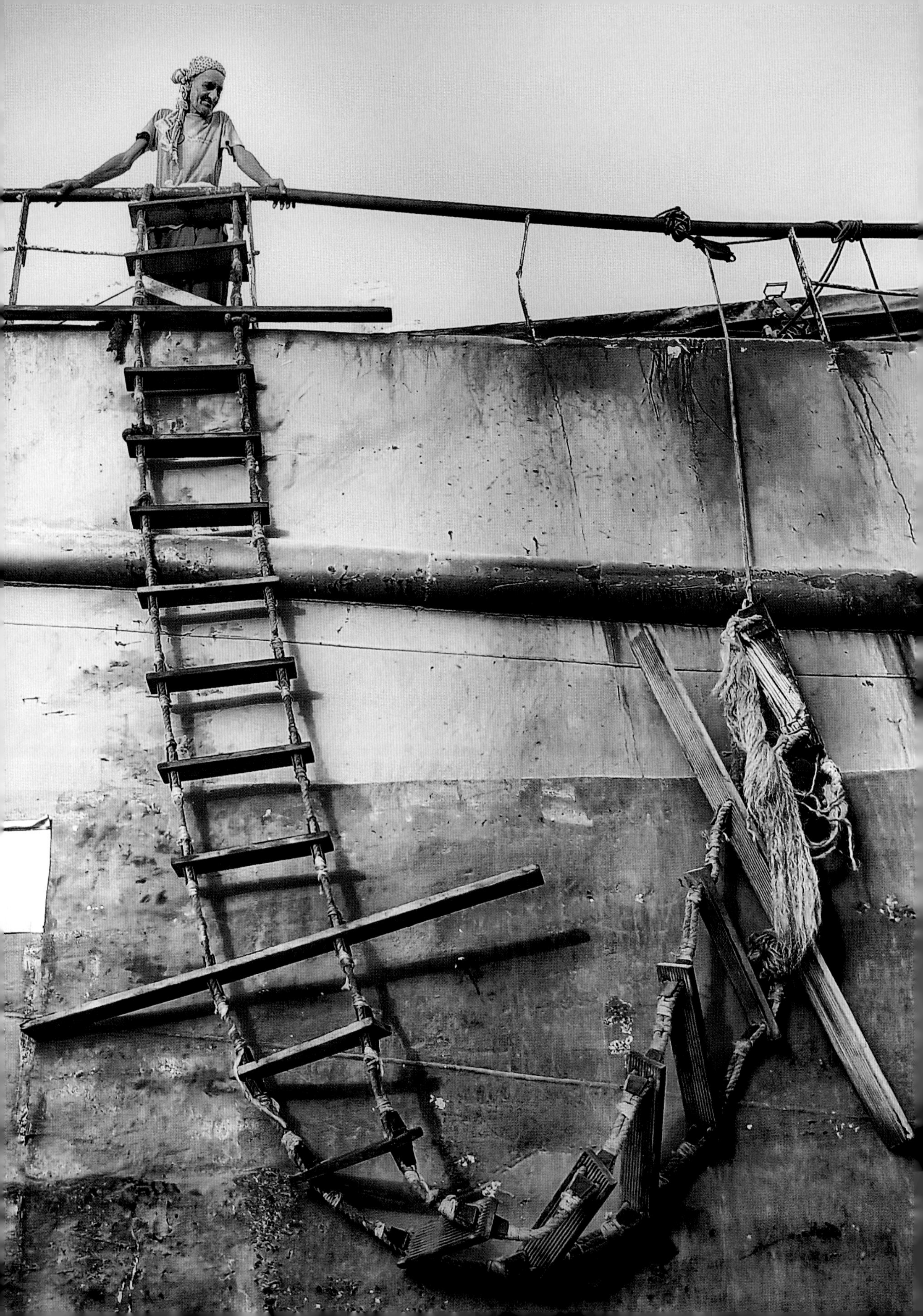

Mobin Mayeli
Bandar Abbas (Gambron), Iran

LEFT: In the early 2000s, following huge investment into the area to support energy supplies for China, Chinese fishing vessels started trawling in the Persian Gulf. China was seeking to catch sufficient fish to meet the demands of its large and growing population. But this meant that local fishermen, like the one here fishing out of Gambron, were able to catch fewer and fewer fish. I used to visit the beach every day to capture this depressing decline. The fisherman has just returned from the sea and appears lost in thought as he mournfully observes his empty fishing nets. I wanted to convey the sense of sorrow conveyed in this picture marking this specific period of the country's history.

As a young person and new photographer, Mobin Mayeli has never actually owned a digital camera and has only ever used his smartphone to take photos. He works in a photographic laboratory checking and printing photos for exhibitions and shows, and has no interest in expensive photographic tools and the burden of owning equipment beyond what he needs to capture his point of view and share it with others. Mayeli finds immense peace through practising the art and action of photography in his daily life. As such, he is a constant photographer. A keen walker, he makes photography that leans towards street and documentary styles. He attempts to capture moments in the lives of the people around him. Mayeli is also a big movie fan; he makes a conscious effort to compose his photos to look like cinematic film stills. Through his photography he provides an unsentimental view of life, the people and all aspects of his home city.

'I have a sentence that I always repeat: "The train goes and the rail stays, death comes, and the memory remains." I always repeat this sentence, because everything will change, and our photos will remain to show the history of a city and a country.'

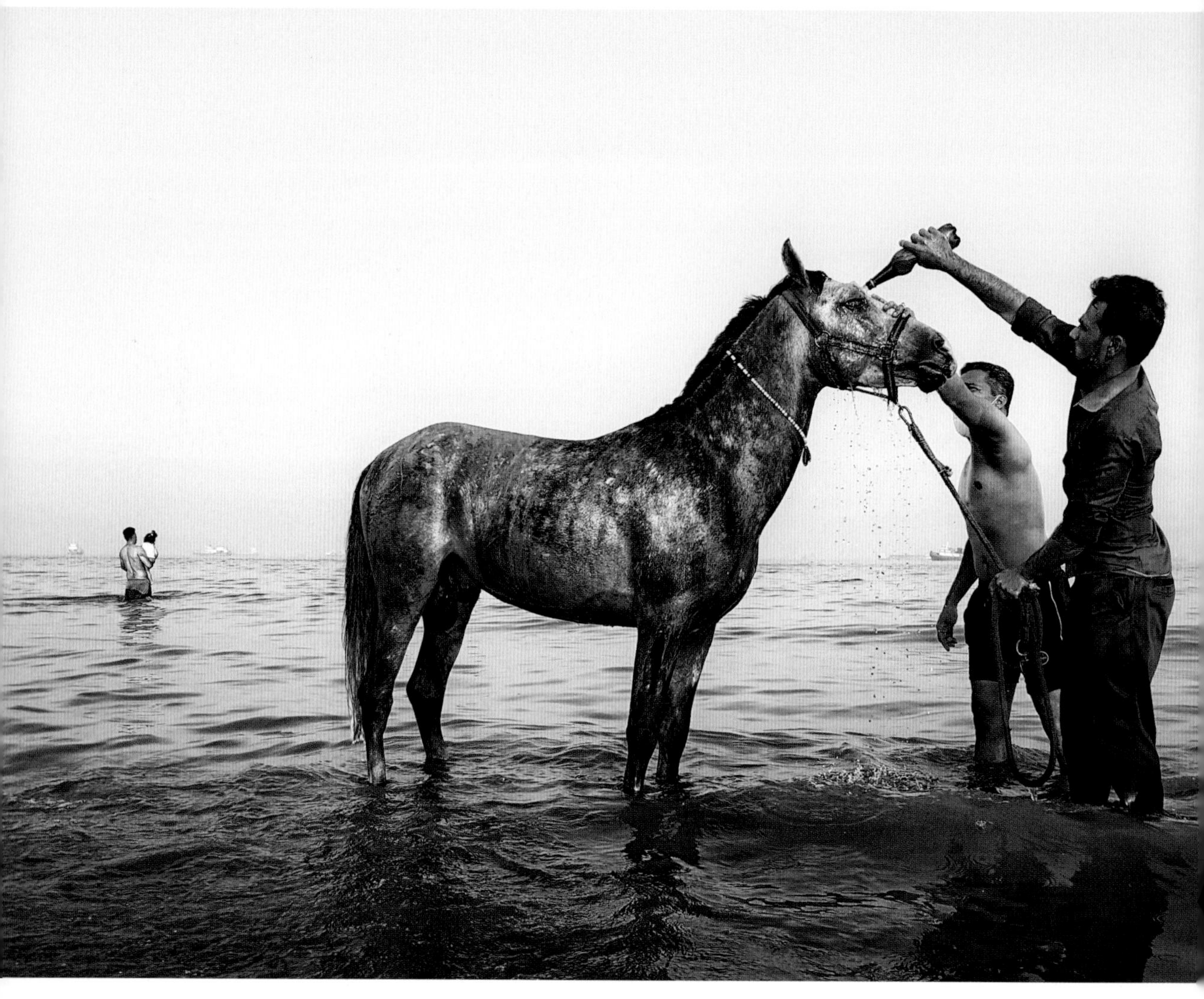

ABOVE: A man bathes his horse at the end of a day's work on a spring day in Gambron. It is often hot during the spring and it is not surprising to see horses on the shore. Their owners make a living by offering visitors a short ride or the opportunity to have their photo taken with the horses. This photo documents a way of life in the south of Iran.

RIGHT: I had gone to the beach
with my friends and we were
delighted by the mild weather.
I was drawn to the young boy
playing on the beach. His direct
eye contact seems to make the
viewer stare back at him.

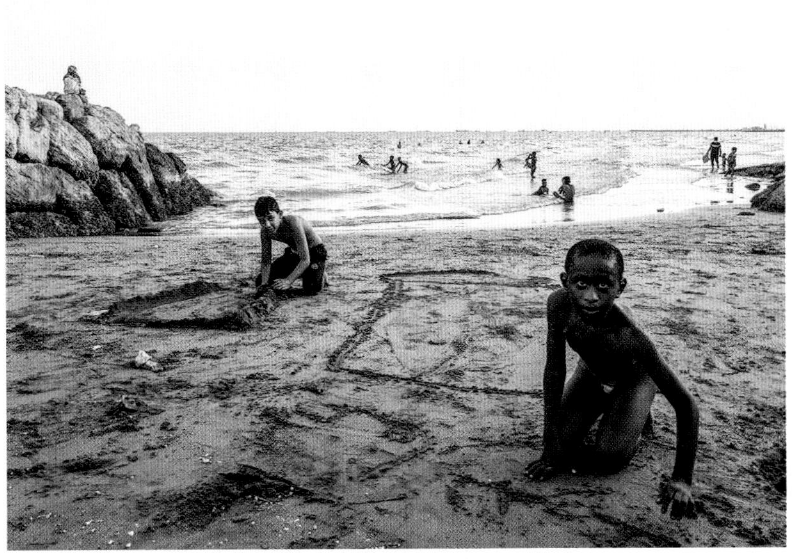

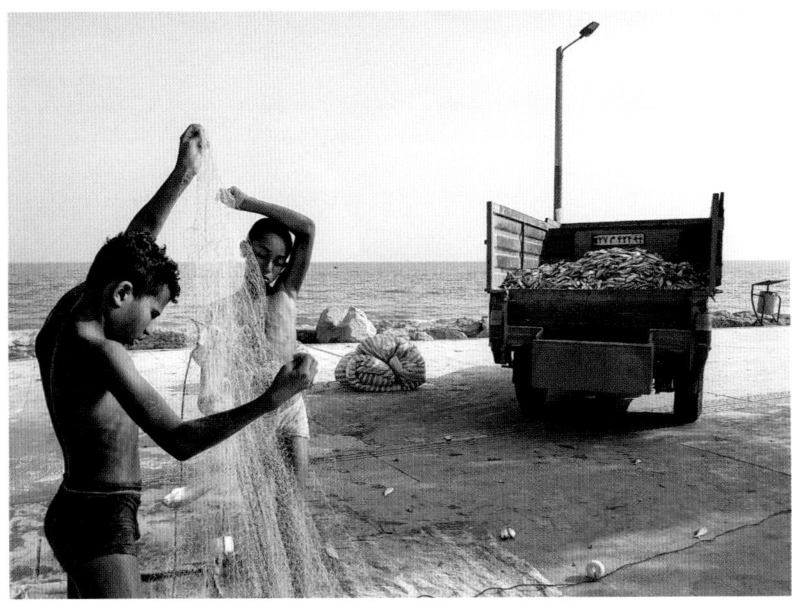

LEFT: I was walking along the
beach in Gambron. The fishing
boats had come back from
the sea and the children were
detaching the fish from the
nets. I was captivated by this
old method of fishing and it
made me think about how
it might be neglected and
ultimately forgotten in years
to come.

Mohammad Nazari
Zanjan, Iran

Mohammad Nazari works in the support department of a road construction project, and is consumed by photography. In his spare time he takes photos with his mobile phone. He likes to plan his photographs beforehand – they come from his subconscious. Nazari says that he sees himself in all his photo stories, so his relationship with them is the same as his relationship with himself. Nazari is especially interested in fog, snow and winter; he wants people to feel the cold in his photos. Horses are a signature of his work. He stages his photos using his friends and their horses as subjects that look like illustrations from folk stories or cinematic stills.

RIGHT: I saw this girl during a religious ceremony that is held in Zanjan, northern Iran, every year to commemorate the anniversary of the martyrdom of Imam Hussein. The ceremony is held at the Great Husseiniya of Zanjan on the eight day of Muharram – the first month of the Islamic calendar. This little girl was without a hijab in the crowd, a unique scene.

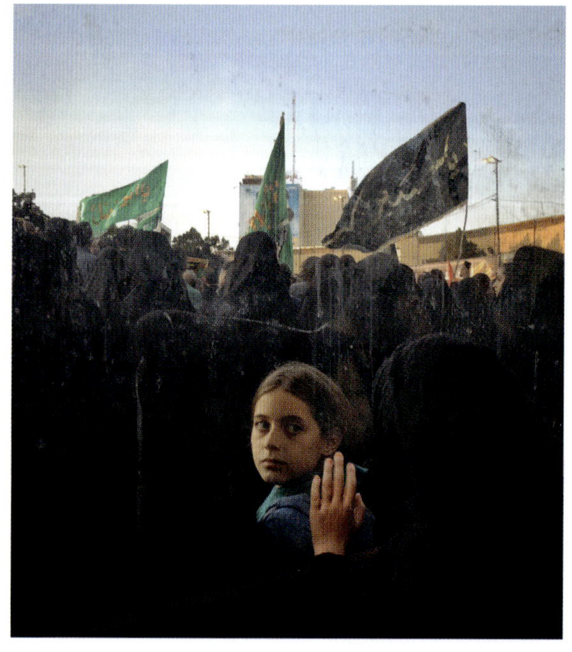

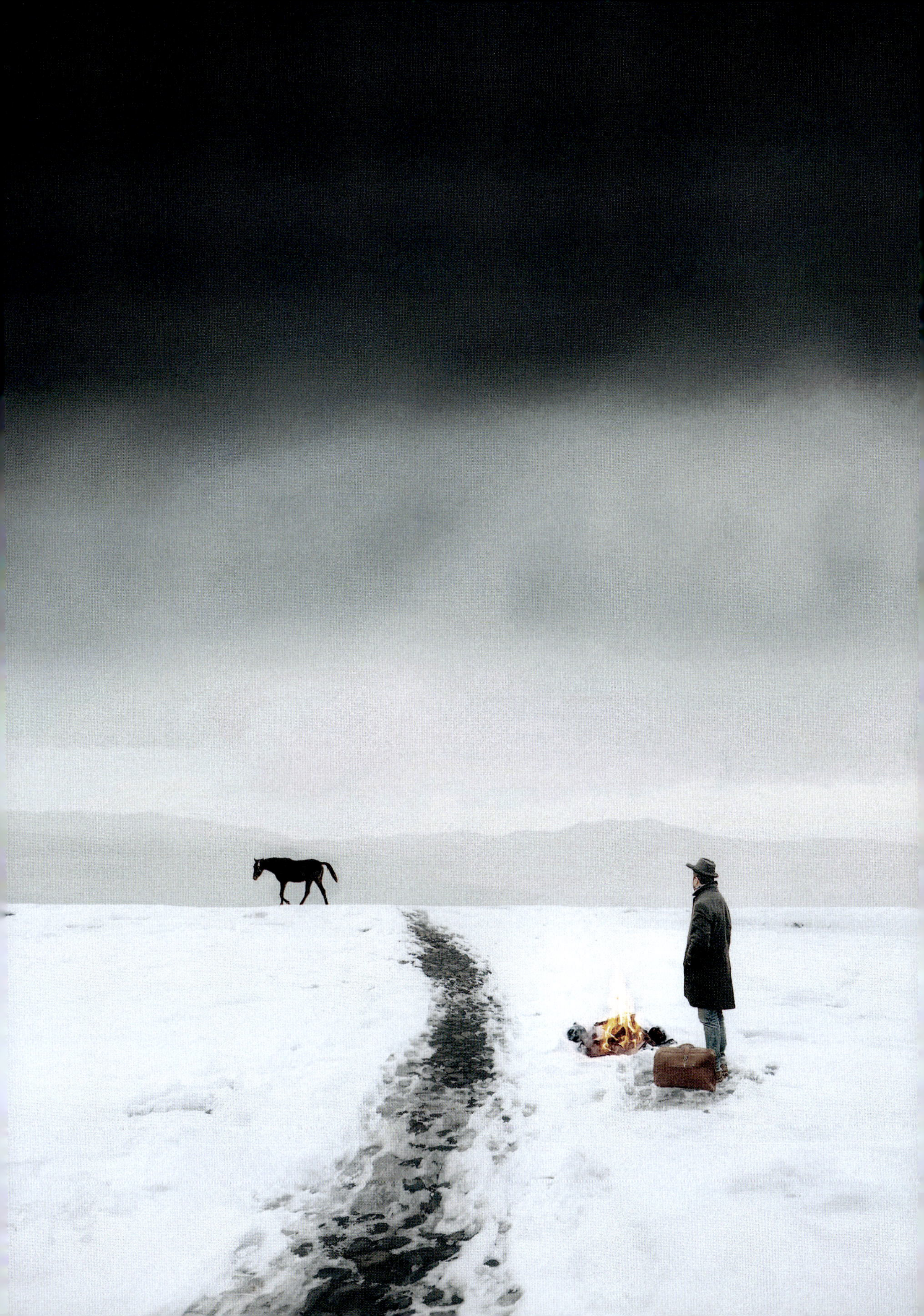

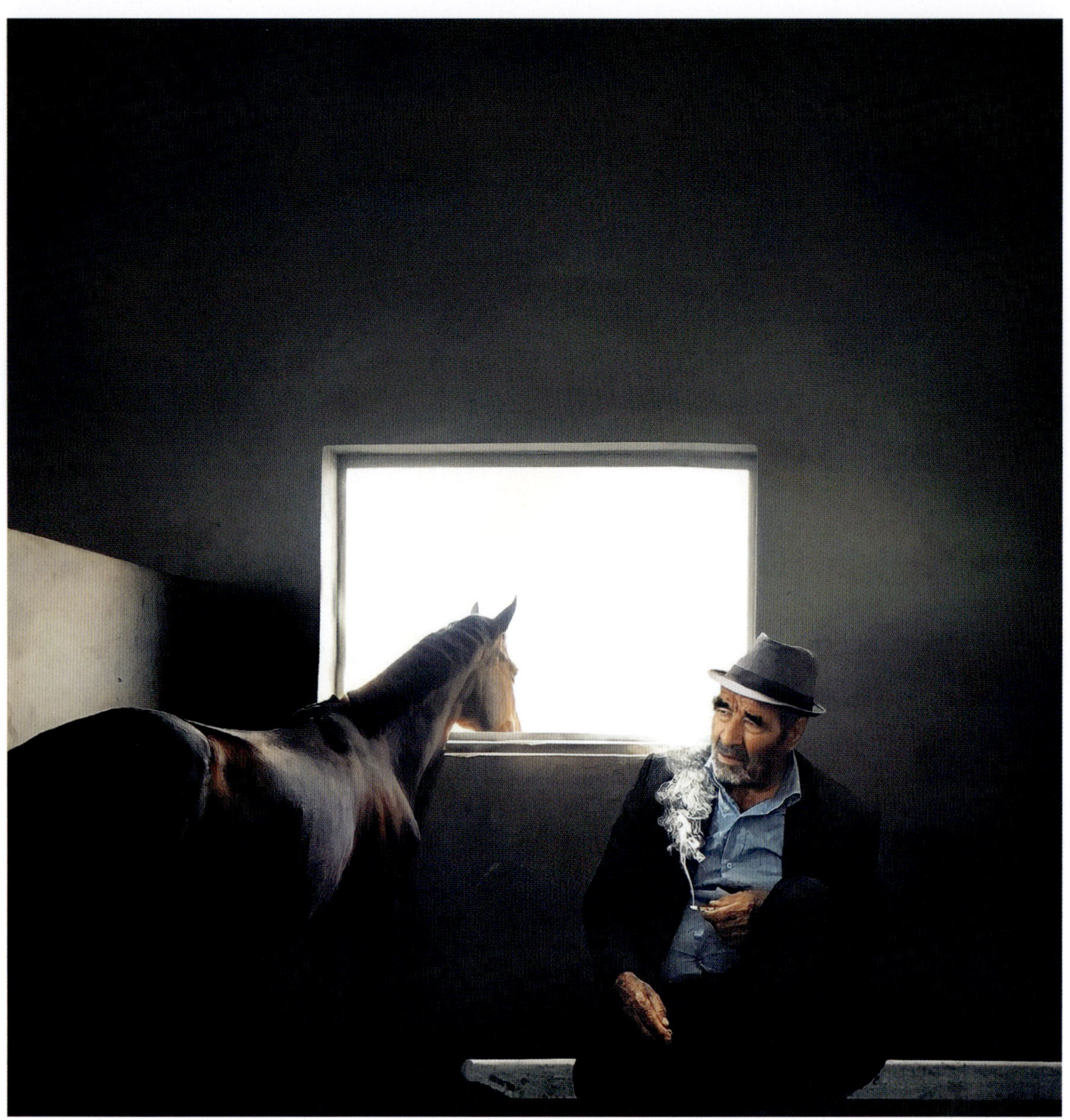

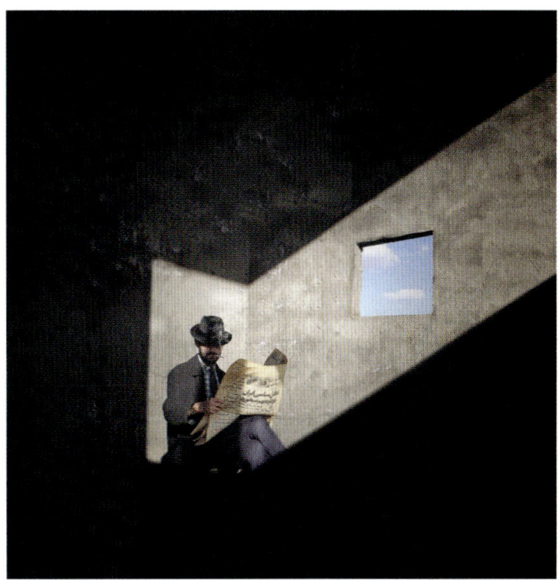

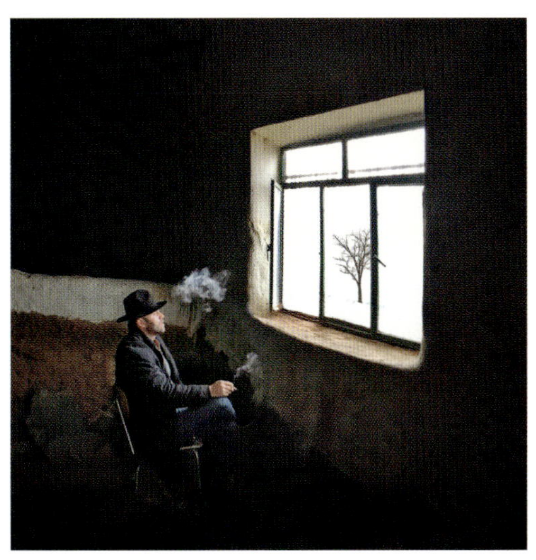

‘I am particularly interested in fine
art and staged photography.’

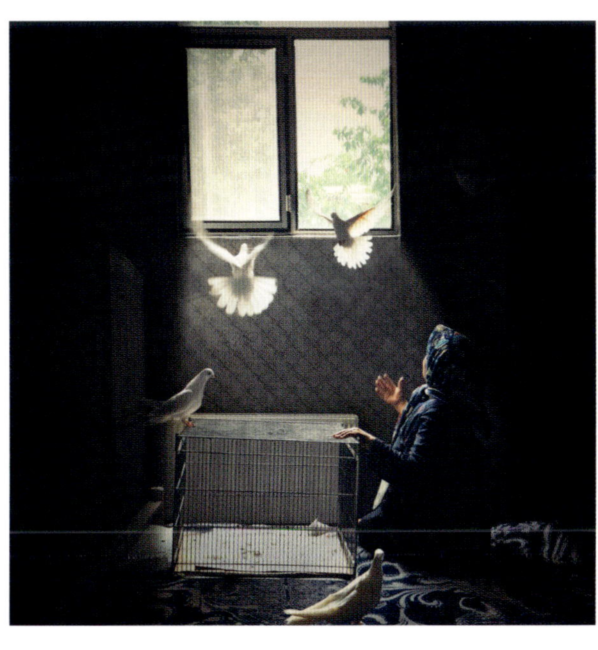

Moises Levy
Mexico City, Mexico

Architect Moises Levy lives and works in the Mexican capital. He designs residential buildings and interiors and loves to paint and produce gravures and platinum palladium prints of his photography. There is little separation between his work and his passions, which he sees as a single whole: 'my work as an architect, photographer and painter is one, each one complements the other in one way or another'. Whatever the medium, Levy's creative output is his way of understanding the world, expressing his thoughts and thinking with his eyes. His architectural background feeds into all his work – he explores perspective, scale and geometry through photography. He uses a Samsung Note 10 and Adobe Lightroom.

Levy's photography encompasses street, landscape and still life, each one offering him something different. His current passion is to find the point where street photography intersects with abstraction. He likes to shoot spontaneous moments, using anonymous people as icons or symbols. He is drawn to a clean aesthetic, and therefore favours the clean backgrounds he finds at beaches and bodies of water. The photos here were taken on the beaches of Mexico, as Levy captured the people enjoying these settings.

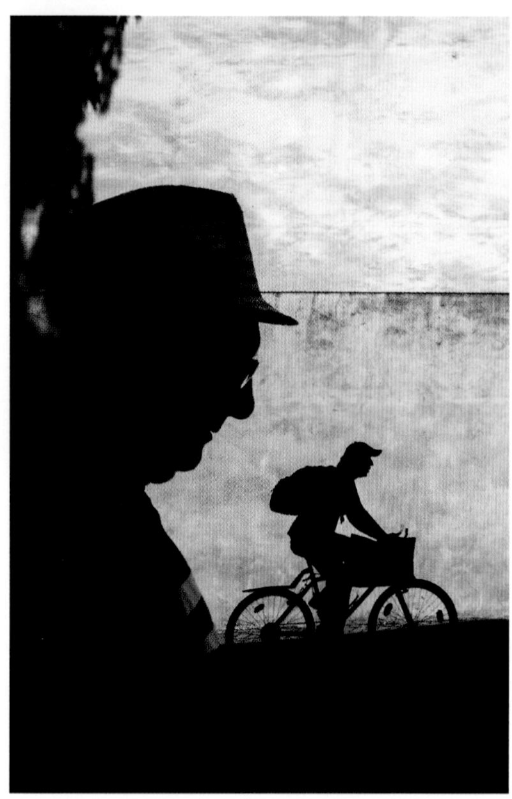

'All my street photography is about finding coincidences in real life in a beautiful and spontaneous way.'

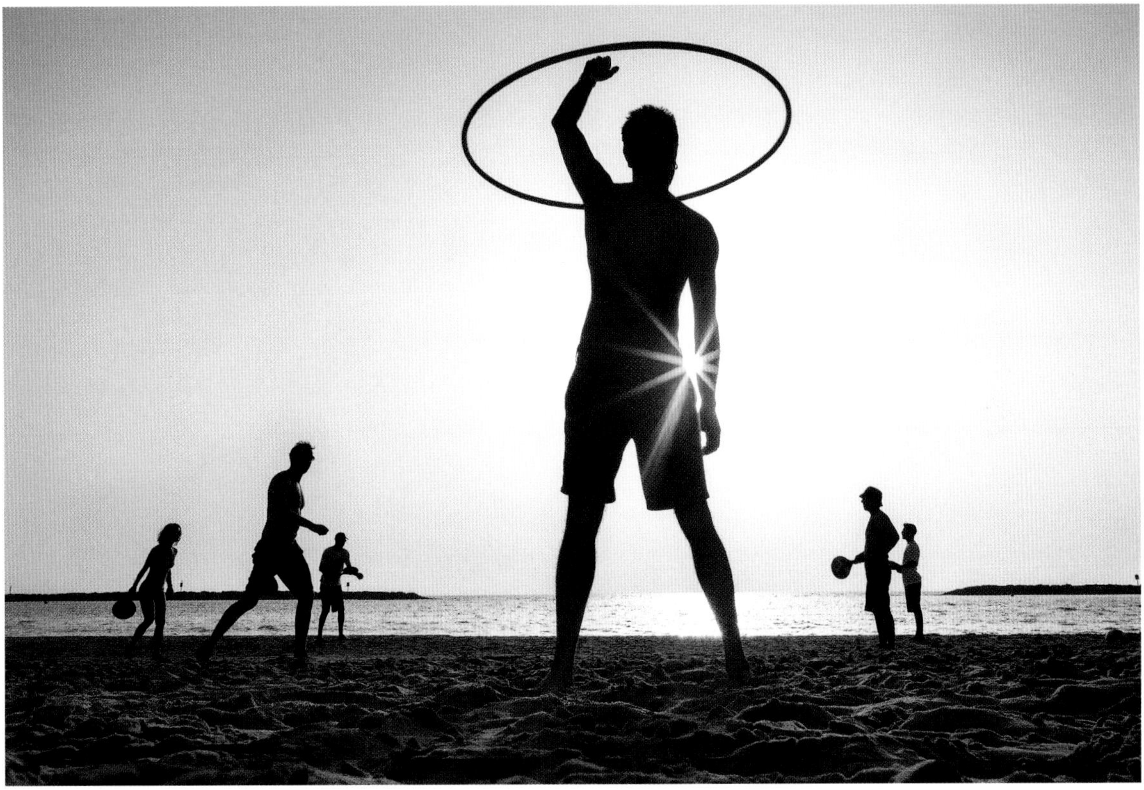

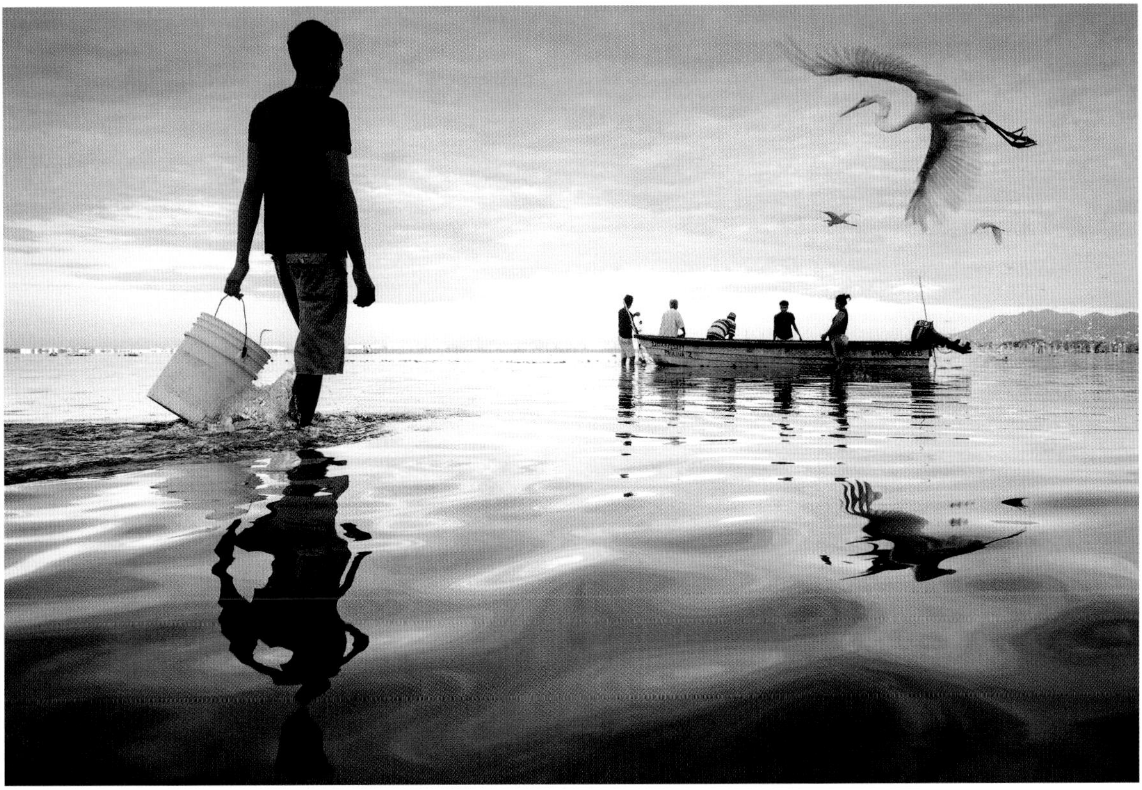

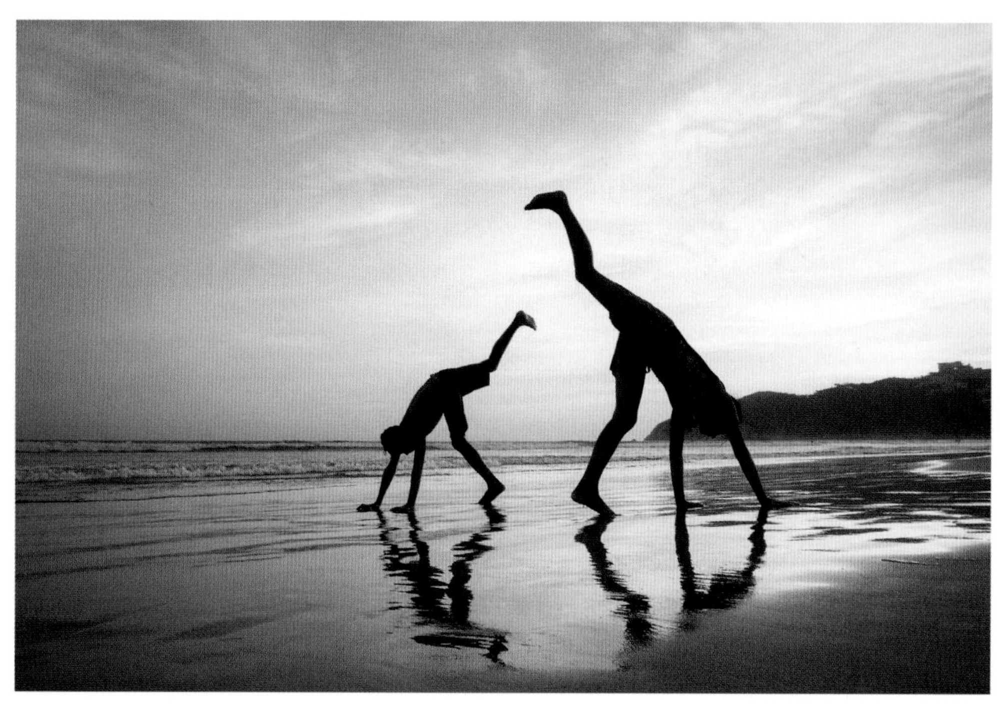

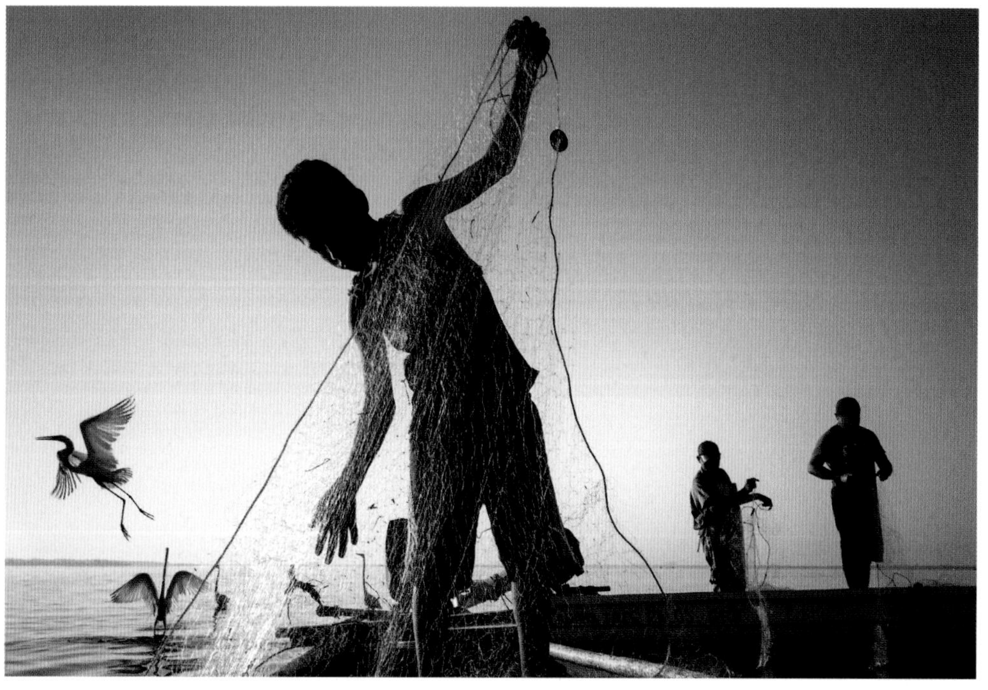

VIEWPOINT

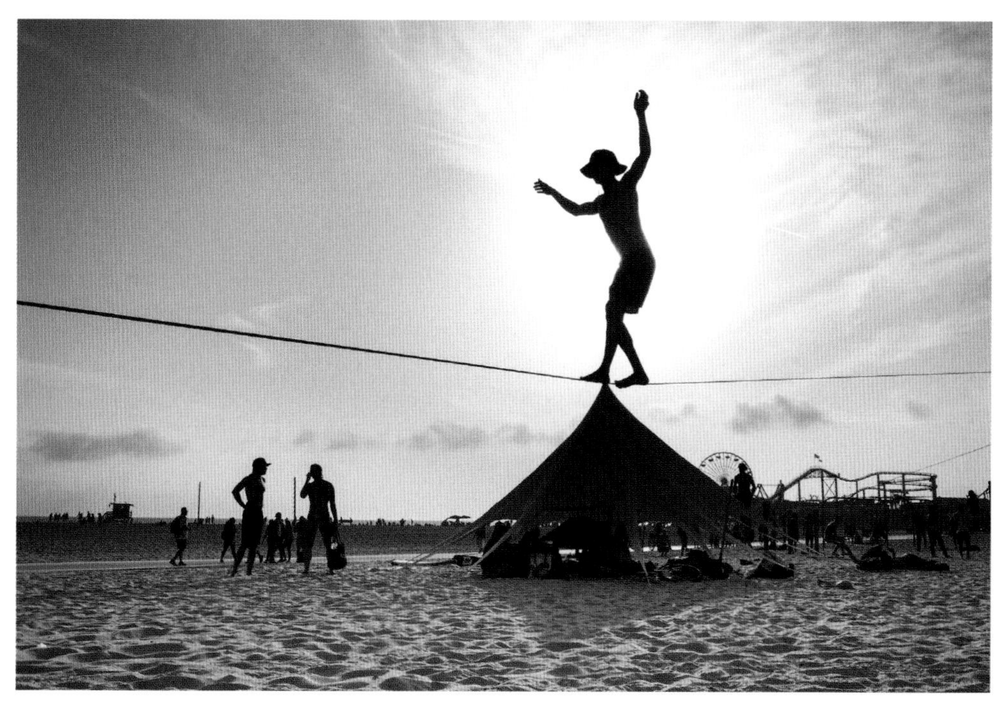

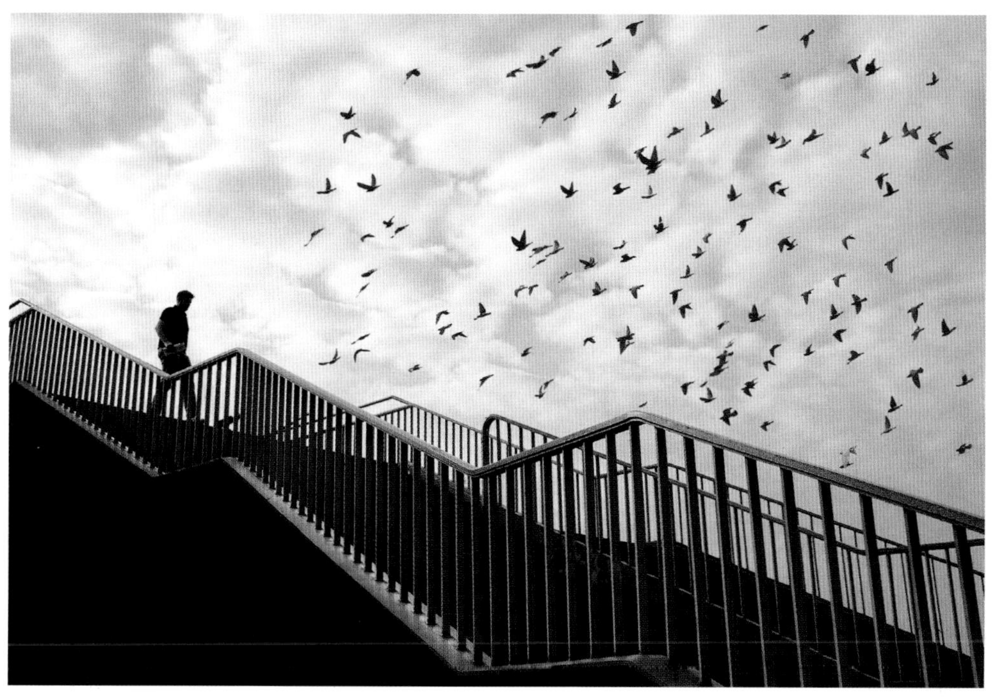

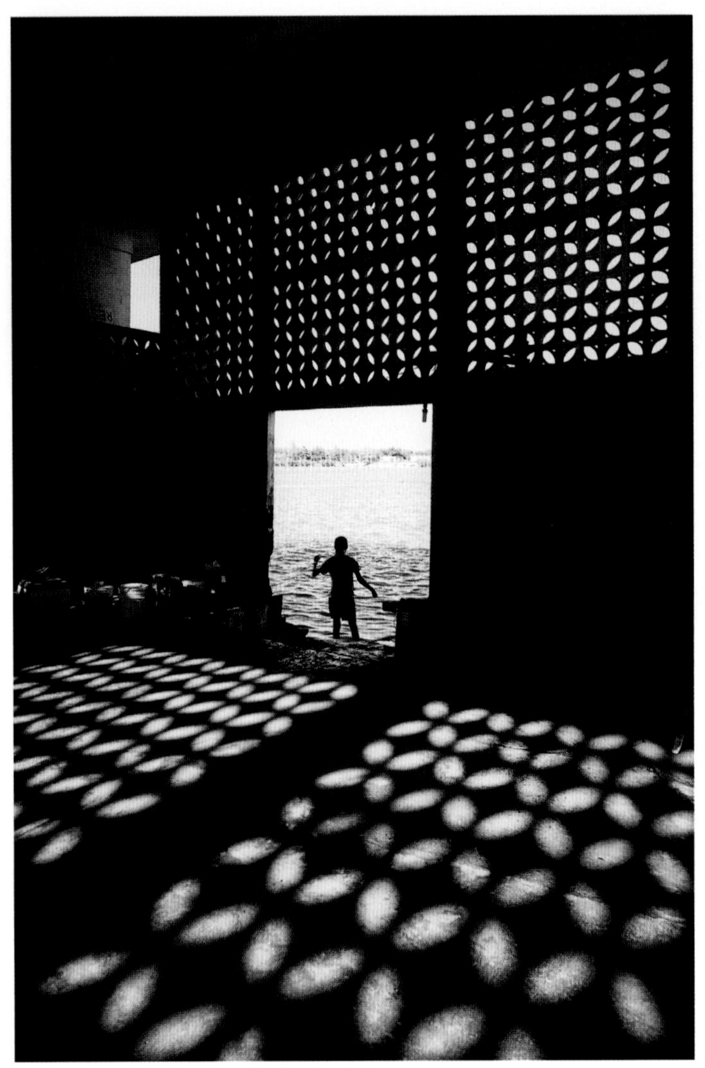

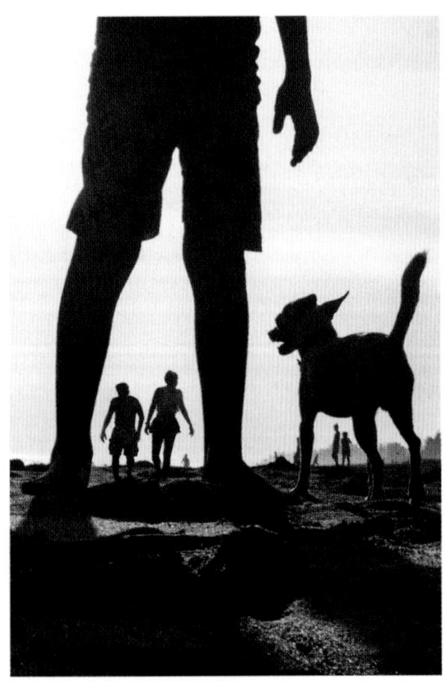

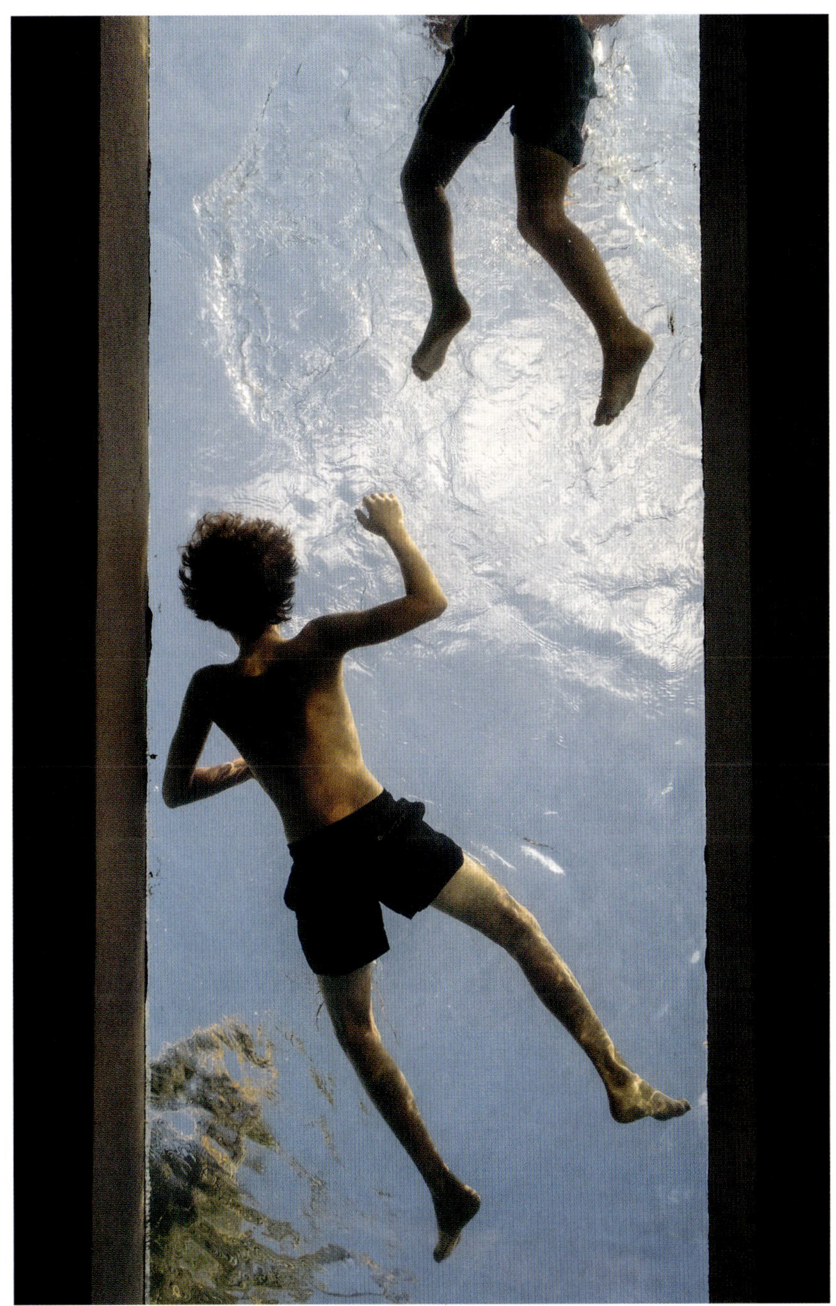

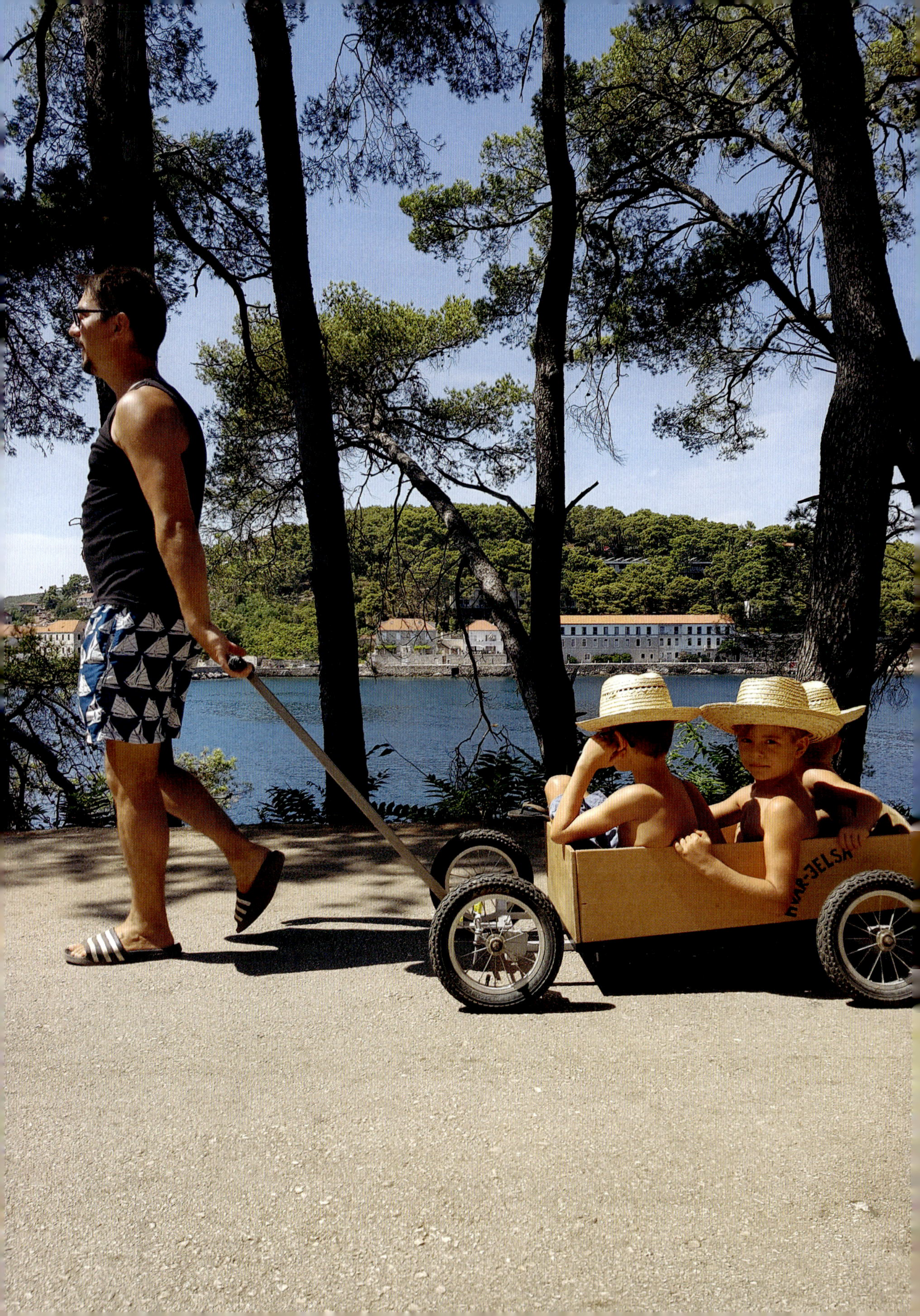

HVAR-JELSA

Paulo Buncuga
Jelsa, Hvar, Croatia

In 2019, after working as a professional music photographer photographing the likes of AC/DC, Leonard Cohen, Arctic Monkeys and Nick Cave for nearly two decades, Paulo Buncuga turned his life around by 180 degrees and moved to an island off the coast of Croatia. He has no plans to leave this new life. The peace and quiet are a long way from his old life on the mainland, where he lived between Croatia's two biggest cities, Split and Zagreb. He likes the slow tempo of seaside life and says he has totally lost his wanderlust because of it. Buncuga inherited some vineyards and olives trees and happily lives surrounded by nature, fresh air and no hustle and bustle.

Buncuga shoots on a Samsung S22 Ultra. He used to edit with Photoshop and Lightroom, but since getting the S22 Ultra he posts his photos to Instagram straight from the camera with just small adjustments to the brightness, contrast, shadows and sharpening. Buncuga loves documentary-style photography, and likes to take pictures of people in their natural habitat, surrounded by the things and people they love. His photos are mostly taken 'in the moment' on his walks around Jelsa.

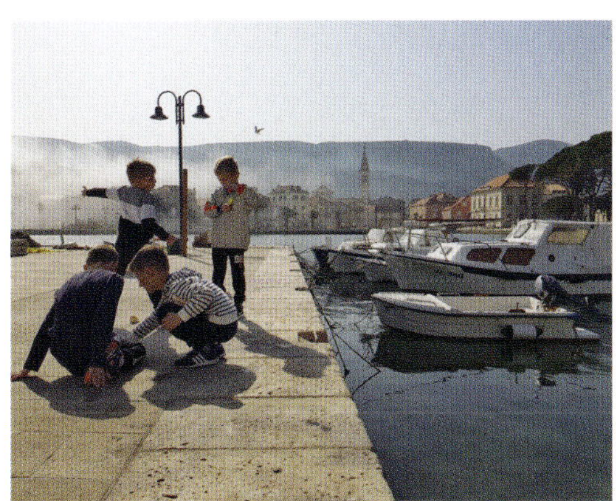

ABOVE: I love the sight of kids living in the moment, something we sometimes forget to do as we get older. There are only about a dozen families left in Jelsa who make a living from fishing, but all the children love to fish and compete to see who can catch the biggest one.

LEFT: A visitor to the island pulling his triplets along behind him.

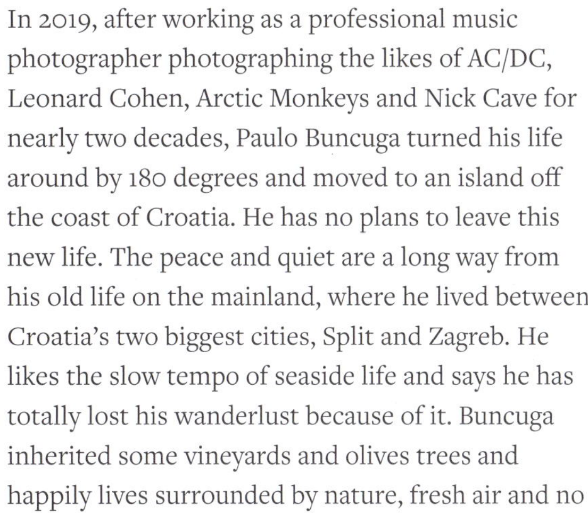

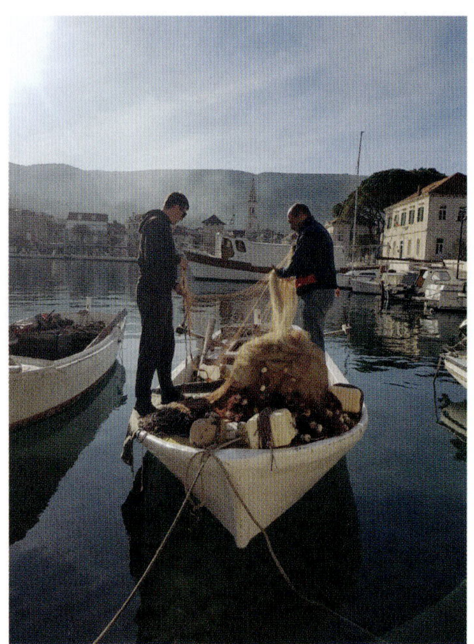

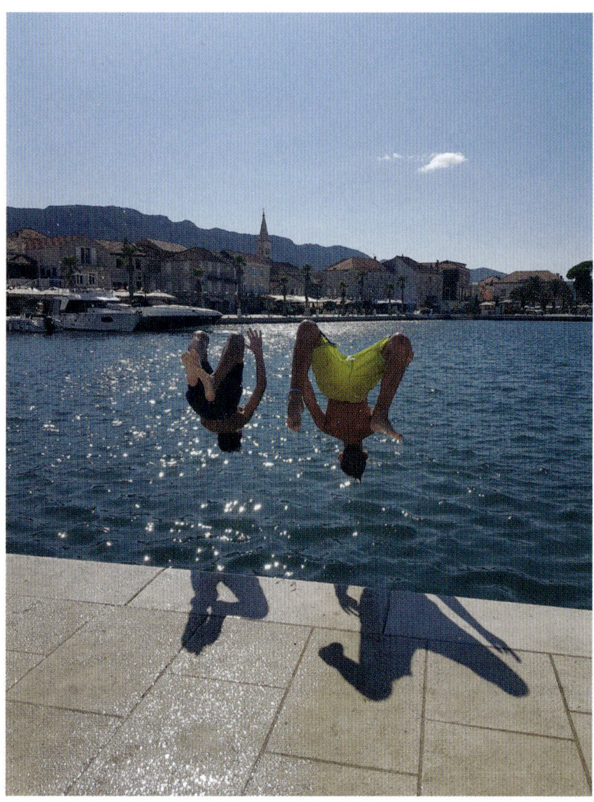

ABOVE: A father and a son from the oldest fishing family in town working as equal partners. The family goes back several generations, and I captured them as I walked by the shore. There isn't much fishing here anymore; most people work in offices, tourism and agriculture. I like to photograph fishing because it is almost a lost skill. Of the fish caught here, 80 per cent is eaten by the families that caught it, while larger catches are sold when the fishing boat arrives in port. Depending on the season, they may catch grouper, John Dory, mullet, squid, octopus and crabs.

ABOVE: Kids just want to have fun, and this is one of the best fun things you can do on Jelsa in the summer. These are local children I spotted on a walk around.

'Photography is 24/7 for me. Everybody knows me as a guy who always carries a camera. When you love photography, there is always something to do, especially in an environment like this. I'm inspired by Sebastião Salgado and Henri Cartier-Bresson. I walk around a lot and, from time to time, in the small pauses between taking pictures, I plant trees in devastated areas of the island.'

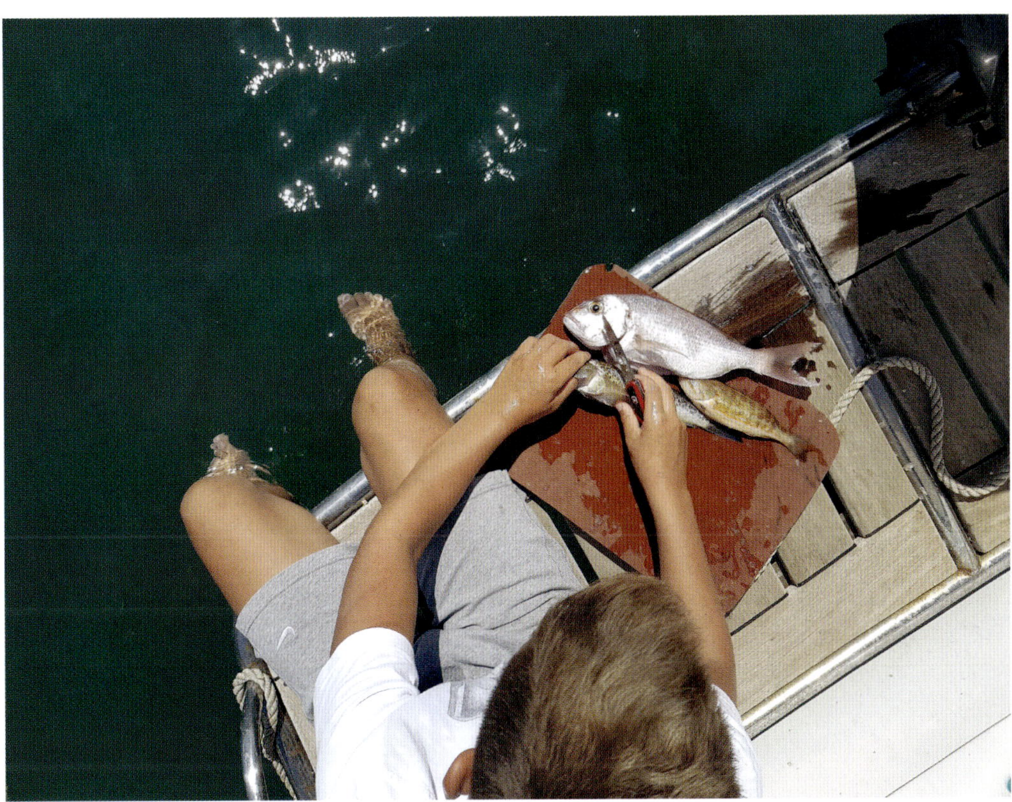

ABOVE: My friend's 12-year-old son had just caught a fish and was cleaning it. I was impressed. To him it is a normal everyday thing. It's not unusual for kids to take a boat by themselves and sail a few miles from the coast to fish.

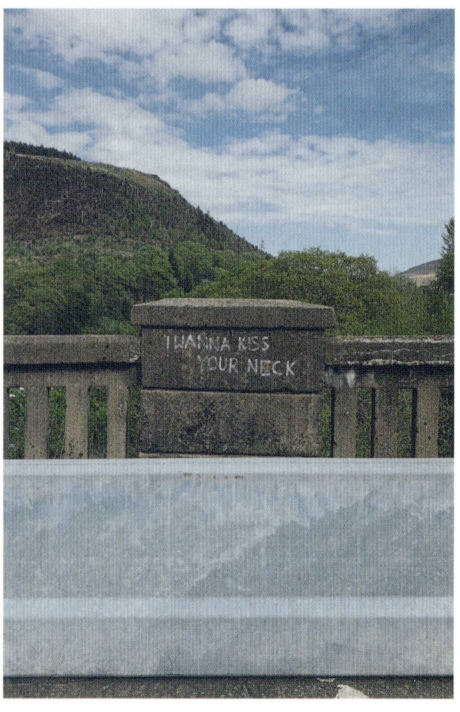

Philip Parsons
Port Talbot, Wales, UK

Philip Parsons works as a clinical scientist at a radiotherapy hospital in Cardiff, near his home in Port Talbot, Wales. He is a keen road cyclist and walker and goes out exploring with his mobile phone camera to capture whatever draws his attention. His favourite scenes are often subjects that can be photographed using negative space to give a sense of stillness and loneliness.

Parsons says, 'I like the idea of looking at things in a different way to other people. I strive to take images that aren't standard or clichéd or just like everyone else. That's if I can – I'm not sure I'm always successful. This can be a good or bad thing. Sometimes a subject is photographed from the same angle over and over because it's just a great shot. In these situations, I generally discard the image altogether. I want to say something different when I take a photo – that's what's important to me.'

Parsons believes that as a scientist, people think he has a rigid, disciplined career, but he feels it's an incredibly creative one. He says that people who work in science often end up being creative outside of that sphere. Photography allows him to express himself – showing people how he views the world.

Parsons is a fan of the Apple iPhone, and has always used them for his mobile photography, but he does have a Fujifilm X-Pro 2 as well. For editing, he mostly uses VSCO, but has also used Snapseed, Image Blender, TouchRetouch, Union, Noir and Cross Process.

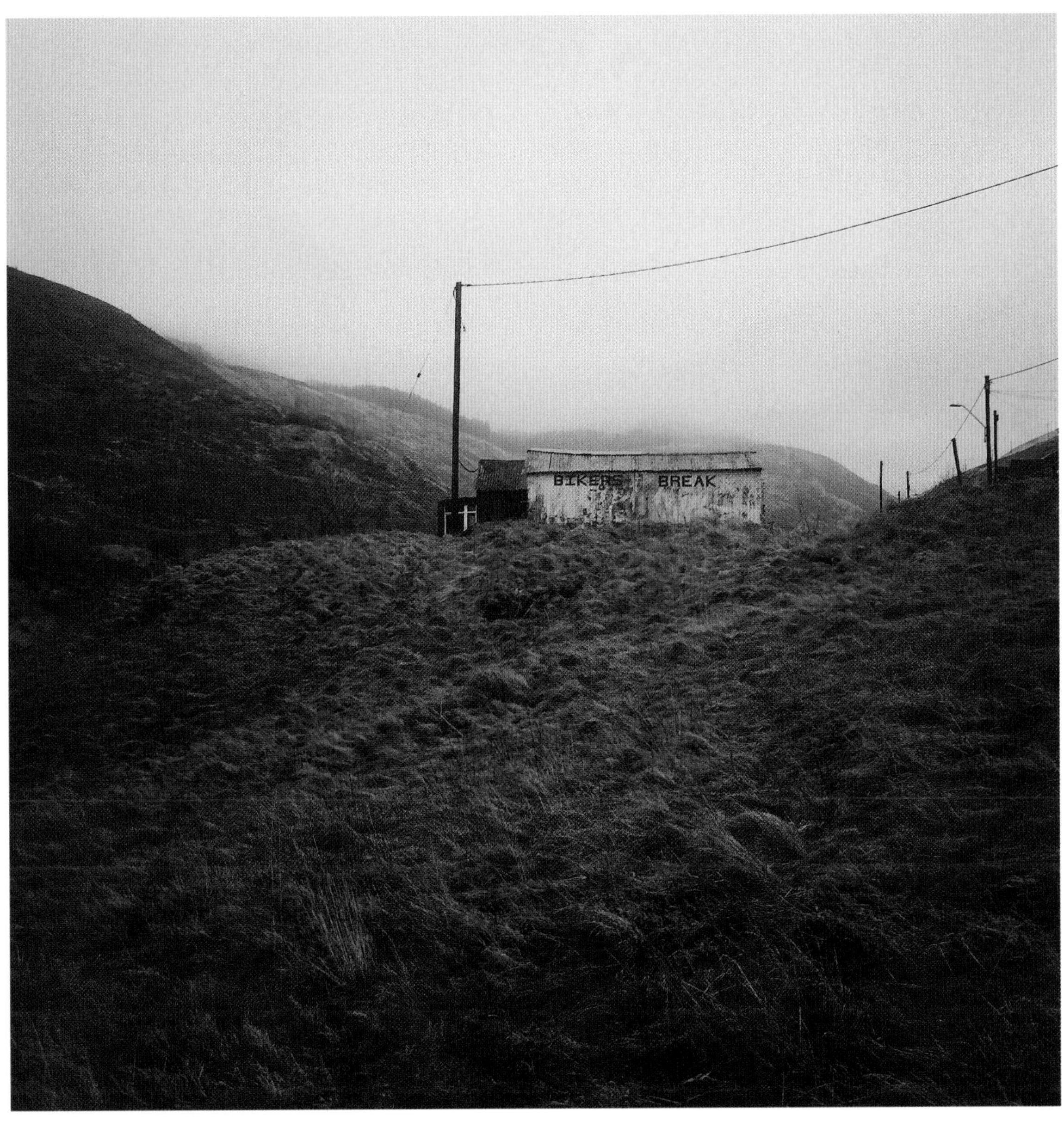

ABOVE: On a rainy day, I went for a drive to the Afan Valley to have a look for things to photograph. I saw this old shed and liked the text, the texture of the ground leading up to it, the worn down and beaten look of the building and the misty backdrop. I parked up and climbed down the mountain to capture it.

'I want to say something different when I take a photo, and that's what's important to me.'

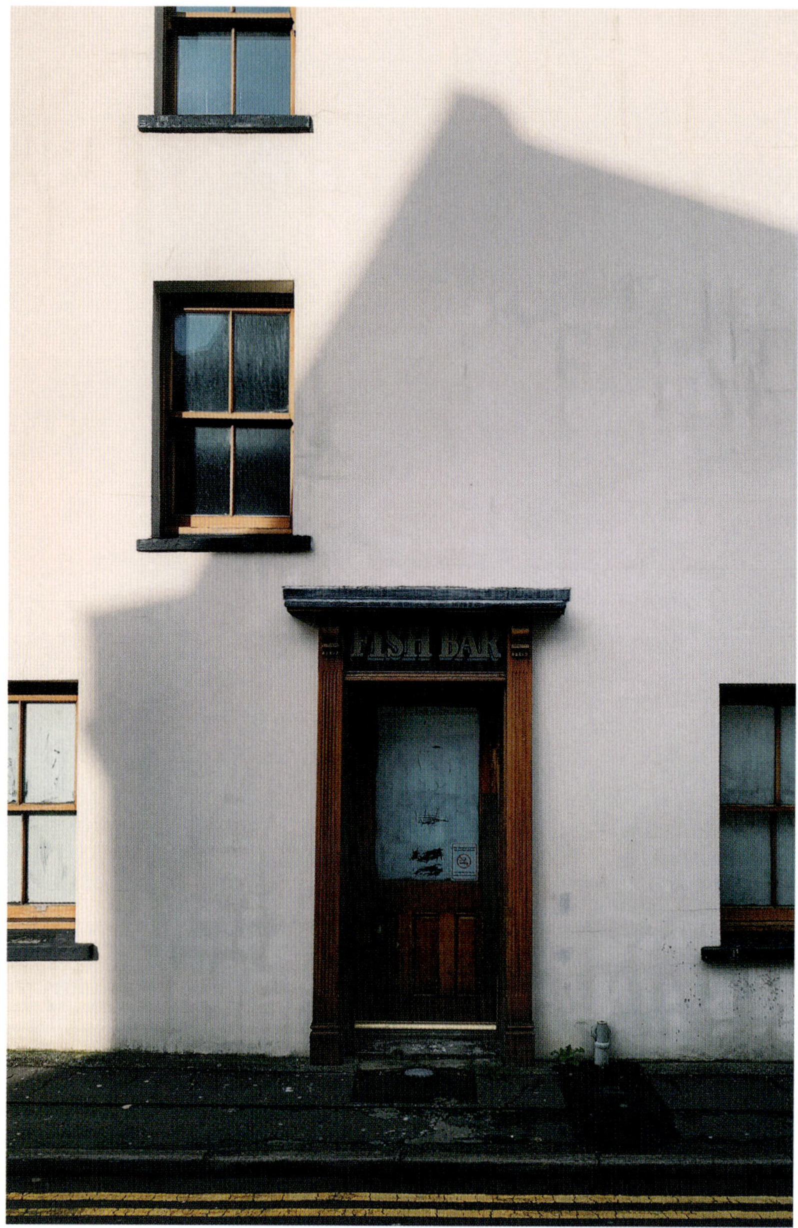

ABOVE: I noticed this fish bar in Neath town centre as I wandered past. I was struck by the interesting shadow of the nearby house and loved the green colour the windows had been painted to stop people looking inside. I loved the way all the elements fit together; I feel it's not a 'standard' or typical composition. The windows are cropped by the edges of the frame, the shadow of the other building dominates the shot, and I love the 'ordinariness' of the scene – even in the most mundane situations there's beauty to be discovered.

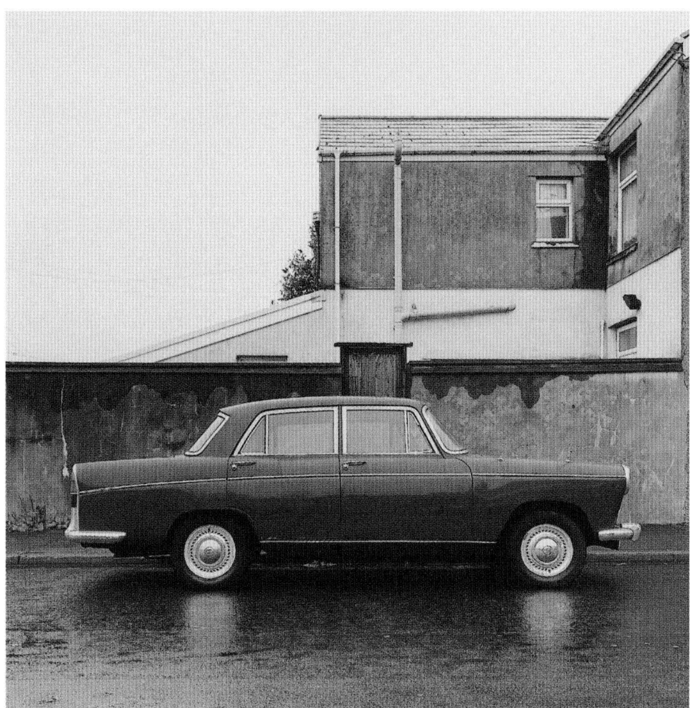

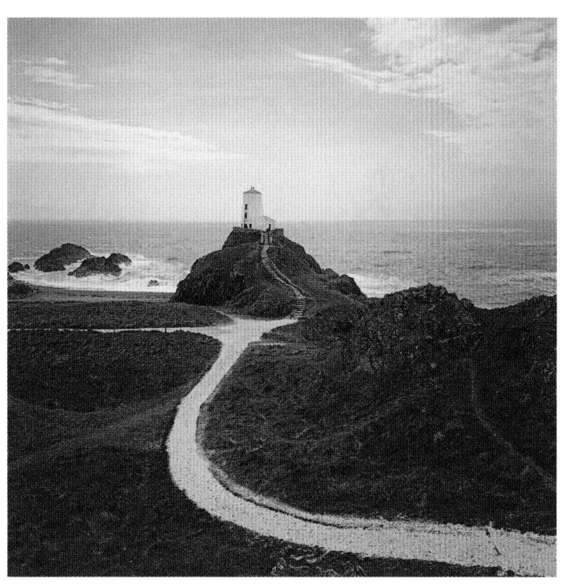

ABOVE: I noticed this car on a back street in Port Talbot a few times, but the position was never right for a photo, or there were other cars too near it. I love old British cars and am always on the lookout for them to photograph. On this day the car was in the perfect position, and it happened to be raining, which created a reflection on the road and meant the water sat on the surface of the car. A bygone beauty in a backseat teaching us to find beauty in unexpected places. We just have to open our eyes and be prepared to look beyond convention.

ABOVE: The sweeping line of the path at this iconic landmark, Tŵr Mawr lighthouse at Ynys Llanddwyn on Anglesey, begged to be photographed.

Rachél Sela
Stockholm, Sweden

Lawyer Rachél Sela works in the IT and contract law department of the Stockholm department of education. She inherited her interest in photography from her mother and grandfather. She got her first camera at the age of eight and, for a long time, her interests were landscape, street and documentary-style photography. Constraints on travel after the birth of her first child, and the further restrictions imposed by the Covid-19 pandemic, pushed her to try out new styles, and she has been exploring macro, portrait, fine art, maternity and family shoots in the last few years. She says, 'Macro, for example, is a fantastic way of 'travelling' without actually leaving home!' She now has two daughters.

'I photograph most of the things I encounter in my life.'

RIGHT: Watching Kent – one of Sweden's biggest bands – on stage at the Tele2 Arena in Stockholm, among some of the 38,000 people at the show. It is a big new arena, but this was the band's farewell show. My fiancé and I hadn't seen them perform before, so decided to go along. I love to take pictures of concerts and shows. Cameras aren't allowed at most indoor shows, so it is essential to be able to take good pictures with a phone. Most mobile photos won't give you that crisp photo unless you're standing in the front row. Standing in the middle of the crowd, with just my phone, gave me the opportunity to think and take interesting pictures with a different perspective. I like the movement and energy in this photo. The artists are only silhouettes – it could be any band – but they let you know it's a concert photo. At the same time the artists are not the important part of the photo, it's the movement. The blurry hands moving and clapping so you can feel the music without hearing it. The image could be cropped, but I find the somewhat hazy ceiling ads to the feeling of movement.

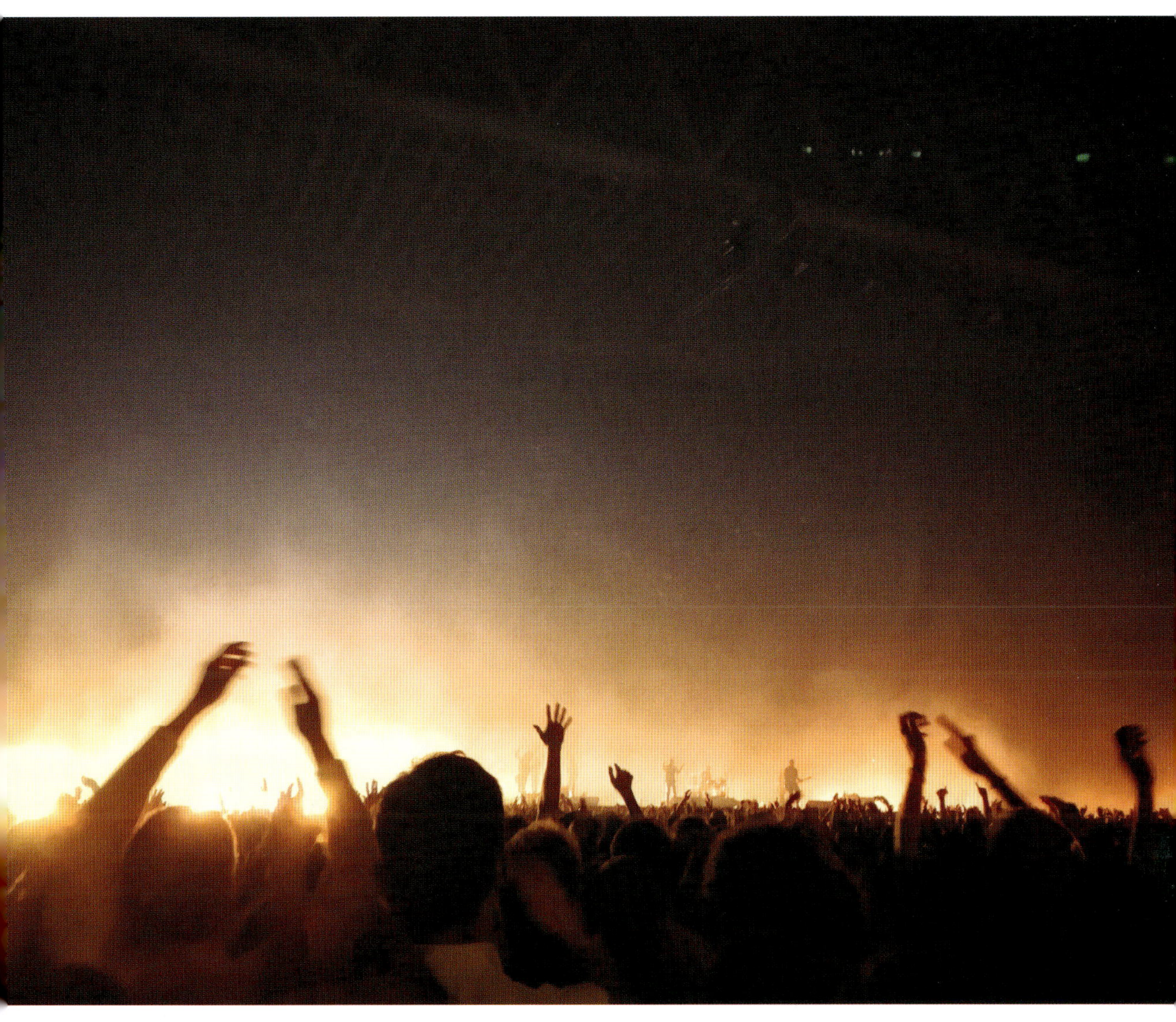

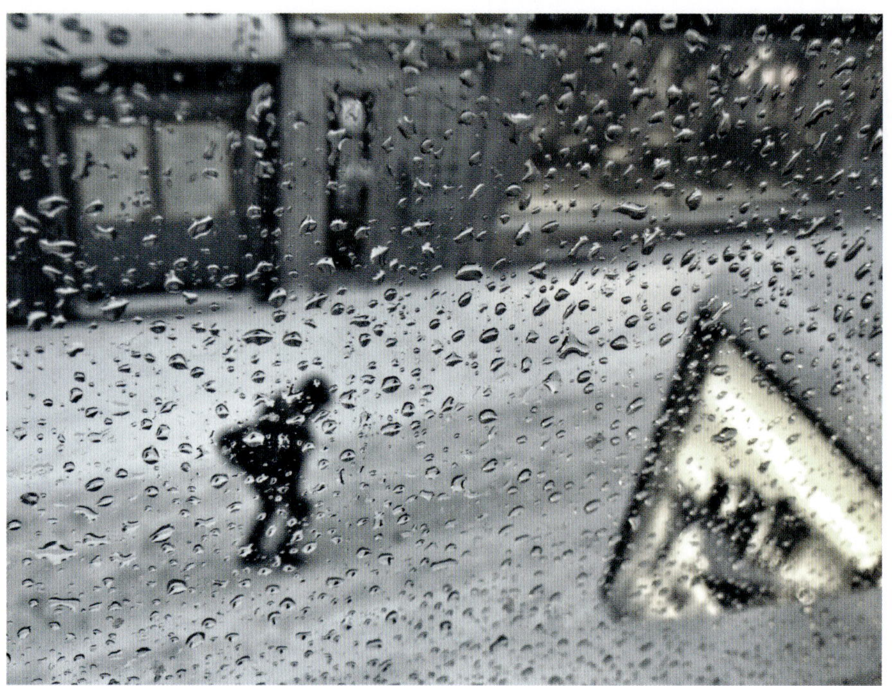

ABOVE: A scene from the window of my office at my former workplace in the centre of Stockholm. The window looks out onto a steep street that leads to Drottninggatan (Queen Street), the city's main street. I was at work on this really snowy day and visibility was becoming very poor when I saw someone trying to walk up the hill in the storm and I wanted to capture it. I took a few shots, some with the person in focus and this one with the waterdrops on the window in focus. Had the person been in focus it would have been more of a documentary shot, so this is more interesting to me. I like the way the waterdrops tell you that the photographer/spectator must be inside behind a window, where it's probably warm and cosy. I think you can tell by the way the person looks and walks that it's cold and windy outside.

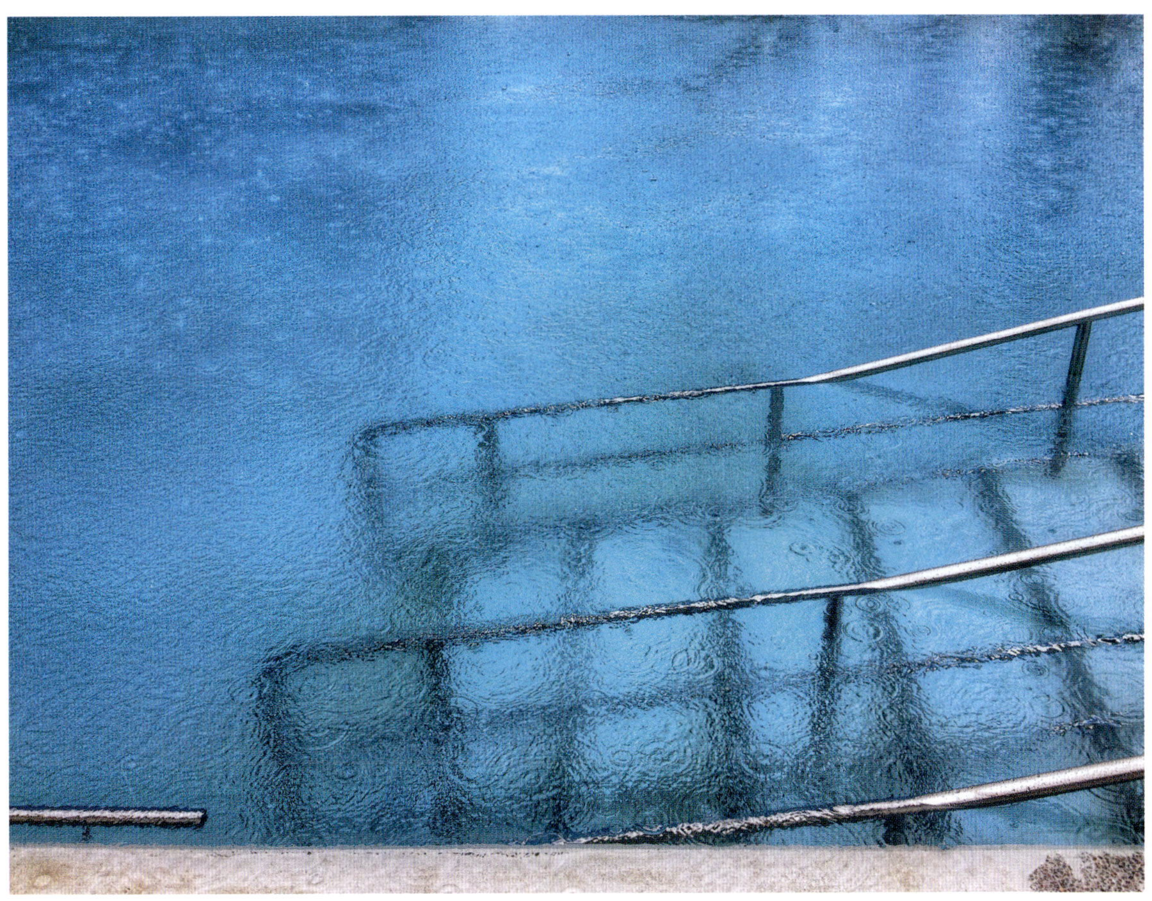

ABOVE: This was taken at a public swimming pool, a short car ride from home, where I go in the summer with my mother and my oldest daughter. It is a heated outdoor pool where you can swim and play, which is nice since the weather in Sweden varies a lot. This particular summer's day was cloudy. Then it started to rain, and everyone except for my mother and I left, so we had the whole pool to ourselves. I love to swim and have been swimming all my life. My grandfather was a swimming teacher for a while and, when I was younger, I went with him to courses – on water safety, ice safety, etc. – arranged by the Swedish Lifesaving Federation (SLS).

I thought it looked so pretty with the clear turquoise colour of the water and the water drops that made the railing and steps fade. I love the bright colour and minimalistic feel. It was taken close up but everyone who sees it will know it's a pool. The water drops seem to give it that sense of the cool summer days we so often have here in the north.

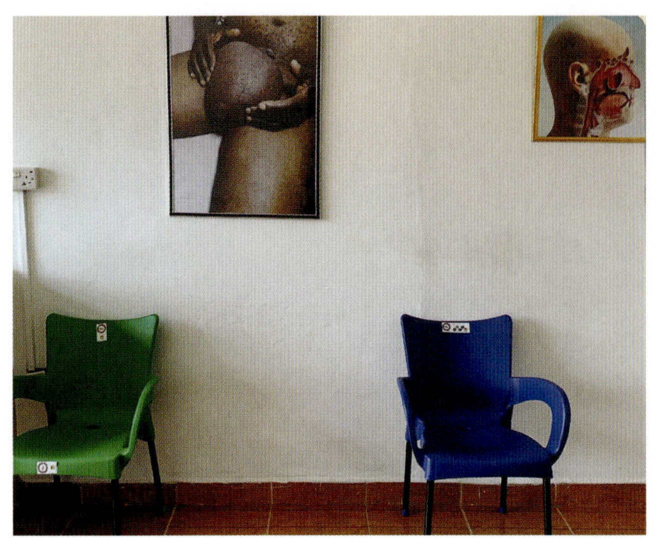

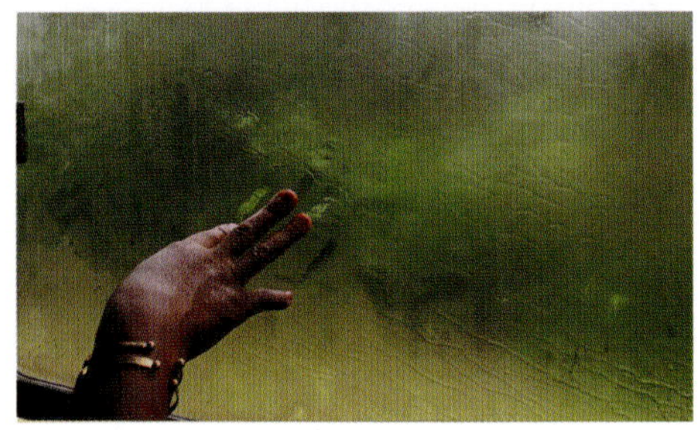

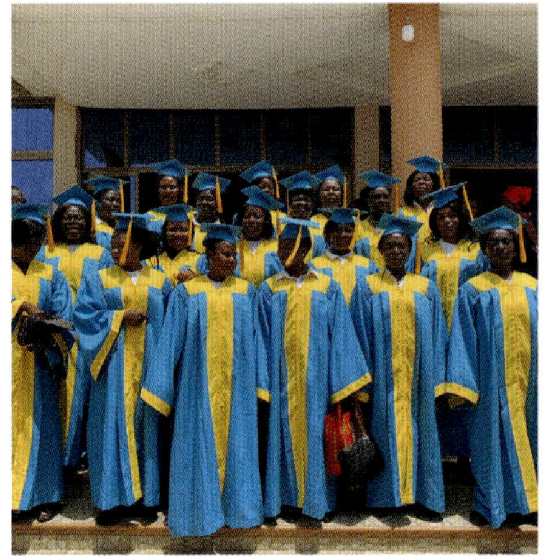

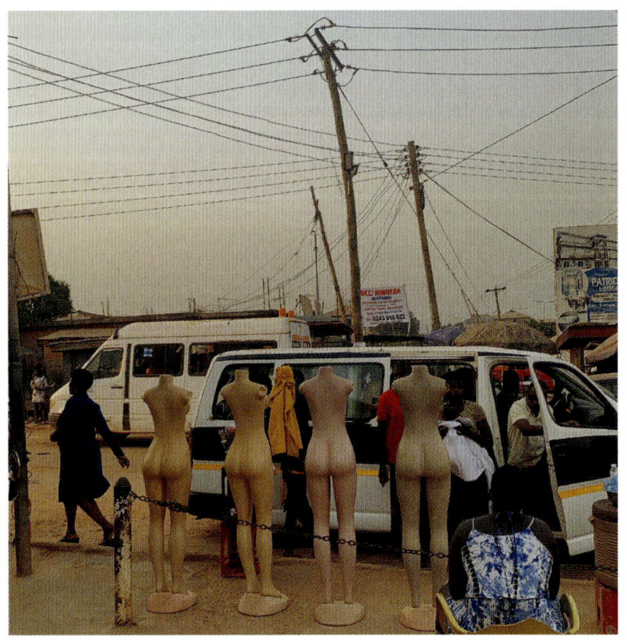

VIEWPOINT

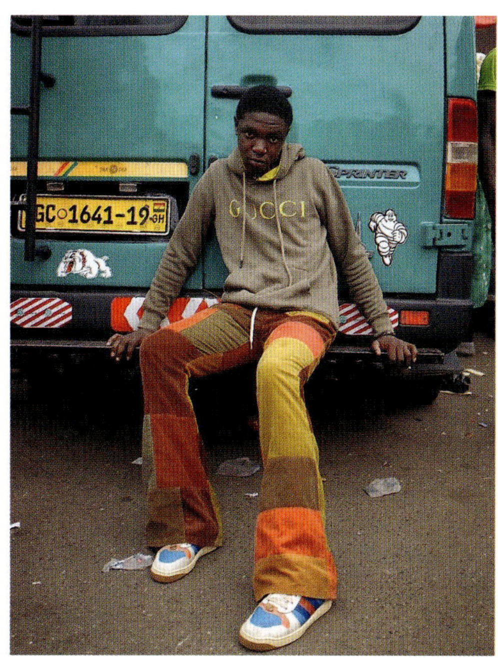

Raymond Baffour
Kumasi, Ghana

Raymond Baffour works as record officer at the Mater Dei hospital in Kumasi and enjoys taking photographs in his spare time using an Apple iPhone XR or Fujiflim X100 F. His interest in photographing daily life comes from a desire to document the place where he lives and events as they happen around him. The act of focusing on a specific time allows him to evaluate how his own life has changed or stayed the same from a past photo to the present day.

Baffour photographs friends, family and strangers as they go about their daily lives on the streets of Santasi, where he lives, and other parts of Ghana. His images are very much 'shot in the moment' without any real planning or staging. His intention is to hold a moment in history for future generations, and to witness tragedy, joy and everything in between.

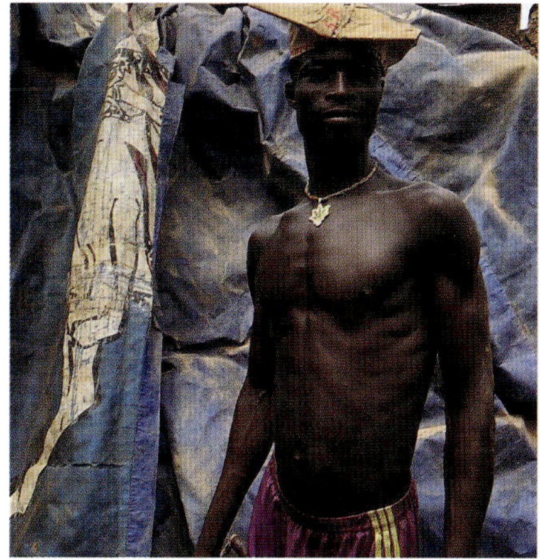

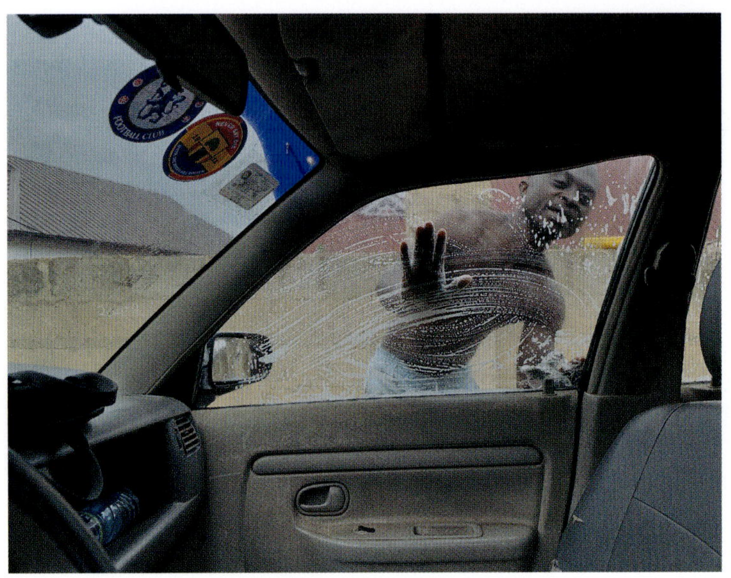

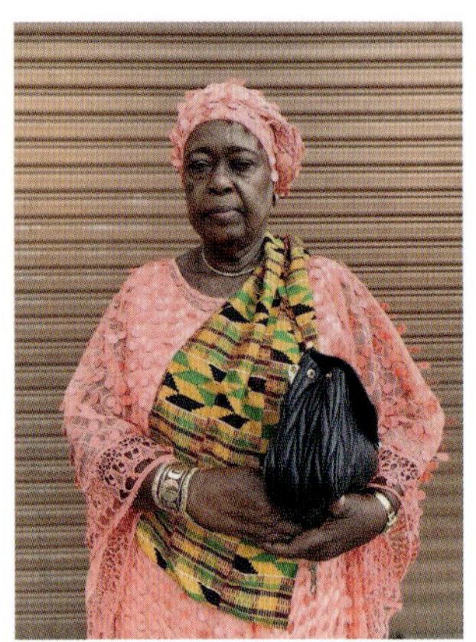

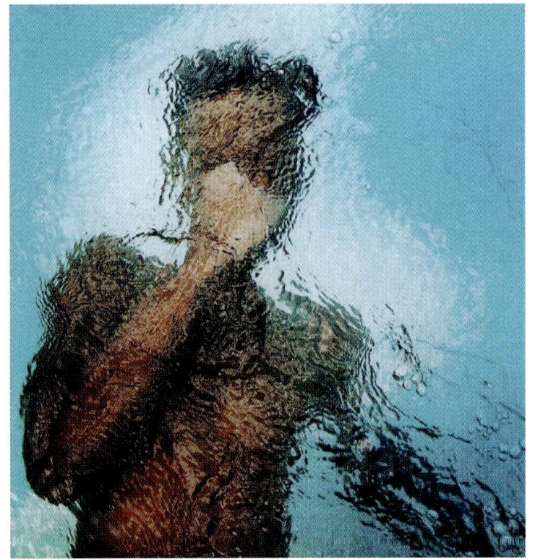

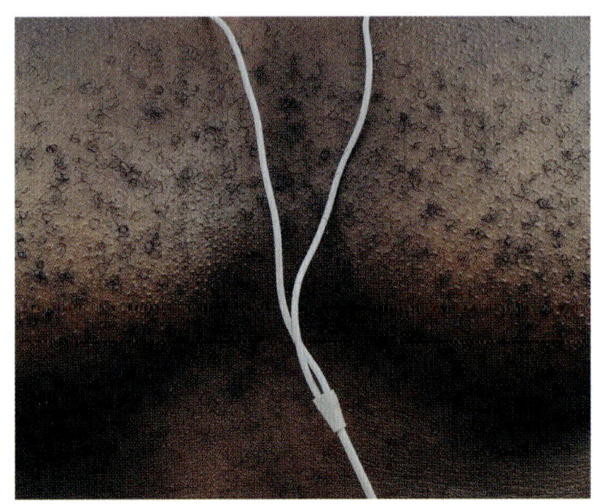

'My photographs help me to pause and reflect on specific experiences.
Birthday parties, weddings, household views, Christmas gatherings,
baby showers, anniversaries, commutes to work, natural disasters
and so on. Whatever the events may have been, in my pictures they
are captured forever in all their beauty and truth.'

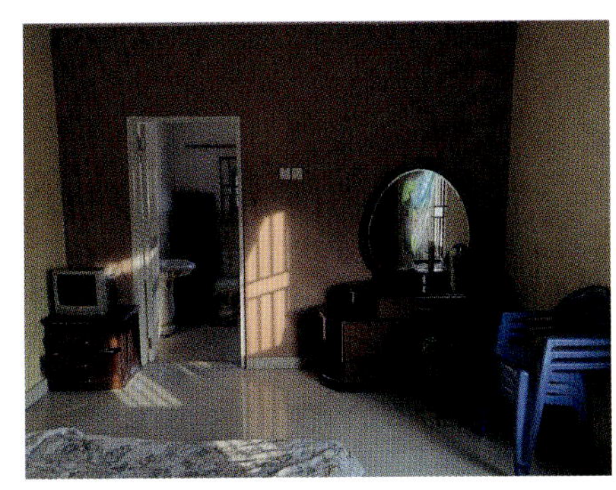

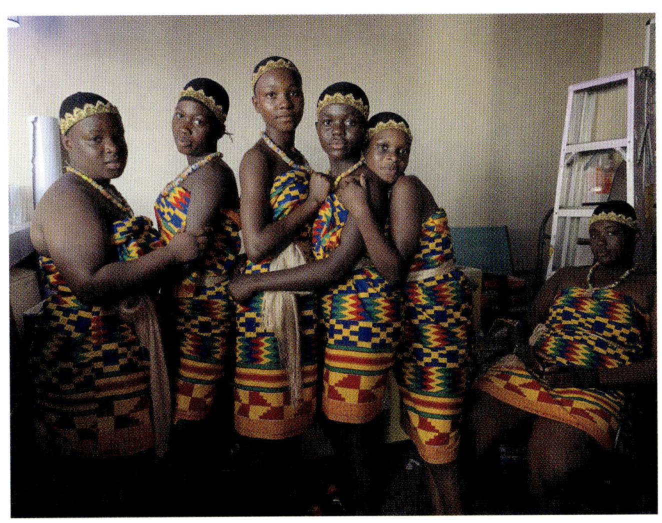

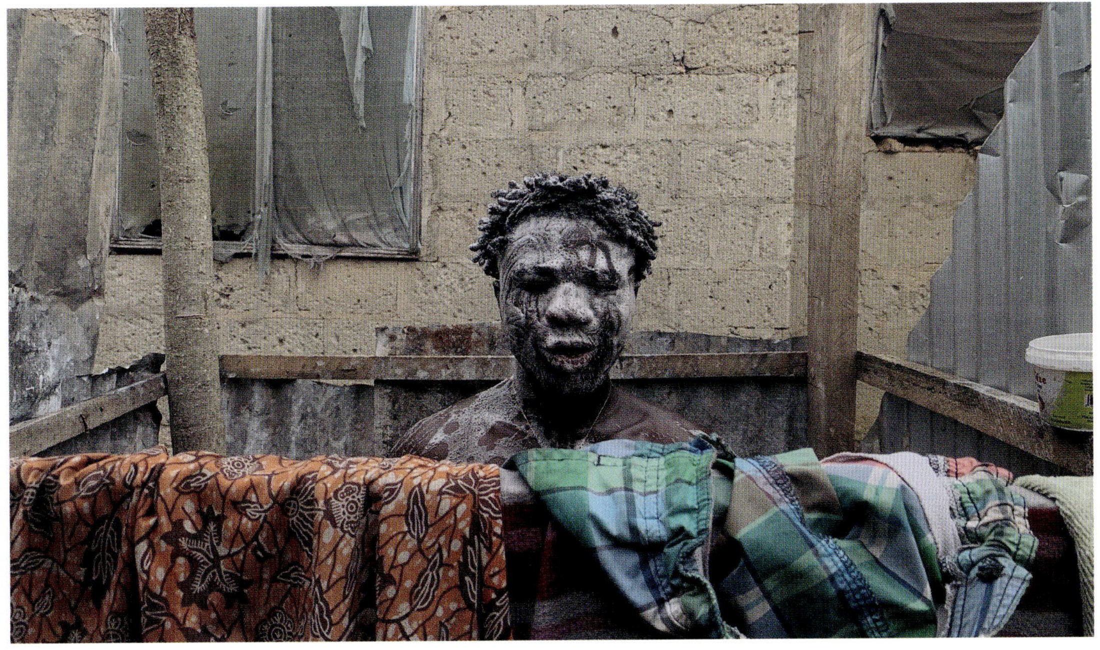

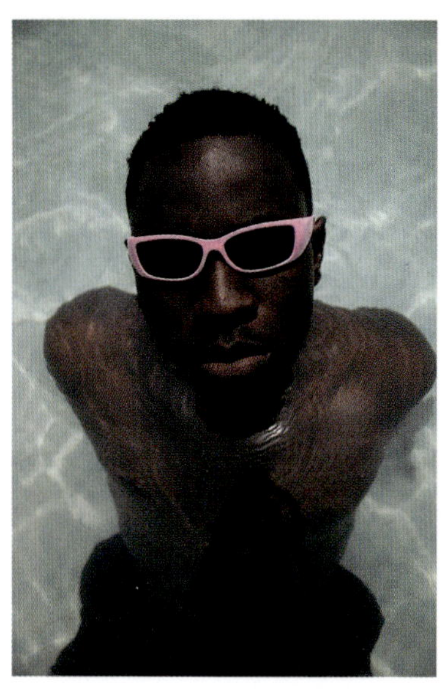

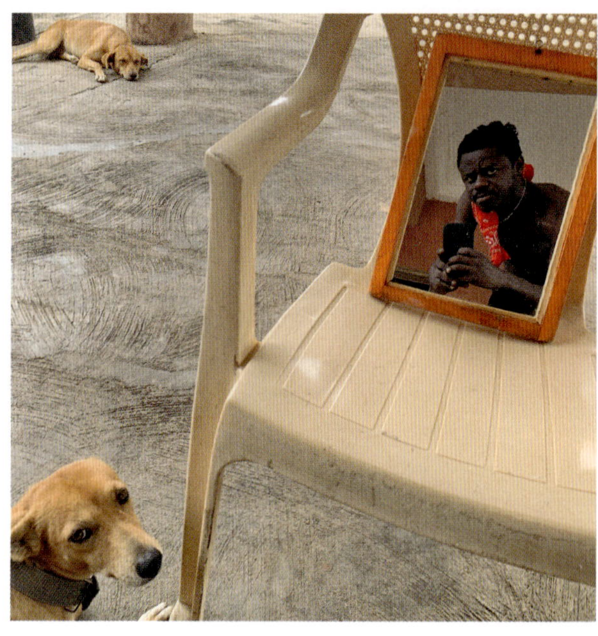

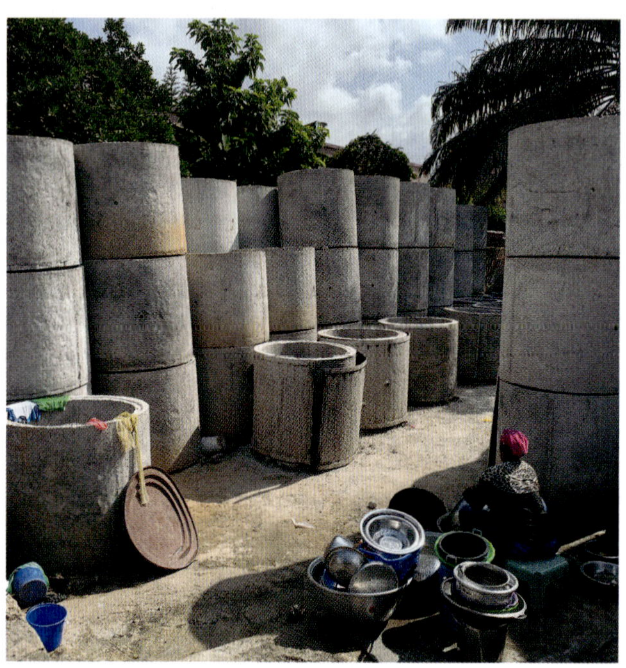

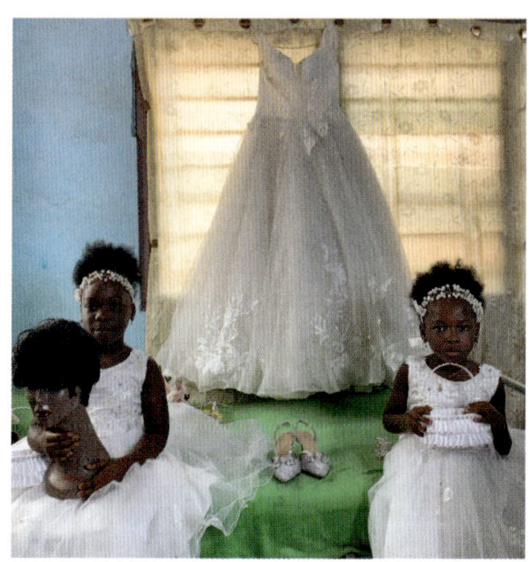

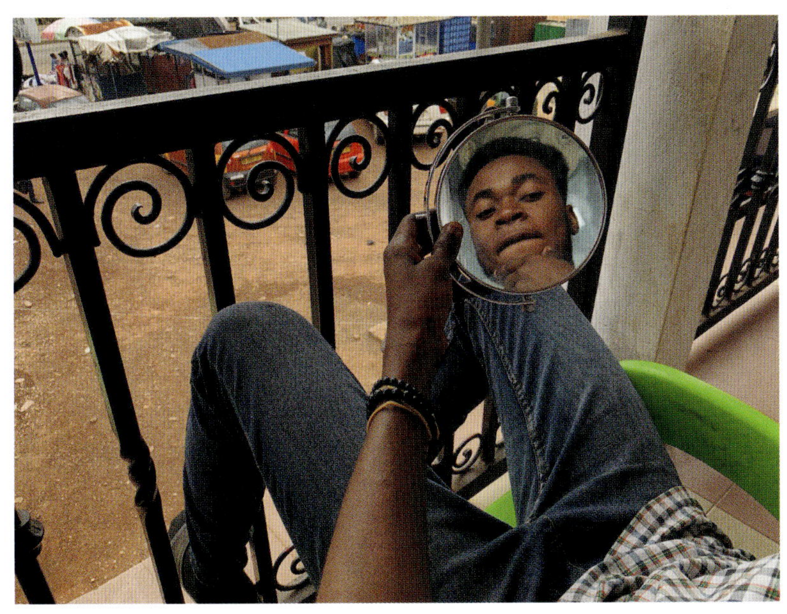

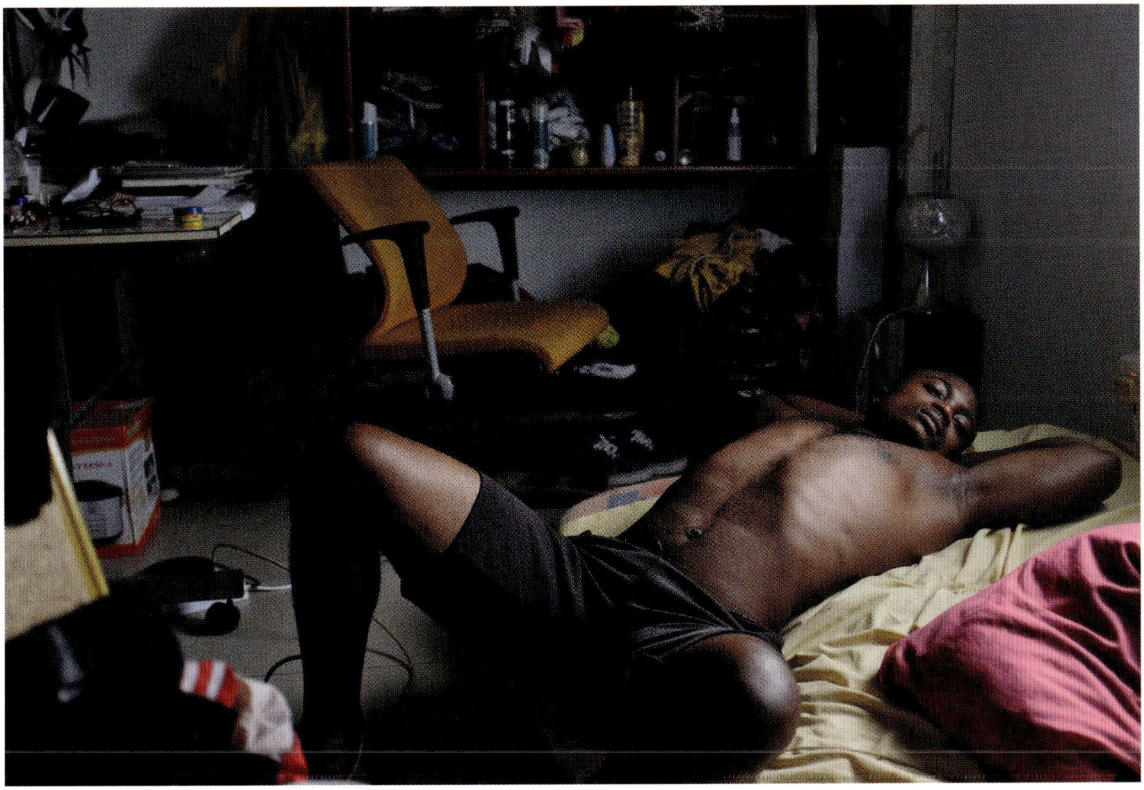

Renzo Grande
Lima, Peru

Originally from Lima, Renzo Grande visited the mountains of Peru to visit his father's family from an early age. He currently lives in New York City and visits his beloved Peru every year. Grande works in the coordination for humanitarian affairs office of a non-governmental organization and is very aware of work towards providing solutions to current humanitarian crises.

Grande's passion for photography began in the early days of the Apple iPhone. He started with an iPhone 3GS and, realizing that there is no perfect camera, learned to work with the imperfections of that phone's camera. He found that using an iPhone allowed him to be present while not disturbing his surroundings as he shot. It started as a therapeutic way to express visually what he could not say with words. Photography has always been Grande's way out, his way to decompress. On a bad day, taking a walk to observe and frame a scene helps him to cope with anything that he is going through. Now he creates documentary photography with an iPhone 13 and a Fujifilm DSLR. Through his work, Grande has visited refugee camps, human trafficking survivor centres and remote clinics in Africa, and because of this he found himself drawn to humanitarian photography.

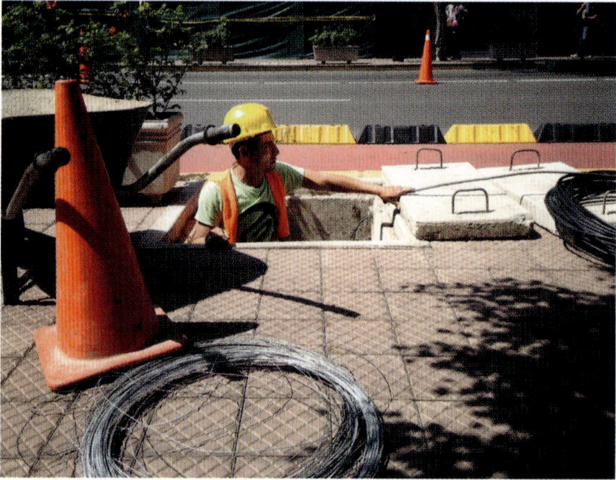

ABOVE: Men at work in Lima, Peru. The city is always focused on improvement.

RIGHT: Locals in the city of Cusco, Peru, enjoying some midday snacks.

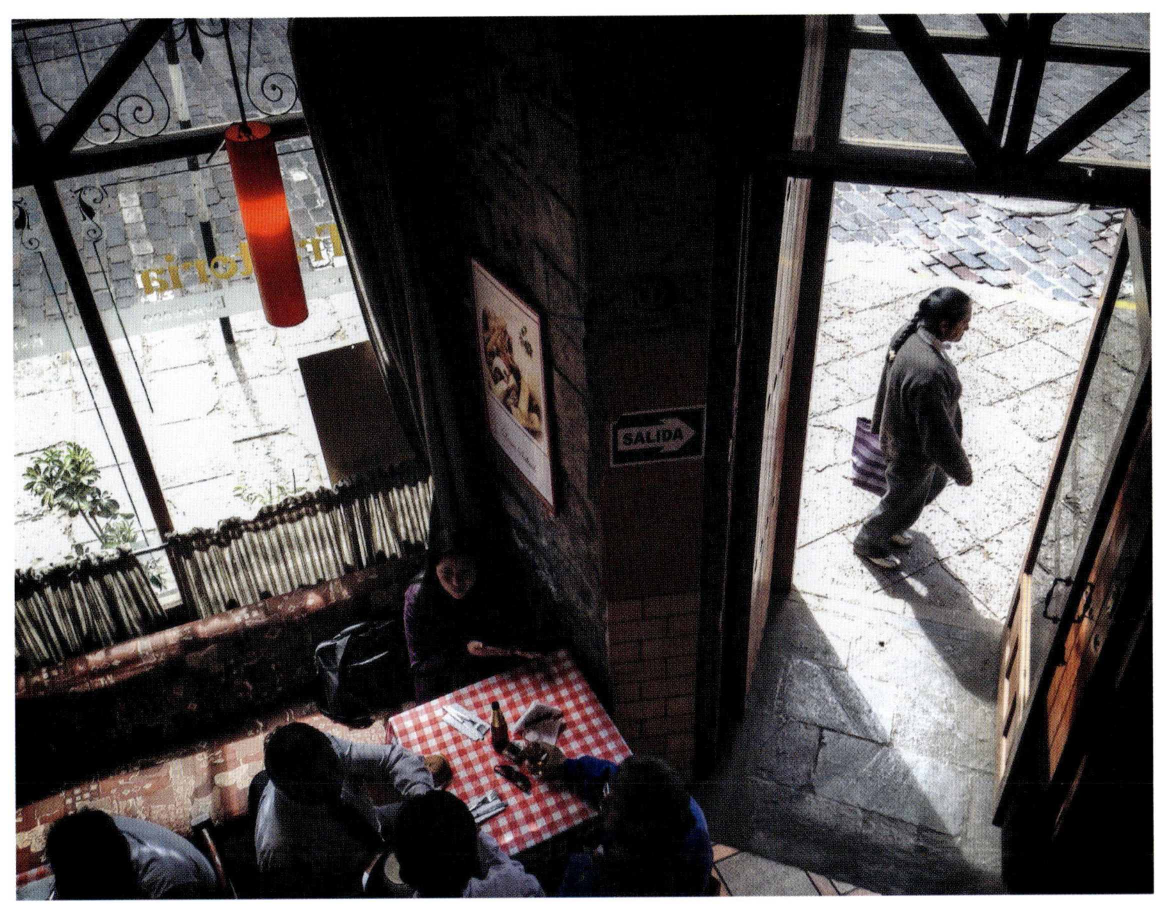

'My work is best described as documentary photography with a purpose.'

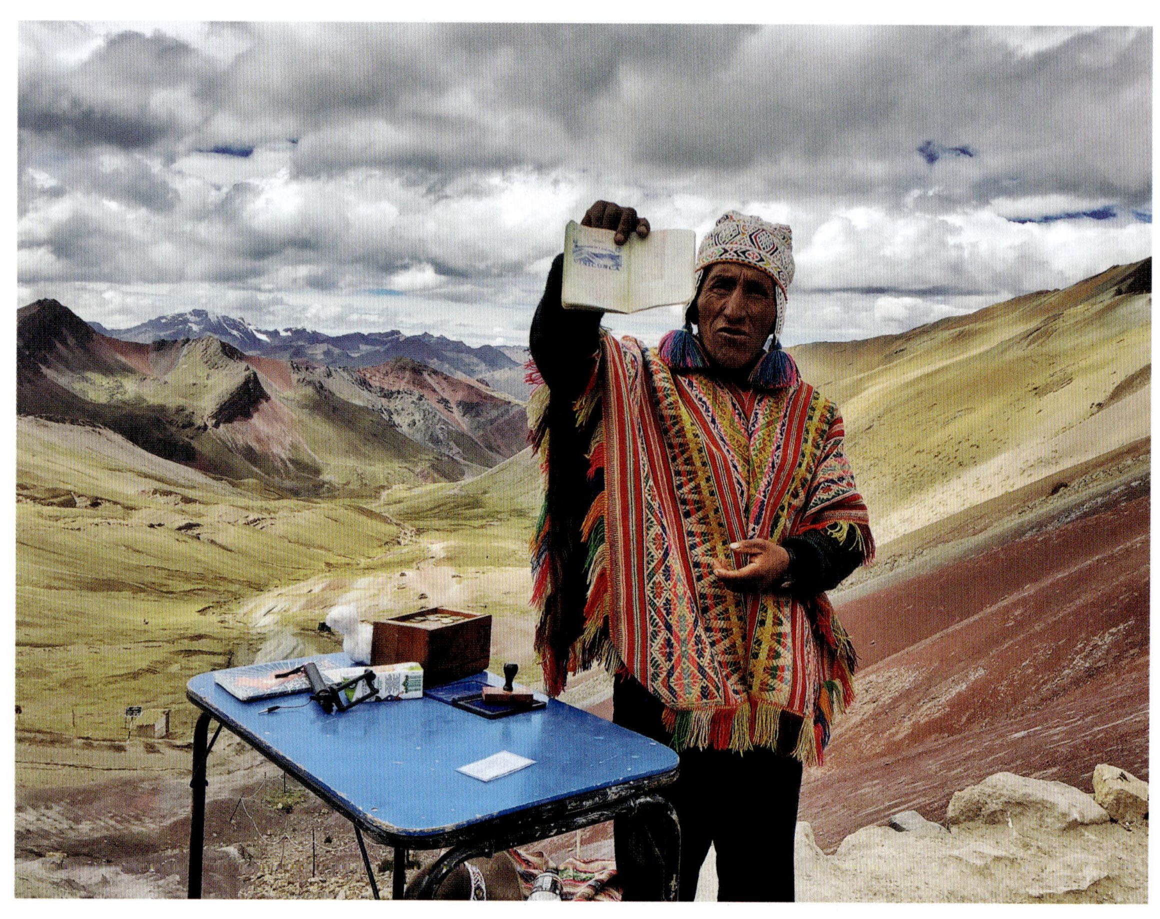

ABOVE: The welcome at the passport-stamping station at Rainbow Mountain, 5,200 metres (17,000 feet) above sea level in Cusco, Peru.

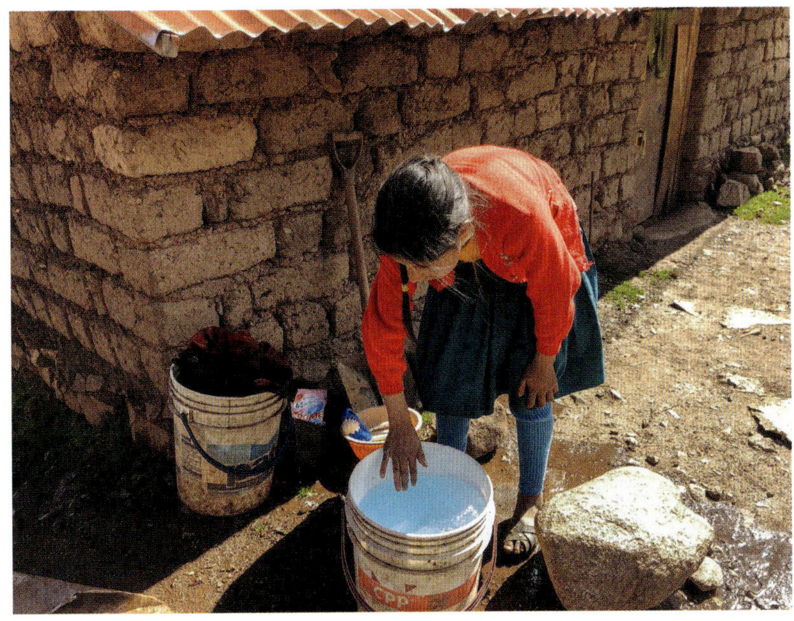

RIGHT: At an early age, girls in Cusco learn to help out at home while their parents are at work. On laundry day, this young girl cleans clothes by beating and rubbing them against a rock.

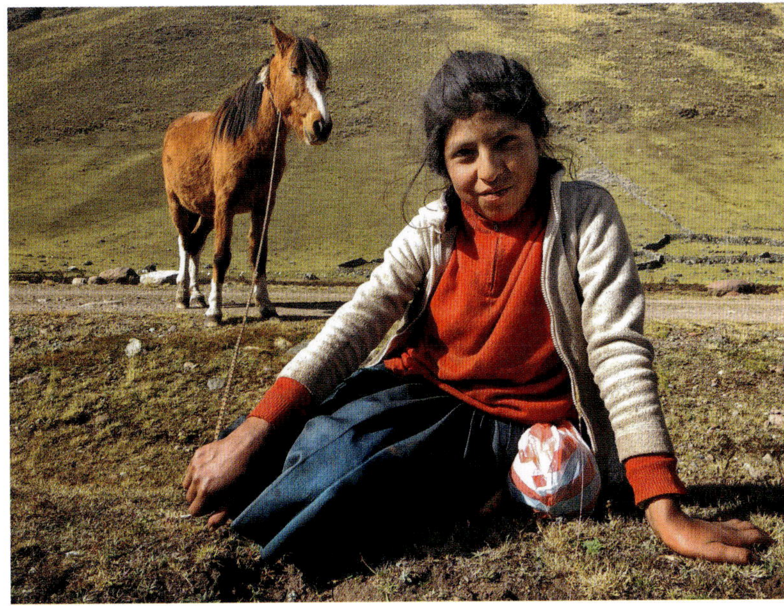

LEFT: Llamas and horses are the main means of transport in the high-altitude area around Cusco. Here, a young girl takes a rest while going from one village to the next at 4,300 metres (14,000 feet) above sea level.

RENZO GRANDE

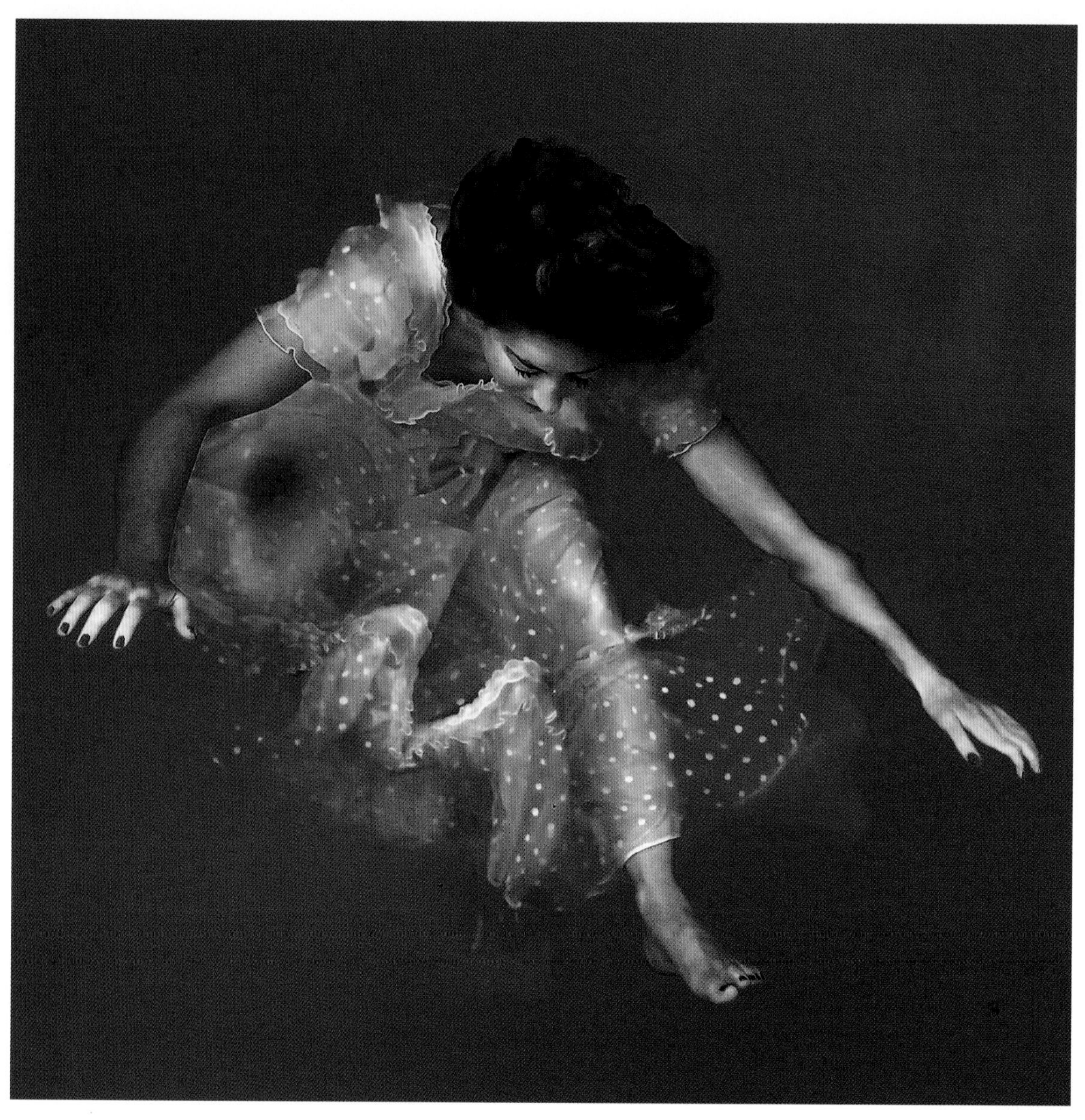

'I have ideas that I try to execute, but they usually
end up taking on a life of their own, which I'm
usually happier with.'

VIEWPOINT

Robin Robertis
Carlsbad, USA

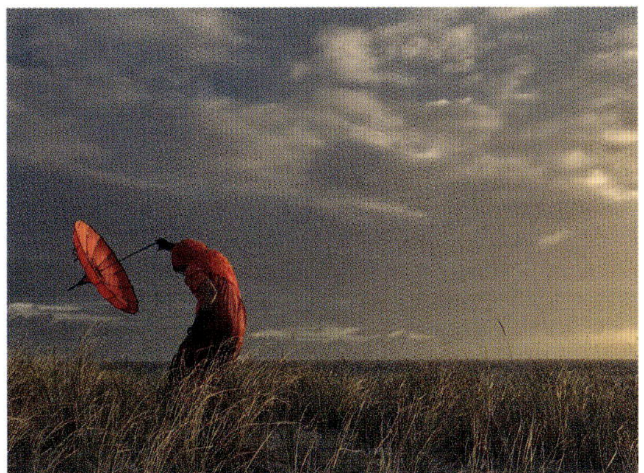

Self-taught artist Robin Robertis works as a flight attendant for a major US airline. She has a busy schedule, travelling all over the world. She wanted to be a painter, but felt she was not very good at completing things, as she has attention deficit disorder. Once a concept was on the canvas and half completed, she would move on to the next, filling the studio with half-finished paintings, sometimes working on many of them the same time. A smartphone camera offers her the opposite – it's a tool for fast photos. Robertis's conceptual photography stands out for its creative potential; it's less a representation of reality, more a distillation of an emotional landscape frozen into a moment in time. Her images can be ghostly, mysterious and ethereal. They represent a slight disassociation from reality, an illusion that begins to suggest new worlds. She says she is interested in making surreal, unexpected, fun, dark, thought-provoking images.

Robertis sees her Apple iPhone 13 Pro Max as being a box of crayons that she can take on the road. For basic editing, her number one, go-to app is Snapseed. Retouch is a must-have for her and she also uses Image Blender and Distressed FX for texture. Robertis enjoys the happy mistakes she makes playing with Hipstamatic. She is inspired by the surreal, people and portraiture, and botanical life, and is influenced by Diane Arbus, Man Ray and Ralph Eugene Meatyard.

'I haven't found my niche yet, but I do mostly portraits and street photography; for now I specialize in that. But I don't limit myself to just one type – I try to experiment with them all.'

Sehin Tewabe
Addis Abeba, Ethiopia

Professional photographer, photo editor and retoucher Sehin Tewabe was born and raised in Addis Abeba. The city is an important cultural hub with a thriving artistic heart and a strong fashion scene, thanks in part to its highly engaged demographic of young people. It has been recently recognized as having the fastest economic growth of any country in the world. Tewabe's professional work covers many types of photography, including portraiture, documentary and event photography. Alongside this, she has a passion for candid street photography and spends as much of her spare time as she can on this pursuit, feeling that it is her life's work. Tewabe uses her Apple iPhone XR for her street photography.

ABOVE: This photo was taken at Meskel Square in Addis Abeba. Our Prime Minister had been appointed for the second time and I was there to photograph the event. I saw these two men walking by; one had the Ethiopian flag on his back, and I thought that was interesting since it was such an historic day for our country. I immediately shared it online and people loved it because it was relatable and timely.

RIGHT: Really beautiful sunlight in the Bole district of Addis Abeba. I was on a 'photowalk' with friends.

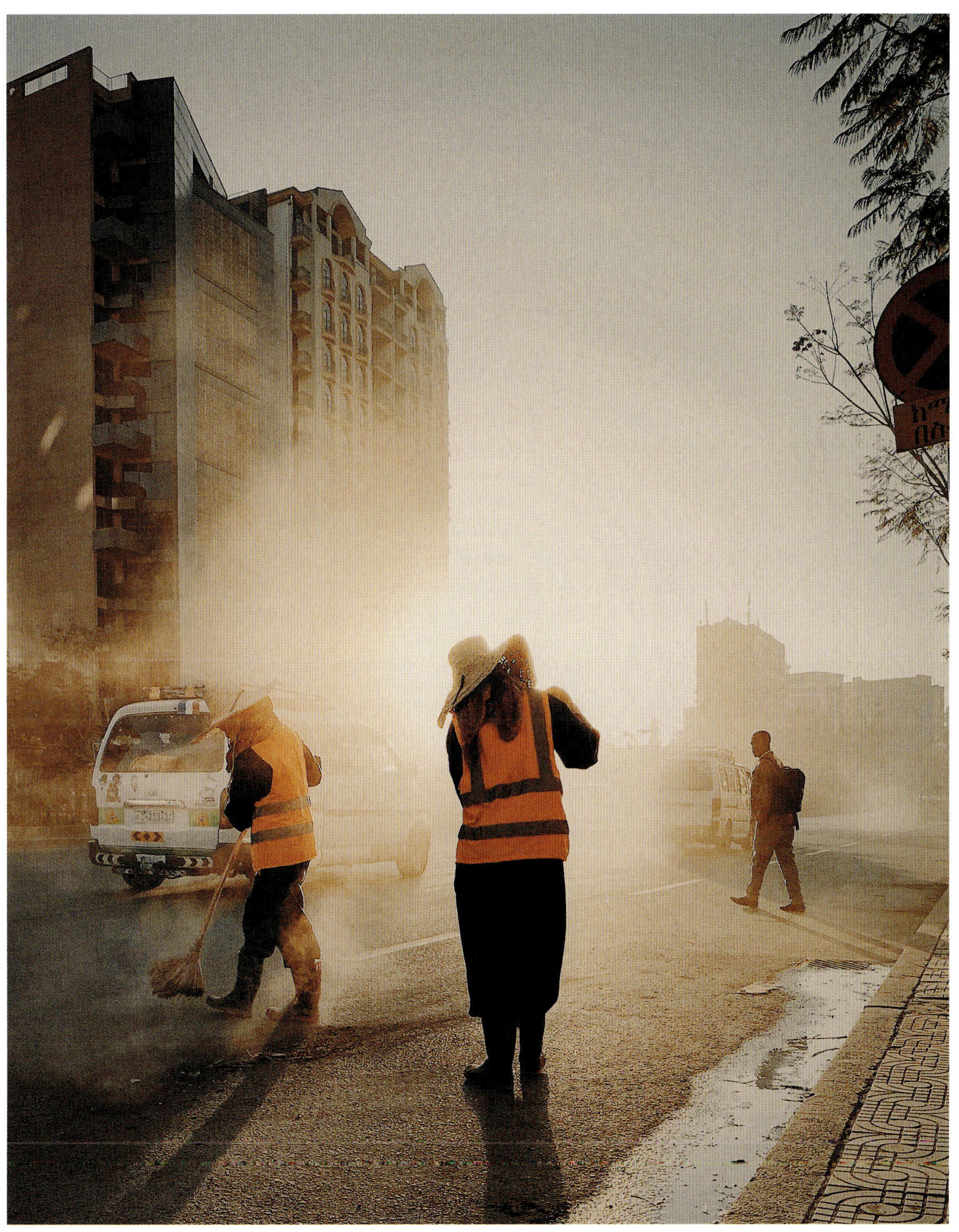

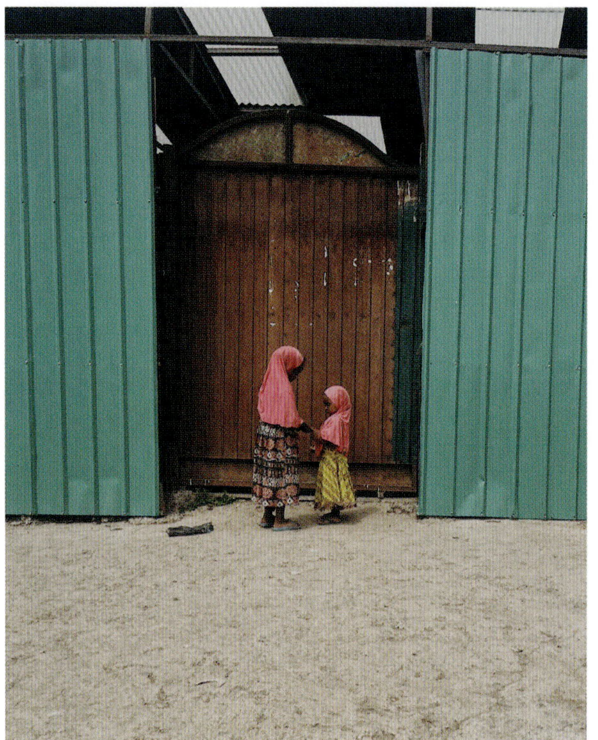

RIGHT: I was in a town called Somali Tera to take photos because I had bought a new phone and I was excited about trying out the new camera. This scene reminded me of the typical morning routine of many Addis Abebans: a girl buying bread for the family breakfast from a nearby bread shop. I also loved the morning light falling across the girl's face as she sold the bread.

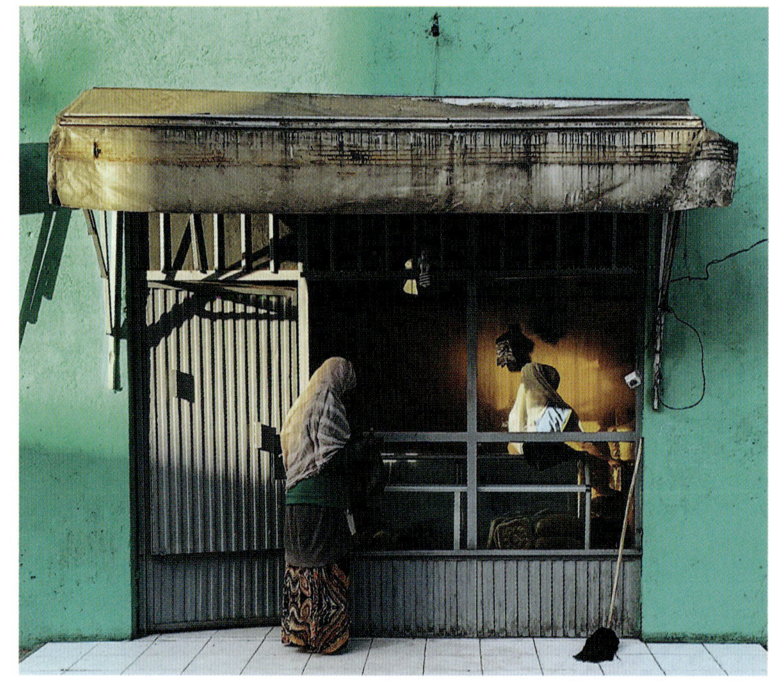

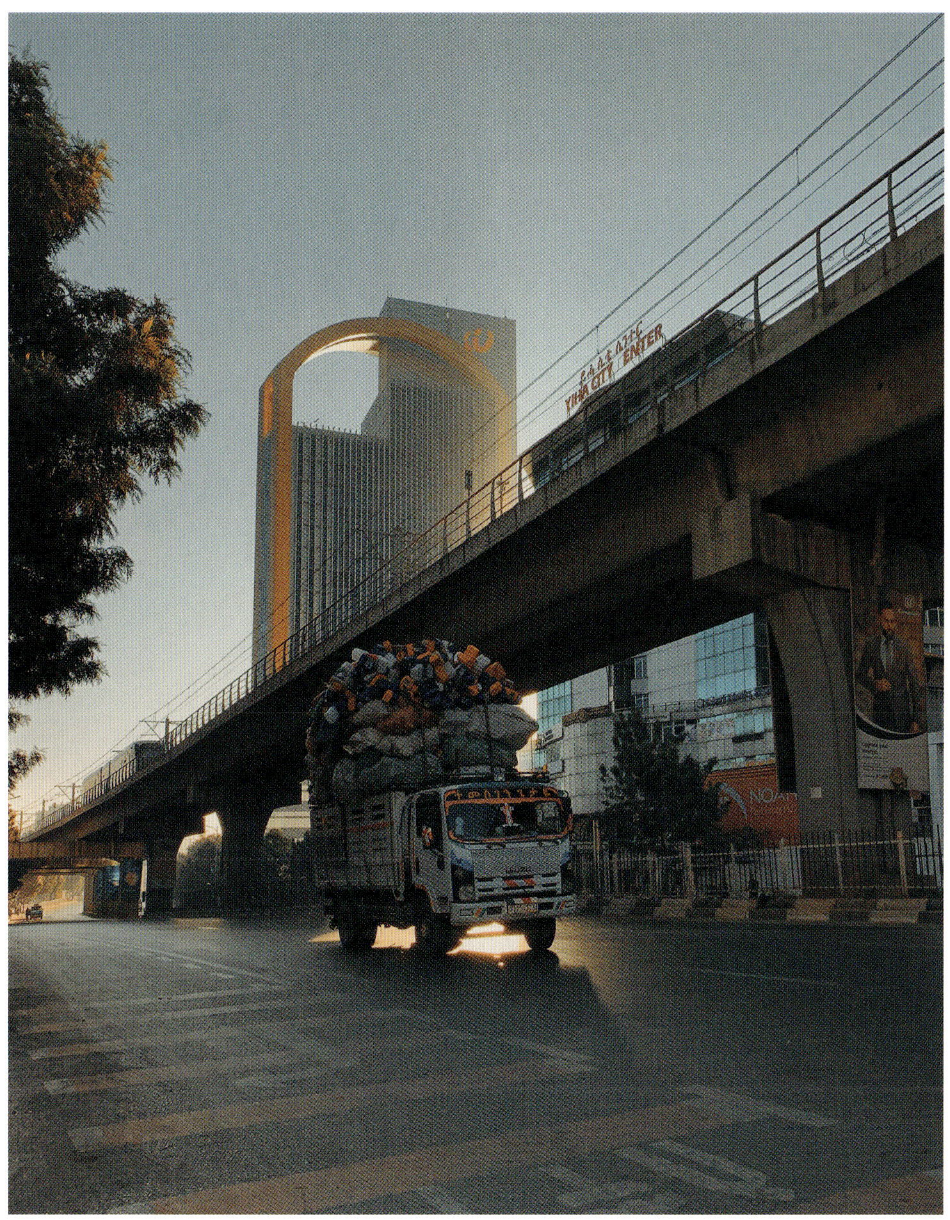

ABOVE: I loved how the morning sunlight glared through that huge car on a random photowalk with a friend in a neighbourhood of Addis Abeba called Mexico.

Shihyu Tsao
New Taipei City, Taiwan

Engineer Shihyu Tsao works in a science research
centre. Perspective, symmetry and geometric
patterns feature strongly in his photography.
He photographs the 'fantastic or funny' around
him, mostly using an Apple iPhone 7.

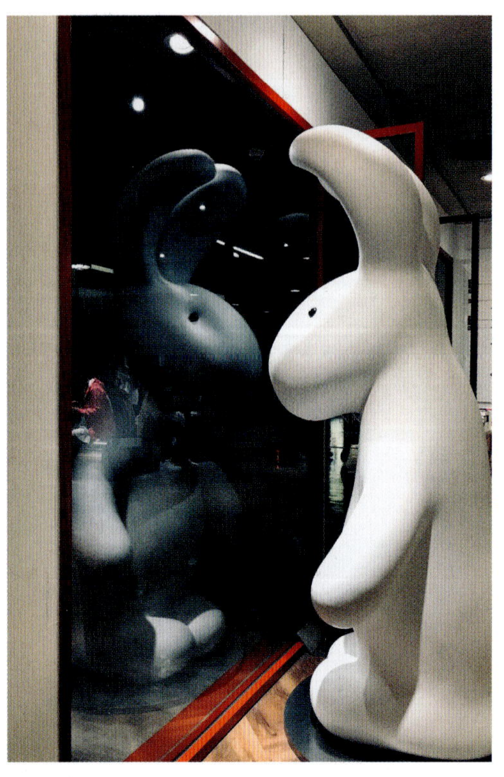

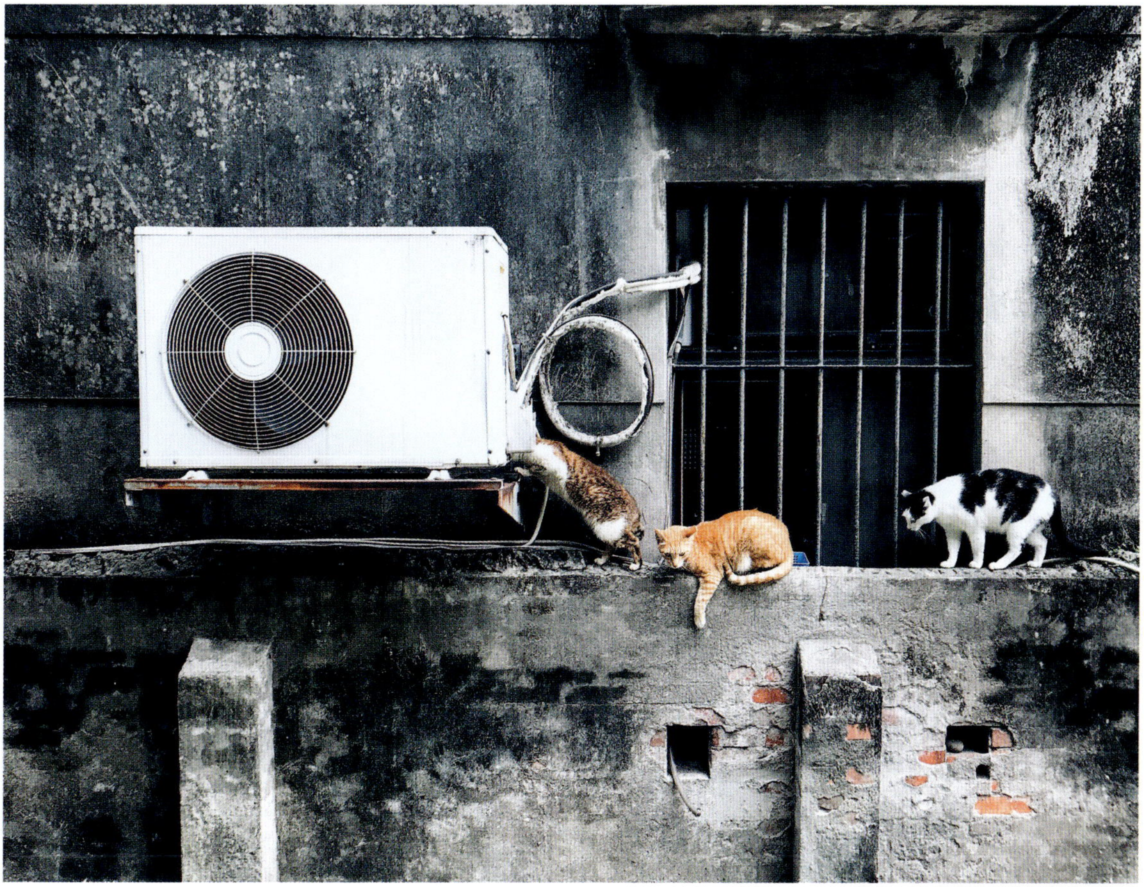

 The Huashan 1914 Creative Park in Taipei was built in 1914 when the country was under Japanese rule. It was originally a private winery and was subsequently owned by both the Japanese and Chinese governments. After production stopped in 1987, the building was left empty for over a decade until it was developed into artists' studios and a venue for non-profit organizations to host exhibitions and performances by theatre groups, film directors, painters and sculptors. I was visiting an exhibition when I walked through this corridor and saw the colourful shadow caused by the sunshine passing through the stained-glass windows.

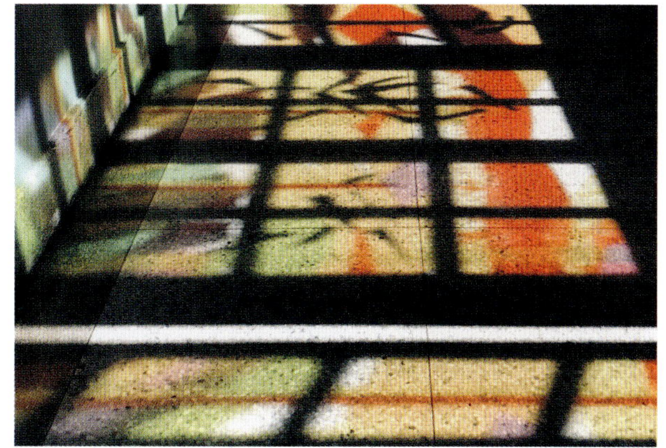

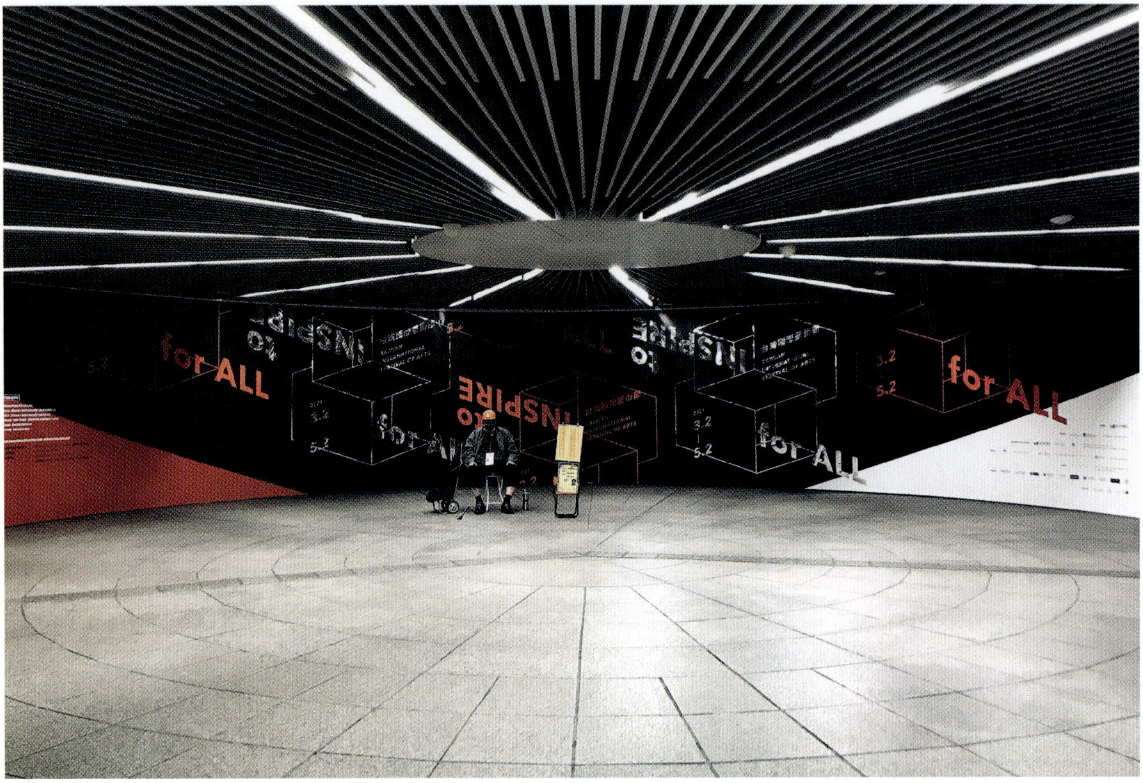

ABOVE: A street violinist sits on a chair, having a nap between songs at the metro station by the Chiang Kai-shek Memorial Hall in Taipei. At the same time, I noticed that the arrangement of fluorescent lamps on the ceiling and the patterns on the ground were both radial, creating visual tension.

RIGHT: This photo was taken at Banqiao Station in Taipei in May 2020. At the time, Taiwan was just beginning to experience the effects of the Covid-19 pandemic. People went out less and so the station concourse became empty. This was a pretty rare sight when I was commuting during 'normal' times so I stopped to take a photo.

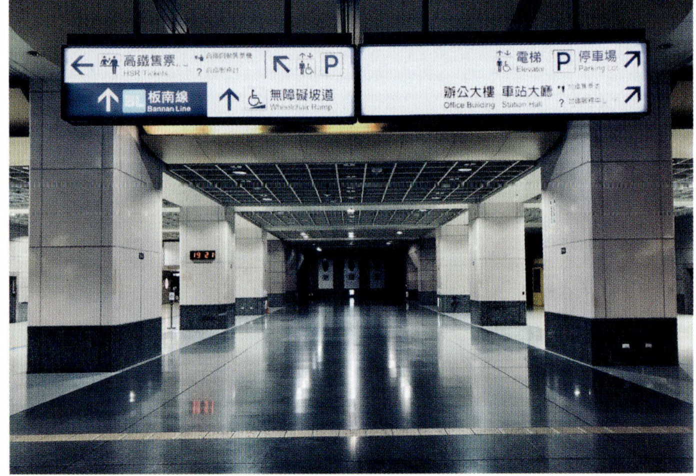

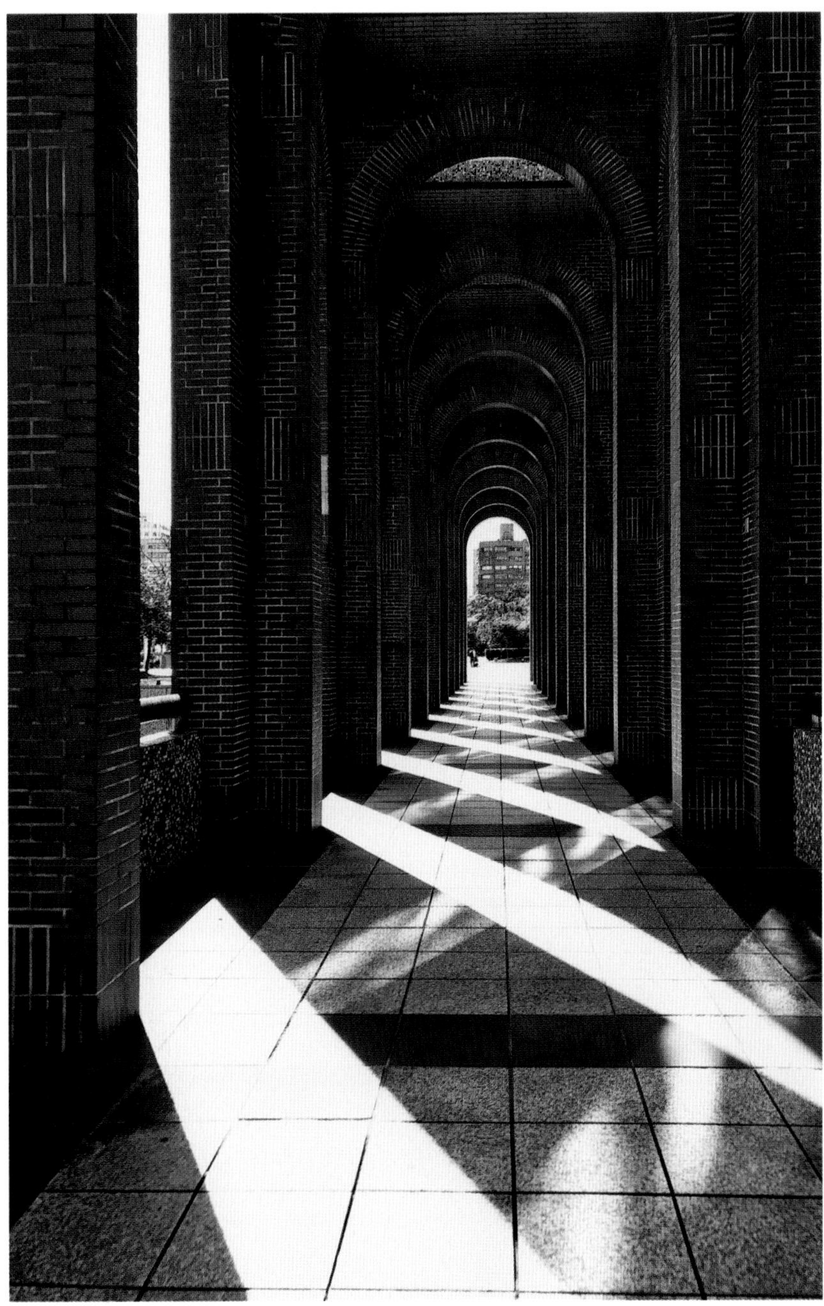

ABOVE: The interweaving of
shafts of light through this arch
at the National Central Library
in New Taipei City reminded me
of the laces on a pair of trainers.

Taru Latva-Pukkila
Helsinki, Finland

Textile designer and freelance photographer Taru Latva-Pukkila lives in Helsinki, but has deep roots in the small town of Kauhajoki on the west coast of Finland. It makes her smile to know that her little brother moved back there with his family and is the town's mayor. Latva-Pukkila has a masters degree in textile design and currently works for a Danish textile producer at their Helsinki office.

Photography is one of the most important things in her life and she sees it as a tool to express her creativity and way of seeing, and to make sense of life as it unfolds around her. Every day Latva-Pukkila walks to catch the tram to and from work and there isn't a day that goes by without her finding something that catches her eye and makes her feel the need to take a photo. It has become a natural part of her daily routine.

Since 2011 Latva-Pukkila has mainly used an Apple iPhone (4s, SE, SE 2nd generation) for her mobile photography. At the moment she is using an iPhone 13 Pro and, when it was new to the market, she tested a Huawei P10. For editing she uses different apps depending on the requirements. Her most-used apps are Snapseed, VSCO, Hipstamatic, Noir and ProCam8.

At the beginning, Latva-Pukkila was drawn to shooting and editing in monochrome, but colour has slowly entered her photographs. Since the beginning, street and documentary photography have been her main interests. She sees beauty in everyday life and even the smallest details make a difference for her. Being from a small town, and then living in nine different places and three countries, has kept her senses strong.

The photos shown here were all taken in Helsinki. They are typical Finnish street scenes showing the changing seasons, which give Latva-Pukkila the chance to create a variety of moods. Light plays an important role in her images, creating dramatic long shadows, and the lack of light is one of the challenges when photographing in Finland. Her images are colourful but there is a certain loneliness and melancholy too. Latva-Pukkila mainly photographs strangers on the streets and in public places. Sometimes she makes connections with people and has conversations with them, especially if they are interested in knowing why she takes photos. When publishing the photos, she uses her own name so people can contact her if they want to talk about them. These images bring her joy, and they tell stories of people's lives. You can see things or details which aren't visible at first glance.

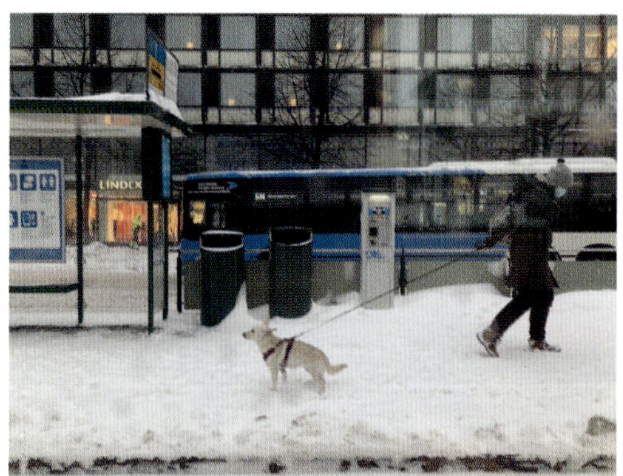

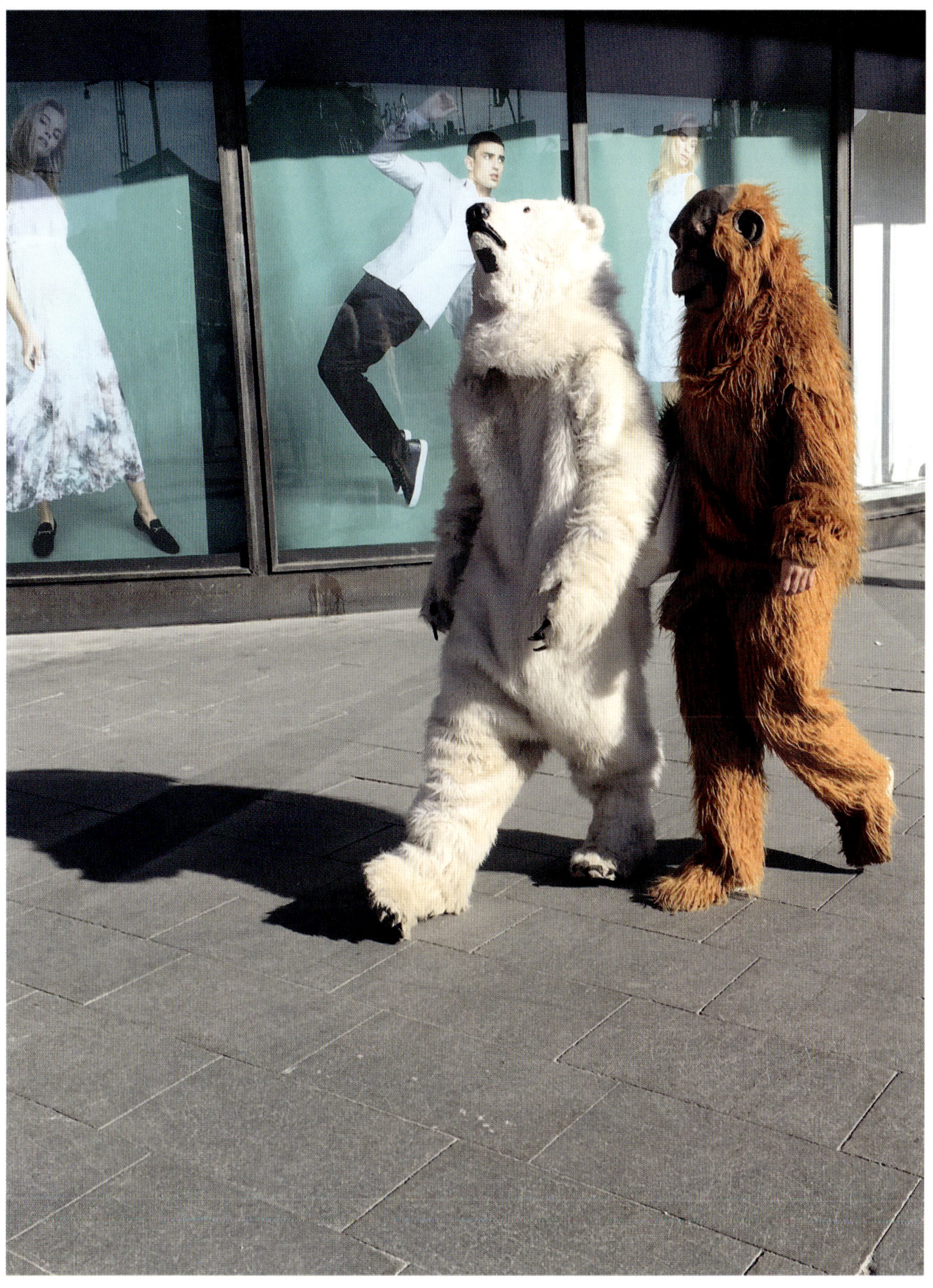

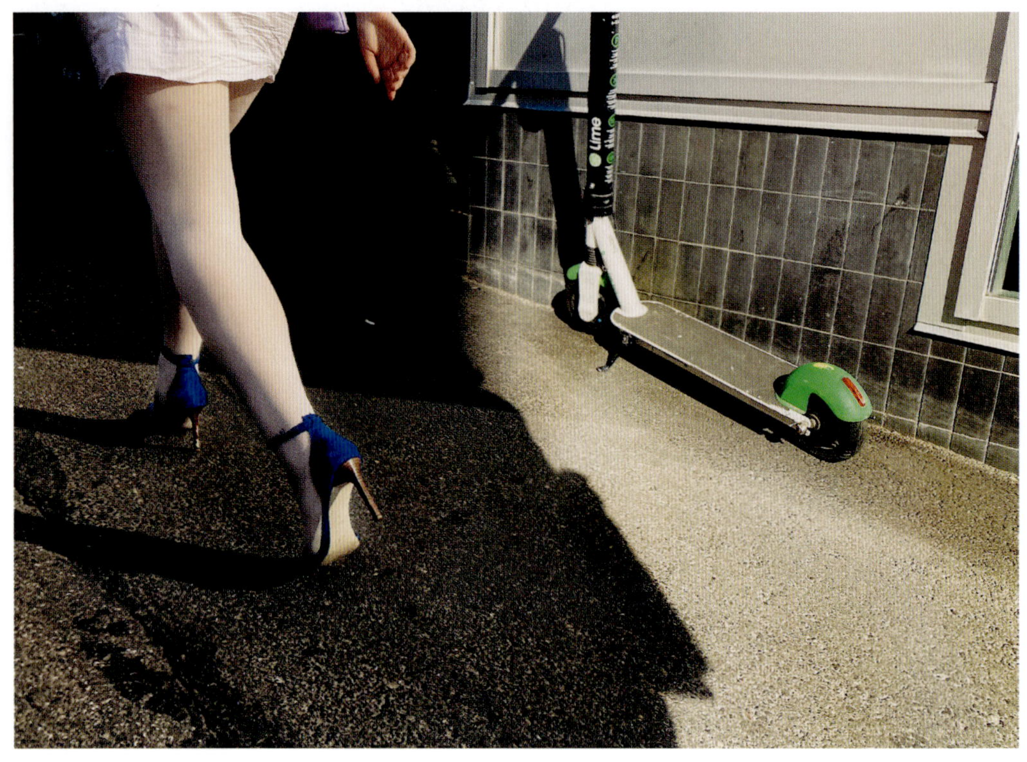

VIEWPOINT

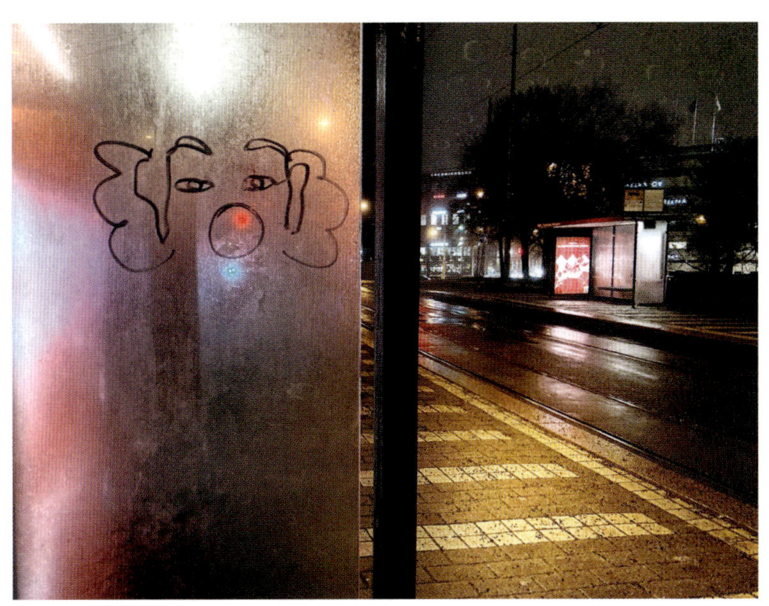

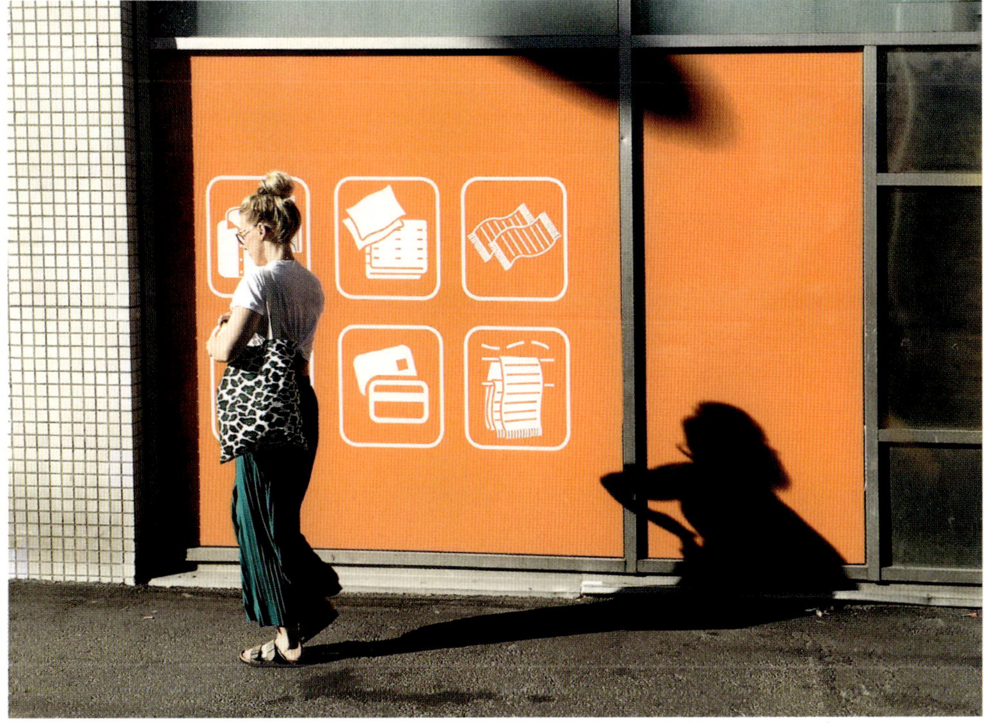

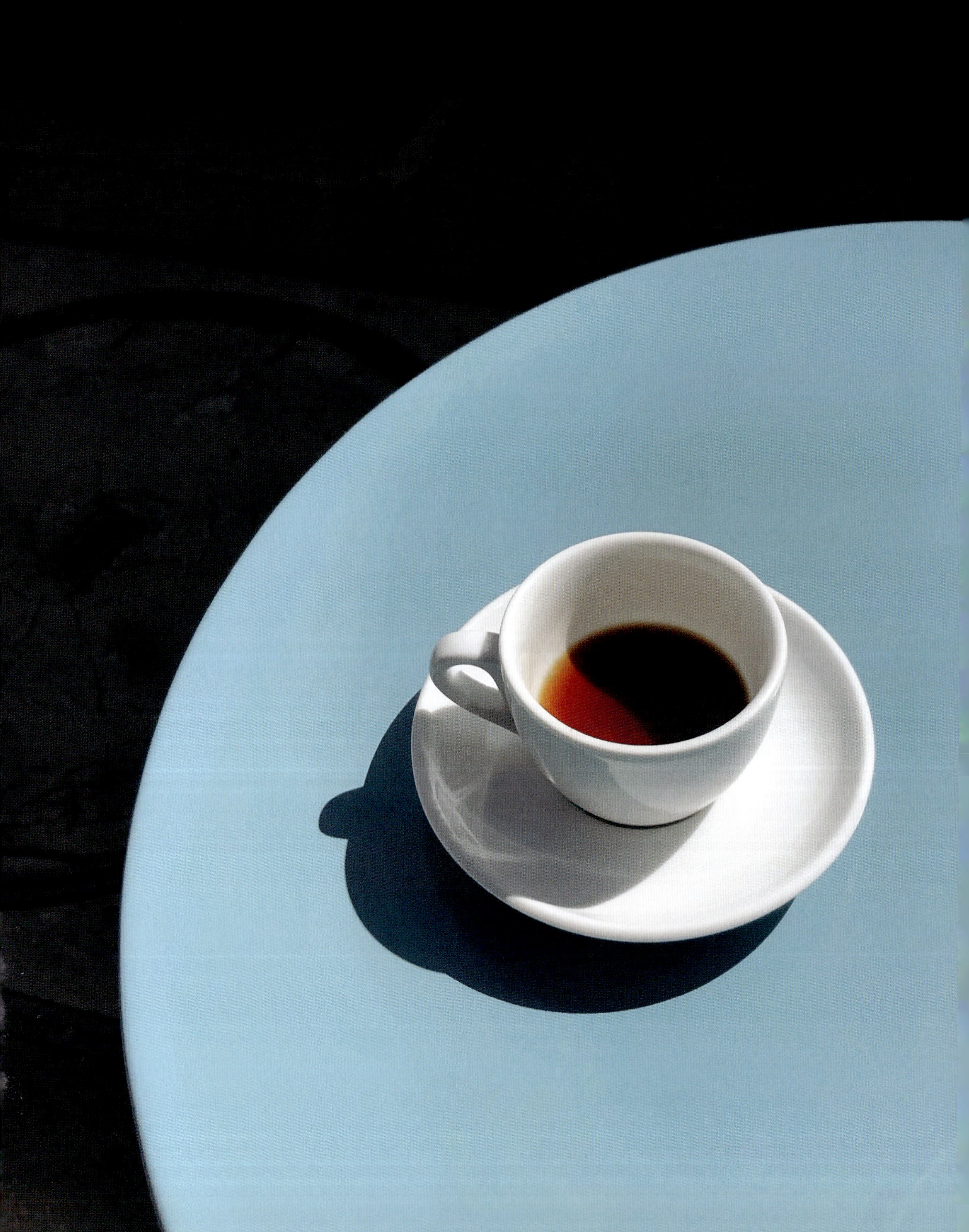

Vincent Patrizi
Montreal, Canada

Photography has been part of Vincent Patrizi's life since 2010 when he got his first camera. Patrizi was born in Normandy, France, and lived in Paris for five years before moving to Canada. He says that photography has become a part of him.

He used to use both his iPhone and his camera, but it evolved to a point where he just shot portraits for his boyfriend's career as an influencer with the DSLR and used his phone for everything else. He slowly re-introduced a hybrid camera into his routine and never looked back.

Patrizi says his iPhone is his 'best partner' for recording memories of his everyday life. He used to edit in VSCO, but now he mostly edits using Lightroom, and sometimes the iPhone's native editing settings for quick adjustments. He loves to play with light and shadow; he used to have a passion for geometry, lines and symmetry but is less concerned with them now. He uses the Lightroom app for editing, aiming to do minimal work as he feels the photos are better with less processing. This aesthetic can be a challenge to achieve, considering how the algorithms in smartphones tend to overprocess photos at the time of capture.

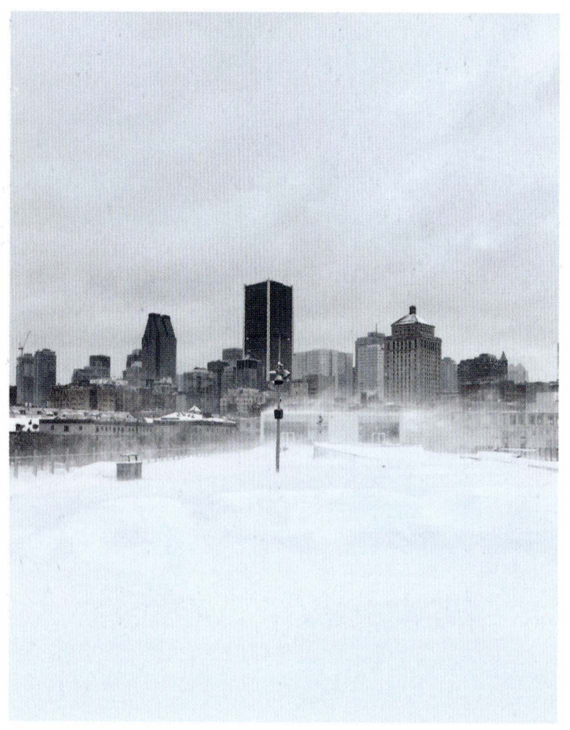

ABOVE: This shot of Montreal's Old Port was taken during the first weeks after we emigrated to Canada. We wanted to enjoy a snowstorm close to the Saint Laurent river because the wind was very intense and created a lunar aesthetic. The view of Montreal from here is one of the best you can get and, in this moment, the floating snow made it feel like the city was fading away in the storm. I love the multiple layers of snow, city and sky.

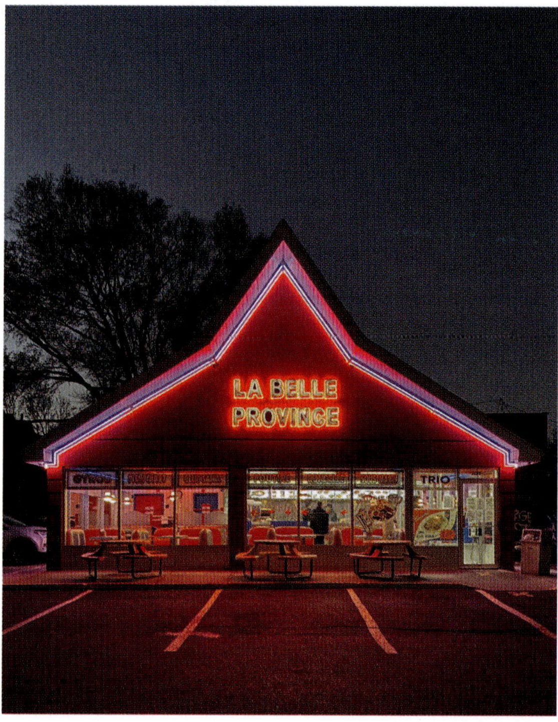

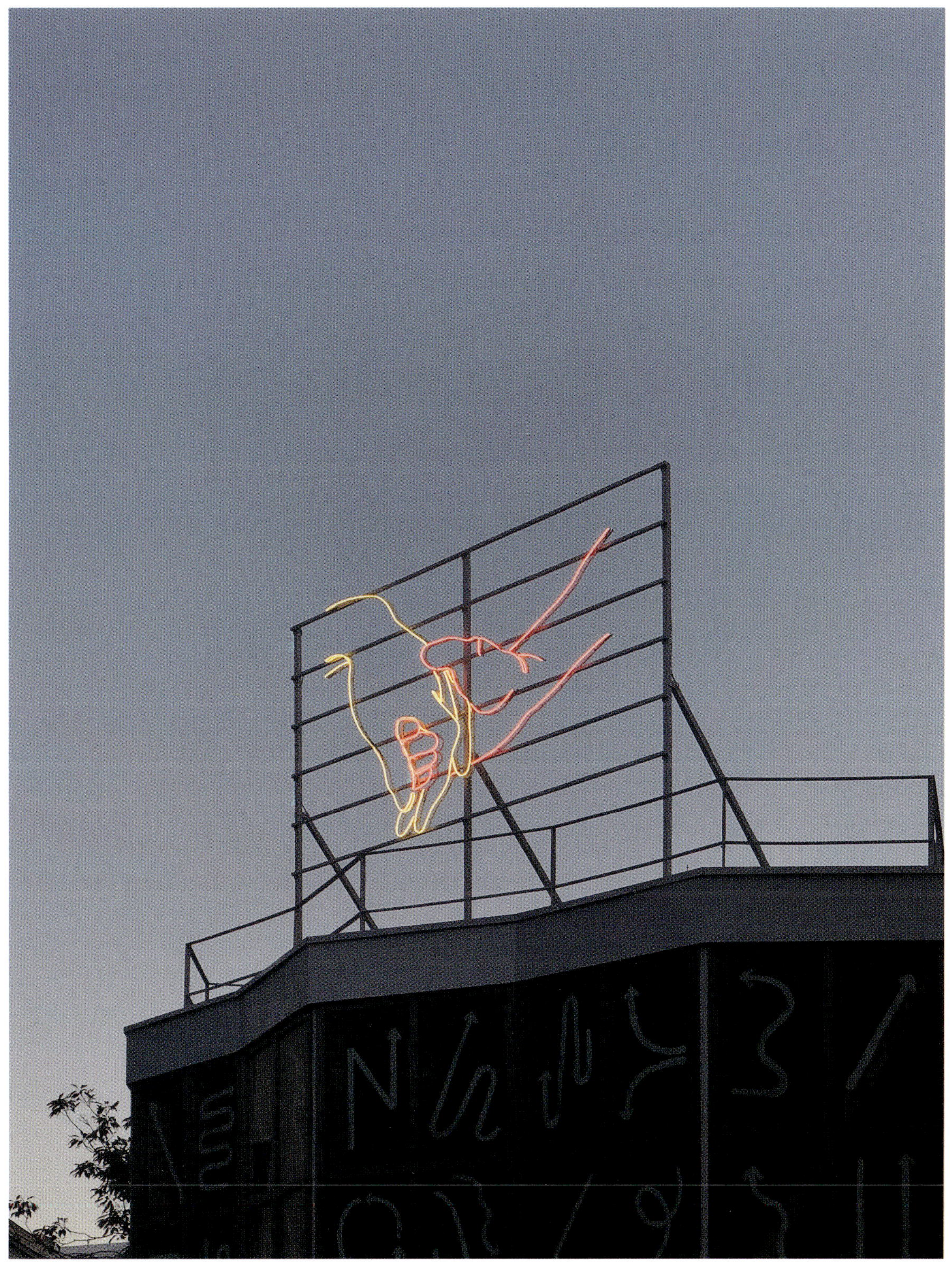

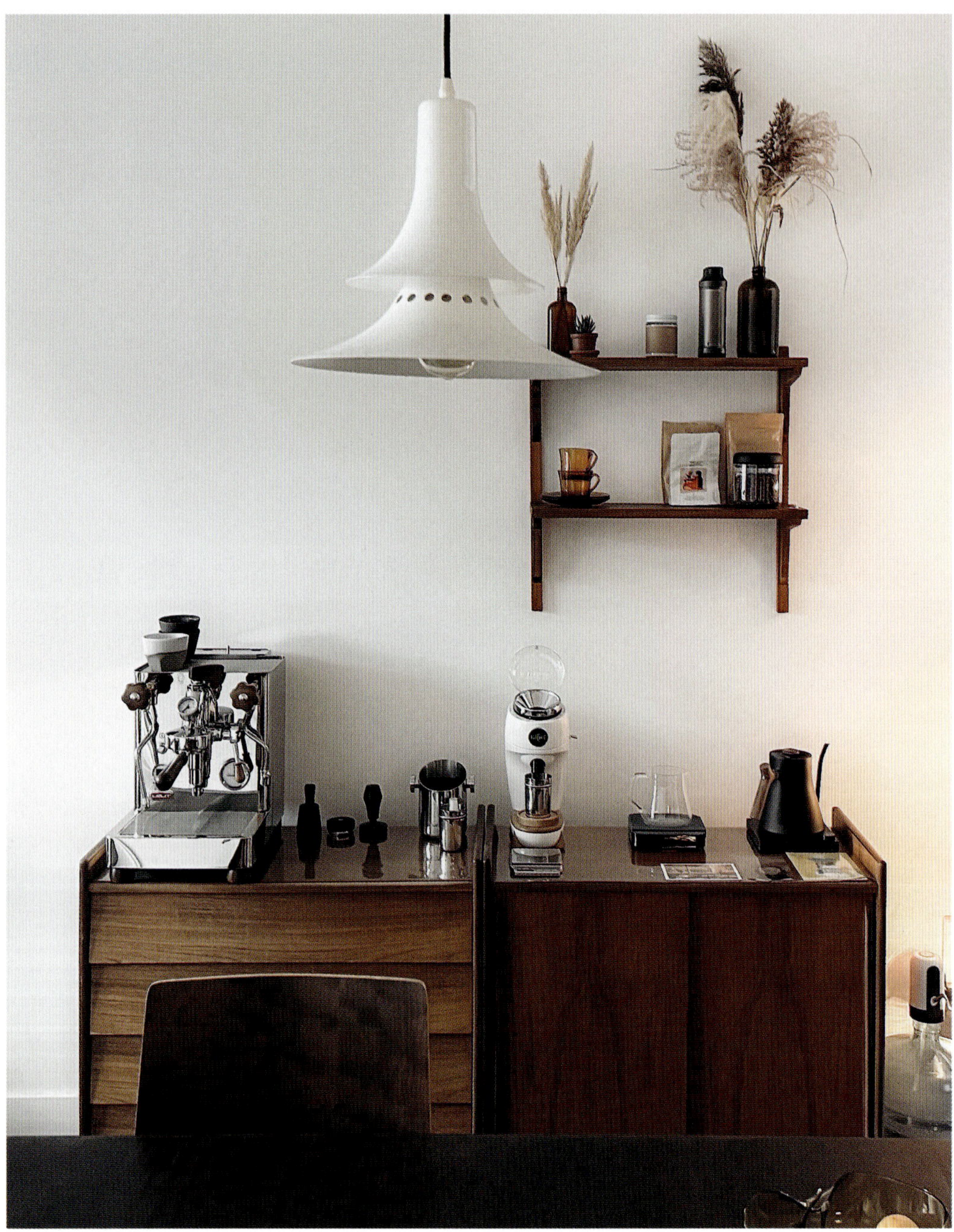

ABOVE: This shot of my home in Montreal showcases my relationship with coffee: my passion for it and the importance of the visual pleasure I get when I get to my coffee station and take time to brew it. For me, coffee is as meditative as photography – it helps me to slow down. I don't care how long it takes to brew the perfect cup. At that moment, I quit the desire for instant satisfaction that is so present in our lives.

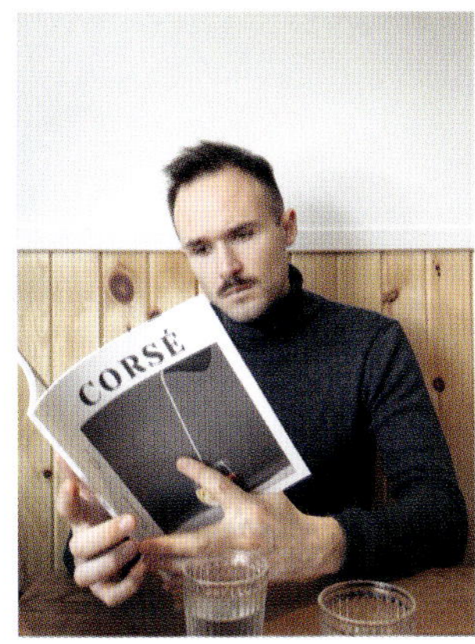

ABOVE: A self portrait at the Duplex café, Trois-Rivières. We visited when we arrived in Québec, and it remains a key moment in our expatriation and relationship with the region. We saw it on Instagram before we got to Canada and wanted to go there to meet the owners as it represented the project we had in mind when we arrived in Montreal – to eventually open our own cafe. I asked Camille to press the shutter on this shot of me reading a local magazine dedicated to Québec's specialty coffee scene. The circle was complete. Coffee is our shared passion, for what it is, how it is consumed, what it represents and the places where we can enjoy it. It's one of the reasons we moved to Montreal because it's a very active place for lovers of speciality coffee. We now both work in the coffee industry. The image is symbolic of the place; plus I'm reading and I like the look of concentration on my face, which is rare.

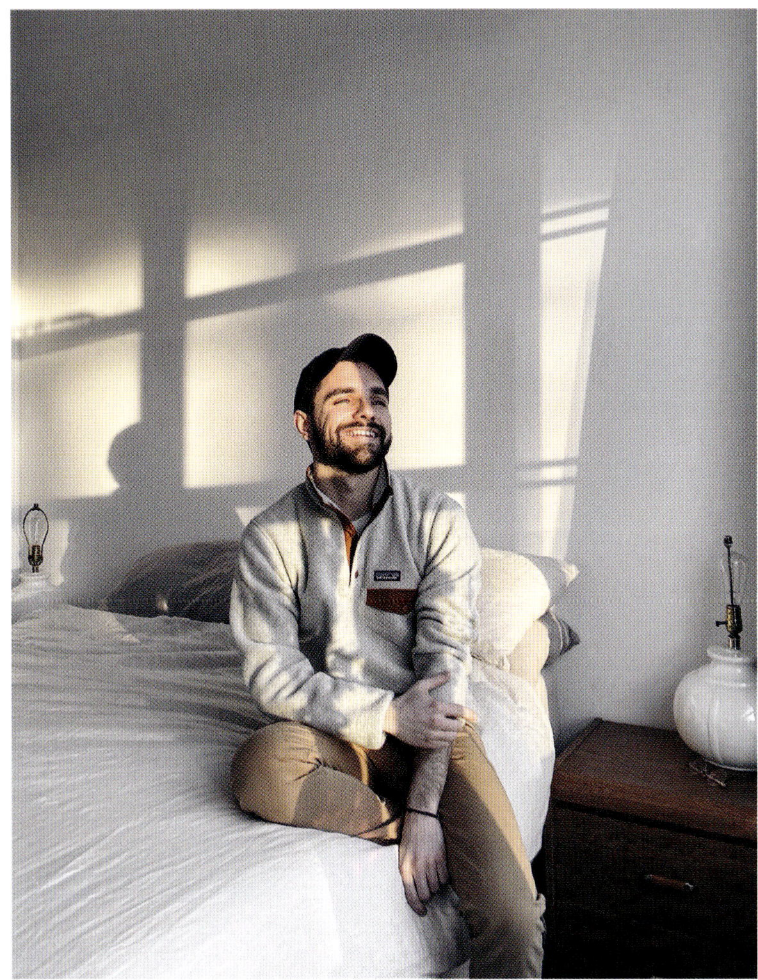

ABOVE: At home in Montreal with my fiancé, Camille. We were getting ready to go out and the light was spot on. It was beautiful, with typical autumn rays and Camille's outfit was a reflection of it too. He just sat on the bed because the whole thing was perfect, particularly with the rays of light on his face.

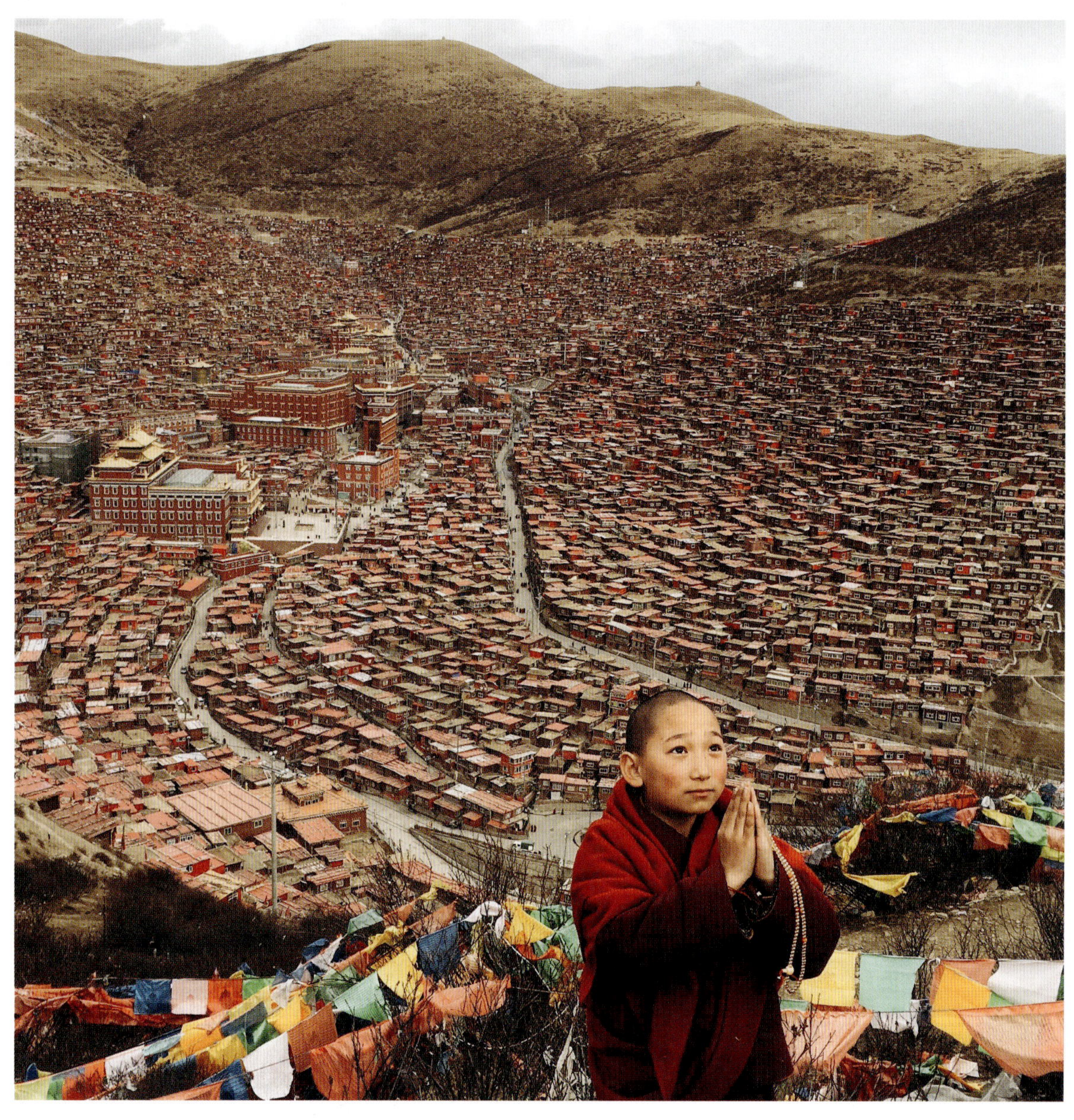

'I take photos to freeze time, to keep memories
 of ordinary life and simple happiness forever.'

 Larung Gar is the largest
Buddhist study institute in the
world. It is built 4,000 metres
(13,000 feet) above sea level
on a hillside in a remote and
treeless valley in eastern Tibet.
It is one of the most significant
Tibetan Buddhist institutes in
the world and home to more
than 10,000 crimson-robed
monks and nuns. It is unusual
to find men and women
studying Buddhism in such
close proximity to each other
as they do here, but they do
live separately in their own
designated areas. The densely
packed huts are sprawled
around the monastic centre.
These colourful homes, each
just large enough for a bed and
a suitcase, are brightly painted
in traditional Tibetan red paint.
It takes five days to build a
house here. The price is cheaper
higher up, so that's where the
children stay.

Wei Xiong
Wuhan, China

The district of Huangpi, where mobile phone
photographer Wei Xiong lives, is a like a small town,
but it is one of the thirteen urban districts that
make up the city of Wuhan. The area around the
Huangpi district is primarily rural and this pastoral
way of life is reflected in some of Xiong's photos.

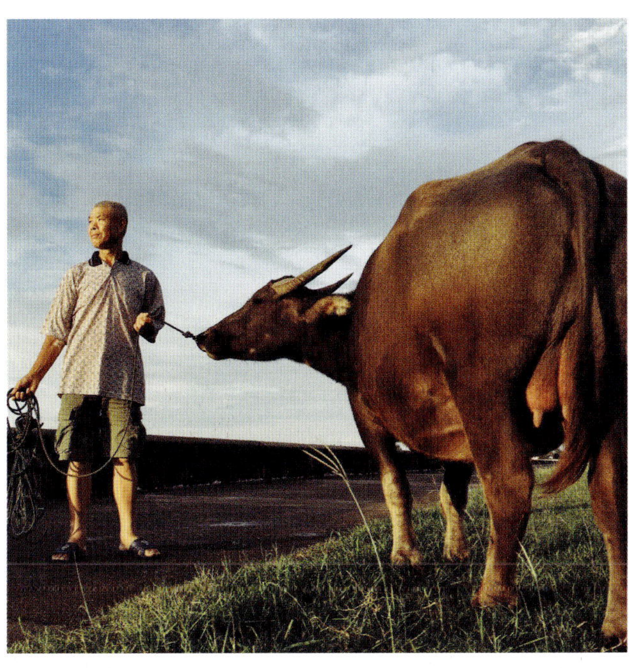

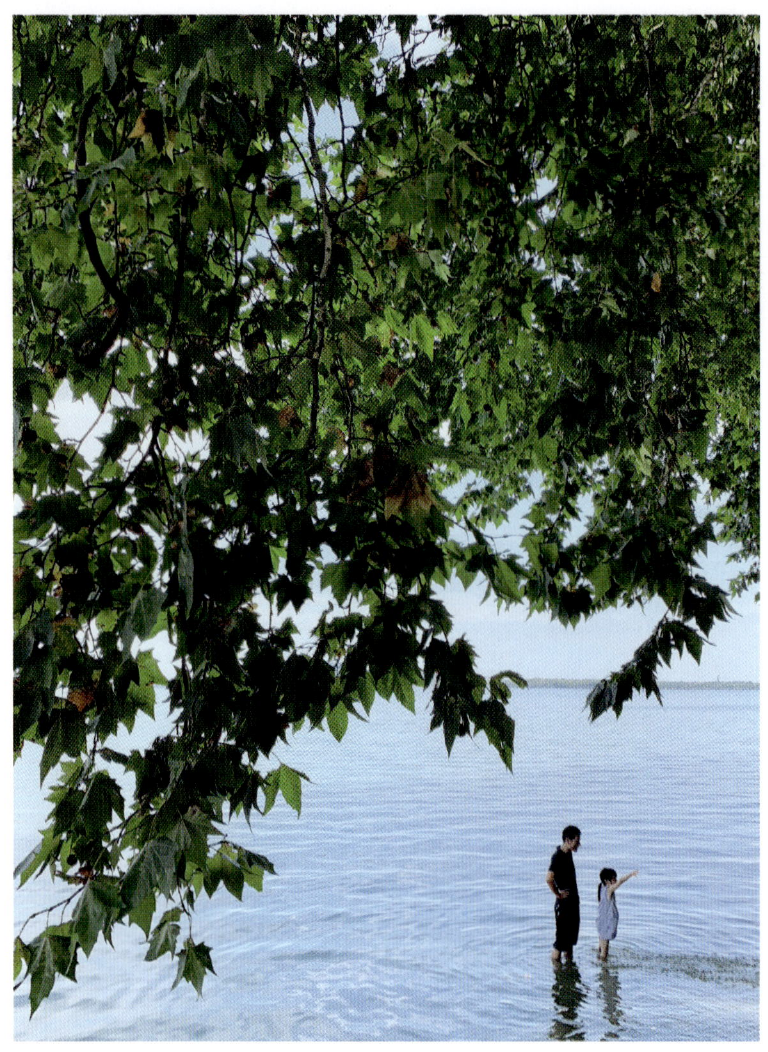

ABOVE + RIGHT: Wuhan is situated
on the northern left bank of
the Yangtze River and has
nearly 200 lakes. Perhaps
not surprising, then, that the
main theme in Xiong's work is
swimming and water.

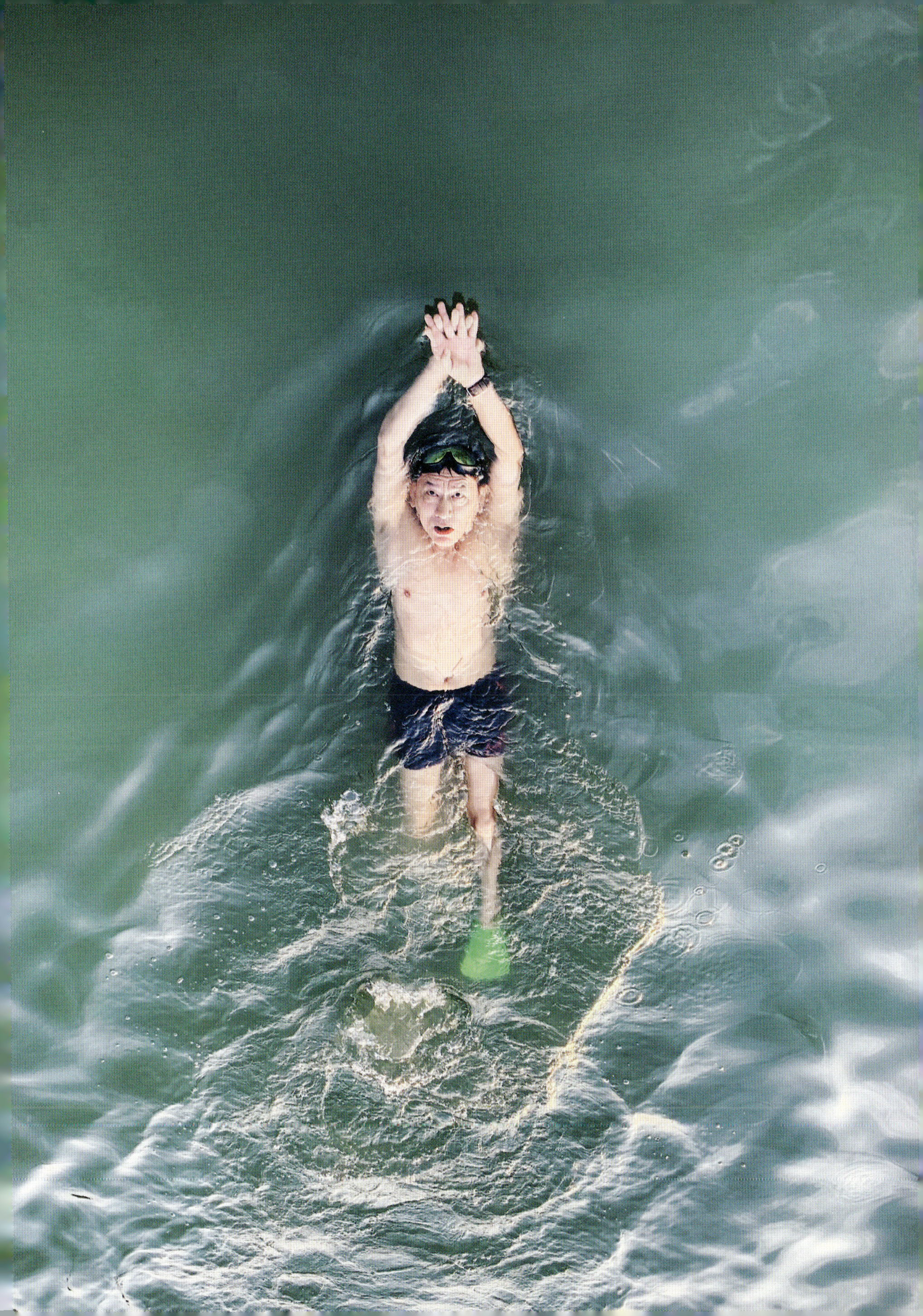

Acknowledgements + List of Contributors

A huge thanks to all the contributors who made this book a reality.

Thanks to Jo Dymond for the assistance in wrangling all the contributor admin into shape.

Thank you for all the hard work, vision and support to Richard Collins, Faye Robson and Ben Gardiner and the whole team at Ilex and Octopus.

My endless gratitude to my agent Jane Turnbull for always bringing positivity and support to the proceedings, and to John Coleman, for gifting me my first darkroom set-up.

Thanks to Taiga Inami and Anna Filonenko for their help with translations and the time they spent helping me hunt for people.

Thanks also to the venerable Andy Butler of Mobiography, who suggested people to look at and for being a long-time supporter of smartphone photography.

But thank you most of all to Grace, Kade, Mum and Dad and all the family and friends who have given me a lifetime of stories to listen to and everyday moments to capture with my camera.

Akhil Vilakkadan
@Akhilvilakkadan
Alessandra Manzotti
@Amanzottifoto
Alexandra Cabral
@alex_cabral02
Ana Carolina Fernandes
@culafernandes
Ann Hecht
@alice1280
Barbara Januszewska-Piróg
@barbara_j_pirog
Brendan Ó Sé
@brendan.o.se
Charlotte Mason-Mottram
@mason_mottram
Dina Alfasi
@Dinalf
Elaine Taylor
@sunflowerof21
Ernest Ankomah
@ankomah_
Ernest Rius Bonet
@erniernes
Forough Alaei
@Foroughalaei
Franc Ortiz Rodrigo
@soldatdp
Glenn Homann
@blueboy70
Harshita Sabnis
@harshitasabnis
Hasan Belal
@hasan.belal.001
Hezron Chen
@hez.c

Inga Dinga
@dinga.diary
Isaac West
@isaacwest
onyongo/@hannah_gilo
Ismail Zaidy
@L4ARTISTE
Joyz Kwok
@joyz_kwok
Julia Shatun
@juliashatun
Juliet Cope
@howtogrowaboy
Jun Imaizumi
@ima_ju
Karl Mansour
@karliseverywhere
Kelley Dallas
@kelleydallasphotography
Kgomotso Neto Tleane
@kgomotso_neto
Kim Abbas
@tenderfoot_photo
Laura Gorun
@gorunul
Laurence Bouchard
@laurence_bouchard
Leonid Pryadko
@Leonid_Pryadko88
LianYu Lu
@666.605
Ludovic Broquereau
@lbrphotographs
Maksim Goncharenok
@maksgelatin
Marcello Raggini
@marcello.raggini

Mariko Klug
@mariko_klug
Martina Loiola
@martiloi
Mehrnoush Negahdari
@_zhinhin_
Mobin Mayeli
@M0bino
Mohammad Nazari
@mohammd.nazarii
Moises Levy
@moises_levy_street
Paulo Buncuga
@paulo.buncuga
Philip Parsons
@HereInMyOwnSkin
Rachél Sela
@rachel_artphoto
Raymond Baffour
@asokwa_seaman
Renzo Grande
@renzogrande
Robin Robertis
@robinrobertis
Sehin Tewabe
@sehintewabe
Shihyu Tsao
@tsy12217
Taru Latva-Pukkila
@tarulp
Vincent Patrizi
@vincent.patrizi
Wei Xiong
@trtits

First published in Great Britain in 2023 by Ilex, an imprint of
Octopus Publishing Group Ltd
Carmelite House
50 Victoria Embankment
London EC4Y 0DZ
www.octopusbooks.co.uk

An Hachette UK Company
www.hachette.co.uk

Text copyright © Jo Bradford 2023
Design and layout copyright © Octopus Publishing Group 2023
Photographs copyright © individual copyright holders

Distributed in the US by Hachette Book Group
1290 Avenue of the Americas
4th and 5th Floors
New York, NY 10104

Distributed in Canada by Canadian Manda Group
664 Annette St.
Toronto, Ontario, Canada M6S 2C8

Publisher: Alison Starling
Commissioning Editor: Richard Collins
Art Director: Ben Gardiner
Designer: Geoff Fennell
Editor: Faye Robson
Copyeditor: Julie Brooke
Assistant Production Manager: Lisa Pinnell

Cover image: Jun Imaizumi
Frontispiece: Raymond Baffour

ISBN 978 1 78157 882 7

A CIP catalogue record for this book is available from the British Library.

Printed and bound in Malaysia

10 9 8 7 6 5 4 3 2 1